THE MAN OF
VILLA TEVERE

St. Josemaría Escrivá: His Years in Rome

THE MAN OF
VILLA TEVERE

St. Josemaría Escrivá: His Years in Rome

Pilar Urbano
Translated by Helena Scott

Scepter

With ecclesiastical approval

The original work, *Hombre de Villa Tevere*, is © Fundacion Studium, published by Editorial Plaza y Janés, Barcelona, 1995. Pilar Urbano, 1994.
© Translation—Scepter (U.K.) Ltd., 2002
© Second edition—Scepter (U.K.) Ltd., 2003
© This edition © 2011, Scepter Publishers, Inc., New York.

Cover and inside photos courtesy of Fundacion Studium, Madrid.

Scepter Publishers, Inc.
P.O. Box 211, New York, N.Y. 10018
www.scepterpublishers.org

Translated by Helena Scott

Text design by Carol Sawyer/Rose Design

Printed in the United States of America

ISBN: 978 1 59417 142 0

Library of Congress Cataloging-in-Publication Data

Urbano, Pilar.
[Hombre de Villa Tevere. English]
The man of Villa Tevere : St. Josemaría Escrivá : his years in Rome / Pilar Urbano ; translated by Helena Scott.
    p. cm.
Includes index.
ISBN 978-1-59417-142-0 (alk. paper)
1. Escrivá de Balaguer, Josemaría, Saint, 1902–1975. 2. Opus Dei (Society) I. Title.
BX4705.E676U7213 2011
267'.182092–dc22
[B]
                    2011013567

CONTENTS

Like Nietzsche, you said you could only believe
"in a God who could dance"
Well, I assure you he can:
I have known a man who danced with God.

1

A Full-length Portrait

September 1966: the poplars at Molinoviejo conference center, near Segovia in central Spain, were turning gold. A painter named Luis Mosquera had set up an improvised studio in a seminar room. He came from Madrid every morning to paint a portrait outside his own studio "as an absolute exception," as he put it, "because this sitter really interests me."

The sitter had to overcome his dislike of posing with his hands folded. "Ten sessions," he complained, "as if I were a film star!" Mosquera wanted even more time. "I need two or three times that many sessions. I'm a slow worker, because I think a lot about each brush stroke." In the end they agreed on five sessions, each two and a half hours.

Mosquera knew the clothing would be a problem in this portrait. Monsignor Escrivá was wearing a plain black cassock, the only relief provided by his white clerical collar and the white cuffs at his wrists. The entire portrait's vitality would have to come from the face and hands.

The painter could see he was faced with a subject of notable contrasts. He had to get onto canvas a mature person who projected the vitality of youth; an ascetic character, tempered by suffering but still joyful. This was a contemplative overflowing with activity; clearly a great intellectual, yet with none of an intellectual's aloofness; a very simple person who could be forthright when he had to but was not brusque. He was pleasantly serious; a peaceful man, but prepared to fight for what he believed in. One had only to look at him. His firm jaw indicated tenacity; his mouth, strength of character and self-control. The deep lines on his forehead showed a character molded by past sufferings—or maybe present ones.

As Mosquera studied his subject he became more and more interested in this personality. For some time he debated with himself how to get this complex priest onto canvas. In the end, as he dipped his brushes into sienna and ochre, he made up his mind: "A priest first, but one who is deeply human."

Mosquera studied the hands: vigorous, strong, capable, expressive. He could imagine them taking up a pen thousands of times, telling the beads of many rosaries, handling the Christian mystery of the Eucharist day after day for years. They were the hands of a craftsman, hard working hands, made for work well done. "Something like the hands of a potter."

Three characteristics stood out in the face. There was intelligence. There was friendliness—or was it an intense capacity to communicate? And there was a third factor, an indefinable element that was to be the painter's main challenge in all five sittings. It was something very subtle, difficult to grasp, let alone recreate on canvas. Nevertheless there it was, not so much seen as glimpsed, from the moment the painter came face to face with his subject each morning at eleven, with the golden-leafed autumn poplars as background.

He was to discover it gradually, observing the priest in silence, scrutinizing his features, listening to him speak while posing, or feeling penetrated by his gaze.

He became very interested in that gaze. In contrast to so many others, those eyes seemed to bring light forth from the interior of the person—like genuine Russian icons which are drenched with the golden light they bear within. That gaze, rather than reflecting images of the world outside, seemed to communicate messages from its own inner depth. It was an attentive gaze that did not scrutinize; neither intrusive, inquisitive, nor questioning. A gaze which, paradoxically, *saw*, yet did not *look*! Those eyes, small, short-sighted, and bright, had the rare trait of piercing through the present, as if observing faraway horizons, while at the same time establishing a close, affectionate rapport. Mosquera found himself confronted with an enigma: it was as if those eyes were holding back out of respect, while at the same time breaking down barriers by coming forward to meet the person before them. It was only later that he would discover that the secret was not so much in the eyes as in their look. How was he to translate that look onto canvas? It was the gaze of an adventurer, a patient voyager who, forging ever farther into the deep, watched the stars and scanned oceans. Where had he seen that gaze before? In which port, on what beach, in which fishing boat had he seen that deep, attentive, concentrated look of a fisherman gazing into the distance?

There were witnesses to these scenes: Alvaro del Portillo, Javier Echevarria, Florencio Sanchez Bella, Emilio Muñoz Jofre, and Alejandro Cantero. One of them made the following notes during those September days.

"So that he could get a fuller idea of his subject, Mosquera asked the Father to talk while he was posing. Yesterday several of us were in the studio with him. The Father was the life and soul of a pleasant, animated, amusing conversation. We were interested to see what was going on, and he spoke to all of us. But, as time passed, he focused more on Mosquera. The Father was 'a docile model' according to the painter. At his suggestion the Father folded his arms and kept them folded, staying quite still, scarcely breathing. When Mosquera at last said 'That'll do,' he carried on talking normally but still didn't change his position. . . . Today I was alone with the Father and the painter, sitting in a corner of the studio for a whole session. The Father was speaking to Mosquera in terms of close friendship. He called him by his first name, Luis. Rather than praising his talent, he applauded the effort and enthusiasm with which he tackled his work. From there he went on to explain how Luis could make his art into 'something holy, something both human and divine.' Then in plain, simple language, he told him what Opus Dei is. And with moving sincerity he told Luis that God had chosen to use him, the Father, as an instrument to carry out the Work in the world. He stressed, with absolute conviction, that he himself was 'a clumsy, deaf instrument' who saw himself as 'full of wretchedness,' 'capable of every error and every horror,' but who at the same time only desired to love Jesus Christ madly.

"The Father spoke for over half an hour. In silence, sitting in my corner, I made use of his words to do my personal prayer.

"The painter went on with his job, absorbed and attentive. You could see he was moved, captivated, by the Father's words, which were prayer done aloud.

"Suddenly, the Father stopped. There was a silence, while Mosquera kept on mixing colors on his palette. Then the painter began to talk about the bohemian life artists live, and about their emotions and passions. He spoke of his recent marriage, his secularist education, and his scanty practice of religion. He was touched into baring his soul, ignoring my presence. The Father stopped him short, with compliments about his art. He cut in on purpose; he wished to avoid this confidential outpouring. At the end of the session, when Mosquera had left, the Father said to me, 'Did you realize that if I hadn't interrupted him he would have made a public confession?'"[1]

Months later, by the time he finished the portrait[2] in his studio in Doctor Arce Street, Luis Mosquera had resolved his doubts about the third factor that had been bothering him so much. It was what had attracted and captivated him, something that had never fully emerged from his palette and had challenged the skill of his brushes in a new way. The fact was that one could paint light and shade, transparency and opaqueness, joy and sorrow, wealth and poverty, order and chaos, the smooth and the rough. These were all chancy, difficult undertakings which nevertheless could be conquered by skill. But who could paint grace? What resources of color could ever be capable of marking the mysterious connection between human clay and grace, which is holiness?

During those five sessions at Molinoviejo, the artist became deeply aware that the priest sitting in front of him was something more than a prelate, chancellor, founder, or illustrious figure. Something more, and something different: he was a saint through and through. He was a saint, clay and grace, from top to toe, but a very human saint.

---

1. Testimony of Dr. Alejandro Cantero Fariña (AGP, HRF T-06308) and Monsignor César Ortiz-Echagüe (AGP, HRF T-04694).
2. Luis Mosquera did two paintings: a full-length portrait which hangs in Diego de Leon (one of the earliest centers of Opus Dei in Madrid), and another, a half-portrait, which is in the Galleria di Fumo, in Villa Tevere (the headquarters of Opus Dei in Rome).

2

On Board the *J.J. Sister*

On the port side of the *J.J. Sister*, Father Josemaría Escrivá and a very young law professor, José Orlandis, a member of Opus Dei, were leaning on the rails breathing in the sea air. They looked at each other and smiled. A passenger nearby commented, "After the storm comes the calm." The platitude described the situation perfectly. They had just been through twenty hours of terrible storm; the little mail steamship had been buffeted by a violent gale from the Gulf of Lyon. The *J.J. Sister*, notorious for pitching and tossing, kept its course despite wind and tide, although the dining room china and glassware were shattered, the waves swept the deck, and the furniture slid up and down. All the passengers and the crew, from the captain to the cabin boy, were seasick. At the height of the storm Father Escrivá quipped, "Do you know what? If we go down and get eaten by fish . . . Perico Casciaro will never eat fish again as long as he lives!"[1] (Father Pedro Casciaro, one of the very early members of Opus Dei, was well known for etiquette.) Soon afterward he referred to the reason behind this hair-raising voyage. "How the devil dipped his tail in the Gulf of Lyon! It's very clear that he's not exactly happy about our arrival in Rome!"[2]

It was 5 p.m. on a warm day, Saturday, June 22, 1946. The sun beat down, but the breeze on the high seas made being on deck very pleasant. The *J.J. Sister* was sailing eastward from Barcelona to

1. Testimony of Father José Orlandis (AGP, RHF T-00184).
2. AGP, RHF 21164, p. 1408–1409.

Genoa. Suddenly the sea surged again. There was a moment of anxiety among the passengers.

"What's up now? Another gale?"

"No, a school of young whales!"

The captain was still looking through his binoculars when he saw the menacing metal bulk of an enormous mine floating near the bows. World War II had ended less than a year earlier and it was not unusual to find this type of 'souvenir.' The boat veered to starboard to avoid it. After that everything seemed to calm down. Father Escrivá and Orlandis ran their gaze along the tenuous line of the horizon. Far away they could see the French coast, misty in the distance, beautiful. They stood in silence, entranced.

Three years earlier Alvaro del Portillo, another young member of Opus Dei, had traveled the same route, but by air, while the war was still raging. His fellow travelers were some friendly, excitable Italian actors. During the flight several fighter aircraft had flown overhead and opened fire on a ship uncomfortably close to them. The terrified actors started shouting, *Mamma mia, c'è molto pericolo! Affoghiamo tutti!*—"This is really dangerous! We'll all be drowned!" Del Portillo, however, did not bat an eyelid. "I was quite sure nothing would happen. I was carrying all the papers."[3] He had with him all the documents he was to present to the Holy See to obtain the *nihil obstat*, the green light for setting up Opus Dei, or the Work, in different dioceses. At the time Opus Dei had just one limited approval: a kind of pass granted by Monsignor Eijo y Garay, bishop of Madrid-Alcalá, to allow it to develop as a "Pious Union." From every point of view this was insufficient for the universal scope its nature demanded.

On the day in June 1943 when Pope Pius XII granted him an audience, Alvaro del Portillo had not yet been ordained a priest. He appeared at the Portone di Bronzo, the entrance to the Vatican, wearing the full dress uniform of a civil engineer, which was adorned with so much gold braid and trimmings that the Swiss Guard jumped to attention and presented arms. Obviously they took him for a field marshal or an admiral—though an astonishingly young one.

---

3. AGP, RHF 21165, p. 177.

The project of Opus Dei, its apostolate of holiness through professional work, with its desire to expand to all points of the compass, was welcomed by the Holy See not just formally but "enthusiastically." A few months later, on October 11, the Church declared that there was nothing in its spirituality that could not be blessed or encouraged by the Pope. This was the *nihil obstat,* the go-ahead they had sought. It was an important step, but only one in the long, steep, wearisome climb on the canonical path that cost the founder of Opus Dei and all its members so much prayer, work, negotiation, efforts, and suffering.

A pathway of hope had opened up. It was to take them forty long years to travel it, like a new exodus across the Sinai desert. But it was a cheerful crossing over a fruitful desert in which, year by year, vocations came by the thousands.

Every century produces outstanding movements, and each has its own intrepid figure who leads the way. Father Josemaría Escrivá was one of the greatest of the twentieth century. In the certainty that he was fulfilling God's desires, he was encouraged to found the revolutionary innovation which was Opus Dei.

Like all genuine revolutions, Opus Dei goes back to the origins. It links the men and women of today with the citizens of the early Christian period who achieved holiness in their work and secular state in the world. Opus Dei did not invent anything: it rediscovered, in a way as simple as it was radical, that Christianity is a leaven which has to impregnate and transform civil society from the inside, setting a course toward God for all human activities, as long as they are clean and honest. But it needed to be established and activated, and lived out in the middle of the world, with no limits other than those of freedom itself. It was as simple and sublime as that; but not that easy.

Opus Dei exists to serve the Church "as the Church wishes to be served." To do this, it was essential from the start that its specific spirituality should obtain canonical recognition only the Church could give. But this canonical confirmation should not distort its secular nature or clip its wings. It was within this difficult balance that Father Josemaría Escrivá had to work to the end of his life, as a faithful son of the Church and a faithful instrument for founding the Work.

Efforts to attain an appropriate canonical formula took Alvaro del Portillo to Rome a second time in February 1946. By then he was a priest. He brought to the Vatican dozens of letters of recommendation from bishops who backed the request for a *Decretum Laudis*—a "decree of praise"—for the Work. However, when it came to setting up a suitable canonical framework for something new in the Church, the project met with rigid resistance on the part of canon lawyers. In the Holy See they told Father del Portillo Opus Dei had been born too soon.

Later on, Father Escrivá would write: "Both to the world and to the Church the Work seemed a great novelty. The canonical solution that I was seeking seemed impossible to attain. But, my daughters and sons, I could not wait for things to be possible. A high-ranking member of the Roman Curia told us, 'You have come a century too soon.' Nevertheless we had to attempt the impossible. I was urged on by the thought of the thousands of souls who had dedicated themselves to God in the Work, with full commitment, in order to do apostolate in the middle of the world."[4]

At the gates of the Vatican

The gates of the Vatican were shut because the caller had come too early. But God's work can't wait. Father del Portillo did not waste a second. Besides negotiations with the Vatican, he made visits and calls to ask for more letters of recommendation from cardinals soon to leave Rome for posts in Palermo, Argentina, Mozambique, and Cologne. He got new letters supporting the request for the *Decretum Laudis* from Cardinals Ruffini, Caggiano, Gouvcia, and Frings.

Even though he had mailed a letter to Father Escrivá, he distrusted the chaotic postwar postal service and gave another to a Spanish diplomat returning to Madrid to be delivered by hand. In both letters he related the response of the Holy See and added: "I can't do any more. It's your turn now."[5] Although Father Escrivá was suffering from severe diabetes, he considered it necessary for him to come to Rome.

---

4. *Letter*, January 25, 1961, 19.
5. AGP, RHF 21165, pp. 985–986. Dr. Juan Rof Carballo, who attended Father Josemaría Escrivá in Madrid, advised him against making this journey.

"I won't be answerable for your life"

As soon as Father Escrivá received Father del Portillo's two letters, he called a meeting of the general council of the Work at a center of Opus Dei in Villanueva Street in Madrid. He read the letters to them, and told them bluntly that his doctors had reacted unfavorably to the idea of his making such a trip; Doctor Rof Carballo had told him, "I won't be answerable for your life." Father Escrivá then went on, "The doctors say I may die at any moment. When I go to bed I am not sure if I will get up again. When I get up in the morning I don't know if I will make it to the end of the day."[6]

The governing body of the Work was made up of young men, but they had the maturity which comes from living an interior life. Against their personal feelings, they gave priority to the needs of a mission greater than all of them. They agreed unhesitatingly to what they felt Father Escrivá wanted to do and encouraged him to set sail as soon as possible.

"Thank you," he responded, "but I would have gone anyway: what has to be done, has to be done."[7]

This took place on Monday, June 17, 1946. The tickets and visas were arranged in a few hours. On Wednesday, June 19, at 3:30 p.m. Father Escrivá left Madrid for Saragossa. From there he went to Barcelona to board the *J.J. Sister* for Genoa, and from there to Rome. Nowadays the trip is one short flight from Barajas Airport in Madrid to Fiumicino Airport in Rome. In those days, with the Second World War just over, there were no commercial flights between Spain and Italy, the French border was closed, and one could only make the trip this way.

"Will I turn out to be a fraud?"

Father Escrivá broke his journey at three shrines dedicated to the Mother of God. First, Our Lady of the Pillar in Saragossa, then Montserrat, and the last stop was in Barcelona, the shrine of Our Lady of Ransom. He sought from his Mother, whom he called "all-powerful

---

6. Ibid.
7. Ibid.

in her petition," all the recommendations, strength, and guidance he would need.

In Barcelona, early in the morning of Friday, June 21, Father Escrivá met a small group of his sons in the oratory of an apartment in Muntaner Street. They did their prayer together. With his eyes fixed on the tabernacle, Father Escrivá appealed in words Christ had heard before: *Ecce nos reliquimus omnia, et secuti sumus te: quid ergo erit nobis?* "Here we are, having left everything to follow you: What is to become of us?"[8]

It was the same question St. Peter had asked as spokesman for the misgivings and anxieties of the Twelve. Father Escrivá paused. There seemed no light at the end of the tunnel but a foreboding of disaster. With the confidence born of love, he continued in a hushed, impassioned voice, "Lord, have you allowed me, in good faith, to deceive so many souls? I've done everything for your glory, knowing it is your Holy Will! Is it possible that the Holy See can say that we have come a century too soon? *Ecce nos reliquimus omnia, et secuti sumus te!* I've never wished to deceive anyone. I've only wanted to serve you. Will I turn out to be a fraud?"[9]

Everyone present knew perfectly well what it meant to "leave everything" and pay for it with their reputation. In Barcelona certain good people had set in motion a ruthless campaign of insults and calumnies against Opus Dei, provoking discord among the families of members and their friends, and warning parents against letting their sons "be snared in the nets of this new heresy." However, Father Escrivá's words were not a reproach, nor was he demanding a reward. They were a plea, uttered almost on the verge of tears by one whose only foothold on earth was heaven.

The *J.J. Sister* arrived in Genoa very late the night of June 22. Father Alvaro del Portillo and Salvador Canals were waiting, walking up and down the quayside. Father Escrivá greeted each with a big hug, then, looking at Father del Portillo over the rim of his glasses, addressed him: "Rascal! Here I am! You got your own way!"[10]

---

8. Matt 19:27.
9. AGP, RHF 21164, p. 1324.
10. Ibid., 1409.

By the time they got to the hotel it was so late that there was no way of getting a meal. All Father Escrivá had had since leaving Barcelona thirty-two hours earlier was a coffee and some biscuits. Father del Portillo had kept a small piece of Parmesan cheese from his dinner, thinking Father Escrivá would like it. It was all he got to eat that night.

3 ✤

Subletting in Città Leonina

They drove from Genoa to Rome in a battered hired car, large and old-fashioned, with a running board, extra folding seats, and a strong, rancid smell of oilcloth. Arriving at dusk on a beautiful Roman summer evening, they were greeted by the sight of the Tiber, pink façades, and the smell of rosebay and cypress. On rounding a bend of the Via Aurelia they saw the dome of St. Peter's. Father Escrivá, deeply moved, broke out into prayer: "I believe in God, the Father Almighty . . ."

It was dark by the time they reached their destination and climbed to the fifth floor. The members of the Work had half a top floor apartment in the Piazza della Città Leonina, sublet to them by a countess who had come down in the world. She had also lent them some pieces of furniture and ornaments that still had a certain elegance despite their shabbiness. There was not much space. They had fitted up the best room as an oratory. The dining room doubled as a sitting room, a study, a workplace, and a reception room, as well as a place for formational talks. At night, they opened up some folding beds in the same room. There was only one bedroom, for Father Escrivá or anyone who happened to be ill. The room used by Don Alvaro (as Father Alvaro del Portillo was normally called) was just a wider part of the corridor, used by everyone during the day. The apartment was very poor, but did have a covered balcony with sliding doors, a kind of gallery that they optimistically called "the terrace," looking onto St. Peter's Square.

As always, Father Escrivá went straight to the oratory to greet "the Master of the house" and prayed for a few seconds on his knees before the tabernacle. Loving care and poverty were both apparent in the way the oratory was furnished. At the first opportunity in Rome, Father Escrivá bought a fine crucifix made of variegated marble, with very stylized lines, on which the figure of Christ looked alive and serene. From then on it presided over the little altar.

After dinner they had a lively get-together. With Father Escrivá were Don Alvaro, José Orlandis, and Salvador Canals (nicknamed Babo). Within a few weeks they were joined by Ignacio Sallent and Armando Serrano. With Vladimiro Vince, this was all there was of Opus Dei in Rome, or in Italy. In that same year, 1946, the Work would begin to spread, with members going to Portugal and England and, in 1947, to France and Ireland.

While the Pope slept

At one stage in the conversation, the people with Father Escrivá pointed across the gallery toward the Vatican, where the lights of the Pope's rooms could be seen. They could imagine him moving about from one room to another. As the Swiss Guard barracks was a fairly low building, they were almost certainly the Pope's nearest neighbors. Father Escrivá decided that on this, his first night in Rome, he would not go to bed. Passing the hours in a vigil there on the balcony, he kept the Holy Father company with his prayers.

Father Escrivá had a deep, sincere, even enthusiastic love for the Pope. It wasn't hero worship but the conviction that the Pope, no matter who he is, is the successor of Peter. He holds the keys. He binds and loosens. In spite of any human frailty he may have, he is the firm rock on which the Church is built. In words Father Escrivá borrowed from St. Catherine of Siena, he is *il dolce Cristo in terra*—"the sweet Christ on earth." Or, still more strongly, he is the Vicar of Christ.

With Pope Pius XII as with his predecessors for centuries, the papacy had trappings of Baroque splendor that elevated and distanced the figure of the Pope, surrounding him with ornament and an almost imperial protocol, perhaps to symbolize his spiritual power and authority. Pius XII radiated holiness and majesty, but he could only be seen from a distance. There was no television; it was not the custom to hold large public audiences; and the Pope didn't travel. Only a few select people had access to him. At solemn ceremonies Pope Pius was carried in triumph on an imposing chair like a throne, erect and priestly, wearing the triple crown of gold and silver. To see, just a stone's throw away, the window of the room where the Pope was sleeping like any other tired man was moving and heartwarming to someone of Father Escrivá's faith and sensitivity.

For years he had pounded the streets of Madrid day after day, wrapped in his cape, saying rosaries "for the Pope and his intentions." Earlier, when Pius XI occupied the Chair of Peter, he wrote, "I used to imagine myself beside the Holy Father when he was celebrating Mass. I did not know then, nor do I now, what the Pope's chapel was like, but at the end of the rosary I would make a spiritual communion, desiring to receive Our Lord from the Pope's hands. You won't be surprised to hear that I feel a holy envy for those who have the good fortune to be physically near the Holy Father, because they can open their hearts to him, and show him their esteem and devotion."[1]

"Thoroughly Roman"

That night of June 23, 1946 not just Rome but the whole of Italy spent a particularly restless vigil: the next day the new parliamentary assembly would meet to elect Alcide de Gasperi as president. King Humberto II abdicated and gave up all his powers. But there was only one matter which concerned Father Escrivá: It could not be true that the Work of God had come too soon, or too late. Opus Dei existed because heaven wished it. No suitable canonical formulas? God would provide a way.

Dawn broke on his reverie. A bird flew fast and low across the Piazza della Città Leonina. Reaching the reddish wall, it fluttered a moment before taking off again. A halo of warm sunlight surrounded the basilica's dome.

---

1. *Letter*, January 9, 1932, 20.

Inside the top floor apartment, there was the noise of beds being folded and showers running. The housekeeper had arrived, a Hungarian not particularly expert at domestic tasks, and she could be heard preparing breakfast.

When Father Escrivá later told an old prelate of the Curia he had spent his first night in Rome keeping vigil "out of love and devotion for the Pope," this good man told others, who made fun. "Lots of people made me a laughingstock. At first I was hurt by their gossip; later on it made my love for the Pope less Spanish—which is a love that springs from enthusiasm—and much firmer, a love born of reflection, more theological and thus far more profound. Since then I have often said that in Rome I 'lost my innocence,' and that incident was of great benefit for my soul."[2]

The wheels in the palace grind slowly

This half-apartment in Città Leonina was an interim base, but they were to spend another thirteen months there. From December 27 on they even had to give up some space in order to provide another totally separate apartment for a group of women of the Work who had come to Rome at the founder's summons to begin their own apostolate and take charge of the domestic management of this center.

A Spanish proverb says, "Wheels in the palace grind slowly," and speed was hardly the outstanding feature of the negotiations with the Curia. Still, Father Escrivá obtained positive results in his contacts with the Holy See. The first words of affection and encouragement he heard from that source in Rome were from Monsignor Giovanni Battista Montini, an intelligent, sensitive Italian from Brescia who, since the end of the Second World War, had been laboring to update the Vatican's diplomatic relations. Years later, he was to become Pope Paul VI.

One day, talking with Salvador Canals and two other members of the Work, he asked them for "a photograph of the founder so as to be able to show it to the Pope." Julian Urbistondo put his hand into the inside pocket of his jacket, took out his wallet, and handed Montini a

---

2. *Letter*, October 7, 1950, 19.

little photograph of the Father. Monsignor Montini could not repress a surprised smile when he read the dedication Father Escrivá had written on the back: "Rascal! How are you treating your parents?"[3]

Pope Pius XII had received Alvaro del Portillo twice and, separately, the law professors José Orlandis and Salvador Canals, as well as the scientist José María Albareda, whose intellectual capacity the Pope found amazing. Since 1943 he had prayed for the founder by name and had a copy of *The Way* among his books.[4] It was time to prepare for the first audience of the Pope with Father Escrivá.

It took place on July 16. Father Escrivá explained to the Pope what Opus Dei was and what it was not. After their conversation, Pius XII asked the responsible parties to resume the juridical studies that finally resulted in a new apostolic constitution, *Provida Mater Ecclesia*,[5] opening the way for secular institutes. As a secular institute, Opus Dei could have a definite canonical status within the Church. It was not a perfect formula because members of Opus Dei neither practiced nor were intended to practice the state of perfection of the secular institutes. But in some way, total self-dedication by lay people who did not change their state in life, job, or place in the world had now been given a formal blessing.

When barely three weeks later Pius XII also published the *Decretum Laudis* approving Opus Dei, Father Escrivá had achieved recognition of the universal call to holiness which the Work promotes for men and women, priests and lay people alike, in one and the same vocation. He did not need to take any shortcuts or easy ways out. He prayed and got other people to pray; he studied and got others to study; he worked and got others to work. He knocked at doors and spent hours in waiting rooms. He spoke with the strength and humility of someone performing a task commissioned by God. However, as would shortly be seen, the constitution *Provida Mater Ecclesia* was not the right "clothing" for ordinary people walking through the world *nel bel mezzo della strada*, in the middle of the street. So, at every opportunity, with Aragonese clarity and tenacity,

---

3. AGP, RHF T-21167, pp. 1323–1324.

4. Testimony of Encarnación Ortega (AGP, RHF T-0574).

5. The Apostolic Constitution *Provida Mater Ecclesia* was dated February 2, 1947. The *Decretum Laudis* giving canonical approval to Opus Dei was dated February 24.

Father Escrivá said he was "giving way without giving up, intent on recovering any concessions later."[6]

"Opus Dei," he would write years later, "has created many canonical and theological problems in the Church and has solved them—I say so with humility, for humility is truth. Once solved, the problems appeared simple; in particular, the fact there is only one class of members, which includes both clergy and laity."[7]

Pius XII perceived a splendid panorama: the personal holiness and personal apostolate which Opus Dei could spread all over the earth. He also observed Father Escrivá's spiritual stature, and the divine scope of his vision, to which the Pope was to give definitive approval on June 16, 1950. Soon after the Pope told Cardinal Norman Gilroy of Sydney, Australia that he had been profoundly impressed by a recent visit from Father Escrivá. "He is a real saint, a man sent by God for our times" (*é un vero santo, un uomo mandato da Dio per i nostri tempi*).[8] No inkling then of the bitter hours, the great suffering, that Father Escrivá would have to endure during his pontificate, though not at the Pope's doing.

Some nights during the summer of 1946 as well as later, Father Escrivá would go down with several of his sons to St. Peter's Square, deserted and silent. They would go to the obelisk which Caligula had brought from Heliopolis and Sixtus V had placed in the huge esplanade; or else they would walk under Bernini's columns. Standing on the dark flagstones Father Escrivá would recite the Creed, emphasizing each word. After saying, "I believe in the holy Catholic Church" he would add with special insistence, "I believe in my mother, the Roman, Roman, Roman Church."[9]

A few months later he introduced another phrase: "I believe in one, holy, Catholic and Apostolic Church . . . in spite of everything!" Later, he told a high-ranking official, Monsignor Tardini, his great confidence about these additions. When he came to the expression "in spite of everything," Tardini asked "Ah, and what do you mean by 'in spite of everything'?"

6. *Letter*, December 8, 1949, 18.
7. *Letter*, August 8, 1956, 5.
8. Testimony of Bishop Thomas Muldoon, titular bishop of Fessei, auxiliary bishop of Sydney (AGP, RHF T-04261).
9. *Articles of the Postulator*, 296 (AGP, RHF 20755, p. 158).

"I mean, 'in spite of your sins and mine,'" replied Father Escrivá.[10]

His negotiations at the Vatican continued unabated. It was a struggle in legal logic, trying to bring down ancient canonical walls in order to open a way for the Work. The hinges of some doors had the rust of centuries. The formulas obtained in 1941 and 1943, and the one now being prepared, which became official in 1947, were the best solutions possible and the most suitable—meaning the least unsuitable. "However, there was no other option; either we accepted everything or we would have to carry on trying to go forward with no path to follow. In reality, we were the needle that pulled the thread through. Experience has confirmed that those institutions which sought approval as secular institutes after us, have found themselves at ease and joyfully accept the things which clash with our secularity, because such is their calling. One can see more clearly every day that, leaving the thread in place, the 'needle' has to leave the cloth which is now called secular institutes."[11]

The Roman dog-days, July and *ferragosto* (the August holiday), passed. Father Escrivá prayed, worked, studied, wrote, walked, talked with people, and practiced patience. He was ill. His diabetes was unpredictable and dangerous, with fever, dehydration, attacks of raging thirst, muscular exhaustion, headaches, weakness, and prostration. Father Escrivá did not complain. Except for Don Alvaro, no one knew what he was going through. He even outdid his younger sons in energy and good humor. Sometimes, coming home to Città Leonina exhausted, they would find a power failure and the elevator not working. Father Escrivá would grasp the stair rail and start the climb. On reaching the landing, he would joke, "They say there are five floors in this house but I think they are exaggerating. There are four—because we've already done one." A little farther and: "What's more, there aren't four, only three." So, merrily, they reached the last steps. There he stopped, breathed deeply, and exclaimed with a mischievous smile, "Sure, this house has only two or three steps."[12]

---

10. Ibid., 297 (AGP, RHF 21503, p. 152). Salvador Bernal, *Monsignor Josemaría Escrivá—A Profile of the Founder of Opus Dei* (London, 1977), p. 249.

11. *Letter*, October 7, 1950, 21–22.

12. AGP, RHF 21172, p. 507.

There was something more than a naturally friendly and optimistic disposition here. This was a man of tenacity who, day after day, for years had practiced a "smiling asceticism" as training in virtue.

Father Escrivá returned to Madrid on August 31. He brought with him two important documents: a brief, *Cum Societatis*, and a letter, *Brevi Sane*, praising the aims of the Work. He also brought a strange, very valuable personal present from the Pope: the complete relics of two young Christian martyrs, St. Mercuriana and St. Sinferus. By this gift, Pius XII showed his understanding of the similarity between the members of Opus Dei and those early Christians.

The relics of St. Sinferus were placed in the oratory of a center for men of Opus Dei. The relics of St. Mercuriana were placed by two priests, Father Alvaro del Portillo and Father José María Hernandez de Garnica, under the altar of Los Rosales, a center for women, in Villaviciosa de Odon, near Madrid. Father Escrivá was present at the ceremony with some of his daughters: Antonieta Gomez, Mari Tere Echevarria, Josefina de Miguel, and others.

He attended to different matters concerning the running of the Work—the general council was still in Madrid—and then went to Molinoviejo, near Segovia, for a few days' rest. Molinoviejo had just opened as a conference center for retreats and courses. During Father Escrivá's stay, a simple ceremony took place in the little shrine of Molinoviejo, following Father Escrivá's wishes. It was of fundamental importance: the first members of the Work took promissory oaths, making a free commitment to the Work in conscience, without vows.

September 24 was the feast of Our Lady of Ransom. Father Escrivá recalled the church near the port of Barcelona where he had gone to ask his heavenly Mother for help before embarking for Genoa. Inside the little shrine at Molinoviejo, at noon, he and a group of his sons said the Angelus together in front of a statue of Our Lady.[13] These were people who had joined the Work at the very beginning, and although they were young, they were very conscious

---

13. This was a statue of Our Lady, not yet restored, which was in the shrine in Molinoviejo at the time. The following year, on the same day and in the same place, the founder once again met with a group of his older sons before a statue of Our Lady, Mother of Fair Love, to undertake the same commitments on maintaining the spirit of Opus Dei in its integrity.

of being "seniors" in Opus Dei. A crucifix stood on the wooden altar, with a stout candle burning on either side. There these members of Opus Dei committed themselves to maintain its spirit exactly as God had given it to their founder. One of the commitments they made was to practice personal poverty, preserving it as it had been practiced at the beginning of Opus Dei; another was to maintain unity with the directors; the third was to help each other with fraternal correction. In fact, the only "mutual benefit" between two members of the Work is prayer, service, and the concern manifested in fraternal correction. This is all the help anyone in the Work should expect from any other. It is the real meaning of the phrase in big letters on a wall-hanging in Molinoviejo and a mural in Villa Tevere: *Frater qui adiuvatur a fratre, quasi civitas firma*: "A brother who is helped by his brother is like a strong city" (Proverbs 18:19).

On the red flagged floor in the little shrine were straw mats to kneel on as protection against the cold floor. On leaving the little shrine, Father Escrivá asked for two or three of these as souvenirs. He was neither nostalgic nor sentimental nor a relic-maker, but he had a historical consciousness of everything that had to do with the shaping of the Work.

One afternoon at the beginning of November, returning to Los Rosales, he announced to his daughters that he had to go back to Rome on November 8. This time he did not know how long he would be away. "Father Pedro is staying here to represent me, for anything you need," he told them. Without more ado he went out into the garden and beckoned to someone waiting outside.

This was Father Pedro Casciaro, a young architect with a doctorate in mathematics, who had been ordained shortly before. From then on he was to be the counselor of Opus Dei in Spain, and as he governed the Work he would try to identify himself "with the mind of the Father."[14] It must have been around that time that a priest in Madrid remarked, "So now he's off to Rome, leaving the Opus in the hands of a few good-for-nothings." The response was: "If this *Opus* is *Dei*, it will last even if the founder is not here. And if it is not a Work of God, with or without a founder it will collapse of its own accord."

---

14. Oral testimony of Encarnación Ortega to the author.

In Rome, work on drawing up the constitution *Provida Mater Ecclesia* intensified. Many visitors came to the apartment in Città Leonina, mostly ecclesiastics working in the dicasteries of the Curia. Father Escrivá felt like a wound-up spring. Not a minute was being wasted, but he still had an inner sense of urgency. The Work could not travel at man's speed but had to go "at God's pace." On December 6 he wrote to the members of the Work in Madrid, "Everything is going very well, but excessively slowly."[15]

Two days later Pius XII again received him in a private audience. On the 16th of the same month, in another letter to Madrid, he pointed out: "Don't you forget it was during the octave of the Immaculate Conception of Our Lady when the Roman 'solution' began to take shape."[16] The founder had discovered that the Holy See was not just willing but anxious to grant the approval of Opus Dei as soon as possible. It was better to make the most of this opportunity, even though it was to be a stop-gap solution. So the negotiations continued.

On December 27, Father Escrivá and Don Alvaro went to the military airport of Ciampino to meet five women of the Work arriving from Spain: Encarnita Ortega, Dorita Calvo, Julia Bustillo, Rosalia Lopez, and Dora del Hoyo. Now the top floor apartment in Città Leonina began to take on the air of a pleasant, welcoming family home. But some of the women boarded for a while in another house and later moved into a residence hall.

They soon began to look for a permanent headquarters of Opus Dei. Monsignors Montini and Tardini suggested to Father Escrivá that he should set up "a big house" near the Holy See. Father Escrivá put his hands in his pockets, and all he found was a handkerchief, a small notebook, and some rosary beads. They were living from day to day. When guests came for lunch, everyone in the house knew that this hospitality would inevitably have to be paid for: there would be either no evening meal or no breakfast. Sometimes there was no money for firewood or gas. Julia and Dora were hard put for cooking, and used a charcoal brazier and bellows.

---

15. AGP, RHF, EF 461206-2.
16. AGP, RHF, EF 461216-1.

No money; but they had never had money to spare. They knew all about eating plain batter fritters; turning an old suit to use the less worn side of the cloth; economizing on lights and heating; keeping count of every nail; and making spaghetti at home because it was cheaper. They had never had the luxury of "saving up." The enterprise they were engaged in was alive and growing, developing and spreading to other countries. This knowledge urged them on and made more demands on them. Yet somehow in a pinch they never lacked essentials. Father Escrivá wrote: "My God, you always come to meet our real needs."[17]

Cardinals, bishops, and priests visited the apartment in Città Leonina very often. Two regular visitors were the canon lawyers Father Arcadio Larraona and Father Siervo Goyeneche. They spent whole days with Father Escrivá and Don Alvaro, discussing points of canon law and working on the drafts of the constitution *Provida Mater Ecclesia*. These visits upset the women of the Work, who had to perform real miracles with meager supplies.

A bunch of roses without thorns

The advice given by Monsignors Montini and Tardini was well founded: it would be best to locate near the Holy See for several reasons. The canonical path had to be opened up. Opus Dei needed to be Romanized. Father Escrivá wanted the Pope to feel his love as a good son at first hand, and to be able to count on the Work as an instrument of secular apostolate which "only wishes to serve the Church, not make use of it." And there was a reason which could not be disregarded: the Work needed to move away from Spain, where there was a climate of hostility and the founder was being defamed as a heretic, a Freemason, a sectarian, a secretive deceiver of young people, someone ambitious for honors, a political opportunist, a miracle-monger, a madman, and much more. Often, while having breakfast after Mass, Father Escrivá would ask Don Alvaro, "My son, where will the insults come from today?"[18] He remarked that he felt

---

17. *The Forge*, no. 221.
18. AGP, RHF 21165.

like "a spittoon which anyone and everyone thinks they have the right to use."[19] Years later he would joke, "I know my fellow country-men very well. As they have mistreated me and continue to mistreat me so much, when I die they will want to carry my dead body from one end of the country to the other on their shoulders; but I will rest here in Rome, in some little corner of this house."[20]

Monsignor Montini, referring to these attacks, remarked to Father Escrivá, "Our Lord has seen fit to make you suffer right from the beginning what other institutions suffer years later when they are up and running."[21] He did indeed suffer greatly, but with no anguish or surprise, because he trusted God with a blind trust, the trust of love.

When he visited the office of Dr. Carlo Faelli, an endocrinologist, to continue his treatment for diabetes, the doctor inquired after examining him, "Have you suffered a lot? Occasionally diabetes occurs when people have serious problems."

"No, I haven't."

Father Escrivá was telling the truth: he always made light of his difficulties. Not out of stoicism or insensitivity, but in the certainty that for those doing God's will, "difficulties are not difficult."[22] After the consultation, Dr. Faelli noted on the clinical history: *E' un uomo che ha sofferto molto, anche se afferma di non aver avuto dispiaceri.* "He is a man who has suffered greatly, although he states he has not had any sorrows."[23]

Long afterward, on June 23, 1971, the twenty-fifth anniversary of his arrival in Rome, during a gathering in the headquarters in Villa Tevere, Father Escrivá recalled events still vivid in his memory. "Twenty-five years of God's goodness, of suffering, joy, learning, and—'losing our innocence'! We created the universality of the Work right here."

Then he concluded by urging them on. "I must insist that we didn't feel unfortunate, not for a second. But you will understand

---

19. Cf. Meditation, *The prayer of the children of God*, April 1955. Cf. also AGP, RHF 21165, p. 20.
20. AGP, RHF 21165.
21. AGP, RHF 21503, note 280.
22. *The Forge*, no. 812.
23. AGP, RHF 21165 and 21171, p. 854. Testimony of Dr. Carlo Faelli (AGP, RHF T-05362).

better now why I used to say so often, '*prima, più, meglio*' [sooner, more and better]. Everything was disproportionate: the human means and the material means. If we don't see God as the cause, it would not make sense. I am grateful, deeply grateful to the Father, the Son, and the Holy Spirit."[24]

That same day, early in the morning, the women of the Work in Italy had sent him twenty-five red roses, without thorns. This had a special significance. On one of his trips to Spain while the government of the Work was still in Madrid, he found that the general council had put aside a complex matter so that he could study it with them and tell them how to resolve it. Father Escrivá, who strongly supported responsible freedom and believed everyone in governance should shoulder responsibility, had remarked, "My children, when you die, you will be canonized, because you are so very good! And when they paint pictures of you, they will paint you looking very handsome and wonderful—as of course you are— and with your hands full of roses, lots of roses! Do you know why? Because you left the thorns to me!"[25]

Now, moved by his Italian daughters' thoughtfulness, he asked to see some of them to thank them. He remarked, "These roses came without thorns. The thorns, lots of them, came first. There were one or two roses as well, but lots of thorns! If I had to live through these past twenty-five years all over again I couldn't bear it."

He paused briefly, then corrected himself.

"Yes I could! With God's help, I could!"[26]

---

24. Testimony of Father Fernando Valenciano Polack (AGP, RHF T-05362).
25. Oral testimony of Begoña Alvarez to the author.
26. Oral testimony of Mercedes Morado (AGP, RHF T-0792) and Marlies Kücking.

4 ✣

The Making of Villa Tevere

The house of the head of a family

They scoured Rome for a house. Not just any old house: they did not want a hut, or a palace, or a mansion, or a barracks, or a hotel, or an office block. It had to be a home for the head of a family, a very large family. It was to be the permanent headquarters of Opus Dei, a dignified place with plenty of room and with the potential for further building, since in the future men and women from all over the world would come to live there, to study and be formed in the spirit of the Work.

In an antique shop in Piazza di Spagna Father Escrivá and Don Alvaro spotted a beautiful Baroque wooden statue of the *Madonna*. It was very cheap—8,000 lire, or about six dollars. Thinking ahead to the new house, it was a bargain they did not want to miss. But it took them more than a month to scrape together enough money.[1]

Father Escrivá did not have an open-handed patron behind him. At that moment vocations to the Work in Italy could be counted on the fingers of one hand. In Spain the Work had been established in Madrid, Barcelona, Saragossa, Valencia, Bilbao, Granada, Valladolid, and Santiago. However, the young women who lived in Los Rosales, besides studying, had to rear chickens and grow vegetables to feed themselves. The men in Molinoviejo likewise combined their studies with building an extension and setting up a small farm. Recently

---

1. Cf. AGP, RHF 20164, p. 862 and AGP, RHF 21167, p. 742.

graduated architects, engineers, physicists, lawyers, and mathematicians were not above battling with hens, pigs, or cows. They swept up coal dust, mixed it with plaster, and used it to feed the boiler for the central heating. In the kitchen they invented some sophisticated hamburgers—made of rice, cooked and mashed. These ways of making do were a true picture of the finances of Opus Dei in those early years.

Postwar Italy was an aristocratic republic where destitute but dignified princesses, dukes, counts, and marquises swarmed in the impoverished salons of what had been high society. Some were well up on news of houses to rent, small palaces being disposed of, furniture going to auction, tapestries, lamps, and pictures for sale, privately and discreetly, by people who did not want their new poverty to show.

One day the telephone rang in Città Leonina. Duchess Virginia Sforza-Cesarini was on the line. The person who answered the telephone, surprised, made gestures of inquiry to the others. No one knew her.

"I have been told you are looking for a villa, a residence," she said. "Maybe I know one that would suit you. I would be delighted to invite you to tea in my house."

Father Escrivá and Don Alvaro paid a visit. The Duchess Sforza-Cesarini was a charming, gracious lady, but the offer she made on behalf of a third party did not interest them. Among the disadvantages, the house was outside Rome. Father Escrivá used the visit to talk to the duchess about the love of God, a life of prayer, and the value of suffering. Then he explained Opus Dei to her, how the range of its apostolates would be throughout the world, and how this task had to be directed from the heart of the Church in Rome.[2]

Virginia Sforza was impressed, and offered to help in their search for a house. A few days later she contacted them again: "I have seen something which I think you will find interesting." It was a large villa, with a garden which could be built on, in the Parioli district of Rome. It belonged to another aristocrat, Count Gori Mazzoleni, who wanted to sell it and leave Italy. The house had been leased

2. Cf. AGP, RHF 20165, p. 836 and AGP, RHF 21170, p. 462.

to the Hungarian ambassador to the Holy See, but diplomatic ties between the Hungarian Communist government and the Vatican State had been broken off. The owner wished to sell as soon as possible, without using agents.

Father Escrivá, Alvaro del Portillo, Salvador Canals, and a fourth person went to see the villa. It was on the corner of Viale Bruno Buozzi and Via di Villa Sacchetti. The garden reached as far as Via Domenico Cirillo. Count Gori Mazzoleni received them in the porter's lodge where he was living, since the main house was still occupied by civil servants and employees of the Hungarian legation, who were staying there illegally (and would continue to do so for two more years). Father Escrivá liked the situation of the house, the extent of the land which could be built on, and the *quattrocento* Florentine style of the main building. He asked Don Alvaro to go ahead with arranging the purchase. As they had no money, they would buy the property by making a symbolic down payment, then get a mortgage and use it to pay off the count.

Don Alvaro, Salvador Canals, and a lawyer friend, Dr. Merlini, negotiated with the owner and came to an agreement. They achieved such a reduction in price that it almost seemed a gift. Two or three years later the property would be worth thirty or forty times as much. But even though it was a small amount, at the time they did not have the money. They resorted to asking everyone they knew for help. They managed to persuade the owner to formalize the sale without any money, giving him as a pledge a few gold coins that they had been keeping to make a sacred vessel with. Not wanting to lose these, they stipulated in the contract that the gold coins should be returned when they paid the total amount. They committed themselves to finalizing the deal within two months. Gori Mazzoleni's only condition was for payment in Swiss francs. He was content to wait until the buyers got the money together.[3] When the contract was finally signed, in the early hours of the morning, Don Alvaro and Salvador Canals returned to the apartment in Città Leonina to find Father Escrivá waiting for them, on his knees praying in the oratory.[4]

---

3. AGP, RHF 20165, p. 836; AGP, RHF 21165, p. 850 and AGP, RHF 21170, pp. 463–464.
4. Cf. AGP, RHF 21170, p. 463.

"He accepted the gold coins—and he's giving us two months!" they said. "His only condition is that the payment must be made in Swiss francs."

Father Escrivá started to laugh and shrugged his shoulders, surprised and amused. "We don't care! We have neither lira nor francs, and one currency is the same as another for Our Lord."[5] Later on, asking his daughters to pray for this matter, he said with a mischievous wink, "Mind you get the currency right: it has to be in Swiss francs."[6]

Payment had not yet been made when Count Gori Mazzoleni met Encarnita Ortega and Concha Andres one day on the streets of Rome. He stopped his car and gave them a lift to Città Leonina. On the way he praised Don Alvaro to the skies: "To me, he's not just an honest person with whom I've made a deal; he's a loyal friend, a wise counselor, and an admirable priest."[7]

Sometime later, when the people of the Work had moved to the villa on Bruno Buozzi Street and were living in the lodge, the count went to visit them. He was taken into what had been his house, and, seeing the floor shining, asked Salvador Canals, "Have you changed the floor?"

"No, it's the same one, but clean."[8]

The Count might have said the same later if he visited the main house: some of the walls had been washed, others had been covered in cloth, though not where big pictures were going to be hung, so as to save material. The people of the Work themselves did most of the decorating, painting ceilings, beams, and door frames. They were the same rooms but they had been thoroughly cleaned and artistically painted.

"Where shall I sleep tonight?"

From July 1947 until February 1949 when the Hungarian "tenants" eventually left the villa, the people of the Work lived on the two

---

5. Ibid.
6. Oral testimony of Lourdes Toranzo to the author.
7. Testimony of Encarnación Ortega (AGP, RHF T-05074).
8. Ibid.

floors of the lodge. Upstairs were the kitchen, laundry, and dining room; downstairs, the residence, "*Il Pensionato.*"

Few rooms and many people. Every square foot was used intensively. There was only one bed with legs and a mattress; at night, people unrolled bedrolls, as if they were camping. Later on, Father Escrivá would recall this strange, cramped way of living without dramatizing the situation and even humorously: "As we had no money, we did not turn on the heating. Neither did we have a place to sleep. We didn't know where we would sleep at night—inside the hall door, in one corner or another. There was just one bed and we reserved it for whoever was ill. Like St. Alexis, we lived under the stairs."[9]

What he omitted was that as soon as anybody got a cold or was threatened with flu, Father Escrivá himself was always first to unroll a bedroll under the dining room table and would sleep there. If his sons plugged in an electric heater for him, he would turn it off because he did not want to be warm while his sons were cold.

During the day, everyone helped with the building and decorating; they also studied, went to classes at the pontifical universities and carried on apostolate with their university classmates. Soon Opus Dei spread to several Italian cities: Turin, Bari, Genoa, Milan, Naples, and Palermo.

The Opus Dei "banker"

In addition to the difficulties of paying for the property and food, there was the expense of the building alterations in progress. For the next few years they lived among scaffolding and pickaxes, as well as the comings and goings of foremen, bricklayers, carpenters, and plumbers. These workmen had to be paid every Saturday without fail, at 1:15 p.m.

Don Alvaro bore the brunt. He obtained credit, signed bills of exchange, and borrowed money. He himself told a little—not everything—of the difficulties in buying building materials and paying the workers. "The first time we managed to pay them without any problems as we had saved up a bit of money, but by the second time,

---

9. AGP, RHF 20162, p. 1055.

we couldn't. So we began to search all over Rome for people who would lend us the money we needed. One person did offer to help, but the next day he came back to say he would have to mortgage his property, which was a step out of all proportion to the amount we were asking for. So we had lost a day. Saturday was looming, and the workers had to be paid come what may.

"In the end we spoke to a lawyer called Merlini, a man with a beard which really suited him, a good, devout Catholic and a competent jurist. He had helped us to buy the house, and in many other negotiations. 'This time,' he said, 'it so happens that I have some money left with me by a client, which he has given me the use of for a year.' He lent it to us at no interest, and it was enough for two weeks' wages. Then Our Lord saw to it that we should manage with bills of exchange and a certain amount of juggling. It was a matter of robbing Peter to pay Paul: a kind of madness, and a source of great stress. How did we manage? It was a miracle. I don't know how, but we always paid."[10]

One day Don Alvaro fell ill. He was running a temperature of forty degrees (104°F). Father Escrivá came to his bedside and, seeing him so ill and worried because "Saturday, pay day, is coming up," he asked, "Alvaro, my dear son, what will happen, what can happen if for once we don't pay them, and let them wait until we have the money?"

"What can happen? I don't mind going to prison. But it's the honor of the Work that is at stake."

"Well then, get yourself up and see if you can find the money, wherever."

While awaiting Don Alvaro's return, Father Escrivá, as he so often did, went to ask his daughters for an intense bombardment of prayers for this intention. He was deeply affected.

"What kind of a swine am I? I'm killing poor Alvaro. But we have no option: he's the only one who can go to the banks and solve the problem, because they know and trust him. With just a little bit, only the tiniest bit of what he's carrying on his shoulders, I'd have died by now."

---

10. AGP, RHF 21171, pp. 1249–1250.

Then, to defuse the situation, he added playfully, "My son Alvaro's illness would be cured instantly if we put a healthy poultice of liras, or better still, pounds sterling, on his liver."

After a little while, Don Alvaro returned. Father Escrivá came out to meet him.

"Have you got it?"

"Yes, Father."

"How did you get it?"

"As always Father, by obeying."[11]

In the end they found a construction company belonging to Leonardo Castelli. He studied the work already underway, as well as the plans of the projected buildings. He could see it was not just a makeshift job, but something that had to be done thoroughly, a project to last for centuries. He trusted Don Alvaro's goodness and honesty, and decided to take over the contract. From then on Castelli would pay the workers' wages. He even increased the number of workmen to speed up the job. Don Alvaro had to pay Castelli's bill every two or three months. The cost was no less, but they had more time to find the money.

They all tightened their belts. They got up at the crack of dawn to walk to the universities so as to save the bus or streetcar fares. On these long walks they wore rope-soled sandals and carried their shoes in a bag so as not to wear the shoes out. On the way, one would read the day's lesson aloud while the others memorized it to the rhythm of their own strides. A packet of twenty cigarettes, sliced with the precision born of long practice, was transformed into sixty mini-cigarettes.

As the villa was so big, it had seven entrances from the street. All but two were now closed off. Money was so tight they did not have enough to pay *lo Zio* Carlo, "Uncle Charles," a carpenter from Città Leonina, to board up all the doors, so he did half of them and finished the job when they could pay. Meantime they stopped the drafts with newspapers and sacks.

About this time, March 1948, Father Escrivá suffered a facial paralysis as a result of the cold, but only three people knew about it.

---

11. Oral testimony of Lourdes Toranzo to the author.

He only referred to it much later, saying in a conversation, "My face went like that too, about twenty years ago. There are three witnesses to it in Rome. But it was not a joke; it was because we had no money for heating and it was very damp indeed there."[12]

Ten years amidst scaffolding and builders

They had taken on a formidable construction project to house the offices and the living quarters of the general council and the central advisory of Opus Dei. Faculty and students of the Roman College of the Holy Cross, for men, also lived there for some years, as they did not move to Cavabianca until 1974; and for some time the students and faculty of the Roman College of Our Lady, for women, had to live there too, until they moved to Castelgandolfo in 1963. There also was quite a large domestic staff. In all, more than 300 people lived there.

One day, while walking through part of the house with one of his sons, a naval officer named Rafael Caamaño, Father Escrivá explained how many of the architectural or decorative features had been copied from other places seen while walking around Rome or traveling in Italy. "We were not trying to be innovative but to get the thing done well." Then, laughing because some people might think the house had the airs of a great mansion, he added lightheartedly, "We have copied so many lovely things from here and there that everything has an 'ancestry' and a 'genealogy.' Besides, when you copy something you can improve on it, do it more cheaply and with fewer defects."[13]

Father Escrivá kept a close eye on the work, both at the planning stage and when it was being done. He often climbed up the scaffolding with the architects and the builders. Sometimes, on days when the men were not working, he took his daughters with him so that they too could enjoy imagining where things would be. It was not just his house but everybody's—a big family house. On one of these visits he showed them a large crucifix hanging in the Galleria di Sotto. "I told the artist to do his very best to make a living, serene

---

12. AGP, RHF 20760, p. 462.
13. Testimony of Fr. Rafael Caamaño (AGP, RHF T-05837).

Christ, not one twisted in agony on the Cross," he said. "I wanted people's hearts to be moved to contrition just by contemplating it."

Then he read the phrase he'd had engraved on a plaque beside it. They were Peter's words when Jesus had asked him three times, "Peter, do you love me more than these?"

Domine, Tu omnia nosti, Tu scis quia amo te—"Lord, you know all things, you know that I love you."

Father Escrivá continued looking at the crucifix. He whispered an irrepressible exclamation, "And how!"[14]

They lived in discomfort, privation, and austerity, through the cold and damp of winter and the suffocating summer heat, often going hungry. Father Escrivá did not try to conceal the truth with euphemisms, and would say to his sons, "You can't become easygoing here! Humanly speaking you have it tough, thank God! Although years ago it was much worse. I've told you so often that many of your brothers have been hungry with me: not for one or two days, but long spells. We did not have a cent."[15]

In time, no one would remember the hardship. They could only talk of Father Escrivá's immense love, tender and firm at the same time, toward each of them, "calling us each by our own nicknames: Pepele, Pilé, Olly, Beto, Wally, Riny, Cipry, Babo, Quecco, and more, because a big and beautiful family is what we were and what we are."

When there was a break in his work, Father Escrivá would often step into a small garden in front of Villa Vecchia and walk up and down while he said a part of the Rosary or chatted with a companion. He could not avoid the company of his children, and he did not want to. He would look toward the windows, open perhaps because of the heat. Everybody was busy studying or working. If he saw someone, he cleared his throat to attract attention and, if the person looked up, beckoned him to join him. Soon he would be surrounded by young men and would have a lively conversation, strolling from one side of the garden to the other. Other times he would sit in a corner at a central area called the Arco dei Venti, perhaps because there was a breeze there. He would talk to his sons about

---

14. Testimony of Encarnación Ortega (AGP, RHF T-05074).
15. AGP, RHF 20163, p. 1025.

supernatural themes and give them the spirit of the Work, letting them drink it from its source while he forgot his tiredness and gave himself to them joyfully.

One afternoon in 1954 he was talking in this way when suddenly he lost the thread of what he was saying. Gazing at them one by one, he asked point-blank, "Do you know, my sons, why I love you so much?" A few seconds went by. The answer came with irresistible forcefulness: "I love you so much because I see the Blood of Christ bubbling through your veins."[16]

Financial problems persisted, a permanent feature of Father Escrivá's life, although lack of money never stopped him from doing what the spread of Opus Dei demanded. He put into practice the old saying: "Spend all you ought, though you owe all you spend."[17]

Worry about ways and means did not destroy his peace of mind for a second. When money worries were at their peak, in October 1948, Father Escrivá directed a workshop for his daughters who held executive posts in the Work. They met in Los Rosales. They studied and worked intensely to get through a week's program in three days. The agenda was very diverse, taking in subjects ranging from the spiritual formation of people of Opus Dei to the maintenance of the centers; from new apostolic initiatives to the need for physical rest.

When they came to a session called "Study of the Financial Situation," the women supposed they would need to produce an analysis of ways to maintain apostolic projects. Folders, notebooks, records of experiences, estimates of expenses and incomes, extracts of domestic accounts, and more, were piled up on the table in the dining room, where sessions were held. But Father Escrivá said, "My daughters, financial questions are solved by personal responsibility and equally personal poverty. Rather than studying the matter here, it is something you each need to discuss in your prayer, face to face with our Lord." That session took place in the evening, in the oratory of Los Rosales, in intense silence.[18]

Father Escrivá believed financial problems had to be solved by making demands on oneself and having total trust in God. As part

---

16. AGP, RHF 21166, p. 63.
17. *The Way*, no. 481.
18. Testimony of Encarnación Ortega (AGP, RHF T-05074).

of his own dialogue with God, he wrote: "My financial situation is as tight as it ever has been. But I haven't lost my peace of mind. I'm quite sure that God, my Father, will settle the whole business once and for all."[19]

He practiced the same personal poverty expected of his children. There are countless examples. Father Escrivá had just two cassocks. One, cut in the Roman style and always clean and well-ironed, was for going out and receiving visitors. The other was for wearing around the house. It had so many darns and patches that he said, "It has more embroidery than a Manila shawl."[20]

His bedroom was a small cubicle with a bed, a table, a plain wooden chair with no cushion, and a tiny built-in wardrobe. Everyone had to walk through it to get to other rooms. The room where he worked was the smallest, darkest room in Villa Tevere. Only through one tiny window, looking on to an interior patio, could a breath of air and a sliver of light get in.

He had a thorough-going determination to have no possessions, nothing of his own, not to complain if he lacked what he needed, and to do without anything superfluous. He also practiced poverty in his body and soul all the time.

One morning, before breakfast, Father Escrivá had gone with Don Alvaro to have a blood test in Via Nazionale. It was 11:30 before they were through. As they had to make a few calls elsewhere, it was not worth going home, so they went into a bar in Piazza Esedra for breakfast. Standing at the bar, they asked for a cappuccino and a bread roll. Don Alvaro paid. As they were about to drink the coffee, a beggar woman came in, went up to Father Escrivá, and asked him for money.

"I have no money. The only thing I have is this. Here you are, and God bless you!" He passed his untouched breakfast to her. Don Alvaro immediately tried to pass on his breakfast to Father Escrivá. "You have this, and I'll get another one for myself."

"No, no, leave it. I've had mine."

Don Alvaro insisted. Father Escrivá refused to budge. The girl at the till joined in, "Father, you have your cappuccino, we'll make

---

19. Cf. *The Forge*, no. 807.
20. AGP, RHF 21166, pp. 59–60.

another for this woman." Father Escrivá, smiling but determined not to give in, closed the episode by saying, "No, no, thank you very much. Relax, I've had breakfast already." He wanted to be poor because he wanted to be Christ. And because he wanted to be Christ, other people's helplessness, suffering, and destitution struck at his conscience. He would have preferred to suffer himself.

An "assault course" by the Tiber

The work on the house in Bruno Buozzi Street increased. They were still living in the lodge which they called *Il Pensionato*, "the boarding-house." Encouraged by the motto "God and Daring" of earlier years, Father Escrivá launched into the building of the Roman College of the Holy Cross. It was madness, a dream. But to commit himself further before God, he gave it the legal formality of a decree, signed on June 29, the feast of Sts. Peter and Paul, 1948. In the text he proclaimed that people from every country would come to the Roman College to receive spiritual, intellectual, and apostolic training. It would be a school where men were formed to be educators in their turn. It would be an "assault course," a rigorous training ground for passing on to others the compelling news of an ideal that could enrich every aspect of their lives.

This mixing and sharing of young people from many nations would open up their horizons, ridding them of any provincial outlook, nationalism, or discrimination by race or class. In the Roman College they would acquire a perspective incompatible with any kind of arrogance: *para servir, servir*—"to be useful, serve."

Repeatedly, Father Escrivá pointed out to men and women that they weren't there to become "supermen" or "superwomen." He told them they would always be "earthenware": brittle clay, easily broken, but able to hold the fine liquor of wisdom.

In a corner of the villa visible from the Cortile Vecchio as well as from the Galleria della Campana, a white marble slab expressed this idea in sober Latin words. The inscription, dated 1952, was addressed to every visitor, resident, or guest. "Consider these buildings you see around you as the rigorous training ground from which a race of strong men and women will go out, who shall always fight joyfully and peacefully, throughout the world, for the Church of God and the Roman Pontiff."

On saying good-bye to some who had finished their studies in the Roman College and were returning to their countries, Father Escrivá expressed what each of them felt: "If you have used your time well, Rome will leave a mark on your soul, a deep, lasting imprint. And you will be able to be more faithful sons of the Church."[21]

The Roman College of Our Lady for the women of the Work was established on December 12, 1953. The number of students grew so fast that by 1959 a proper college had to be built for them with all speed. Villa delle Rose was built outside Rome, at Castelgandolfo, on land which Pius XII had made over temporarily to the Work and which John XXIII donated permanently.

Villa delle Rose was finished in 1963. Now Father Escrivá launched the building of the campus for the Roman College of the Holy Cross, also on the outskirts of Rome near Via Flaminia: Cavabianca. He had no mania for building. The cause, rather, was the tide of vocations responding to the "universal call to holiness."

Keener on finishing things than beginning them, he always refused to bless foundation stones. In the case of the building on Bruno Buozzi Street, he held a simple ceremony to bless the last stone of the group of buildings that made up Villa Tevere. It consisted of the sign of the Cross and recital of a *Te Deum*, followed by a cheerful "*Auguri*, everybody! *Siamo arrivati!*—we're here!" It was January 9, 1960, and pouring rain.[22]

The result of all this effort was a fine, large house, simple and unpretentious in style. What had been a large garden was now built over. More levels had been added, and several floors below ground level. The complex was neat and well balanced, by no means monumental or imposing. The classic Florentine style of the original "old house," Villa Vecchia, had been maintained. The different levels meant lots of staircases, short bridges, and connecting corridors.

Literary invention came to the fore in choosing a name for every corner. The *cortili*, tiny inner courtyards, took their names from ornamental details: *del Fiume, della Palla, dei Cantori, delle Tartarughe,*

---

21. AGP, RHF 20162, p. 598.
22. Testimony of Fr. Carlos Cardona (AGP, RHF T-06138).

del Cipresso—river, ball, singers, tortoises, and cypress. The ensemble was as varied as it was compact.

For those who lived in Villa Tevere, each place had its intimate history. Every stone held memories of Father Escrivá. "This is where the Father told me. . . ." "How often the Father, standing in front of this image of Our Lady, would. . . ." "When we painted the fresco on that wall, the Father helped. . . ." Here was the background of his life, inseparably linked to the epic of the Work itself: a marble slab; bare footprints, showing the start of a route; the guardian angel of Opus Dei; the cheerful inscription *Omnia in bonum* telling the viewer that "everything is for the best."

Altogether, Villa Tevere comprised eight houses. For the women, there were La Montagnola, Villa Sacchetti, La Casetta, Il Ridotto, and Il Fabbricato Piccolo. For men, there were the Casa del Vicolo, Uffici, and Villa Vecchia where Father Escrivá lived with the members of the general council.

"We pray more than we eat"

On one occasion, referring to the fact there were only four dining rooms as against twenty-four oratories, Father Escrivá said, "That's good; we pray more than we eat!"[23] The whole complex had a name which he had given it even before the scaffolding was raised: Villa Tevere (Tiber). He was thinking, perhaps, of the allegory of the old river Tiber which embraces Rome, surrounding her as if lovingly.

Sometimes, having gathered for a get-together in the evening, the men would start singing. Everyone sang, some better, some worse. They sang popular songs, songs full of genuine love. One of them might be borne through the windows to float on the warm air of the Roman night.

Roma, che la più bella sei del mondo, il Tevere ti serve da cintura . . . Rome, you are the most beautiful city in the world, girded by the Tiber . . .

Rome had penetrated the hearts of these young men, leaving not a melancholy nostalgia but a deep impression on their souls.

---

23. Oral testimony of Salvador Suanzes.

Like a Giant

Ut gigas

xultavit ut gigas ad currendam viam.[1] "He was filled with joy and, like a giant, rose to run the course." Father Josemaría Escrivá often used to repeat these words, emphasizing the rhythmic flow of the Latin. This rather strange verse from the Book of Psalms sometimes impelled him to find time where there was none, other times to fight still harder in his interior struggle, and still others, to give of himself wholeheartedly. He never realized that these six Latin words were a graphic description of his own life.

Great men, a very different species from mere "celebrities," provide the biographer and the historian with an interesting problem. On the one hand, they are men of their time, well acquainted with the mentality, customs, and events of their age; on the other hand, they are men who look forward, and are spurred on by their vision of the future. They are ahead of their time, swimming against the tide of inertia of their own generation.

They propose bold, imaginative, untypical solutions to problems. Because they can see what is invisible to others, they dare to take on the impossible. Because they can see ahead, they are prophetic. Because they have nothing to lose, they are rebels. Public opinion either ignores them or misunderstands them. Those who live in the comfortable greyness of ordinary life feel upset and bothered by such troublemakers.

---

1. Ps. 18(19):6.

One day in August 1941, in semi-darkness in the oratory at 14 Diego de Leon Street, Madrid, Father Escrivá was leading a meditation. He spoke about faith, boldness, and daring to ask for the moon, in the unshakable confidence that God can give it.

"Afraid?" he said. "I'm not afraid of anyone! Not even of God, because he is my Father." He turned and looked at the tabernacle, and added, as if speaking directly to someone there in the same room, "Lord, we're not afraid of you, because we love you."[2]

Father Escrivá unfolds a dream

Ut gigas . . . On an afternoon in November 1942, also in Madrid, Father Escrivá arrived at 19 Jorge Manrique Street. It was a center for women of the Work. At that moment there were just ten women in Opus Dei: Lola Fisac, Encarnita Ortega, Nisa Gonzalez, Lola Jiménez-Vargas, Amparo Rodriguez-Casado, Enriqueta Botella, Laura and Conchita López-Amo, Maria Jesús Hereza, and Aurora Oliden, who was from Leon and was a friend of Nisa.

Father Escrivá met with the three who were at home, Encarnita, Nisa, and Lola Fisac, in the sitting room-cum-library. He unfolded a paper and spread it out on the table. It was like a chart, a graphic plan setting out a variety of apostolic tasks. The women of the Work would carry them out all over the world, either as personal initiatives or corporate works. He explained the chart enthusiastically, pointing to each of the headings in turn: agricultural schools for country people; university halls of residence; maternity clinics; centers for the professional training of women in different areas—hospitality and catering, secretarial work, nursing, teaching, languages, and others; activities in the field of fashion; mobile libraries; bookshops. The most important thing of all was the apostolate of friendship, developed on an individual basis with their families, neighbors, acquaintances, and colleagues, "and that will always be impossible to register or measure."

Father Escrivá repeated every now and again, "Dream, and your dreams will fall short!" The three looked at him, thunderstruck,

---

2. Testimony of Encarnación Ortega (AGP, RHF T-05074).

astonished. It did not occur to them that they were to do all this themselves. It seemed more as if the Father were unfolding a wonderful dream for a faraway future. They felt unskilled, devoid of means or resources, and incapable.

Father Escrivá could read in their faces both desire and fear, a cowardly "If only we could. . . ." He picked up the paper very slowly and started to fold it. His face had changed. He was very serious now—perhaps upset, or disappointed, or saddened.

He had been struggling for more than twelve years to give form and life to the ideal of having women in Opus Dei. This ideal was what he had *seen* God wanted on February 14, 1930. The first women to come to the Work had prayed a lot but never lifted a finger. They were very good, but of a mystical disposition: Father Escrivá had to tell them they were not suitable. Later on came others who talked a lot and bustled about, but did not pray. They left. The present ones belonged to "the third batch." Could it be that, at the moment of truth, they were going to sit there paralyzed with fear?

Choosing his words carefully, he said, "When looking at all this, you can have one of two reactions. That of thinking it is something very fine but unreal and unrealizable. Or else that of trust in our Lord—that if he is asking us for all of this, he will help us follow it through." He stopped. He looked at each of them individually, as though trying to transmit his own faith, communicate his own conviction. Before turning toward the door, he added, "I hope you will have the second reaction."[3]

Breaching frontiers

They did. In the next forty years the women of Opus Dei spread over both hemispheres, and set up and put into action more than 40 university halls of residence, 200 cultural centers, 16 secretarial and language schools, 79 schools which were parents' initiatives and another 12 as corporate projects, 94 institutes for professional training, and 13 agricultural schools for women.[4] They also started countless dispensaries, primary health care centers, literacy programs,

3. Ibid.
4. 1984 statistics: provided to the author by Marlies Kücking.

campaigns for cultural and social development, food distribution services in rural areas, evening courses for primary and secondary education in working-class districts, and much more.

Ut gigas . . . Forty years on, those three women had multiplied by more than 10,000. As the men's side of Opus Dei had spread, the women's had too, in parallel, and was established in cities and towns in more than seventy countries and on every continent. In 1984, they were soon to begin their apostolate in Sweden, Norway, Finland, Taiwan, Hong Kong, South Korea, Macao, Ivory Coast, Zaire, Cameroon, Santo Domingo, New Zealand, Poland, Hungary, and Czechoslovakia.

Father Escrivá had a powerful, muscular faith. "A champion of the faith," Cardinal Tedeschini called him.[5] He preached and worked hard. He was never intimidated. He chipped away at difficulties with his demanding mottoes: "More, more, more," "Don't be content with what is easy." He was never satisfied. "You see: it has nearly all died out . . . will you not help to spread the blaze?" (*The Way*, no. 801). He was ambitious: "Our apostolate is a sea without shores." He was always ready to set out anew: "So much has been destroyed! There is so much still to do!" He was fired with an unquenchable ideal: "*Regnare Christum volumus!* We want Christ to reign!"

Once when some of his sons were talking to him about the University of Navarre, he noticed a certain sense of complacency in their achievements, and at once warned them not to rest on their laurels. "This is only the beginning—within a short time there will be ten or twenty similar universities."[6] And so there were: following on the University of Navarre in Spain, came the University of Piura in Peru, the Pan-American University in Mexico, La Sabana in Colombia, the Austral in Argentina, the Andes University in Chile, and the University of Asia and the Pacific in Manila, the Philippines. And plans were well under way for Strathmore University of Nairobi, Kenya and the Libero Istituto Universitario Campus Biomedico in Rome.

On November 17, 1969 in a gathering of university students,[7] someone mentioned La Moncloa University Hall in Madrid. Father

---

5. Testimony of Encarnación Ortega (AGP, RHF T-05074) citing Cardinal Tedeschini.
6. Testimony of Monsignor César Ortiz-Echagüe (AGP, RHF T-04694).
7. Get-together on November 17, 1969 at Colegio Mayor Aralar, Pamplona, Spain.

Escrivá recalled how this hall had cost a lot of prayer. The owner of the building they rented and ran as a hall of residence in Jenner Street in Madrid had given them notice. The day it expired, Father Escrivá set out very early and went to the owner's house, getting him out of bed. He had brought with him a check for 5,000 pesetas, at the time, 1943, a considerable sum. He gave it to the owner as a deposit to extend their lease until they could find another place.

Now it was back to square one. He searched high and low. He prayed with all his might. Before the lease expired, an industrialist called Messeguer from Murcia, in the south of Spain, turned up, and committed himself to help turn two neighboring houses, badly damaged by bombing during the civil war, into a hall of residence big enough for 100 students, and a third detached house into the base for the catering staff. The refurbishing was carried out in record time. Father Escrivá finished this account by saying, "Everything was sorted out, with no miracles; but I must say, with a lot of prayer."

Just then, Father Jose Gil, a priest of the Work present at the get-together, spoke up with some good news. "Well, right now in La Moncloa we *are* seeing a miracle: out of 104 residents, ninety are coming to daily Mass. Just think, Father: ninety!"

"But aren't they also bringing friends of theirs from other halls of residence?" asked Father Escrivá.

"Well, Father . . . we're working on it."

"We've been working on it, my son, since 1928! So that if each of them isn't bringing another ten along with him, we can only talk about *half* a miracle."[8]

A strange bourgeois: far-seeing, never satisfied, daring

He had the dissatisfaction of a burning spirit who wanted to set fire to everything he touched. In Rome one day he was shown a recently published book by a son of his, the lawyer and theologian Father José Luis Illanes, on "sanctifying work." He flipped through it, and

---

8. Testimony of Monsignor César Ortiz-Echagüe (AGP, RHF T-04694).

then, without wasting time on expressions of satisfaction, told the people with him in the sitting room, "Other books like this can and should be written, on the spirit of service, on loyalty, friendship, human virtues, and so on. They would do souls a lot of good."[9]

Ut gigas . . . The plans for the construction of the shrine of Our Lady of Torreciudad were under study. Father Escrivá knew that, from a human point of view, it was crazy to consider building a basilica of monumental dimensions among the ridges of the Pyrenees. It was a challenge to those agnostic, materialistic times of soulless commercialism when pragmatism demanded that every cubic meter of concrete show a profit. Nevertheless he saw with the eyes of faith multitudes of pilgrims there.

"Build confessionals, lots of confessionals, because people will come from all over the world to get rid of their sins!" he said. He also gave the architects some challenging advice: "Don't be afraid of size!"[10]

Seeing the need to start human and spiritual training and development before adolescence, he encouraged the setting up of schools, and youth clubs for younger children, "not because at that age it is easier to win them over, but so that from an early age they can acquire the Christian principles they will need later on in order to preserve their faith and lead good lives."[11]

He insisted on the importance of providing professional, doctrinal, and moral training and support for women in all walks of life, at the university, in the home, in the countryside, in industry, and so on. He said "anti-Christian militants" were tirelessly promoting materialistic and atheistic ideas in this sphere. "And once the woman is corrupted, the family is corrupted, and then society is too."[12]

In a January 1968 interview with Pilar Salcedo, a journalist, in Villa Tevere he made ground-breaking statements which were published in *Telva*, a Spanish women's magazine.[13] He talked about human love, marriage, the family, women in the home, and in the

---

9. Ibid.
10. Ibid.
11. Testimony of Mercedes Morado (AGP, RHF T-07902).
12. Ibid.
13. *"Women in Social Life and in the Life of the Church,"* interview published in *Telva* (Madrid), February 1, 1968; and in *Conversations with Monsignor Escrivá* (Sydney: Little Hills Press).

workplace, and about "not blocking up the sources of life." Reading his replies with the benefit of hindsight, it is clear that Father Escrivá was anticipating a frontal attack by the feminist movements then in fashion; he was trying to cushion the blow, to absorb the impact of unpopularity which the encyclical *Humanae Vitae*, about to be published, would unleash on Paul VI. It was a way of serving the Church. Father Escrivá risked injury to himself by treading the path beforehand to clear the way.

He was also anticipating by twenty years Pope John Paul II's reflections in the Apostolic Letter *Mulieris Dignitatem* on women and their role in society. The *Telva* interview underlined the dignity of women and their double vocation: to give life to humanity and humanity to life.

In a world of specialized technical know-how, Father Escrivá realized the need to promote the study of the humanities. This was not just because "it is essential to be a whole man," but to counter trends which diminished the human person, leaving people unable to claim their historic, artistic, philosophical, and literary heritage.

Many of those who heard his talks and get-togethers during the 1960s recall how Father Escrivá pressed them "to wage war on poverty, ignorance, illness, suffering, and against the saddest of all forms of want: loneliness,"[14] while he encouraged them to channel the generosity of young people "into the great project of charity and justice whose aim is to ensure that there is no one who is poor, illiterate, or ignorant."[15]

He considered ignorance a great impediment to freedom that enslaves people by impeding their access to the truth. He did not hesitate to describe as "the worst kind of crime"[16] the activities of powerful people who rendered those under them defenseless by keeping them uneducated, misinformed, and in ignorance. "The greatest enemy of souls, of the Church and of God, is ignorance . . . which is not confined to one particular social class: you can find it everywhere."[17]

---

14. Testimony of Mercedes Morado (AGP, RHF T-07902).
15. Ibid.
16. Ibid.
17. Testimony of Marlies Kücking. Get-together on March 18, 1964 at Castelgandolfo, Italy.

He drew a practical conclusion: "The Church of Jesus Christ is not at all afraid of scientific truth. And we, children of God in Opus Dei, have a duty to make our presence felt in all the human sciences. Backed by sound doctrine, how much good we will do to souls! How much ignorance we will dispel!"[18] "People who appear to be far from God only seem so. They are fine, good people...but they are ignorant. Even their sins are like blasphemies on the lips of a child: they don't realize what they are doing. People are not bad. People are good. I don't know any bad people. I do know ignorant people. That is why I never get tired of saying that Opus Dei is not anti-anything. We have to love everyone a lot: evil can only be drowned in an abundance of good."[19]

Ut gigas . . . He opened his arms wide to the lonely, the downtrodden, the weak, the mistaken, the defenseless, without excluding anyone. "And if you ask me whether I love communists, I will say yes, communists too! Not Communism, though. It is a heresy full of heresies, a brutal materialism which leads to tyranny; but I do love communists, because they are in great need."[20]

In one gathering he talked about someone from Central America, a well-known Jewish Freemason, who had come to see him in Rome. "I asked him, 'Why do you love the Work so much?' He answered, 'Because I've found a lot of understanding and openness in the Work.' Then I said to him, 'My friend, all the Freemasons I've met in my country are fanatics; but you're not a fanatic, and that is why, although you're not a Catholic or even a Christian, you are helping us.' Then I promised him I would pray for him very much. And I explained why I love Jewish people such a lot: 'My first love is a Jew—Jesus Christ. And my second love is also Jewish: his most holy mother Mary.' I gave him a medal of Our Lady. He was delighted!"[21]

However, because of his conviction that the Catholic faith he held was the true faith, his limitless understanding for everyone did not lead him to compromise on doctrine, or to debase the content

---

18. Ibid.
19. Ibid. Get-together on September 4, 1967 at Villa Tevere.
20. Ibid.
21. Testimony of Monsignor César Ortiz-Echagüe (AGP, RHF T-04694). Testimony of Marlies Kücking. Get-together on September 14, 1967 at Villa Tevere.

of truth by leaving out difficult bits, which would have been a false ecumenism. Whether in public or private conversation with Muslims, Protestants, Jews, or Buddhists, he would say: "You do not have the whole truth. I am going to pray that one day you will achieve the gift of the true faith. But I assure you that you do have all my respect: I respect you and I respect your freedom."[22]

Father Escrivá's respect for freedom was born of and nourished by respect for each person, because each possesses the supreme dignity of being a child of God. Once when reading the morning news during a trip to Spain in October 1968, he was deeply troubled to see that a publication where some of his sons worked was making a personal attack on someone. He commented, "I cannot defend my children's freedom out there, if my children don't first of all defend the freedom of others. You can speak the truth, criticize things which are going badly, and offer well-thought-out resistance at a high level of debate, but you cannot stoop to blows below the belt. We cannot have two different moral standards, one for ourselves and another for other people. No, my sons. We have just one moral standard: Christ."[23]

Father Escrivá made his daughters and sons in Opus Dei realize that the centers of the Work and their activities were to be open to all classes of people without any discrimination on grounds of belief, race, social class, or ideology. But each activity did need to be appropriate to the social group and cultural level it was intended for, "because Opus Dei does not take anyone out of their environment."

In Africa, too, he was ahead of his time and of the socio-political changes later to come about in Kenya with independence, which was not even dreamed of when people of the Work first went there. The founder held firmly that the two corporate educational projects developed in Nairobi by women and men of the Work had to be interracial. This aroused not only the opposition of the white British residents, but also the suspicions of the Africans and of the Indian colony, none of them integrated with the others. Kianda College and Strathmore College were finally built in an area which enabled people of different races, creeds, and social classes to be educated together.

---

22. Cf. AGP, RHF 21159, p. 926.
23. Testimony of Monsignor César Ortiz-Echagüe (AGP, RHF T-04694).

Option for the poor and rich alike

The same thing happened in other countries where integration at first seemed impossible. Where Chicago runs into West Side, he encouraged a club for the education and training of boys and young men. Midtown Center is open to boys, whose environment is a mix of drugs, sex, idleness, crime, violence, and poverty. The center staff labors to prevent boys from starting on the downward spiral called "there's nothing to be done."[24] With the same aim women of Opus Dei work in the heart of the Bronx to give girls who live in this area of crime, rootless lives, and foul language something their schools have defaulted on and their families cannot supply.

Father Escrivá often said, "Charity does not mean giving loose change and old clothes. We have to give love! We have to give our hearts!"

One day in January 1969 in Rome his eyes shone as he talked about the rehabilitation and social integration gradually taking place among the black people of Harlem. "All of us human beings are made of the same clay. We all speak the same tongue. We are all the same color, as children of the same Father. We are all children of God! We're all equal! This project makes me very happy. Treat them as equals, looking them in the eye, face to face, never looking down on them. Are they less educated? Well, let's give them an education! The cleverer ones can do a university degree. We can give the less clever ones the teaching they need so as to lead decent lives."[25]

In May 1970 during a catechesis in Mexico to a group of people from the United States, he said: "I have something very harsh to say to you. I understand the great problem you have with black people in your country. If we look for the root of the problem, we will find that both sides have been and are at fault. The result is that there is great resentment toward the whites. You need to be prepared to spend two or three years working without expecting anything in return. If you are constant, you will win their confidence, by working with devotion and affection. . . . About 200 years ago, there

24. Cf. Rafael Gomez Perez, *Opus Dei: An Explanation* (Madrid: Rialp, 1992), pp. 175–176.
25. Testimony of Marlies Kücking. Get-together on January 13, 1969 in Rome.

were more black people in Mexico than in the U.S. It did not cause any problems. If there were any problems, they have been able to overcome them in these two centuries, with divine love and human love, unafraid of mixing races. We have to be convinced of this reality which I will not tire of repeating: there aren't lots of different races—Caucasian, black, yellow, brown. There is only one race: the race of the children of God!"[26]

He said that again in Mexico at the old estate of Montefalco, where since the early 1950s people of Opus Dei, with many others, had been carrying out an enormous social, cultural, and apostolic project among local Indians. "No one is greater than anyone else—no one! We are all equal! Each one of us is worth the same: we are worth the blood of Christ."[27]

"Those at the bottom have to come up"

At Villa Tevere on November 11, 1966, an upper-class family from Barcelona named Vallet came to visit him. It was a big group. Among them was a boy wearing the smart uniform of Viaro School. Father Escrivá took the lad aside and told him something he might previously not have known: his parents were paying the school so that another boy from a poor family could study there too. That was sharing. That was practicing social justice and human solidarity.

Turning to the adults, he stressed the same point. "We have to achieve the disappearance of the poor by raising them up; not by pulling down the upper classes."[28]

On countless occasions Father Escrivá explained the Christian criteria of social justice. It was "not what the Marxists say; it is not a class struggle: that is a great injustice. . . . Social justice is not achieved by violence, or shooting, or forming factions."[29] And again: "Those at the bottom have to come up. Those on top will fall of their own accord if they are no good."[30]

---

26. Cf. AGP, RHF 21159, p. 928.
27. Ibid., p. 936.
28. Testimony of Mercedes Morado (AGP, RHF T-07902).
29. Cf. AGP, RHF 20793, pp. 44–45.
30. Testimony of Monsignor César Ortiz-Echagüe (AGP, RHF T-04694).

One day in May 1967 he said to some of his sons: "We want there to be fewer poor, fewer people with no training, fewer suffering from illness or disability, or suffering in old age. That is our aim. But you won't achieve that by setting people against each other. Besides, I insist, the ones at the top will fall of their own accord. What we have to do is advance those at the bottom. We are enemies of violence."[31]

He went to see the building work at Molinoviejo and walked around the site on foot. Seeing Juan Cabrera, the foreman, he waited for him with open arms and they greeted each other with a big hug. Then, during the tour of the site, he talked with the workers he met. "It's only fair, isn't it? They have to pay you well for your work. And if they don't, you must say so."

A carpenter reassured him, "Father, don't worry: they pay us very well here."

"Look here, my son, I would like all your children to be able to study. And that's not just talk; I spend a lot of effort on making it happen."[32]

In the autumn of 1968 he had to go to Spain from Rome. To save time he agreed to travel by boat instead of going by car as was his habit. He drove from Rome to Naples, intending to embark on the *Michelangelo* for Algeciras. But a strike by the crew forced him to stay in Naples for a week. He did not get impatient. When he eventually reached his destination, he talked about his adventures. "It seemed absurd to me, with all that there is to be done, to waste a week in Naples. But very often in life I have experienced how things happened to me that I didn't understand at the time; but years later our Lord has made me see that they did make sense. If God wills, I will understand the Naples episode. If not . . . they will explain it to me in heaven, if all of you help me to get there!"

As for the strike: "As far as I know, having spoken to several of them, these men had reason to complain. To save money, the shipping company was operating with the minimum of staff. Because of that, many sailors and stewards, most of whom were very young, could only spend one month a year with their families. That's not

31. Ibid. Get-together on May 1, 1967 in Molinoviejo, Segovia, Spain.
32. Ibid., April 1970.

just, and it isn't human either!"[33] Later they learned that he had hardly left his cabin during the voyage because of the worldly atmosphere on board.

He was a priest who did not interfere in politics, or argue about current issues that were open to free debate. He only spoke about God and what could bring men to God. Still, some of his texts could be used as guidelines for a substantial program of political, economic, or social action. For instance: "We have to uphold the right of all to live; to own what they need in order to live with dignity; to work and to rest; to choose a particular state in life; to form a home, to bring children into the world within marriage and bring them up; to be able to face times of sickness and old age in security; to have access to education and culture; to join with other citizens to achieve legitimate ends; and, above all, we have to uphold the right of all to know and love God in perfect freedom."[34]

One afternoon in December 1971, in Villa Vecchia, Father Escrivá was talking to two of his sons who had just come from Spain, Pablo Bofill and Rafael Caamaño. The subject of "the option for the poor" arose. Slowly, as if exploring the depths of the mystery, he concluded, "All souls are poor. But the Church is rich. Yes. And her riches are the sacraments; and her doctrine; and all the merits of Christ. . . ."[35] He sprang to his feet smartly. A moment before, while talking about other matters, he had seemed like an old man, weighed down by a heavy burden of suffering. Now he was transformed: he was standing tall, looking cheerful, strong, and courageous, as if about to set off on a cross-country run.

---

33. Ibid.
34. *Friends of God*, no. 171.
35. Testimony of Fr. Rafael Caamaño (AGP, RHF T-05837).

6 ✤

"Why this useless murmuring?"

Psalm 2 on Tuesdays

Since 1932 people in Opus Dei have recited Psalm 2 every Tuesday. It is a powerful psalm which speaks of rebellion, broken bonds, yokes cast away, mutinies, and plots among princes to harass the Lord and his Christ. God jeers at his enemies, submits them to his will, breaks them in pieces like a potter's vessel, and rules them with a rod of iron. It is also a tender psalm, in which this same God declares his love for his Son, whom he begets "today"—every day. The psalm starts off with a challenging question: "Why among peoples this useless murmuring? Why do the people devise vain things?"

In the Middle Ages the Knights Templar also recited Psalm 2 before going into battle. Emblazoned on their shields was the image of two warriors riding on one horse: possibly one knight had picked up the other. Here was a symbol of robust fraternity.

Father Escrivá always referred to the Work as a twofold reality, "family and militia." It was a family of welcome, trust, and companionship. It was a militia, making demands, imposing discipline, involving struggle.

Almost all Father Escrivá's preaching speaks of struggle: a vigorous, constant struggle against oneself, not anyone else. From the beginning he conceived Opus Dei as a militia of Christians who, far from making war, would make peace. They would sow joy and peace in the world—or, more precisely, joy *with* peace. At the heart of this joy with peace is struggle, effort, self-denial, war. "Man's life on earth is warfare," Father Escrivá used to say, echoing Job.

Pax in bello, peace in war. That is how a day or a life in Opus Dei could be summarized. The family greeting used by this militia is "*Pax!*"

Our Lady of Peace

The Prelatic Church of Opus Dei in Rome is several meters underground in Villa Tevere, and is dedicated to Our Lady of Peace. It is not by chance or a mere whim of the decorators that a glass case at the back has swords on display. These swords have never drawn blood: they are ceremonial swords, dress swords, swords of peace. This collection of weapons represents *Pax in bello,* peace in war. This is the peace that comes of personal struggle, always in battle array and constantly on guard.

The three battlefronts of Opus Dei

For many years the people of the Work have been battling on three fronts simultaneously, waging a canonical battle, an ascetical battle, and a battle for training and development.

The ascetical battle, each individual's personal battle for holiness, for people of Opus Dei is a struggle not generally focused on evil desires but on virtue. They don't consider themselves incapable of sinning, but they are intent on finding love.

The "battle for training and development" took up a lot of Father Escrivá's time and effort. It was a one-to-one affair in which he formed those who would form others. ("You are the bridge. You are the continuity," he would say to the students of the Roman College in the 1950s.) His aim, which he achieved, was to offer everyone in the Work the chance to make a serious study of philosophy and theology. The classes had to be pitched at the right intellectual and cultural level. This was not about creating a set of intellectuals, but enabling every person in Opus Dei to acquire deep religious devotion with a firm theological base, and enough sound moral criteria to be able to act freely in their own sphere.

The phrase "Opus Dei is a great catechesis" means that everyone in the Work has to be able to give their fellows a sure, attractive, and very clear notion of God. They have to be able to say what their faith is about, whom they love, and why they hope.

People in Opus Dei do not settle for simple faith—even manual workers need to read, study, and develop their understanding of what they believe. They will apply the same skills to their study of the fundamental truths of the Catholic faith as they do to their work. None should have an illiterate piety devoid of sound arguments, a religion of emotional spasms, morality based on blindness.

Aspirations and his guardian angel

One of the aspirations Father Escrivá passed on to his children was *Deo omnis gloria!*—"all the glory to God!" But it would be a gross error to conclude that people in Opus Dei have a relationship with God based on Latin. Father Escrivá taught his children to relate to God naturally. Himself a lover of fine Latin, he enjoyed making free translations, not allowing an adverb or a gerund to stifle the heart's expression.

On the stone lintel of the door into the sitting room of Villa Vecchia he had engraved the words, *Respiciat nos tantum Dominus noster et laeti serviemus.* Sometimes, on passing through, he would stop and say aloud, "If Our Lord just casts a glance our way, we will work cheerfully!"[1] He translated well; not with a dictionary but with his heart. With the same freedom of spirit, and because he loved God with all his soul, he treated him with the trust of a son who knew he was loved.

"Be like children before God," he said. "I spend the whole day saying childlike aspirations—childish ones. If you heard them you'd laugh! Or maybe you'd cry!"[2]

On occasion he recommended, "When you are doing your personal prayer, if you see you are not capable of praying, not even by turning your distractions into prayer, then meditate once again on those splendid prayers we Christians possess: the Our Father, the Creed, the Hail Mary, and the others. They are like an open book! One word—wait a little, another word—wait another while, and so on!"

---

1. Cf. AGP, RHF 21162, p. 700. Testimony of Helena Serrano (cf. AGP, RHF T-04641).
2. Testimony of Monsignor César Ortiz-Echagüe (AGP, RHF T-04694).

He himself discovered strands of gold in each Hail Mary of the Rosary. Sometimes he would emphasize one word, reciting "pray for us sinners, *now*"; other times, "*at the hour of our death.*" Or, as he said "the Lord is with you!" he would be enthralled by the discovery of Our Lady's likeness-unto-God.

One day he was traveling by car with Don Alvaro and two other sons. When they got to Bologna he saw a church's bell tower. His heart and mind flew toward the distant tabernacle; he spontaneously cupped his hands round his mouth and called out, "Hey, Lord! An affectionate greeting from all of us here in this car!"

This "piety of a child" was not an imitation of children's silliness but their spontaneity, their candor and openness. It found very natural ways of dealing with supernatural realities. For instance, Father Escrivá cultivated a close friendship with his guardian angel. He was so conscious of his angel's company that every time he went through a door, no matter how much of a hurry he was in, he made a gesture unnoticeable to anyone who did not know about it: he stopped for a split second, to let his guardian angel go through first.[3]

People of the Work do not pray about intellectual theories or arid theology. They pray about their real lives, and they live by their prayer.

One of Father Escrivá's concerns was to avoid doctrinal errors or any weakening of moral conscience among people of the Work. He urged them to be vigilant and not "swallow" any book without taking precautions beforehand. Those were times when many Catholics were losing their moral and doctrinal criteria, or letting the foundations of their faith crumble, because they were dazzled by the idea of "progress."

"Watch out," he warned them. "This warning comes from a man who knows a lot, not because of his doctorates, but from years of experience. It comes from an old priest. It comes from me, and I'm not one to be overcautious." He himself always sought advice before reading treatises of high theology. Humbly and straightforwardly, he consulted whoever had the post of spiritual director of the Work at that moment.

---

3. Written narrative of Bishop Javier Echaverria given to the author.

How to become a "director"

Father Carlos Cardona, who studied metaphysics and had an impressive intellectual capacity, clearly recalled the day in September 1961 when Father Escrivá told him he had been appointed spiritual director of Opus Dei throughout the world. It happened in Villa Tevere, in a meeting room known as "Commissions." Father Cardona's feelings showed in his face: he was obviously overwhelmed and had a natural fear of not being up to the job. Father Escrivá was gifted in "discerning spirits." He realized that his son's sense of panic might result from the mistaken belief that he was to rely on his own strength and talents to carry out the task.

Father Escrivá looked Father Cardona in the eye and said, "I haven't appointed you for positive reasons, because there aren't any. I've appointed you because the negative reasons, of which there are plenty, aren't of sufficient weight to impede it." Father Cardona had been living under the same roof as Father Escrivá for five years and knew how much he loved him, how well he knew him, and how he missed no chance of making demands on him, correcting him, and lovingly hitting him where it hurt—any sign of intellectual arrogance.

There was a moment's silence. Then Father Escrivá went on. "There are brothers of yours who would do it better than you, but I need them where they are. And on the other hand you couldn't do their jobs." Then all at once there was a change of mood, and Father Escrivá smiled. His whole face beamed. He opened his arms wide and, taking his son by both shoulders, he rocked him lovingly to and fro, calling him by name and making light of his troubles. "But Carlos, you're not to worry. We'll help you! And between us all, it will work out—with God's grace." As he left the room he said half-jokingly, half in earnest, "'Spiritual Father,' pray for me to God our Lord! Amen."

Father Cardona went directly to the oratory of the Holy Apostles. He threw himself on his knees and spoke to our Lord trustingly and daringly. "I'm transferring the appointment. You be the spiritual director. I'll work for you, at your bidding: I'll be your clerk."[4] This was the "piety of a child" Father Escrivá had taught him. Father

---

4. Testimony of Fr. Carlos Cardona (AGP, RHF T-06138).

Cardona could not help feeling amazed when, shortly after, Father Escrivá consulted him about some doctrinal books he was reading and, in all simplicity, asked for a list of theological treatises on the Trinity, adding, "But be careful what you give me! They need to be books of sterling doctrine, sound to the very last letter. By no manner or means would I want to put my faith in danger!"[5]

The canonical battle

The third "battle" people of Opus Dei had to fight was an external battle, fought with prayer, study, waiting, and keeping quiet. This was the canonical battle. It was a question of opening up an appropriate canonical path through the general law of the Church so that the Work could exist, work, and spread in accordance with its secular nature.

The inscription over the door into the general council's sitting room in Villa Tevere and described how to win the third battle: *In silentio et in spe erit fortitudo vestra.* "Your strength shall lie in your silence and in your hope." They had not come "a century too soon" but more than half a century elapsed, from 1928 until 1982, before Opus Dei obtained a suitable canonical formulation as a personal prelature of universal scope.

"They fit in too!"

On January 13, 1948 Father Escrivá and Don Alvaro were driving from Rome to Milan. It was a cold, dark day with a dense fog. Less than a year earlier, in February 1947, Pius XII had conferred the *Decretum Laudis*, a preliminary approval, on the Work, and they were waiting for definitive approval to be granted. The car was going slowly with its headlights on. They had got as far as Pavia when Father Escrivá, who had been quiet and absorbed in his thoughts, suddenly exclaimed, "They fit in too!" He had just discovered the canonical solution whereby married people could also join Opus Dei.[6] Quite a few were ready to join, aspiring to be saints in their

---

5. Ibid.
6. Cf. AGP, RHF 21169, p. 71.

married lives, their daily work, and their social environment. They were already fulfilling the norms and customs of Opus Dei. They only needed to find a canonical way to join.

Father Escrivá presented his petition to the Holy See on February 2, 1948.[7] The doors were opened to married people without delay. Victor Garcia, Tomas Alvira, and Mariano Navarro were the first three to join. Several more followed a few months later.

Within an ace of stepping down

Father Escrivá started to feel a growing urgency to help diocesan priests. His conscience was stirred by the absence of spiritual attention or cultural enrichment, and also loneliness, of so very many priests.

The solution would be for those who had a vocation to join Opus Dei. But how they could combine belonging to the Work with their dependence on their own bishops? Father Escrivá reached the point where he honestly thought God was asking him to make the enormous sacrifice of leaving the Work to start a foundation dedicated to diocesan priests.

At that time, not just in Spain but almost everywhere in Western Europe, the clergy in big cities had lost the place formerly theirs in society, and found themselves marginalized. Many country priests were badly cared for and spiritually isolated, without support or incentives. Father Escrivá suffered over the harsh loneliness endured by priests in big city parishes and country priests. Without support their vocation either withered or went soft; or, if they stood firm, it was only by dint of heroic stoicism.

That same year, 1948, on a trip to Spain from Rome, Father Escrivá told his sister Carmen and brother Santiago of an important decision he had made and had already made known unofficially to the Holy See. With the definitive approval of the Work in hand and its publication now imminent, he was going to set about organizing an association concerned exclusively with priests. "After all your help and all you have done for the Work," he told them, "I think you have the right to know about this new step as soon as possible."[8]

7. RHF, EF-480202-1. Request of Monsignor Escrivá to his Holiness Pius XII.
8. Testimony of Encarnación Ortega (AGP, RHF T-05074).

Don Alvaro and the members of the general council of the Work were told, but Father Escrivá needed extra fortitude to tell his daughters. One day he summoned Encarnita Ortega and Nisa Guzman to Villa Vecchia.

"Our canonical solution is on the point of coming through. I think the Work can go ahead without me. Our Lord is making me feel the loneliness of so many of my brother priests. I am going to give up the post of president general of Opus Dei, to dedicate all my efforts and time to a new foundation exclusively for priests. The spiritual, ascetical, cultural, and even human abandonment in which our priests live, scattered among villages and city parishes, is heartbreaking. They have a very great mission to carry out. A priest never goes to heaven alone or to hell either: for good or for evil, he always drags a long trail of souls with him. But how lonely and neglected they are here on earth!"

Encarnita and Nisa were stunned. Father Escrivá, seeing the shock his news had caused, said, "You have to be very peaceful, very serene, and very secure: more so than ever. I want you to pray! Don't talk much about this business. But I wanted you to know. You had a right to know!" They did not understand how the Work could continue without the founder. Only he had received the full message of Opus Dei from God. Overwhelmed and crushed, they kept silent, not saying a word even to one another.[9]

Around the same time in 1948, Father Escrivá made a strange request of one of his sons who was keen on photography. He asked him to take a special picture. No face was to appear. It was to be an image full of symbolism: a close-up of Don Alvaro del Portillo's hands, palms outstretched, receiving some wooden donkeys from Father Escrivá's hand. Father Escrivá considered himself a donkey. Very often, to tell a son in the Work that he was going to entrust him with a new task of forming others or a post in governance, he would say, "My son, I am going to make you a pack donkey."

Later this photograph was reproduced in internal publications of Opus Dei with no commentary other than the brief caption "Photograph taken in 1948. Our Father placing some donkeys in

---

9. Testimony of Encarnación Ortega (AGP, RHF T-05074) and oral account to the author.

Don Alvaro's hands." This photograph was intended to reflect the handing over of responsibilities. Father Escrivá was on the point of leaving his post at the head of the Work, and his successor was clearly Don Alvaro. Not for nothing Father Escrivá since 1939 had called him *saxum*, "rock."

A few months later in August, in Molinoviejo, Father Escrivá summoned Encarnita and Nisa again. He knew they were having a rough time. He took them to see the building alterations. They passed through a gallery decorated with painted maps and a bas-relief in wood representing the scene of Achilles being wounded in his heel. When they came to a small grey granite fountain built into the wall in the form of a fish with water gushing out of its mouth, he pointed to red letters engraved around the fountain and read, "*Inter medium montium pertransibunt aquae.* Through the mountains the waters shall pass." Taking up the thread of their earlier conversation in Rome, he said again, "You have to be very peaceful, strong, serene, and assured. This—'through the mountains the waters shall pass'—this is what our Lord has said to me!"

His tone let his emotion show through. They did not ask any questions, nor did he add anything. But right then both Nisa and Encarnita felt a clear conviction that nothing would go wrong. Heaven had pledged its word: "Through the mountains the waters shall pass."[10]

In his notebook, *Intimate Notes*, there was an entry for December 13, 1931: "I had lunch with the Guevaras. While I was there, not while I was doing the prayer, I found myself saying, as at other times, *Inter medium montium pertransibunt aquae* (Ps. 103:11). I think these days I have had these words on my lips at other times, for no apparent reason, but that doesn't matter. Yesterday I said them with such emphasis that I felt forced to write them down: I understood them: they are the promise that the Work of God will overcome the obstacles, the waters of his apostolate passing through all the difficulties that might crop up."[11]

From that day on, Father Escrivá had carried within him the firm conviction that he had God's promise, God's own guarantee. This was what Encarnita and Nisa realized beside the fountain at Molinoviejo.

---

10. Ibid.
11. *Intimate Notes*, no. 476.

Toward the end of 1949 Father Escrivá was in a room in Villa Tevere filled with builders and their noise. With one of his spiritual sons, an architect, he was studying plans spread out on a desk before them. Suddenly, as if unable to contain something which surged up inside him, he said, "My son, the Work is well under way, and I'm not necessary at all."

Then he explained that he was only waiting for the Holy See to publish the decree of definitive approval, to set to work immediately on a foundation for priests.[12] He would be back at square one, facing the gossip, the criticism, and the calumnies all over again!

But the definitive approval which Pope Pius XII was to sanction was delayed. Finally, when all the favorable opinions had been presented to the Curia, on April 1, 1950 an unexpected postponement arose. During that spring of enforced waiting, Father Escrivá understood clearly that there was a place in the Work for diocesan priests too. Or, more precisely, he understood how to make the Holy See understand what he himself had understood on October 2, 1928, when he *saw* the Work, made up of priests and laity.

For married people, the hinge on which their holiness turned was their vocation to marriage, the duties of their state in life, and their work. The same was true of the clergy: the basis for their link with the Work was the fact that they could sanctify themselves by living their vocation to the priesthood to the full and carrying out the ministry itself. There was nothing to invent in the Work.

As for the apparent problem of "double obedience," it also melted away. The diocesan priests would have only one superior, their bishop. Their dependence on Opus Dei would be in regard to their spiritual director, who clearly had no governing function: to help them to be saints he could advise, but never give orders.

The mutilated statue

As the building at Villa Tevere progressed, the architectural team kept seeking out places where they had enough light to work and did not disturb anyone else. One cold December morning in 1952,

---

12. Cf. AGP, RHF 21181.

Father Escrivá met two of the architects in the room they were working in at that time. He leaned out of the window and saw below—in what had previously been a garden and was now a clutter of bricks, iron bars, and tools—some old decorative stones: fragments of tablets, brackets, a couple of capitals, and several bits of pillars. He had recommended that they acquire these stones cheaply and keep them until they found a good place for them. Among them he pointed to a statue lying on the ground. It was the robed figure of a Roman nobleman, but the head, arms, and half of one foot were missing.

"Father, where did you get that mutilated gentleman?" asked one of his sons.

"I call him 'the headless man,'" replied Father Escrivá. "It's a fake, one of those imitation antiques. We bought it in Jandolo, in Margutta Street, for next to nothing."

"Ah, a 'new ruin.' Where shall we put it?"

"That's up to you. In one of the little courtyards, perhaps, or to finish off the 'river terrace.' Wherever you think best."

During those Rome years, Father Escrivá spent many nights awake until the small hours in the sleeplessness of prayer, study, work, and suffering. One of those nights he got up and opened a book by St. Bernard of Clairvaux. His attention was drawn to words which he had often read before. *Non est vir fortis pro Deo laborans, cui non crescit animus in ipsa rerum difficultate, etiam si aliquando corpus dilanietur.* "There is no strong man working for God whose courage does not increase when faced with difficulties, even though his body is sometimes torn apart."

He took a piece of paper from his pocket diary and copied the words in his bold, vigorous handwriting. Next day, when he passed by the architects' studio, he gave the paper to one of his sons saying, "Look at this. You might like to have these words engraved on the pedestal where you put 'the headless man,' the mutilated Roman."

A breathless *Te Deum*

The pontifical approval of Opus Dei was published on June 16, 1950, in a decree called *Primum Inter.* From Father Escrivá's arrival in Rome up to the time of this approval, he had had to cope with the economic difficulties of procuring Villa Tevere and starting the building alterations there, and at the same time endure fiercely hostile criticism. This originated in Spain and always came from "good people who spoke ill"; they set themselves up in Rome, Milan, and another Italian city, even achieving easy access to the Curia. Their efforts, however, were ineffectual: Opus Dei had grown and spread. In 1946 there were 268 people in the Work (239 men and 29 women). By the early months of 1950 this figure had increased more than tenfold to 2,954 (2,404 men and 550 women). At the beginning of 1946 there had been only three priests besides Father Escrivá; in 1950 there were already 23, and another 46 laymen were preparing for ordination. The priests in the Work had joined the Work as laymen, had been practicing their professions, and had freely accepted Father Escrivá's invitation to be ordained to the priesthood after obtaining at least a doctorate in an ecclesiastical subject. Many already had a doctorate in a civil subject as well.

When the Work received the pontifical seal of approval, it had already spread to Spain, Portugal, Great Britain, Ireland, France, Mexico, the USA, Chile, and Argentina. People of the Work were packed and ready, so to speak, to go to Colombia, Peru, Guatemala, Ecuador, Germany, Switzerland, and Austria. Just eight years later came the big leap to Asia, Africa, and Australia. Life was moving faster than legal processes.

In the summer of that same year, 1950, the Holy See informed Father Escrivá that he could publicize the definitive approval. Father Escrivá instructed all the centers of Opus Dei, about 100 by then, to celebrate it with solemn benediction and to sing or recite the *Te Deum* in thanksgiving.

He himself went to Villa delle Rose, a women's center in Castelgandolfo, to preside over the ceremony with Don Alvaro and Salvador Canals, who had by now been ordained a priest. Later, one of the women wrote in her notebook: "Just like on February 2, 1947 in the flat in Città Leonina, when we heard the news of the Pope's first approval of the Work, today the Father looked very cheerful, though very tired: as if every step the Work takes in the Church leaves its mark on him. When he took the monstrance in his hands to give us benediction with the Blessed Sacrament, his hands trembled. He was not agitated. His whole face showed deep serenity. He was very moved, though. Indeed, on singing the *Te Deum* his voice was less clear and strong than usual, and seemed on the point of breaking."[13]

More like a disguise

Now about to start, or rather intensify, was a struggle to prevent man-made law from stifling a spirituality inspired by God. Either this spirituality was totally secular, or it would be of no use either to God or to man.

It soon became clear that the canonical framework of a secular institute was not appropriate for Opus Dei—not merely a badly fitting suit but more like a disguise. Opus Dei was not in reality as it was described in canon law.

Pius XII had drawn up the papal document called *Provida Mater Ecclesia* (Provident Mother Church). No further juridical-pastoral innovation could be hoped for in his pontificate. John XXIII had a huge task in hand: the summoning and setting up of the Second Vatican Council. Besides, plans were being made to update the Code of Canon Law. All that could be done was settle down for a long wait.

Yet people of Opus Dei were persistently compared to members of religious orders. This forced Monsignor Escrivá to attempt to have the canonical status of the Work revised. Between March and June 1960, several conversations and unofficial notes were exchanged between Don Alvaro del Portillo and Monsignor Scapinelli, and between Monsignor Escrivá and the secretary of state, Cardinal Tardini. On June 27, at the end of an audience, Cardinal Tardini made a wide gesture with his arms, expressing pessimism, and said to Monsignor Escrivá, "*Siamo ancora molto lontani. . . !* We still have a long way to go!" Monsignor Escrivá replied, "Well, that's true. But the seed has been sown, and it will not fail to bear fruit."[14]

---

13. Testimony of Encarnación Ortega (AGP, RHF T-05074) and oral account to the author.
14. *The Canonical Path of Opus Dei* (Princeton, NJ: Scepter), p. 309. AGP, Sezione Giuridica, VI/15611.

Opus Dei was asking for a canonical framework which fitted what people in the Work were and how they lived. They were not interested in a "state of perfection"; what they wanted was freedom to seek perfection within their own state in life—their civil status and the practice of their profession or job. However, an application for a revision of the Work's canonical status, made at the suggestion of a high-ranking figure in the Roman Curia, was destined to gather dust. Cardinal Tardini told Don Alvaro openly, "I won't even look at it. It would be a waste of time."[15]

They tried again in 1962, because Cardinal Ciriaci advised them to. This time the application went officially to Pope John XXIII. The reply was, "The obstacles are virtually insurmountable."[16]

Like his predecessor, Pope John XXIII also gave audiences to Monsignor Escrivá. On one occasion he said to his secretary, Monsignor Loris Capovilla, later to become bishop of Loreto: "*L'Opus Dei è destinato ad operare nella Chiesa su inattesi orizzonti di universale apostolato*" (Opus Dei is destined to open up new horizons of universal apostolate in the Church.)[17]

In June 1963 Pope John XXIII died. The conclave elected Giovanni Battista Montini as Pope Paul VI, and Monsignor Escrivá reopened the negotiations.

A note for the Pope's own eyes from Monsignor Escrivá

Don Alvaro had meetings with several Vatican authorities, informing them that the institutional question of Opus Dei was not yet settled. One of them was Cardinal Confalonieri; holding the papers in his hand, he said in bureaucratic Church Latin: *Reponatur in archivio*—"to be filed." The application for a new status seemed to have been consigned to oblivion.[18]

---

15. Cf. AGP, RHF 21171, p. 1295.
16. Get-together with Bishop Alvaro del Portillo, November 28, 1982. Cf. AGP, RHF 21171, p. 1411.
17. Letter to Pope Paul VI from Monsignor Loris Capovilla, prelate of Loreto, May 24, 1978.
18. Cf. AGP, RHF 21171, p. 1424.

Pope Paul VI himself gave Monsignor Escrivá two very cordial private audiences. At the end of the first, Don Alvaro came in to greet the Pope for a moment. Paul VI received him with a smile, and held out both hands to him, delighted to see him again. "Don Alvaro, Don Alvaro! We have known each other for such a long time."

"Twenty years, Holy Father."

"I've become old since then."

"Not so, your Holiness: you have become Peter!"[19]

Because he had known Opus Dei for twenty years, Paul VI understood that what Monsignor Escrivá was fighting for was his people's secularity and freedom. They were "ordinary faithful and ordinary citizens," as he said, and needed to function autonomously in all the honest activities of civil society.

"I want my children to have the same freedom as other Catholics in social, political, and economic affairs: neither more nor less,"[20] Monsignor Escrivá would say. All these civic activities would be obstructed by having to carry the secular institute banner.

On the basis of the faculty granted him by the Holy See to make changes in the constitution, Monsignor Escrivá proposed some modifications to Pius XII. There were thirteen in all, all concerning the women in the Work and aiming to strengthen their self-government at the same time as strengthening the unity of the Work. The Holy See had given its assent immediately. The proposal was made on July 16, 1953 and the go-ahead from the Pope took less than a month, arriving on August 12. This point is worth making because it refutes some published misinformation according to which in 1953 Monsignor Escrivá and Don Alvaro used the small printing press in Villa Tevere "to alter the texts of the constitution without the Pope's knowledge." Though he could have used his privilege as founder, Monsignor Escrivá never made changes to the statutes without the Pope's prior knowledge. In 1953 he asked Pius XII for his permission, and in 1963 he asked Paul VI.[21]

---

19. AGP, RHF 20121, p. 16.
20. Cf. AGP, RHF 20089, p. 37.
21. *The Canonical Path of Opus Dei*, p. 330, footnote 148.

On February 14, 1964 Monsignor Escrivá wrote an *Appunto riservato all'Augusta Persona del Santo Padre,* a "conscience note" to the Pope. Among other things he proposed some modifications to the text which had governed the Work since 1950.

The first official reply was "*dilata*" (delayed). In Vatican diplomacy, this brief, delightfully vague word did not mean no, but not yet. All the same, Paul VI pointed out to Monsignor Escrivá that the developments of Vatican II might open up new routes to the solution of the canonical situation of Opus Dei.

This was in fact what happened. The conciliar document *Presbyterorum Ordinis* (1965), and the texts which explained its resolutions, *Ecclesiae Sanctae* (1966) and *Regimini Ecclesiae Universae* (1967), contained the loom, so to speak, on which the material for Opus Dei's "new suit" could at last be woven: the canonical institution of personal prelatures. Prelatures, in the plural, because it was not something created exclusively for Opus Dei.

When Paul VI's *Motu Proprio,* entitled *Ecclesiae Sanctae,* was published, Monsignor Escrivá was delighted. He told his sons in the Work, "No sooner had the document come out, than the secretary of the council sent it to Don Alvaro with his congratulations. Anyone with eyes in his head can see that it is a suit made to measure for Opus Dei."[22]

Father Arrupe's visits

On September 12, 1965, Monsignor Escrivá received a visit in Villa Tevere which he had looked forward to. It was from Father Arrupe, general of the Society of Jesus. Monsignor Escrivá returned the visit on October 10 of the same year, having lunch at the Jesuits' mother house in Borgo Santo Spiritu. On that occasion Father Arrupe asked for some photographs to be taken of both of them together on the flat roof with a panoramic view over Rome.

There had been numerous incidents of subterfuge, hostile attitudes, contemptuous comments, and malicious gossip on the part of some Jesuits against Opus Dei. These were always people acting in

---

22. Get-together, October 24, 1966.

isolation, representing nobody but themselves. Monsignor Escrivá wished to clear things up. It was absurd that the increase of vocations to the Work should provoke jealousy among religious orders. The Work can never invade the terrain of any religious institution, because the call to Opus Dei can only arise among those who do not feel and have never felt the slightest inclination toward the religious state. There was no room for rivalry. On many occasions Monsignor Escrivá himself directed young men and women who had approached the Work on the way toward finding their true vocation in a novitiate or monastery. He did not consider that he was losing a "candidate." It was simply that for that man or woman Opus Dei was not the right place. "Everyone in their own place, and God everywhere," was his view.

Father Arrupe came to Villa Tevere again, accompanied by Father Iparraguirre, another Jesuit. The day before, Monsignor Escrivá had gone to Villa Sacchetti and spoken to the cooks, Begoña Mugica and Maria Urrutia. "Father Arrupe is coming for lunch tomorrow. I don't need to tell you to put a lot of care into it, because you always do. But this time, if possible, I would like you to put your heart and soul into the effort, not just your skills but also your motherly hearts. I would like this man to feel truly how much we love him. Let's see what you come up with!"[23]

In the little guest dining room in Bruno Buozzi, Monsignor Escrivá told Father Arrupe, "Some years ago, some representatives from B.A.C., the Catholic publishers in Spain, came to see me. They told me they had published the constitution of the Society of Jesus, and wanted my consent to publish the *ius peculiare*, the particular law, of the Work. I replied that I could understand them publishing your constitution because it had been written 400 years ago, and so it was something settled and firmly established. But on the other hand, our particular law is still very recent. I assured them that, in time, it would also be published. And I added, 'I can safely say that we won't make you wait as long as the Jesuits did!' "

Father Iparraguirre confirmed what Monsignor Escrivá had said. "Exactly. We had the first edition of our constitution published

---

23. Oral account of Maria Urrutia to the author.

100 years ago. In other words, it took us three centuries to show it to the world!"[24]

The solution—on an epitaph

Monsignor Escrivá, a fiery and impetuous man by nature, had developed a huge capacity for patience, schooled by life's hard knocks. He was filled with a sense of urgency, but he knew that what was urgent could wait, and that if the urgent matter was also something important, it *needed* to wait. He said to his children one day in October 1966, "I have to tell you that the question of our canonical path has already been solved. But for the present, we are not going to put on the suit. When the right time comes, we will put the suit on, both jacket and trousers."[25] He was not interested in a resounding triumph; he was prudent.

Both in conversations with a few people and in large gatherings, he explained that the "motorway" was ready, but that it was up to him to "decide when it should be opened to traffic."[26] "We are waiting for the time to be right," he said. "We want to live Christian lives and commit ourselves with a commitment of love, based on our honor. This is how we have already lived for many years."[27] On another occasion, reaffirming the same idea which he had always seen clearly in his mind's eye, he said, "I am longing to be able to come full circle! We will get back to being what we were at the beginning. No vows at all. We will make a contract, which is what I always wanted."[28]

In the early 1930s, while still living in Madrid, Father Escrivá had noted some tombstones on the floor of the Church of St. Elizabeth's Foundation, where he was rector. One day in 1936, before the outbreak of the Spanish Civil War, he pointed them out to his spiritual son Pedro Casciaro, and said, "There, that is the future canonical solution for the Work." Casciaro did not understand. He did not know what the two tombstones meant. They belonged to two Spanish

---

24. Testimony of Fr. Fernando Valenciano (AGP, RHF T-05362).
25. Get-together, October 24, 1966.
26. Testimony of Monsignor César Ortiz-Echagüe (AGP, RHF T-04694).
27. Get-together, June 29, 1969.
28. Get-together, March 27, 1966.

prelates who had both been chaplains to the king and vicars-general of the army. By virtue of their army posts, they had possessed a special personal jurisdiction, wide in scope and not based on territory. Here, in outline, was the configuration Father Escrivá saw clearly for Opus Dei: prelatic in character and universal in scope.

A strange prophetess

At different times, Fernando Valenciano and Rafael Caamaño both heard Monsignor Escrivá relate a curious event. One day in 1929 he had received a rather strange letter. It was strange because it was written by a Salesian nun, from France, not known to him, who signed her name Sulanitis. She was engaged in spreading devotion to the Merciful Love as Margaret Mary Alacoque had propagated devotion to the Sacred Heart of Jesus. It was also strange, because this nun could not even have known about the existence of Opus Dei, which at that time was only "what God wants," "what God is asking me," "God's affair." The Work, which Father Escrivá had seen for the first time a few months earlier, had neither structure nor base, neither name nor address. Strangest of all, the letter said this: the final solution for the Work would come, exactly as God wished, but after much searching.

When Monsignor Escrivá spoke of this, he did not add any explanations. He only added the incontrovertible fact: "The letter is in our archives."[29]

The day Father Escrivá joined Opus Dei

Normally it is taken for granted that Monsignor Escrivá belonged to the Work simply because he was its founder; or that, precisely as founder, he was exempt from having to join the Work. However, this was not so. Monsignor Escrivá hated exemptions, exceptions, or privileges and was very much in favor of legality. He joined Opus Dei just like everybody else.

---

29. Testimony of Fr. Rafael Caamaño (AGP, RHF T-05837) and of Fr. Fernando Valenciano (AGP, RHF T-05362).

He talked about this one day in September 1967, during a short stay in Elorrio, a village in the province of Vizcaya in northern Spain, speaking to a group of his spiritual sons who were directors of the Work in Spain. It was an informal family conversation, punctuated with anecdotes and jokes. At a particular point, someone inquired how the "special intention" was coming along. Father Escrivá talked about the difficulties and risks "when you have to leave the side road and come onto the highway." And he gave them to understand that Opus Dei, despite so many delays and canonical problems, "had always followed a straight track."[30]

"In these past few days," he said, "Our Lord has reminded me of something I had almost forgotten. When I joined the Work...why, what did you think? That I never actually joined it? Well, I did. I made a formal commitment to the Work in October 1943, in front of Bishop Leopoldo Eijo y Garay, who was the bishop of Madrid. He was the bishop who gave us our first approval. And I did it just like any of you, by reciting the formula for the fidelity: *Domine Iesu, suscipe me tibi*—'Lord Jesus, accept me for yourself.' A simple, heartfelt prayer with no vows of any kind. Bishop Leopoldo just loved it, it was so natural."[31]

But the delay before "joining the high road" would last for several years more. Monsignor Escrivá guessed this might happen. Perhaps he offered God the sacrifice of not seeing the "last stone" of the edifice of the Work. He said, "I may leave this life without seeing the Work finished. But Our Lord has let me see things he doesn't usually let people see. It's most unusual for anyone who has started up an enterprise—and I didn't intend to do it, it had never occurred to me to found anything!—to be allowed by God to see so many of its fruits here on earth."[32]

There had been an abundant harvest of vocations on every continent. At that point, in 1967, Monsignor Escrivá knew that to speak about Opus Dei was to speak of tens of thousands of people working in about seventy countries. The Work was a field rich with crops. Psalm 2 had again been fulfilled: "Ask of me, and I will give thee the

30. Testimony of Fr. Rafael Caamaño (AGP, RHF T-05837).
31. Ibid.
32. Get-together, July 9, 1967.

gentiles for thy inheritance, and the utmost parts of the earth for thy possession."

A strong man with a mutilated body

On one of those delightful Roman evenings, at sunset, when the slanting sunlight was striking on the ochre and reddish stucco walls of Villa Tevere, Monsignor Escrivá was looking out a window toward the terrace of the Fiume building. It was there that his sons in Opus Dei had placed the statue of the noble senator, which was headless and armless. The stony folds of the tunic, falling smoothly and harmoniously, gave the figure an air of elegant serenity. Monsignor Escrivá read the Latin words engraved on the marble pedestal: "*Non est vir fortis pro Deo laborans, cui non crescit animus . . .*" He translated rapidly: "There is no strong man working for God, whose spirit is not lifted, whose courage is not fortified, even in the midst of difficulties, even though now and again his body is torn apart."

It was as if he were recounting to himself the story of his own life. A vigorous, courageous journey, requiring a similar kind of fortitude. And a fight without weapons, in which he had suffered difficulties with the patient fortitude needed to endure them. That had been his life: *pax in bello,* peace in war.

7

Hunchbacked

Hunchbacked

n the main sacristy of Villa Tevere is an old oil painting by Del Arco, a fourth- or fifth-rate Spanish painter who was a contemporary of Velazquez. It shows Christ after his scourging, almost naked, collapsed, and bent double. Monsignor Escrivá used to call it "the hunchbacked Christ." Passing it once he stopped to remark, "Years ago, this painting seemed exaggerated to me—to see our Lord so bent over with suffering he looked like a hunchback. But now it doesn't, because when I'm tired, I also feel that my body is bent over, and I find it hard to stand straight. I've often seen myself like this by the end of the day—bent double, hunchbacked, tired, exhausted. It consoles me to see Jesus Christ—he who is all beauty, strength, and wisdom—broken, crushed, at the limit of his endurance."[1]

Often those living in Villa Tevere watched Monsignor Escrivá go upstairs very, very slowly, unaware that he could be seen. He would go up one step, then pause. Then another step. It was as if he had not the strength to support his body.

Often too, toward nightfall, he would come to the laundry room at Villa Sacchetti where Julia, Dora, Rosalia, and Concha were working. He would sit on a small, low sewing chair and whisper in all confidence, "I've come today so you can tell me things. . . . Today the Father is absolutely 'whacked.'"

---

1. Cf. AGP, RHF 21162, p. 606 and AGP, RHF 20770, pp. 398–399.

This same man early in the morning looked radiant, dynamic, smiling, and vigorous as he walked briskly along a corridor. He did not wear a watch because his day was a continuous going from one thing straight to the next, without a minute in between.

He displayed an amazing capacity for work, at a pace difficult to keep up with. Asking someone to do a job he would say, "Do it whenever you can." Within an hour he would dial the two digits of the relevant office and inquire, "My daughter, is it ready?" or "My son, have you finished what I asked you for?"

Every day was too short for him. When he came to examine his conscience in the evening, he used to feel squeezed dry like a lemon, bent double. He would say to our Lord, "I haven't had time to think about myself today."

A long, continuous sum set out on one line

The elements of his life were all lived together. The biographer cannot speak of his years of study, years of apostolate, years of travel, years of prayer, years of suffering. All came together every year and every day in Monsignor Escrivá's life.

There was the task of governing the Work, which was growing day by day, plus the slow, delicate negotiations with the Vatican, and the exhaustive studies and canonical procedures. There were the journeys abroad: rapid, intensive trips to establish Opus Dei in other countries. There was the unremitting construction work, because before one building was finished another had been started; plus the always unpredictable and precarious question of how to pay for them. Then there were the many and varied visits he received daily, in which he combined speed, affection, and his deliberate desire "to speak only of God"; and the guests for lunch, nearly always prelates— bishops, cardinals, or council fathers—to whom he explained with untiring patience, over and over again, what Opus Dei was and what it was not; or else discussed with them the thorny question of the needs of the Church.

There was his preaching, plus the constant work of writing spiritual texts, which he produced faster than the printing department could cope with. Then there were the informal gatherings, a constant in his oral teaching, which he used to form the people of the Work, and their friends and relations, in the spirit of Christianity, plus his personalized attention to each spiritual son and daughter who needed it, whether nearby or far away. There was his life of piety, prayer, union with God; in Monsignor Escrivá this had become, from his earliest youth, a way of living with harmonious rhythm of established daily practices. There was family life, including appointments, chance meetings, and moments spent together, all at the appropriate times.

In addition, there was the burden of concern Monsignor Escrivá felt for all the many people who had turned their backs on God; for a whole civilization becoming de-Christianized whose very foundations were crumbling. He suffered for the Church, which was going through a sort of long tunnel of difficulties. During the last ten years of his life he offered up absolutely everything—even breathing or smiling, his most trivial gesture or his most laborious task—so that "the time of trial should end soon" for the Church. Finally, there was a continuous volley of insinuations, calumnies, and complex inaccuracies from all sides. When they were personal they did not cause him to lose any sleep, but when they were aimed at the Work, he found them heartbreaking.

There was also the fact that Monsignor Escrivá was ill, although to outsiders he looked hale and hearty.

"I once went blind when I had diabetes," he said years later. "No one knew except Don Alvaro. My body was covered with skin eruptions, and sometimes I had no choice but to take a little sugar, because I felt a compelling need."[2] Ordinarily he felt tired, so thirsty that his tongue was cracked like a piece of old leather, and he was subject to splitting headaches. But only Don Alvaro and two other sons in the Work, José Luis Pastor and Miguel Angel Madurga, doctors who cared for him, knew anything about it. He was never heard to complain. When cured of his diabetes, he said in surprise, on discovering an almost unknown well-being, "I'd got used to it . . . but now I feel as if I've come out of jail!"[3]

---

2. Cf. AGP, RHF 21171, p. 1520.
3. Cf. AGP, RHF 21173, p. 1094.

And, to the physical pain and mental and spiritual sufferings he already had, he added a generous amount of voluntary mortifications: small ones like not leaning back in an armchair, not crossing his legs, not looking wherever he felt like looking, not drinking water when he was thirsty, going without salt, sugar, wine, or sweets, and much bigger ones like using cilices, sleeping on the floor, beating himself with a scourge or leather whip, "to tame the savage," as he put it.

"If I didn't have a heart, I would sleep like a log"

But what gave life to everything else was the fact that he had an enormous heart, which passionately loved God, mankind, the world, and all creation. Because his heart loved a lot, it suffered a lot. By sunset, his very heart felt hunchbacked.

One morning Monsignor Escrivá met José Luis Pastor in a corridor in Villa Vecchia. He took him affectionately by the arm and asked him, "Son, will you join me in saying a *Memorare* to the Madonna?"

"Of course, Father!" replied José Luis. Then, speaking as a doctor, he asked, "How did you sleep last night, Father? Were you able to rest?"

Monsignor Escrivá did not answer as a patient. "Look, because I love you all so very much, I always have one or other of you to think about. I love you with the heart of a father, a mother—and a grandmother! Sometimes I get all confused inside between what a father ought to demand, what a mother has to understand and what a grandmother can indulge. And occasionally I miss little things: the odd letter, some detail of affection from my children."

He paused, then went on. "I have prayed about all this. And I have seen that parents are for their children, and not children for their parents. This is what I tell other people so often, and I have to apply it to myself first and foremost. If, like the prophet Ezekiel, I were to ask our Lord to change my heart, I wouldn't ask him to change my heart of stone into one of flesh. Maybe the opposite: that instead of this heart of flesh he would grant me one of stone. And then, my son, *then* I would sleep like a log every night!"[4]

---

4. Oral account of Fr. José Luis Pastor, to which the author had access.

The Work has no coat of arms

Looked at from every angle, Monsignor Escrivá's life was sealed with the sign of the cross. He understood that it had to be like that on February 14, 1943 in a house in Jorge Manrique Street, Madrid. He was celebrating Mass in the oratory his daughters had there, when he *saw* with utter clarity the badge or seal of the Work—"seal, because the Work has no coat of arms," as he said later.[5] It was "the cross in the very center of the world."[6] As he saw it, the cross was always a sign of contradiction, scandal to some, madness to others; a paradox in a world that had come to identify good with pleasure and evil with pain.

A drawing made from dictation

There and then, he asked for pen and paper and drew a circle on the page they gave him. Within it he drew a cross with the horizontal beam placed very high. Later, when he got home to Diego de Leon Street, he drew it again on a page in his diary.

One day in 1963, in Rome, Monsignor Escrivá called two of the directors of the general council, Juan Cox and Fernando Valenciano. Don Alvaro del Portillo was also there. Monsignor Escrivá, with obvious delight, showed them "what they've just sent from Spain:" the diary. He opened at the page for February 14, 1943. The seal of the Work was there, drawn in his own hand. His heart missed a beat. He had before him the witness to something he had never considered an idea of his own, but a drawing dictated to him.[7]

"What's up between us, Lord?"

The Cross marked his life. He took as his daily motto, "*Nulla dies sine cruce*: no day without the cross." A touchstone whose truth had been proved by experience. But he brightened it up by adding two words in front: *in laetitia*, in joy, which denoted a disposition, a grace, for

---

5. Testimony of Encarnación Ortega (AGP, RHF T-05074).
6. Ibid.
7. Testimony of Fr. Fernando Valenciano (AGP, RHF T-05362).

his way of living. His personal aspiration was thus "In joy, no day without the cross." If ever a day passed without some note of adversity, Monsignor Escrivá would go to the tabernacle and ask, "What's up between us, Lord? Don't you love me anymore?" Not that he liked pain. But he was convinced that the cross was the royal seal of the works of God. "To me, a day without the cross is like a day without God," he used to say;[8] he did not want there to be a single day without it as a stamp of authenticity.

"I can be won over with a sardine bone"

He was not a sad, sorrowful, long-suffering man. By nature he was a lover of life, exultant and joyous. He had a tremendous capacity for enjoying the wonders of the world. To someone who lives on grace, everything in life is an unexpected gift.

Monsignor Escrivá often used to say, "Teresa of Avila could be won over with a sardine; I can be won over with a sardine bone." A simple donkey, which a son of his had made out of silver paper, was a present prized so highly that he felt it deserved to be put on display in a showcase—which he did.

The psychology of a happy man

He enjoyed everything that was good, no matter how insignificant: a song, a sunset, a poem, a friendly joke, a letter from an old friend, a chat, the concentration of an athlete before the pole vault, or the sheer beauty of a Capitoline Venus.

When the attacks on the Work increased, his cheerfulness was even more noticeable. It was real joy. In case any of his children should feel discouraged, he said to his spiritual daughters, "What if they knock our heads off? Why then, we'll carry them in our hands. We've been carrying them on our shoulders for long enough. And what does it matter in the end? Nothing at all!"[9]

Monsignor Escrivá only spoke about himself in order to pass on to his children new discoveries in his interior life which could

---

8. Testimony of Encarnación Ortega (AGP, RHF T-05074).
9. Ibid.

help them in their own relationship with God. He was not keen on psychological introspection. Begoña Alvarez, surprised to hear Monsignor Escrivá talking on a personal level, took particular note of a comment he made one day with reference to a difficulty that had cropped up: "Not through my own merit but through a light from God, I have had and still have the psychology of never feeling alone. Never. Neither from a human nor from a supernatural point of view. I've never felt that I was alone! And this has helped me to keep silent on many occasions. I've preferred to be silent, for the sake of other people. That is one of the reasons why I've been cheerful all the time, despite having suffered so much. Always cheerful! Although it may seem to be a paradox. I can tell you that I've only had reasons for being very happy. They've never made me feel misfortunate, still less a victim!"[10] He was well aware—having learned it from the crucifix—who the only Victim was.

"I never went to get certificates"

He was ruled by God's point of view, which dominated his outlook completely and gave him an indestructible sense of security. One day Itziar and Tere Zumalde told him about the difficulties they had encountered in the places where they were working—one in Abruzzi, Italy, the other in Santiago, Chile. In the light of his own experience, he advised them to disregard the difficulties.

"I'm going to tell you something. In the early years of the foundation of the Work, when lots of people thought I was crazy, I didn't go and get a doctor to give me a certificate saying I was sane. No, I kept on doing what God wanted of me, ignoring the gossip, not caring a whit what they thought of me. Some people said I was a heretic. But when I was being slandered like that, I didn't set out to get theologians—and I did have some among my friends—to certify that what I was teaching was not heretical. I continued working for God, in the absolute assurance that what I was doing was the Work which God had asked me to do. My daughters, you have to act according to God's viewpoint, and then you'll see the results!"[11]

---

10. Testimony of Begoña Alvarez (AGP, RHF T-04861).
11. Testimony of Mercedes Morado (AGP, RHF T-07902).

The Way thrown on the fire

He was familiar with the pattern of slander, sidelong glances of envy, the stolid incomprehension of those who did not understand because they did not want to, the cowardly whisperers who never showed their faces but sowed confusion from the shadows.

He was also aware of the substance of the worst slanders. They started in Spain. They were led by certain heads of lay, confessional movements, "official Catholics"; by certain religious who were very active and influential just before and after the Civil War; and by groups and individual members of the *Falange* and the National Movement, Franco's political party and the only one he permitted to exist. They were the ones who started things, and then spread the disease among other good but misguided people. In Barcelona, reviving the old practices of the Inquisition, they even held a public "*auto-de-fé*," with all the ceremony of liturgical anathemas and a fire, condemning and then burning copies of *The Way*.

From the time when Opus Dei opened its first student center in Luchana Street in Madrid, the people of the Work always put a wooden cross on the wall in their centers, without a figure of Christ—a plain, unvarnished black cross. Point 178 of *The Way* referred to this: "Whenever you see a poor wooden Cross, alone, uncared-for, of no value . . . and without its Crucified, don't forget that that Cross is your Cross: the Cross of each day, the hidden Cross, without splendor or consolation . . . the Cross which is waiting for the Crucified it lacks: and that Crucified must be you."

This foreshadowed the idea he would preach in 1974 in his catechetical gatherings in Central and South America: "For some, there are too many crosses . . . whereas for me, I need more Christs!"[12]

Soon after the end of the Spanish Civil War, a center for university students was set up in Balmes Street in Barcelona. The people of the Work put up a wooden cross, a very big one. Some unscrupulous people spread the rumor that "blood rites" and "human sacrifices" were carried out there. They believed, or wanted to make others believe, that the cross was an instrument of torture. The rumor was noised about on an alarming scale, especially among the families of

---

12. Bishop Alvaro del Portillo, *Letter*, December 8, 1976, 17.

some young men of Opus Dei, Rafael and Jaime Termes and Rafael Escola. When Rafael Termes, the director of the center, told Father Escrivá of these rumors, he was also able to give him the good news that his sons were facing up to this difficulty "very peacefully and without offending against charity toward anything or anybody."[13] Father Escrivá immediately suggested the cross should be replaced by another one, "so small that not even a newborn baby could fit on it, so that they will realize what lies they are telling. Then they won't be able to say that we are crucifying ourselves, because we simply wouldn't fit on it!"[14]

Father Escrivá was particularly pleased after his first audience with Pius XII in 1946 to find that in the brief *Cum Societatis*, the Pope granted the privilege of a partial indulgence to anyone who kissed or said an aspiration before the wooden cross in Opus Dei's oratories.[15]

Cabalistic signs?

It was also in the aftermath of the Spanish Civil War that certain people tried to interpret liturgical and Eucharistic motifs decorating a frieze as "cabalistic signs" for Masonic rites. This frieze was in the oratory of the residence hall in Jenner Street, Madrid. It bore the following texts: *Congregavit nos in unum Christi amor* ("the love of Christ has joined us together in one"), taken from the well-known Eucharistic hymn *Ubi Caritas* traditional in the church since ancient times, and the phrase *Erant autem perseverantes in doctrina Apostolorum, in communicatione fractionis panis, et orationibus* ("And they were persevering in the doctrine of the Apostles, and in the communication of the breaking of bread, and in prayers") from the Acts of the Apostles (Acts 2:42). Ears of wheat, the vine, the light of Christ, the dove of peace—symbols common in Church usage—separated one text from another. These were the "dangerous cabalistic signs" and "cryptic hieroglyphs."

---

13. Testimony of Fr. Carlos Cardona (AGP, RHF T-06138). Cf. S. Bernal, *Monsignor Escrivá—A Profile of the Founder of Opus Dei* (London: Scepter, 1977), p. 266
14. Ibid. Cf. AGP, RHF 21165, p. 766.
15. Monsignor Escrivá asked for a short notice to be placed beside each wooden cross. It carries the following text: "His Holiness Pope Pius XII by the Apostolic Brief *Cum Societatis* of 28th June 1946 graciously deigned to grant an indulgence of 500 days each time this wooden Cross is devoutly kissed or a pious aspiration is said before it."

The Abbot-Coadjutor of Montserrat (an important center of religious influence in Catalonia), Dom Aurelio M. Escarré, wrote to the bishop of Madrid requesting reliable information about Opus Dei. The reply was a detailed, authoritative, and conclusive letter from Bishop Eijo y Garay, which settled the gossip for a while and relieved the worries felt by families of people of the Work.

The calumny-makers' bag of tricks

This may be a good place to examine the process of creating a defamatory lie. A slanderous rumor nearly always starts from something real, in itself innocent, but deliberately misrepresented—the wooden cross, the point in *The Way*, the words and symbols on the frieze, and so on. It is then easy to create a scandalous story, a suspicious theory, a culpable conjecture. Monsignor Escrivá was subjected to each of these modes of attack.

Half-truths and distorted facts

One method is simply to take a text out of context. That was the case with the liturgical symbols. It was also the case with misrepresentations from highlighting point 28 of *The Way*, "marriage is for the rank and file, not for the officers of Christ's army," while ignoring other points (e.g., point 26, "Matrimony is a holy Sacrament. . . ." and point 27, "Do you laugh when I tell you that you have a vocation to marriage? Well, you have just that: a vocation").

Cracked copper with rivets

Or again, people accused Monsignor Escrivá of telling his children, boastfully and arrogantly, "You will have to render an account to God for having known me, because there have been and will be plenty of Popes, cardinals, and bishops, but there is only one founder of Opus Dei." These people distorted his phrase and took it out of its context. Monsignor Escrivá was calling his children's attention to their historic responsibility as "co-founders," and their present and future obligation to transmit the spirit of Opus Dei wholly and without alteration as they had received it from its source. He was very conscious of the unique importance of a foundational charism, something unrepeatable, nontransferable, and inalienable. Nevertheless, he was reluctant to be treated as "the founder." He argued that he was "a founder without a foundation," saying, "I didn't want to found anything. I've never been anything but a nuisance." He even said, "The only good founder I know comes bottled," referring to a brandy called *El Fundador.*

In a meditation he gave on September 11, 1960, he said: "My children, I have to make you consider something that when I was young, I did not dare either to think or to express; but now I feel I ought to tell you. In my lifetime, I have known several Popes, lots of cardinals, and a host of bishops. On the other hand, there is only one founder of Opus Dei, even though it's a poor sinner like me—I am quite convinced that our Lord chose the worst thing he could find, so that it could be seen more clearly that the Work is his doing alone. But God will ask you to render an account for having been close to me, because he has entrusted me with the spirit of Opus Dei, and I have passed it on to you. He will ask you to give an account for having known that poor priest who was with you, and who loved you so very much—even more than your own mothers did! I will pass away, and the people who come to the Work later on will look on you with envy, as if you were relics: not because of me, because I am, I insist, a poor man, a sinner who loves Jesus Christ madly; but for having learned the spirit of the Work from the lips of its founder."[16]

There is no need to look far in the things he said or wrote to find references to the fact that he was made of clay, "common clay that is easily broken"; or to his being poor metal, or "a clumsy, deaf instrument." But he always distinguished between the man and the mission, between his own weak nature and the divine greatness of his message. So, in 1973, he said, "I've never deceived you. I'm not gold and I've never said I was. I'm not silver, and I've never said I was. I'm not copper and I've never said I was. Maybe cracked copper with rivets. But what I say to you . . . is pure gold!"[17]

---

16. Meditation, September 11, 1960.
17. Fr. José Luis Soria, quoting Monsignor Escrivá, in Torreta (Madrid), January 5, 1973.

Another method of falsifying truth is by using half-truths. In this way gossipers talk about "capturing young people," alleging that the apostolate by people of Opus Dei among the young takes advantage of boys' and girls' immaturity and inexperience, proposing to them an ideal of self-giving to God when they are too young to make free decisions. Such people either do not know or else conceal the fact that even if a boy or girl wishes to join the Work at the age of fourteen or fifteen, and even if they are already practicing the habits and customs of the Work, they cannot legally join until they are eighteen. At eighteen people have sufficient discernment to vote, choose a career, buy and sell, go to war, marry, get divorced, be elected deputy, councillor, senator, lord mayor, even become sovereign. Moreover, the contract made by someone who joins Opus Dei can be freely canceled.

Loud speakers not microphones?

Another tool used by fabricators is the distorted fact. It has been said and written that there are "concealed microphones" in Villa Tevere. Those who say it know it is not true. There are loudspeakers, not microphones, which are not concealed but clearly visible, installed, not in small rooms or offices but in big sitting rooms, the laundry, and one or two oratories. They can be seen by anybody. Their purpose was to enable Monsignor Escrivá to lead a get-together or give a meditation with big groups of his sons or daughters in the Work. They were used two or three times on family occasions or celebrations to send Christmas wishes, to ask what presents they had had for Christmas, or to have them hear some songs.

The trip to Greece

The interpretation of the journey Monsignor Escrivá made to Greece with Don Alvaro del Portillo and Father Javier Echevarria in 1966 was a sensational example of misrepresentation. The purpose of the trip—like so many others he made to countries of Central Europe—was to explore firsthand the possibilities of setting up the Work there. Monsignor Escrivá traveled with the knowledge and express consent of the Holy See. He consulted the Vatican several times, through Monsignor Dell'Acqua, Deputy Secretary of State. It was no secret journey, and he sent several postcards from Athens and Corinth that have all been kept.

Before he left, people in the Roman Curia told him starting Opus Dei in Greece would not be easy as "there is a very close link between the Orthodox Church and the government of the country, so much so that the life of Greeks who are not members of the Orthodox Church, at least nominally, is very hard."

Many years later, Father Javier Echevarria retained a very vivid impression of the coldness, even hostility, they encountered. "From the time of our arrival at the port of Piraeus," he said, "we noticed an atmosphere of distrust; you could say a physical rejection of the Catholic Church. The fact that we were wearing clerical clothes led the Customs officers to hold us up for over an hour and a half, making a detailed examination of our visas and passports and subjecting us to a completely unnecessary third-degree interrogation. . . . We realized we were going to be in an atmosphere suspicious of Catholicism. . . . When we got to Athens, the Father decided to go to the cathedral to do the afternoon prayer. We spent some time in the cathedral, feeling a certain sense of desolation because it was empty, and not a single person came in to greet our Lord in his church. . . . We also had a sensation of emptiness along the streets of Athens, Corinth, and Marathon: people looked at priests distrustingly. In some places they drew aside as we passed, making it clear that we were outsiders.... On our return to Rome, the Father relayed to the Holy See his view that it would be better to wait until there were Greek people in Opus Dei. These views were totally shared by the office of the secretary of state."[18]

Monsignor Escrivá brought back two small icons for his daughters and sons in the Work: one of Our Lady and another of St. Paul embracing St. Peter, symbolizing the unity and oneness of the Roman, Catholic, apostolic Church. He also brought back two of better quality that he presented to Pope Paul VI and Monsignor Dell'Acqua.

---

18. Written narrative of Bishop Javier Echevarria given to the author.

On returning he told his children he had sensed a certain clerical-ism, a sort of religious nationalism among the Greek Orthodox, which would make conversions difficult. "The switch by these Christians to obedience to the Roman Pontiff needs to be encouraged among Greeks living abroad." Because of this, Monsignor Escrivá returned from Greece convinced that setting up apostolates of Opus Dei in that country would be much slower and more problematic than he had thought. "Religion and the nationalistic conscience are so inter-twined that changing from Greek Orthodox to Roman Catholicism is seen almost as a betrayal of their country." Dr. Marlies Kücking heard him make this sort of comment on his return from his Greek trip.[19]

Where does the story that Monsignor Escrivá wanted to "con-vert" to the Orthodox Church come from? There is only one pos-sible explanation. The trip was made between February 26 and March 14, 1966. Among the twenty-four men of the Work who were to be ordained priests in the summer of that year was one called Jalil Badui, son of a Lebanese couple who had emigrated to Mexico. There were also other professional men in Opus Dei who were Catholics of Arab origin (Lebanese, Palestinian, and Syrian). At one point, it was thought that because of their race and culture, these people could begin the Work in the Middle East, bearing in mind the only requirement would be the authorization of the Holy See to change from the Latin Rite to the Maronite Rite in the liturgy, and such an authorization would be easy to obtain if the obvious guarantees were given.[20] To confuse a fairly normal procedure like change of rite with a break from Rome has to be the result of crass ignorance or evil intent.

Some glasses of Malmsey wine

In addition to distortion of a fact, another fraudulent method often used consists in attributing to a real scene some spurious phrase or false episode. The detailed description of a room, a piece of furni-ture, or even of real people lends credibility to the fictitious event narrated. This procedure has been used a lot against Monsignor

---

19. Oral account of Marlies Kücking to the author.
20. Cf. H. de Azevedo, *Uma luz no mundo* (Lisbon: Ediçoes Prumo, Lda.), p. 295.

Escrivá by people who, having lived in centers of the Work, later left Opus Dei. Thus in the sitting room of Villa Vecchia, for instance, they represent Monsignor Escrivá furiously scolding some young women of Opus Dei for creating a cloud of dust while cleaning. They begin with facts: Some women did a major cleaning job when the work on Villa Vecchia was finished; by not taking the precaution of sprinkling water on the floor before sweeping, they lifted a huge amount of plaster dust; Father Escrivá was passing through and called their attention to this in no uncertain terms.

Up to here everything is true. But the truth is falsified by omitting what exactly Monsignor Escrivá pointed out: that the cleaners had dirtied a large, intricate chandelier, already hung, that would now need special cleaning. What was more, the dust was sticking to the vaulted ceiling, which had been painted and was still wet. But Father Escrivá, right there and then, became their guide to the building, explaining the meaning of the eight scenes represented in the medallions of the ceiling: some depicting the story of Joseph, and others, scenes from the Book of Tobias. He joked with them about the fish carried by young Tobias, whom he referred to as "Tobias Junior." That same night there appeared some glasses and a bottle of malmsey, a wine made from sweet, fragrant grapes, with a note in Father Escrivá's handwriting: "For my daughters, who have swallowed so much dust."[21]

Everyone who knew Monsignor Escrivá agreed that he had a strong character, a lively temper, and dynamic fortitude when correcting people. But without exception they also agree in underlining his cordiality, approachability, friendliness, and the tender affection that never left anyone feeling hurt, slighted, or simply upset after a reprimand. His normal way of settling such episodes was to send his daughters a packet of sweets or give his sons a kiss on both cheeks.

Julia Bustillo was a housekeeper, one of the oldest in the Work. Someone asked her, "Julia, tell us about some of the mistakes you made, when the Father told you off." Julia replied, "The Father didn't 'tell us off.' The Father corrected us, and showed us how to do things well. And he did it with a lot of patience, because at first we didn't get a single thing right!"

---

21. Testimony of Helena Serrano (cf. AGP, RHF T-04641).

One afternoon Monsignor Escrivá invited two or three of his sons to go for a walk in Rome with him and finish by "having something in a trattoria." As they set off, Monsignor Escrivá inquired, "Do you know why we are going?"

Turning to one of them with a gesture very much his own—it consisted of sticking his tongue out a tiny bit through closed lips, as if biting it—he said mischievously, "Because I told you off this morning."[22] So much for Monsignor Escrivá's "scoldings."

Another method of spreading calumny is to add a few words that were never said to some which were real. For instance, Monsignor Escrivá had given strict instructions, written and oral, to avoid even the semblance of social contact between men and women in centers of the Work. To ensure that priests—the only men of Opus Dei who go to the women's centers, to carry out their ministry—never stayed longer than absolutely necessary, he said on several occasions, positing two equally undesirable alternatives, "I would prefer a daughter of mine to die without the last rites than for my sons, the priests, to stay in a women's center unnecessarily."[23]

This sentence has been revised as "I would prefer a daughter of mine to die without confession, than for her to confess to a Jesuit." The manipulation and false addition are obvious—but only if you have the original text.

Another deceitful method is to take a part for the whole. People conclude that if a banker is in Opus Dei, Opus Dei "owns banks;" or because four or five people of the Work once held high posts under a particular political regime, they project this onto tens of thousands of other people living in eighty different countries and affirm that Opus Dei "is a political force."

When it is pointed out that in Spain under Franco people of the Work were both in the government and in the opposition, some holding public office and others in exile, they answer: "Ah, this shows the fine Machiavellian spirit of the Opus; it is a strategic ambivalence which enables them to have a foot in both camps."

A clever reply for a television debate. But it would not stand up to analysis in Germany, where there are people of the Work who vote

---

22. Cf. AGP, RHF 21181, p. 495.
23. Cf. AGP, RHF 20776. Get-together at Altoclaro (Venezuela), August 28, 1974.

and/or work for the Liberal, Christian Democrat, Social Democrat, or Green parties; or in the United States, where there are people of the Work among the Republicans and Democrats; or in Mexico where some people of the Work are lifelong supporters of the *Partido Revolucionario Institucional,* and others are lifelong supporters of the opposing party. This is completely beyond the scope of old clichés always trying to explain history by conspiracy theories, hidden alliances between the cross and the sword, the altar and the throne, the Vatican and the White House.

Another tool in the lie-makers' kit consists of saying one thing, then the opposite—"white" today and "black" tomorrow. Some people spent years calling Monsignor Escrivá a heretic, an innovator, and an ultra-progressive, for preaching that the laity were called to be saints without needing to leave the world. After a while, without any change in Monsignor Escrivá's message, those same people accused him of being traditionalist, reactionary, and ultra-conservative.

There were also those who, seeing the discreet way people of the Work acted, said "You can't hear them, you don't notice them: therefore they must be a secret society." These same people, when they later saw the presence of the apostolates of Opus Dei, did not hesitate to assert, "They are Pope Wojtyla's new crusaders, advancing, invading, and destroying!"

Gossipers who recently accused Monsignor Escrivá of sympathy towards the Nazis and of anti-Semitism forget that years ago they or their fellow-travelers called him a Jewish Mason and accused Opus Dei of being "the Jewish branch" of a Masonic lodge.

While on this point, it may be asked what Monsignor Escrivá actually thought of Hitler and Nazism. Francesco Angelicchio, one of the first Italians to join Opus Dei, wrote, "I always heard him express very clear, severe condemnation of totalitarian, tyrannical regimes which killed freedom, no matter what color they were."[24]

Mario Lantini said, "*Per lui non era concepibile il partito único. . . . Era quindi contra ogni totalitarismo, razzismo, nazionalismo, ecc.* For him a single-party system was inconceivable. . . . He was completely against all totalitarianism, racism, Nazism, etc."[25]

24. Cf. testimony of Monsignor Francesco Angelicchio (AGP, RHF T-03322).
25. Cf. testimony of Monsignor Mario Lantini (AGP, RHF T-03339).

Pedro Casciaro said, "With regard to Fascism and Nazism there were no cases of confrontation, as Opus Dei began its stable activity in Italy and Germany when those regimes were no longer in power. On one occasion I heard him [Monsignor Escrivá] speak admiringly of Cardinal Faulhaber, who during the Nazi period had had the courage to publish some Advent lectures given in Munich cathedral."[26] (The lectures warned against the dangers of the Nazi system and showed its anti-Christian roots.)

José Orlandis recalls that on September 15, 1939, the day after he had asked for admission to the Work, during a spiritual retreat in the Burjasot residence hall in Valencia, "I was alone with the Father in his office and without my asking him anything, he confided to me, 'This morning I offered Mass for Poland, a Catholic country, which is suffering terribly under the Nazi invasion.' I could see that this intention—the fate of Poland—was close to his heart and he was very distressed in those days, when Polish resistance was collapsing everywhere in the face of the invaders' superior strength."[27]

Domingo Diaz-Ambrona has left written evidence of a chance meeting with Monsignor Escrivá on a train between Madrid and Avila in August 1941. "I had just returned from a trip to Germany, where I had sensed that Catholics were afraid to show their religious convictions. This made me suspicious of Nazism; but, like many Spaniards, I couldn't really see the negative aspects of the Nazi system and the philosophy behind it, because I was blinded by German propaganda, which presented itself as the force which would annihilate Communism. I wanted to know his opinion. I was very surprised by the priest's uncompromising reply. He had accurate information about the state of the Church and Catholics under Hitler's regime. Monsignor Escrivá spoke to me in strong terms against this anti-Christian regime, with a forcefulness born of his great love for freedom. In Spain at that time, when the Nazis' many crimes were not yet known about, it was uncommon to find people who condemned the Nazi system so roundly."[28]

---

26. Cf. testimony of Fr. Pedro Casciaro (AGP, RHF T-04917).
27. Cf. handwritten note of Fr. José Orlandis, Rome, November 13, 1992.
28. Letter of Domingo Diaz-Ambrona to Bishop Alvaro del Portillo, Madrid, January 9, 1992.

Amadeo de Fuenmayor described Monsignor Escrivá's attitude—
"his condemnation of Nazism was decisive"—and gave a long list of
"expressions referring to Hitler and his racist system which we heard
him say on many occasions." The following were some of them:

"I abominate all totalitarian regimes. Nazism is a heresy, as well
as being a political aberration. I was delighted when the Church
condemned it: all Catholics had been thinking the same thing about
it in their hearts. Every kind of racism is contrary to God's law, the
natural law. I know there have been many victims of Nazism, and it
hurts me. Even one person made a victim for his faith or race would
have been enough to make me condemn the system. I have always
thought Hitler was an obsessive, miserable man. A tyrant."[29]

How did Monsignor Escrivá react? From the time he was called
mad, unscrupulous, a heretic, or a Mason, to the time people started
telephoning Villa Tevere in the small hours and asking whether it
was true that Monsignor Escrivá was dead, he practiced, and taught
his children in Opus Dei to practice, a reaction he summarized in
five steps: "pray, keep silent, understand, forgive . . . and smile."

Enemies who are really benefactors

Mercedes Morado and Begoña Alvarez, who were among those
who worked with Monsignor Escrivá for years, wrote that his spirit
of forgiving and understanding toward those who slandered him
grew progressively, to the point where he could say in all simplicity,
"I don't feel any resentment toward them. I pray for them every day,
just as hard as I pray for my children. And by praying for them so
much, I've come to love them with the same heart and the same
intensity as I love my children."[30]

He was putting onto paper something of his own personal experience when he wrote, "Think about the good that has been done to
you throughout your lifetime by those who have injured or attempted
to injure you. Others call such people their enemies. . . . You
are nothing so special that you should have enemies; so call them

---

29. Cf. handwritten note of Fr. Amadeo de Fuenmayor for this book, Rome, December 2, 1992.
30. Testimony of Mercedes Morado (AGP, RHF T-07902) and of Begoña Alvarez (AGP, RHF
T-04861).

'benefactors.' Pray to God for them: as a result, you will come to like them."[31]

On another occasion, Encarnita Ortega witnessed how he reacted when told that Father Carrillo de Albornoz had left the Society of Jesus, later apostatizing from the Catholic faith. Monsignor Escrivá was visibly moved and deeply sorry. He buried his head in his hands and fell silent, withdrawing into himself, praying. Salvador Canals reminded him that this same man had once organized a very serious campaign of slander against the Work. Monsignor Escrivá interrupted him bluntly, "But he is a soul, my son, a soul!"[32]

While he recommended this disposition of genuine understanding—"we have to understand even those who do not understand us," he said[33]—he encouraged his children "not to remain silent where defending the Work is concerned, because the Work is God's, and we have to stand up for it." One day in Rome in January 1967, while chatting with César Ortiz-Echagüe, who had just come from Madrid, he criticized the lack of political liberty in Spain at the time. He added, "I've written a strongly worded letter to Minister Solis. I don't expect him to reply, but if he does, I have even more things to say to him! And as for you, you cannot permit state newspapers, which are government-controlled and therefore paid for by all of you as citizens, to insult the Work gratuitously."[34]

On the other hand, when the abuse was personal, he did not hesitate to recommend peaceful silence and forgiveness. In 1962, Rafael Calvo Serer went to see him in Rome. He unburdened his heart and told him about the calumnies and persecutions he was being subjected to by petty officials of the Franco regime. Monsignor Escrivá listened and then said, "My son, it is hard, but you have to learn how to forgive."

He was silent for a little and then, as if thinking aloud, he added, "I didn't need to learn how to forgive, because God has taught me how to love."[35]

31. Cf. *The Forge*, no. 802.
32. Testimony of Encarnación Ortega (AGP, RHF T-05074) and oral account.
33. Ibid.
34. Testimony of Monsignor César Ortiz-Echagüe (AGP, RHF T-04694).
35. Cf. AGP, RHF 21165, p. 924.

He made a clear distinction between personal attacks and attacks on Opus Dei. He said on occasions, "And if they never understand, the day will come when they die—and then all their resistance will be over. God will judge their actions! We should never judge."[36]

Telephone calls in the early hours of the morning

In 1972 Monsignor Escrivá was on a grueling apostolic trip around Europe and America. The people living at Villa Tevere started getting strange telephone calls asking if he had died, or inquiring about "his grave state of health." When he heard about this, his response was simply, "They are the same people who wanted to throw me out of the Work in 1951. If they had succeeded, they would have killed me. Now they still want to kill me off, by spreading rumors of imaginary illnesses. I don't know what they're going to gain by that, because when I really do die I hope that with the help of your prayers, the Lord will receive me in his mercy. And from heaven, I'll be able to help you much more!"[37]

As this disturbing tactic of phoning in the early hours of the morning continued, he told his spiritual daughters in La Montagnola about it, in case any calls came during the day and they were to pick up the phone. His comment was brief. "It's what some people want—and what would suit the devil." Turning to another subject, he went on working.[38]

"The usual people"

So as not to give rise to resentment, Monsignor Escrivá always drew a veil of anonymity over the identity of people who attacked Opus Dei. He would talk in general terms about "opposition by good people" and in very specific cases he would simply refer to "the usual people." He knew who they were. Moreover, he wrote down, and had others write down, all the more significant attacks against Opus Dei and had them printed by the printing press at Villa Tevere,

36. Testimony of Encarnación Ortega (AGP, RHF T-05074).
37. Testimony of Monsignor César Ortiz-Echagüe (AGP, RHF T-04694).
38. Testimony of Mercedes Morado (AGP, RHF T-07902).

conscious that they were a very important part of the history of the Work. He did this on the strict understanding that the story of these events would not see the light until years after his death, and after the death of the people involved. His judgement of these events appears in point 804 of *The Forge*: "Opposition from good people? It's the devil's doing."

They wanted to expel Monsignor Escrivá

This opposition from good people became very bitter between 1951 and 1952, just after the Holy See had granted full approval to the Work. It was more than pieces of gossip or calumnies. A full-scale campaign had been set in motion. Its organizers had compiled an inflammatory collection of false dossiers. There were serious accusations, including one alleging promiscuity between the men and women of Opus Dei.

These people knew where to strike a mortal blow at the unity of the Work, which was, and has always been, the great "secret" of Opus Dei's effectiveness: a juridical, spiritual, and ascetic unity, together with total separation of life, regime, government, and apostolates. It was not enough to amputate a member or cut off a branch: the conclusive way was to decapitate the Work. All the schemes were aimed directly at Monsignor Escrivá and his expulsion from Opus Dei. With him out of the way, the men and women of the Work would scatter. It would be as in the Gospel passage: "I will strike the shepherd, and the sheep will be scattered" (Matt 26:31).

Don Alvaro del Portillo, who measured his words carefully, would say years later: "It was a very well-prepared trap, poised like a dagger exactly over the heart. With just a slight application of pressure, the heart would be pierced."[39]

A blind man flailing the air with his stick

Monsignor Escrivá could guess that something serious was afoot, but he had no idea what it was. For weeks and months he was anxious

---

39. Cf. AGP, RHF 21165, p. 1925 ff.

and restless, full of foreboding. He prayed, without knowing what to pray for. Now and again, well into the summer, he would go down to the garden of Villa Vecchia to take a little exercise, have a breath of fresh air, say the Rosary or chat with one of his sons. He said at the time, "I feel *tamquam leo rugiens*, like a roaring lion, on watch, on guard. I feel like a blind man who is being attacked but can only flail the air with his stick, because I don't know what's happening, but something is going on."[40]

He said the same thing more than once to Don Alvaro, his favorite son, confidante, confessor, "guardian," and strong rock. "Alvaro, I don't know what's going on, but something is happening."

Don Alvaro was silent. His eyes would fill with tears, but he could not help. Monsignor Escrivá said to himself, "Alvaro knows something. He isn't telling me what it is because he isn't allowed to." Through his work in the Vatican, Don Alvaro may have had knowledge of ill-natured comments; but he was unaware that a strange operation was being planned that would affect the founder.[41]

One day in August 1951, not knowing whom else to turn to, he turned to the only source of help available to him. He said to Don Alvaro, "Alvaro, I have always used supernatural means—prayer and mortification. So I am driving to Loreto on the fourteenth. I want to be there on the fifteenth to consecrate the Work to Our Lady. Being the middle of August, it's very hot; the roads will be terrible. No matter. That way we'll do some real mortification."[42]

Don Alvaro went with him. Putting up with the terrific heat of mid-summer, they drove to the province of Ancona. There, in the shrine of Loreto, after celebrating Mass, Monsignor Escrivá consecrated Opus Dei to the Most Sweet Heart of Mary. The essence of his prayer was short and to the point: *Iter para tutum!* "Prepare us a safe path!"

---

40. Cf. AGP, RHF 21171, p. 880 ff.
41. Bishop Javier Echevarria told the author in a conversation in Rome on April 9, 1994: "Don Alvaro did not know anything about what was being plotted against the Work. I once asked him if he had kept quiet because he was bound to silence by his job. But he said no, and that if he had known anything when the plot was in motion, he would have acted on his own account to try to deactivate the scheme, and to defend the Work and our Father."
42. Cf. AGP, RHF 21165, pp. 195–196.

The answer was not long in coming. In September, Juan Udaondo, one of the people in Opus Dei living in Milan, informed Monsignor Escrivá of "something vague but very disquieting" which Cardinal Schuster had just told him. Cardinal Schuster, a Benedictine monk and Archbishop of Milan, a very important person, had told him certain things that were being said about the Work, adding, "I don't believe them at all myself. I am very happy for Opus Dei to be working in my diocese."[43]

Months later, in January 1952, in conversation with Juan Udaondo and Juan Masia, Cardinal Schuster inquired, "How is your founder?"

They answered simply, "He's very well!"

The cardinal insisted, "How is he carrying his cross? Doesn't he have a big problem, a heavy cross?"

"Well, you see, if that is so, he'll be very happy," one said, "because he's always taught us that if we're very close to the cross, we're very close to Jesus."

"No, no!" exclaimed Cardinal Schuster. "Tell him to be careful. Tell him to remember his fellow countryman, St. Joseph of Calasanz, and also St. Alphonsus Liguori. And to get moving!"[44]

The two holy founders named had suffered fierce attacks at the hands of men of the Church. One of them, St. Joseph of Calasanz from Aragon, was expelled from the congregation he had founded by its own members. Cruelly wronged and viciously slandered, he had to undergo a lawsuit and a public trial before a tribunal of the Inquisition. St. Alphonsus Liguori, a lawyer from Naples and founder of the Redemptorists, drank the bitter cup of misunderstanding, criticism, and persecution. Udaondo wrote to Monsignor Escrivá at once, telling him of Cardinal Schuster's warning. He was crying as he wrote. The letter is in the archives of the Work and it can be seen how in one or two paragraphs the ink ran where his tears had fallen.

As well as writing, Udaondo himself traveled from Milan to Rome. On March 12 he was in the oratory of Via Orsini, a center of Opus Dei, when Monsignor Escrivá came in and knelt down beside

---

43. Testimony of Juan Udaondo (AGP, RHF T-03360).
44. Testimony of Juan Masia (AGP, RHF T-05869).

him. He whispered to him, without taking his eyes off the tabernacle, "My son, how often have you heard me say, quite truthfully, that I would like *not* to be in the Work, so that I could ask for admission straight away and be the last one of all, and be the first to obey—obey everybody! God our Lord knows I did not want to be the founder of anything. But that was what God wanted. My son, have you seen how they wish to destroy the Work and how they are attacking me? It's the same story over again, 'Strike the shepherd, and the sheep will be scattered.' I tell you, here in front of the tabernacle, that if they throw me out of the Work, they'll kill me!"[45]

Monsignor Escrivá's voice broke. He hid his face in his hands. He was utterly distraught, a man of sorrows.

Since receiving Udaondo's letter, Monsignor Escrivá had gone to ask for explanations from the highest authorities in the Holy See. He talked with Cardinals Tedeschini, Larraona, Piazza, Tardini, Ferretto, and Baggio. He protested, "If you expel me from Opus Dei, you are criminals. The Work is my life, and if you separate me from it, you'll kill me. You'll murder me!"

They replied evasively, "But Monsignor . . . there is nothing, there is nobody . . ."

Monsignor Escrivá did something unusual in the court protocol of the Roman Curia of that time. Taking as intermediary Cardinal Tedeschini who on February 24 had been appointed Protector of Opus Dei,[46] he handed him a letter, filial and respectful but crystal clear, in which, rather than defending the rights of the Work or his own rights, he warned of the "grave sin of injustice which is going to be committed" if the plot went ahead. Although the letter was addressed to Cardinal Tedeschini, it was really for the eyes of a higher recipient: the Pope.

Cardinal Tedeschini promised to read the letter to Pius XII personally at the first opportunity. On March 18, 1952, the opportunity

---

45. Ibid.

46. The position of "Protector" was an honorary title which the Holy See conferred, according to ancient tradition, appointing one to every ecclesiastical institution. This position, which has now disappeared, was held on behalf of Opus Dei by Cardinals Tardini and Tedeschini, among others. After their nomination by the Pope, the institution 'under protection' made an express act of obedience to the Protector.

presented itself. Pius XII reacted quickly. Despite the fact that things were at an advanced stage of planning and the scheme was just on the point of overthrowing the founder of Opus Dei, it all stopped dead.

Monsignor Escrivá wrote on one of the pages of his pocket diary, "Without wanting to, persecutors sanctify. . . . But alas for these 'sanctifiers'!"[47] He was well aware who his adversaries were. He did not name them or point them out. But he could not help thinking of them when twenty years later, in 1972, people in Villa Tevere starting getting those sinister telephone calls.[48]

A witness in stone in the Cortile Vecchio

On one of those days of uncertainty and anxiety, when conspirators against the Work and against himself were breathing down his neck, he had come out into one of the little courtyards of Villa Tevere, to meditate alone for a while. Leaning on the railing of the Arco dei Venti, he wrote a brief text that he would later have engraved on a simple marble slab. "While these buildings were being raised for the service of the Church by dint of daily greater self-denial, God our Lord permitted severe, hidden opposition to arise externally, while Opus Dei, consecrated to the Most Sweet Heart of Mary on 15th August 1951 and to the Sacred Heart of Jesus on 26th October 1952, strong, compact and sure, was strengthened and expanded. *Laus Deo* (Praise God)."

The slab was placed in one of the galleries around the Cortile Vecchio, but it was covered with a metal plaque hung on hinges, like a small door. For some years the little bronze door stayed shut. At that time the turbulence of the storm, which had just failed to break, was still in the air, so that some prelates advised Monsignor Escrivá "to keep a low profile," to "give up all external activity," and "not even to breathe too deeply." A high-ranking member of the Curia told him, "On occasion it is expedient to pretend to be dead, so as not to be killed."

---

47. *Furrow*, no. 246.
48. Testimony of Monsignor César Ortiz-Echagüe (AGP, RHF T-04694).

A foreigner in Rome

Monsignor Escrivá became a voluntary recluse in Villa Tevere, something which went against the grain for someone of his outgoing, sociable character, and even more given his impatient zeal for souls. These were years of very active enclosure, devoted to forming the people of the Work, writing homilies and doctrinal letters, and vigorously encouraging the apostolate. He was not seen out and about in Rome, but he traveled all over Europe, making tiring journeys by car. He felt the sting of loneliness in Rome. He who had once said to Francesco Angelicchio, "I'm more Roman than you are,"[49] now came to feel like "a foreigner in *my* Rome."[50]

One day he prayed about Psalm 68: "More in number than the hairs of my head are those who hate me without cause. . . . For it is for thy sake that I have borne reproach, that shame has covered my face. I have become a stranger to my brothers, an alien to my mother's sons."

He took a pencil and scribbled notes, full of bitter sorrow. He did this, not to unburden himself, but so that some day others could learn what he had learned, without suffering so much. "Plots, wretched misinterpretations cut to the measure of the base hearts that fabricate them, cowardly insinuations. . . . It is a picture that, sadly, we see over and over again, in different fields. They neither work themselves, nor let others work. Meditate slowly on these verses of the Psalm: 'My God, I have become a stranger to my brothers, an alien to my mother's sons. Because zeal for thy house has consumed me, and the insults of those who insult thee have fallen upon me.' And keep on working."[51]

On a cold day in November 1959, during a get-together with students of the Roman College, one, hoping to draw him out on a subject close to his heart, asked him, "Father, tell us what happened in 1951 and 1952 when they wanted to divide the Work into two branches and expel you. Who was behind that persecution?"

---

49. Testimony of Monsignor Francesco Angelicchio (AGP, RHF T-03322).
50. Ibid.
51. *The Forge*, no. 797.

Monsignor Escrivá pointed with his chin in the direction of the stone slab. "Look, my son, out there in the Cortile Vecchio there is a tablet you can read, which is quite clear. It is written in plain Spanish. I wrote it myself, sitting on a pile of stones, while all of that part was still being built. My heart was full of sadness—but at the same time I was very happy! Not even then did I lose my joy. Alvaro and I put a stop to it. But you're saying to me, 'Father, tell us who was behind it.' And I have to tell you that you will discover many things in heaven. Not on earth. Better not."[52]

---

52. Testimony of Fr. Carlos Cardona (AGP, RHF T-06138).

8 ⁜

The Communicator

A strange slide

One evening in February 1960, Monsignor Escrivá and several women of the Work were in Villa Tevere looking at some slides from Kenya. There were landscapes, sunsets, people wearing exotic clothes, wild animals, and exuberant vegetation. Suddenly a strange image was projected onto the screen. It was hard to make out what the dark, cracked mass might be. A large rock? The bark of a tree trunk? An animal's head? While the projectionist was trying to get the slide into sharper focus, Monsignor Escrivá wondered aloud, "But what is it? A plant? An animal? A person?"

Several voices joined in the conjecturing. As it came into focus, a very black and rugged human figure could be seen. But was it a man or a woman? Then Monsignor Escrivá's voice rang out. "Whether it's a man or a woman, it is a soul! A soul that's worth all the blood of Christ! It would be worthwhile our going to Kenya for that one soul only!"[1]

For Monsignor Escrivá the value of every human being, the reason for their overwhelming dignity, was that each had an immortal soul. "To save one soul," he said, "I would go to the very gates of hell." These were not mere words. At a time when he was the focal point of all kinds of gossip, he had not held back from going to a

---

1. Testimony of Helena Serrano (cf. AGP, RHF T-04641).

brothel to hear the confession of the owner's dying brother, and administer the Sacrament of the Anointing of the Sick. As a precaution, he took an eminently respectable elderly man with him, since he was a young priest in his twenties. He had also exacted a promise that for that whole day there would not be an "appointment" there.

A hug for a Mason

Nor did he mind opening the doors of his house in Rome to an illustrious Mason, riddled with cancer, who secretly wanted to be reconciled with the Church. This man began by calling him "Sir" and ended up calling him "Father." When Monsignor Escrivá enveloped him in a big hug, he felt that his evil past had disappeared in an instant into the ocean of understanding of a God who forgives.

Approaching each soul on one's knees

Monsignor Escrivá was driven by two passions, both anchored in one love: a passion for God and a passion for souls. The heart of his "business" was bringing souls to God. Since God is always near human beings, what was necessary was that each person decide to listen to God and his or her conscience. His task as an apostle was to bring about silence in souls so that God could make himself heard.

When Monsignor Escrivá said he was interested in a hundred souls out of a hundred, he was not thinking of crowds so he added, "one by one"—"handling each soul like a unique pearl," entering consciences "on one's knees," always conscious of treading on sacred ground.

From A to Z

One day in 1967 in Pozoalbero, Seville, he was told that the stones in the beautifully cobbled courtyard had been set by a gypsy called Ignacio and his gang. He said, "Well, I'd really like to meet him! See if you can find this artist in paving, and tell him that if he can come, I'd be very happy to spend some time with him!"

Diego, the guard at Pozoalbero, found him, a bit tipsy, at the horse fair in Jerez.

"Monsignor?" said Ignacio when he heard the news. "Monsignor wants to meet me? Well, right now I've had one or two drinks too many, but I'll go straight home to have a little snooze and sweat it off. I'll get washed, put on my Sunday best, and be ready to meet Monsignor. . . . Hey, Diego, can I bring my family with me?"

When Ignacio and his family turned up, dressed to the nines, they immediately dropped the "Monsignor": it was "Father" this and "Father" that the whole time. Suddenly, the gypsy asked point-blank, "Father, do you love us a lot?"

"Yes, my son. I do," replied Monsignor Escrivá. "Look, I'm talking to you here in exactly the same way as I talked to the Duke and Duchess of Alba. I'm saying the same things to you as I said to them. Because I am a priest who only knows how to talk about God. I have only one cooking pot for all. I would love to come back and spend more time here, and organize meetings and get-togethers for you and your mates in which we could all talk: you would ask me things and I would talk, not preach! And we could do it in a very friendly way, over a few drinks. Well, you could have the drinks, I'd have coffee. Besides . . . you're very shrewd! When you want to work, you do it very well, putting lots of art and beauty into it. And when you don't want to work . . . what can I say? You do that very well too! No one can get cross with you!"[2]

The lament of Cayetana de Alba

The comparison with the Duke and Duchess of Alba, Luis Martinez de Irujo and Cayetana, was no exaggeration. Monsignor Escrivá had just received Martinez de Irujo in Rome. Three years later, spending a few days in Madrid, he returned the visit in the Liria Palace. When Cayetana lamented over the problems the Church was going through at the time, Monsignor Escrivá, having "only one cooking pot," said what he said to everyone else. "What you are telling me is the sad truth. But you and I have the obligation to keep silent and pray hard. And sometimes we will have to behave like Noah's good sons, who covered up their drunken father's nakedness."[3]

---

2. Testimony of Monsignor César Ortiz-Echagüe (AGP, RHF T-04694).
3. Ibid.

"Anyone would think I was the Emperor of Abyssinia!"

He put the same zeal and commitment into listening and talking to the cardinal of São Paulo as into making an opportunity to spend time with one of the construction engineers at Torreciudad. This was on a rainy day in April 1970. Monsignor Escrivá was on a rapid visit to Torreciudad, the shrine of Our Lady in northern Spain, to make a pilgrimage to Our Lady and see the construction work. As he was greeting the caretakers of the old hermitage, Miguel Manceras and his wife Antonia, a car pulled up with a squeal of brakes. It was Jose Manzanos, the construction engineer, still wearing his site helmet. Monsignor Escrivá gave him a big hug. Later, being driven to another part of the building site, he asked about this young man. "He's a magnificent worker," was the answer, "but lately he's been out of sorts as he fell out with his fiancée when they were just about to get married." Monsignor Escrivá made no comment.

They arrived at a huge excavated area where the future buildings were to be. It began to rain, and they put on raincoats and hats. At the construction hut the architects, Heliodoro Dols and César Ortiz-Echagüe, started to explain the details of the foundations being laid. "The crypts for the confessionals will be down there. . . ." Monsignor Escrivá looked around, as if seeking someone. Then he saw Jose Manzanos standing a little apart from the group and chatting to Teofilo Marco. Monsignor Escrivá slipped away from the architects and went to join the other two. He took them by the arm, one on the right and one on the left, and joking together in the friendliest fashion they began to walk slowly along, paying not the slightest attention to the rain. Ortiz-Echagüe came up behind them with an umbrella and tried to hold it over Monsignor Escrivá. He turned round quickly and said, "For goodness' sake, César. . . ! You and your umbrella! Anyone would think I was the Emperor of Abyssinia!"

Monsignor Escrivá kept on walking along with Jose and Teofilo, amid all the site activity—the deafening noise from the excavators, the muddy ground, the pouring rain. What did they talk about? None of the three ever said. The fact is that that conversation calmed Manzanos down, he made up with his fiancée, and they soon married. But not before he had written a moving letter to Monsignor Escrivá in Rome thanking him "for all that you said to me that rainy day in Torreciudad."[4]

Walt Disney looking at *The Way*

One day he called for Maria Luisa Cabrera and Helena Serrano, who were responsible for photographs in the Villa Tevere print room. He showed them a photograph of two men looking at a copy of *The Way*. Monsignor Escrivá pointed to one of them and said, "I bet you don't know who that is!"

The face looked familiar, and so did the smile, but they could not quite put a name to him.

"It's Walt Disney!" said Monsignor Escrivá. "And the other person is a son of mine who works in show business. He tells me Walt Disney is delighted with *The Way*."

"Your colleague wastes no time!"

In the summer of 1966 Monsignor Escrivá, Father Alvaro del Portillo, and Father Javier Echevarria went to Florence. There they went to a big wholesale store, where they managed to persuade the shopkeeper to sell them three pairs of trousers at a very cheap price. While Don Alvaro and Father Echevarria were trying them on, waiting for them to be wrapped, and paying, Monsignor Escrivá took one of the shop assistants aside. They talked together about the young man's work and leisure, his family, his Christian life. The shop assistant did not know with whom he had been speaking, but he was moved and encouraged that a priest was concerned about his life and his soul. When they said good-bye, he remarked to Don Alvaro and Father Echevarria, with a friendly wink, "*Il vostro compagno non perde il tempo, eh, ma lo fà molto bene*" (Your colleague wastes no time, does he? But he does it very well).[5]

---

4. Ibid.
5. Account of Bishop Javier Echevarria given to the author.

The friend

Monsignor Escrivá had an amazing faculty for making friends. Father Pedro Cantero Cuadrado, later archbishop of Saragossa, was one from the time of their first chance meeting in 1930 in the big old building in San Bernardo Street which housed the Central University of Madrid. It was on a September day, during the frenzy of exams, when the two young priests met. Father Cantero recalled, "A bond of mutual trust was established between us at once. We exchanged addresses. Thus began a friendship which was to last a lifetime. . . . It was a strong, close friendship. Josemaría entered my soul, little by little, doing a true priest-to-priest apostolate."[6]

On the afternoon of August 14, 1931 Father Escrivá turned up unexpectedly at his house in Madrid. It was very hot, and the smoke of churches and convents which had been attacked and burned still hung in the air. Father Cantero had decided to work on his doctoral thesis. When Father Escrivá entered the room, he found him absorbed in his books. Father Cantero told him his plan, and Father Escrivá listened. Then he said, "Look, Pedro, you've become selfish! You're thinking of nothing but yourself and your studies. You only have to open your eyes to see what sort of state the Church in Spain is in today—and what state Spain itself is in. These are difficult moments, and you and I should be thinking of the personal service we can and ought to offer the Church. Your thesis? Your books? Let me tell you that what we have to do right now is to busy ourselves with other, far more important things."

At the end of that summer Father Cantero decided to leave aside his academic career. He went to see Angel Herrera Oria and told him that he was at his disposal to work for the recently created Propagation of the Faith association. "Josemaría's words urged me on. When I saw him again and told him about my decision he was delighted. Our friendship deepened. He encouraged me to work incessantly."[7]

---

6. *A Man of God—Testimonies on the Founder of Opus Dei* (London: Scepter, 1992). Cf. AGP, RHF T-04391.
7. Ibid.

Summoned before the Holy Office

Monsignor Juan Hervas, Bishop of Majorca and Ciudad Real, who had a doctorate in law and was promoter of the Short Courses on Christianity, had been a friend of Father Josemaría Escrivá since the 1930s. When Monsignor Escrivá died, Bishop Hervas wrote: "I had never stopped to think to what extent my friend Josemaría was really so much *mine*; so close to me, that his disappearance has left me feeling stricken with an enormous sense of bereavement. I had always been able to count on him when I needed him."

On many occasions Monsignor Hervas had stayed with Father Escrivá in Diego de Leon Street in Madrid where he was treated as one of the family. Without belonging to Opus Dei, he saw and lived the life of the Work from the inside. When he went to Rome, he always found the doors of 73 Bruno Buozzi Street open to him.

Bishop Hervas remembered particularly well one of the "Roman conversations" he had with Father Escrivá. He called it "the conversation of the dark night of my soul." Misunderstandings had been whipped up against the Short Courses on Christianity and their promoter. The author of the campaign turned out to be Father Carrillo de Albornoz, the same person who had attacked Opus Dei in 1941–42. On this occasion, he placed dreadful allegations before the Holy Office. Bishop Hervas came to Rome to face these accusations. He was heartbroken. He thought it was too much to expect Father Escrivá to console him for the same sort of attack as he himself had suffered, caused by the same hand, too. Nevertheless, he came to Villa Tevere.

Father Escrivá enveloped him in a bear hug, then sat down and listened attentively, and priest opened his heart to priest. Monsignor Hervas did not need to go into details. Father Escrivá saw the problem and, without wasting time, showed the true solution.

"Don't worry, Juan. They aren't enemies but benefactors, because they help to purify us, to sanctify us. We have to pray for them, and *love* them! I've been through the same thing. I can talk to you as one brother to another about something I've been through myself, which you're now going through in your turn. Don't let resentment or bitterness lodge in your heart. Don't fear anything from your Mother the Church. Only good things can come to you from her! Keep calm, only listen to the voice of the Church, and turn a deaf ear to street gossip."

Father Escrivá did not limit himself to encouraging words. He came out in his defense, interceded and argued on his behalf. Hervas testified, "Only God knows in what measure Josemaría Escrivá contributed to straightening the paths of Providence."[8]

A Christmastime present

Along with opening his heart, Father Escrivá also opened his wallet—as far as he could—and gave generously to a friend in need. Nor did he wait to be asked. Particularly impressive is a letter he wrote one Christmas to his good friends, Brother Jose de Lopera and the community of monks of El Parral, Segovia. Dated December 26, 1943, it said,

> My dear brother: You cannot imagine how grateful I was for your good wishes for the *nihil obstat*. May God reward your kindness and your affection. We will always remember you with joy. Particularly during this holy season, we have often been speaking about you and your community.
>
> The Three Kings[9]* called here and left 500 pesetas for some Christmas sweets for the monks of El Parral, which I am sending you today.
>
> A big hug for you all. Help us be saints.
>
> Another hug for you yourself from this sinner, who begs for your prayers. Josemaría.[10]

In those days, 500 pesetas was the equivalent of a captain's pay for a month. Father Escrivá was burdened with debt and had to do juggling acts with his finances to restart the students' residence lost during the Civil War. Yet friendship led him to turn his pockets inside out.

---

8. Op. cit., Testimony of Bishop Juan Hervas. Cf. AGP, RHF T-04697.
9. *Translator's note: The Three Kings traditionally bring Christmas gifts in Spain instead of Santa Claus.
10. EF-431226 (Letter of December 26, 1943 to Fr. Jose de Lopera and the monks of El Parral).

Cardinals have feelings too

Friendship was not reserved for big occasions. One New Year's Day he asked some of his daughters to give Cardinal Ildebrando Antoniutti a surprise—a present of little material value, but one which the old cardinal would enjoy.

> Look: although today's a holiday, the sweet shops will be open. Prepare a nice box with pretty Christmas wrapping, a really attractive package with a whole lot of sweets. But mind, they have to be a specific kind: MU toffees. They're not expensive, but Cardinal Antoniutti loves them. See if you're lucky enough to find them! You have to realize that at his age the people who knew his likes and dislikes are no longer with him. Cardinals are children at heart, too, and can be moved by a few simple sweets. Write him a nice friendly card to go with it and sign it yourselves. He'll be bowled over.[11]

Cardinal Dell'Acqua's sister, Rita, now an old lady, had been mentally deficient since birth. Monsignor Escrivá wished to alleviate Cardinal Dell'Acqua's sorrow in some way. He decided to ask two of his daughters to do something to help.

"The cardinal's a friend whom I love very dearly," he explained. "And I am going to ask you to do something for him that I can't, although I'd like to. His sister, poor lady, is mentally retarded. Although she looks old, she's really like a good little ten-year-old girl. She's called Rita Dell'Acqua, and she lives in the cardinal's house in the Lateran Palace. Sister Scolastica Pavanel looks after her full-time, because people who are mentally retarded need a lot of loving care. I'll give you Sister Scolastica's telephone number so you can contact her. Sister Scolastica herself could also do with a break and a little affection. You can invite them home one afternoon for tea, whenever it suits them. But don't do it because you have to: it's a favor I ask of you, as if I were doing it myself for the cardinal, who's a friend of mine. Let them come and go as they like here, have a good time, and enjoy themselves. Then another day, you go and visit them, and take them some sweets or a homemade cake. Put your

---

11. Testimony of Mercedes Morado (AGP, RHF T-07902).

hearts into it—give them the love I would give them myself." From then on he would often remind them to go or telephone. It was not a task he handed on and then forgot about.[12]

The theology of coincidence

One morning in November 1965 Monsignor Escrivá entered in the print room in Villa Tevere with an old gentleman. He introduced him by his full name to the people working there, adding, "an English publisher." In one particular area he saw they were binding a collection of letters from people of the Work—laborers, farm workers, and manual workers—to the Pope. Monsignor Escrivá said in amusement, "These sons of mine are simple, noble fellows. They write without a trace of protocol: 'Dear Pope . . .' or 'Yours sincerely.' But the Pope is going to love them. He has too many things that make him suffer!"

He came closer to see how Maria Jose Rodriguez, known as "Puchi," was gilding the pontifical seal of Paul VI on the cover. Then the publisher exclaimed, "This is wonderful! Tomorrow I've got a private audience with His Holiness. I'm taking him some leather-bound books. I've searched all over Rome for a gilder who had a die of the papal arms, but no one had one—and now I see you have one here!"

"Well, when you want something that shows affection for the Pope, you don't have to scour Rome: look for it in a center of Opus Dei. Come on, where are those books?"

"In the car, Father."

"Well, bring them in, and these daughters of mine will put the shield on them in a moment!"

The visitor, delighted, hurried out to his car. Meanwhile Monsignor Escrivá sat down, visibly tired, crippled with fatigue. In a little while the publisher came back with his books. Monsignor Escrivá stood up with the same vitality as before. Puchi and Helena busied themselves with engraving and gilding the shields onto the books. Meanwhile Monsignor Escrivá and his British friend were chatting.

---

12. Testimony of Marlies Kücking.

"Father," said the man, "I think someone ought to write a 'theology of coincidence.' Listen to what happened to me . . ."

"Not a theology of coincidence," interrupted Monsignor Escrivá, "but a theology of providence. And it's already been written."

"All right. But let me tell you what happened to me yesterday. I wanted to interview a particular African bishop, and I couldn't find him anywhere in Rome. I've been going to the Vatican every day, when they were coming out of the council, but there was no sign of him! I'd given up hope. Yesterday I was in the center of the city when suddenly it started to rain, so I stopped a taxi. Just as I was getting in, an African priest appeared. He told me, in English, that he was in a terrible hurry and asked me to let him have the taxi. You know, Father, how difficult it is to find a taxi in Rome, in the rain. I said to him: 'Look here, I'll take you wherever you want to go, but I won't give you the taxi because I need it too.' So we got in together. The 'coincidence' or 'providence' was that he turned out to be the very African bishop I'd been looking for! As I didn't know he was a bishop, I'd been calling him 'Father' all the time."

"Don't let that worry you. If he's a good bishop, he has to be a father before anything else."

Puchi had stamped the papal shield on the books, but the impression on one was a bit faint. The publisher thought it was "perfect, great!" Monsignor Escrivá, however, turned to Puchi and said, "Would you mind doing it again, please? In the Work," he added to the publisher, "we try to finish all our jobs with the greatest possible perfection. It isn't an obsession, it is the essence of the love of God. Besides, these books are going to end up in the hands of the Vicar of Christ."

As the Englishman was leaving, he remarked, "Tomorrow the Pope will hear about the love Opus Dei has for him. I'm going to tell him myself. Father, how will I be able to repay you for all this? And your kindness to me all morning?"

"What do you mean, repay? In my country there is a very wise saying: 'Love is repaid with love.' You've done many good things for the Work, as I don't need to remind you. And I'm trying to respond to all of that a little, with the only thing I have: my prayer and affection."[13]

---

13. Testimony of Helena Serrano (cf. AGP, RHF T-04641).

An honest marketing strategy

Monsignor Escrivá carried out his friendly apostolate with every kind of person, from agriculturists to zoologists. He spoke to each in his own language, without adulterating the message. In private conversation and public preaching, in the dark of the confessional and under stage lights, he reached people's hearts. But he set no value on his leadership qualities. All that interested him was how to bring people to God.

What marketing strategy did this awakener of consciences employ? His 'technique' was to tell the truth, with a gift of tongues. "It's not a question of 'simplifying the message to get through to the masses,' but of speaking words of wisdom in clear Christian speech that all can understand."[14]

The poet in wine

Without adulterating the word of God, he 'materialized' the doctrine he taught by drawing examples from real life.

When someone said that in putting their heart into work they lost all track of time, Monsignor Escrivá said enthusiastically, "The very same thing happens to me, when I am doing the 'work' of the Mass! I lose all notion of time, and I think that while I am there, at the altar, all clocks should stop."[15]

He taught Fernando Carrasco, a wine producer, to put "the same care, the same art, the same loving attention" into his periods of prayer as into his wine-making, "because you are a poet in wine."[16]

Domecq's steed

He spoke to a friend, Alvaro Domecq, about the final leap to pass from this life to heaven, "leaping over purgatory regardless." He said he envied him his Arab stallion: "A horse like yours, Alvaro, is just what I need to make that final leap! I need the steed of God's love to leap clean over purgatory."[17]

14. Cf. *The Forge*, no. 634.
15. Oral Testimony of Javier Mora-Figueroa.
16. Testimony of Monsignor César Ortiz-Echagüe (AGP, RHF T-04694).
17. Ibid.

A gift for Olinda

On another occasion he was going to talk with Olinda, an old servant of the Sartos, St. Pius X's family. Monsignor Escrivá had received her several times before, and was very fond of her. Carmen Ramos asked Monsignor Escrivá if she should prepare a little present for her, such as some sweets or a rosary.

"No, don't worry. Don't prepare anything. I have something for her."

When Olinda arrived, Monsignor Escrivá came into the room carrying a small packet. After the visit was over, Monsignor Escrivá explained to Carmen, "You see, I was wondering what she would like most. A rosary? No, because she has one already. She must have heaps of them! I myself have given her several on other occasions. Some chocolates? No, she's diabetic. Then, as I was thinking about her, I remembered a picture of the Virgin Mary as a child which we have here in this house, given to us by St. Pius X's nephews. It occurred to me that Olinda would like to have a copy, because it's a family souvenir, and she must often have prayed in front of this picture when she was young and working for the Sarto family. Her face lit up when she saw it, so I think we got it right."[18]

Destroyer of stereotypes

He had the gift of knowing how to think from the other person's point of view. In 1941, when he was thirty-nine, preaching a retreat in Alacuas, a small town near Valencia, he already knew how to talk to that particular group, finding their natural strengths in order to build supernatural virtues on them. He always preferred to stress what was good rather than what was bad. Encarnita Ortega was in Alacuas for the retreat, and she was surprised at how Monsignor Escrivá turned stereotypes inside out.

"People say that Valencians act on the spur of the moment, that with them it's all sheer improvisation and lack of continuity," he began. "I've found that that's not true. Farmers here make good use of the land on the banks of the River Turia to plant crops. When the river floods, the crops are ruined. But do you think they're put

---

18. Oral testimony of Carmen Ramos.

off? They start planting all over again! That's not improvisation: it's continuity, effort, and perseverance. Well, in your interior life, you have to do the same."[19]

Issuing challenges

All good educators try to bring out the best in people, and this is what Monsignor Escrivá did. He possessed an undeniable "gift of tongues," not only because he could say the same things in different ways depending on his listeners, but because without either scandalizing or wounding people, he managed to bring a demanding message home to them.

He encouraged some Irish women to "take revenge" for the ill-treatment they had received from the English "by sending them a heavy downpour of prayers," while at the same time telling them not to consent to feelings of victimization, still less vindictiveness.

He made clear the solidarity and affection he felt for the first Germans who came to study with him in Rome soon after the Second World War, "because you have suffered under the yoke of a tyrant, a genocidal cur." But some years later he warned them and other Germans that their passion for work could lead them to turn their lives into selfish preserves shut to anything not materially profitable.

He made people from the United States think about the implications of their economic power and world leadership, and see these as a challenge to responsibility toward others.

When he came in, the room lit up

He could also make himself understood by people who did not speak his language. Marlies Kücking, who could speak many languages, recalled her experience as a translator for foreign visitors who came to see Monsignor Escrivá at the end of his morning's work in Villa Tevere.

When the visitors had arrived and were waiting for Monsignor Escrivá, there was often a feeling of uncertainty, especially if they

---

19. Testimony of Encarnación Ortega (AGP, RHF T-05074).

had come to see him for the first time. They would ask things like, "Will he speak or do we speak? What can we talk to him about? How are we going to understand each other? How do we greet him? Will he mind if we take some photos?"

When Monsignor Escrivá came into the sitting room, he was smiling. He called them by their nicknames, his arms outstretched toward them, as if he had come to meet each of them individually. In a moment the strained politeness of a formal visit had vanished. Everyone felt at ease and the atmosphere was one of cordiality, understanding, and trust. The translator hardly had to do anything, while Monsignor Escrivá took the lead, talking, asking questions, joking, and moved to pity when a piece of bad news came out. Afterwards, putting it all into their own language, they were amazed that they had covered so many subjects, intensely and in such depth, in such a short time.[20]

Monsignor Escrivá's gift for people went hand-in-hand with a total incapacity for treating visitors with conventional politeness, pronouncing a few set phrases to get the visit over with. He went to the heart of people's concerns, and never treated them as trivial. For him, such times were unrepeatable moments, and he applied all his talents and put his heart into them.

Dictionaries were not needed

But the real reason for the lasting effect of even the shortest visits lay elsewhere. Monsignor Escrivá never talked to his visitors from his position as president general of the Work, Monsignor, or founder. At every moment he was totally a priest—someone who had been set there to make contact between men and God.

One spring morning in 1970 he received nine or ten Japanese women, not all of whom were Catholic. Loretta Lorenz, an American woman in Opus Dei who was living in Osaka, was one of the group.

In their conversation, Monsignor Escrivá praised the good things of Japan, the delicacy of their customs, their tenacity and diligence in cultivating their tiny *bonsai* gardens, and their skill in the world of electronic technology. Then he went on to talk to them as a priest.

---

20. Testimony of Marlies Kücking.

"In a few minutes I am going to celebrate Holy Mass," he told them. "Those of you who are not Christian won't be able to understand its importance, but it is of infinite worth. I am going to offer it up today for everyone in Japan. And now I will give you my blessing." He stood up and raised both arms as though laying his hands on them. The women also got up. Some remained standing and bowed their heads. Those who were Catholics knelt down.

"The blessing of a priest is a good thing, like the blessing of a father, which can only bring good. May the Lord be in your hearts and on your lips . . ."

At this point, Monsignor Escrivá placed his left hand on his chest while he made the sign of the cross in the air slowly and clearly with his right.

". . . In the name of the Father and of the Son and of the Holy Spirit. Now, I want to ask you for something. Pray—you who are Catholics, to Jesus Christ, and the others to the Supreme Being in whom you believe—pray, all of you, each in your own fashion, for me to be good and faithful!"[21]

As a farewell gesture he made a profound oriental-style reverence, bowing from the waist and placing his hands on his knees.

This was another characteristic of the way he always acted: with an indestructible certainty that he had found the truth in the small number of matters which are the core of the faith. For these questions and no others, he used the words "I believe." In matters left to opinion, he was always ready to give in, but he would not compromise, as he said, "even out of good manners!"

"I have touched God"

The times he lived in were times of "adaptation," even "barter," for priests who lacked the courage of their convictions. Facile labels were invented and applied which pigeon-holed people and destroyed the freedom of consciences to make a stand on matters of faith or morals. Monsignor Escrivá turned them around and showed how void of real meaning they were. He did this quite naturally before massive audiences made up of people he did not know so that he could not

---

21. Testimony of Mercedes Morado (AGP, RHF T-07902).

tell how they might react. As he himself acknowledged, "You could tell me: 'Go home, priest!' "

Monsignor Escrivá had too much respect for God to give way to human respect. He could not care less whether he was popular or unpopular or having a good or bad press. He told the truth plainly to anyone who wanted to hear it. He proclaimed openly, "I am a Thomist, a paternalist, and a triumphalist. Of course I am! I want to triumph with Christ on the Cross. People do not want to triumph, because the glory of Christ was the Cross, sufferings, and the worst possible torments. I love the throne where Christ triumphed: the Cross of Calvary. . . . Now that so many people go around broadcasting their opinions against St. Thomas Aquinas, I love and admire him and I'm grateful to him. I am a Thomist. And when they speak badly of paternalism, I get cross. Paternalism can only upset those who don't know who their own father is! I knew and loved my father, as a good son. And we all know that God is our Father, and we love him. . . . A providentialist? I'm not a miracle-monger; I believe in God's providence. And as I have actually touched it with my hands, I can truthfully say that I hardly need faith—and sometimes you can leave out the 'hardly,' because I have touched God."[22]

He also spoke out against the oversimplification which split humanity into traditionalists and progressives in every field. This dichotomy was both false and deceptive. Those who maintained it dictated in advance the direction which progress, according to them, was obliged to take.

Monsignor Escrivá did not beat about the bush. " 'Traditionalists' are like Egyptian mummies. 'Progressives' are like badly brought up children who smash everything they touch. But above all these two words are criminal: the effect they have is that many people don't dare say what they really think, for fear of being labeled as one or the other of them."[23]

He went on, "I am neither traditionalist nor progressive, just a priest of God and a lover of truth. I possess the freedom of God's children, which Christ won for us on the Cross. I feel as free as a

---

22. AGP, RHF 20761, pp. 743–744. AGP, RHF 2077, pp. 26, 56, 188. Testimony of Fr. Carlos Cardona (AGP, RHF T-06138).
23. Testimony of Monsignor César Ortiz-Echagüe (AGP, RHF T-04694).

bird that looks for good food wherever it can be found. We love sound doctrine, and we leave people utterly free in matters of opinion. So if anyone calls us traditionalists or progressives, it isn't true! We are children of Christ's Church. We feed on sound doctrine, and no one can take that freedom away from us!"[24]

Confronting impostors in the pulpit

In the last years of his life, from 1972 to 1975, Monsignor Escrivá changed his habits. He had turned seventy. Before he had almost always kept his preaching for small groups, preferring to do a one-to-one apostolate. Now he set out on marathon tours to teach as much sound Christian doctrine as he could to huge audiences in Europe and South America. He spent long, exhausting days traveling or preaching. But even though he might be speaking to more than 5,000 people in a big theater, the occasion was magically converted into a family gathering. Monsignor Escrivá invited people together for dialogue, and the initiative lay with the audience. "Ask me questions," he would say. "I haven't come here to preach to you! I'm here to talk about whatever you choose."

Why did he do all this? Because the teachings of the Second Vatican Council had been badly explained and poorly assimilated. There were too many closed mouths, too many geniuses who had lost their brilliance, too many imposters in the pulpits, too many disused confessionals, too many catechisms growing moldy in attics, too many empty seminaries, too many divided parishes, too many of the faithful losing their way. Monsignor Escrivá decided to jump defenseless into the arena and take on the bulls.

"Too aggressive"

He put all he had into the task. He said, firmly and categorically, that Christian dogma and morals remained unaltered, that the truths of the faith were what they always had been, the commandments were the same, the sacraments had not changed, the Church was the same Church, and God was the same as he always had been.

---

24. AGP, RHF 20761, p. 712.

For these events Monsignor Escrivá drew upon all the resources of his "gift of tongues" and his "gift for people," with expressiveness in words and gestures, light-hearted banter and a seriousness that drove home the doctrinal message. To whom? A mother from Caracas, a diplomat from Quito, a kiosk-holder from Rio de Janeiro, a university student from Bogota, an invalid from Barcelona, a gypsy patriarch from the Triana district of Seville, a businessman from Santiago de Chile, an ice cream seller from Maracaibo, a postman from Vallecas in Madrid, an Indian peasant from Morelos in Mexico, an army man from Buenos Aires. He dipped his spoon into the "one same cooking pot" for each. After each event he did not ask, "How was I?" but "Have any of them decided to go to confession?"

A beginner of eighty-three

During one of these get-togethers in Argentina, an eminent scientist was sitting in the stalls, lost in the crowd. He was eighty-three and notorious for disbelief in religion. While listening to Monsignor Escrivá, he felt his agnosticism crumble away. He looked around and found a priest of Opus Dei nearby. Quite suddenly, he asked if he could speak to him in the confessional. There he announced, "I want . . . I would like to make my First Communion."

The priest, not wanting to rush things, said, "Steady on! First of all we have to find out if you are baptized." It turned out that he was not. He started preparing for it, including learning the penny catechism. Soon afterward, having been reborn by Baptism, he was going around with the innocence of a beginner.[25]

At home one day with a few of his sons, Monsignor Escrivá was leafing through a book, *Dos meses de catequesis* ("Two months of catechesis"), which reproduced part of the preaching he had given. He read a bit here and a bit there. Then, looking at the others and laughing, he said, "All this is God's providence, God's will. It did not happen by chance, nor was it something willed by you or me; Our Lord took the initiative. And I thank him for having given me such sound doctrine . . . and so little embarrassment at explaining it in public!"[26]

---

25. AGP, RHF 21165, p. 90.
26. Testimony of Monsignor César Ortiz-Echagüe (AGP, RHF T-04694).

9

When God Takes a Hand

Which is more important or worth more to a holy man: what he does for God or what God does for him?

What the man does for God invites us to imitate it; inside the saint there is always a hero fighting battles, and we feel drawn to watch the drama. What God does for the man belongs to the unfathomable mystery of grace. We admire it, envy it, even fear it; but we can easily imagine it is not meant for everyone, but given to some by God's free choice. However, this is not true. God gives every single person the favors of his grace. Why does he give more to the saints? Doubtless because they ask more insistently. Holiness is built up and nourished by constantly begging from our Lord and constantly receiving his graces.

A saint?

Saints are misers who fill themselves with God. And God lets himself be pillaged by his saints. In the end, sanctity is a matter of trust: what a person is prepared to let God do in him or her. Saints neither love, believe, or hope on their own: they always count on the Other. Monsignor Escrivá was one of those who trusted in God. In October 1950 he wrote, "God's wisdom has been leading me, as if playing with me, from the darkness of the first inklings, to the clarity with which I now see every detail of the Work."[1]

---

1. *Letter*, October 7, 1950, 3. AP, HRF, 20755, p. 279.

"I did not want to checkmate"

In a letter dated January 1961, he again referred to this "divine game" in which God took the initiative and he let himself be led with willing docility. "God led me by the hand quietly, little by little, until his 'castle' was built. 'Take that step,' he seemed to say. 'Now put this here. Take that away from in front and put it over there.' That's how our Lord built his Work, with firm strokes and fine outlines, a work both old and new, as the word of Christ is. The divine game I am talking to you about appears very clearly in the history of our canonical path within the life of the Church. I have not had to calculate things in advance, as if I were playing chess; among other things, because I have never tried to work out the other person's moves so as to be able to checkmate him later. What I have had to do is to let myself be led."[2]

For forty years Don Alvaro del Portillo was a privileged witness of Monsignor Escrivá's life of prayer: of his efforts, his searching, his periods of darkness and drought. Don Alvaro was also a witness to Monsignor Escrivá's unexpected discoveries, surprise meetings, and the big and small gifts or new lights, with which God rewarded his tenacious struggle. Monsignor Escrivá described such gifts as "being given a fingerful of honey to suck." He never forgot them, but savored them continuously and passed them on to his children so that they too could benefit from these insights. But he never boasted of having been so favored. "It is only human, and indeed supernatural, to conceal God's favors!" he said.[3]

God speaks quietly

On October 2, 1968 he celebrated the fortieth anniversary of the founding of Opus Dei at the Pozoalbero Conference Center, near Seville and was bombarded with questions by his sons. He explained, "I purposely haven't wanted to tell you about it. I've been trying to avoid it. But I'd be lying if I said that our Lord hadn't given me extraordinary favors. He has always done so when it was necessary

---

2. *Letter*, January 25, 1951, 4-5. AP, HRF, 20755, p. 280.
3. *Letter*, January 9, 1932, 10. AP, HRF, 20765.

for the Work. Those happenings are something I would not wish on anybody, because although they fill the soul with peace, they are also enormously demanding. But, especially on a day like today, I don't want to tell you anything about this because I want you to understand clearly that our way lies in ordinary things: sanctifying our ordinary everyday actions, making our daily prose into heroic verse."[4]

"Let me read!"

Often Don Alvaro saw how, after they shared the morning paper between them over breakfast, Monsignor Escrivá had hardly begun to read when he became lost in God. Resting his forehead on the palm of his hand, he would put the paper aside and start to pray.

After Monsignor Escrivá's death, Don Alvaro was putting his writings in order. Reading the *Intimate Notes*, he was struck by the discovery that this facility for letting himself be flooded by God was something Monsignor Escrivá had from his youth. In one notebook this short note appears: "Prayer: even though I don't give it to you, you make me feel prayer at the wrong time, and sometimes, reading the newspaper, I have had to say to you: 'Let me read!' "[5]

I heard the word "gloriae"

At times it was as though there were an imperious knocking in his heart. Monsignor Escrivá was having a few days' break with Don Alvaro and Father Javier Echevarria in Caglio, a small town in the north of Italy. On August 23, 1971, while having breakfast after Mass, Monsignor Escrivá was again reading the newspaper when he was deeply struck by an inner locution from God in these exact words: *Adeamus cum fiducia ad thronum gloriae ut misericordiam consequamur!*— "Let us go therefore with confidence to the throne of glory: that we may obtain mercy." Immediately Monsignor Escrivá told Don Alvaro and Father Echevarria what had happened. He pointed out that the phrase he had "heard" was not identical to the one in the Epistle to the Hebrews (4:16). The scriptural text says *ad thronum gratiae*, to the

---

4. Testimony of Monsignor César Ortiz-Echagüe (AGP, HRF T-04694).
5. J. Escrivá, *Intimate Notes*, no. 1130.

throne of grace, but what Monsignor Escrivá heard was *ad thronum gloriae*. His eyes shining with joy, he explained that *thronum gloriae* should be taken as referring to Our Lady, the Throne of God, in the same sense in which she is called *Sedes Sapientiae*, Seat of Wisdom.[6]

Theologians and market stalls

From 1965 on Monsignor Escrivá prayed, and got everyone in the Work to pray, for Christ's Church, which was being shaken by the postconciliar agitation of those who called themselves progressives but who were in fact old-fashioned and regressive. Theologians, liturgists, and moralists were bringing out centuries-old errors and heresies. The only novelty was that in the pulpit or at the altar they sported ties or sweaters instead of cassocks.

Monsignor Escrivá offered his life "for an end to the time of trial" in the Church and asked his children, "Join with me in the Mass, in your prayer, and throughout the day. I am constantly centered on God: I am more outside the earth than on it."[7]

On May 8, 1970 he heard another clear internal locution: *Si Deus nobiscum, quis contra nos?*—"If God is with us, who is against us?" (Romans 8:31). He traveled to Mexico that same month to pray and do penance at the shrine of Our Lady of Guadalupe. He went to the shrine on nine successive days and spent hours kneeling in front of the picture of Our Lady, urging her, "Show us you are a mother" and "you can't fail to hear us!"[8] Prior to this, he had been to many of the major shrines of Our Lady in Western Europe, praying for the Church and the Work: Lourdes and Notre Dame in France, Sonsoles, Our Lady of the Pillar, and Our Lady of Ransom in Spain, Fatima in Portugal, Loreto and St. Mary Major in Italy, Einsiedeln in Switzerland, and Maria Pötsch in Austria.

August 6 of the same year brought an invitation to beg relentlessly until he got what he was asking for: *clama, ne cesses!*—"cry aloud, spare not!" (Isaiah 58:1). Keep on praying, he understood it to mean; turn your life into a clamor of prayer. Monsignor Escrivá

---

6. AP, HRF, 21171, p. 881.
7. AP, HRF, 20160, p. 894.
8. AP, HRF, 21171, p. 1357.

transmitted God's wish to his children numbering thousands upon thousands all over the world.

"I love you more than these"

From his early days Monsignor Escrivá had taken the path of prayer that involved listening with the heart. He felt an affectionate inner reproach on February 16, 1932. Distributing Communion to some nuns in the church of St. Elizabeth in Madrid he had been saying mentally, "I love you more than this one . . . or this one . . . or this one. . . ." Then he "heard" the words, "Love means deeds, not sweet words."[9] Forty years later, talking to his spiritual daughters in Rome, he told the story in the third person: "I know a poor priest who was once giving Communion to some enclosed nuns. . . ." At the end he stated, "I can vouch for the truth of this case."[10]

The 1930s were difficult for young Father Escrivá, urged on by God to be a founder without material means and surrounded by misunderstanding and loneliness. A very small number of people understood him. Others liked the ideal, but when the time came to put their shoulder to the wheel they backed off, disappearing without saying good-bye.

Father Escrivá also came up against belligerent anti-clericalism, normal in the Spain of those years. He felt dismayed and powerless. He had neither strength nor resources nor a "middle way" he could take, and the whole Work was still to be accomplished. Once again, however, God was going to take a hand.

The young priest was on a streetcar in Madrid in 1931. Suddenly he experienced with extraordinary force the categorical certainty of being a child of God. He had never felt it like that before. The words were fragments from Psalm 2, "*Thou art my Son, this day I have begotten thee. . . . You are my Christ.*" He found that he had gotten off the streetcar and was wandering through the streets, as if delirious,

---

9. Cf. *Intimate Notes*, no. 606 (dated February 16, 1932); *The Way*, no. 933 and *The Forge*, no. 498. Monsignor Escrivá would never forget that 'locution,' that 'reproach' from his jealous God. He would often return to it: cf. *Intimate Notes*, no. 912 (dated January 20, 1933), and no. 1120 (dated January 20, 1934). AP, HRF, 20166, pp. 1231–1232; HRF, 20760, p. 137; *Articles of the Postulator*, 1222, 370.
10. Testimony of Marlies Kücking.

drunk with joy, repeating another word the Holy Spirit had poured into his heart, the affectionate name Jewish children used for their father: *Abba, abba!* "Dad, Daddy!"

From that moment on, divine sonship was stamped on the spirituality of Opus Dei like a genetic pattern determining an attitude of trust, unselfishness, security, and joy, plus a certain legitimate pride.

From his apostolate during those months and years came an experience noted in *The Way*. " 'Father,' said that big fellow, a good student at the Central University (I wonder what has become of him?), 'I was thinking of what you told me—that I'm a son of God!— and I found myself walking along the street, head up, chin out, and a proud feeling inside . . . a son of God!' With a sure conscience I advised him to encourage that 'pride.' "[11]

On August 7, 1931, while celebrating Mass, Father Escrivá heard God speaking words that defined another major feature of the Work: to put Christ in triumph at the summit of all human activities. This time the locution was a fragment from the Gospel of St. John: *Et ego, si exaltatus fuero a terra, omnia traham ad meipsum.* "And I, if I am lifted up from the earth, will draw all things to myself."[12] He understood that "it will be men and women of God who will set the Cross, with the teachings of Christ, at the summit of all human activity."[13]

In his *Intimate Notes* that day, after narrating what had happened, he wrote something that sheds light on his personal reaction to this type of spiritual experience. "Normally, in the presence of supernatural events, I am afraid. Afterwards comes the *Ne timeas!* (Luke 1:30) 'Do not be afraid: it is I.' "[14]

At this time he was vigorously pursuing a personal apostolate in the districts of Madrid where pain and poverty were most abundant, looking after those suffering from infectious and incurable diseases, the destitute, children with runny noses, confirmed homeless.

He covered the whole city, walking from one end to the other in old, worn-out shoes that had been used when he acquired them. He fasted and mortified himself. He spent nights in vigil. He lived

---

11. *The Way*, no. 274.
12. John 12:32.
13. *Intimate Notes*, no. 217 and AP, HRF, 21166, pp. 17–19.
14. Ibid.

a life of utter dedication and gave himself to prayer whether he felt like it or not. All this was what the man gave. And God repaid him by giving himself.

Here is another passage from his personal diary of 1931: "Yesterday afternoon at three I went to the chancel of the Church of St. Elizabeth to do a little prayer in front of the Blessed Sacrament. I had no desire at all to pray. But I stayed there like a puppet. At times, I would come to my senses and think, 'You can see, my good Jesus, that if I am here, it is for you, to please you.' I couldn't manage anything else. My imagination was off on its own, far from my body or will; just as a faithful dog, dozing at his master's feet, dreams about racing and hunting and friends (other dogs like himself), and gets excited and barks in his sleep, but never leaves his master. There I was, just like a little dog, when I realized I was repeating some Latin words, without meaning to; words I had never noticed and had no reason to keep in my memory. Even now, to recall them, I will need to read them from the piece of paper I always carry in my pocket to write down what God wants. (Instinctively, out of habit, I wrote the phrase down on this piece of paper, right there in the chancel, without giving it another thought). The words of Scripture that I found on my lips were *et fui tecum in omnibus ubicumque ambulasti, firmans regnum tuum in aeternum*—'I have been with you wherever you went, confirming your reign forever.' I applied my mind to the meaning of the phrase, repeating it slowly. Then, later, yesterday afternoon, and again today, when I re-read those words I understood clearly that Jesus Christ wanted me to comprehend, for our consolation, that *the Work of God will be with Him everywhere, affirming Christ's Kingdom forever.*"[15]

When the clocks explode

The phrase "You are my Son, you are my Christ" overwhelmed him with joy in 1931. Monsignor Escrivá was still discovering new depths when he went over the same words in 1963. He explained, "All I could answer was '*Abba Pater! Abba, Pater! Abba! Abba! Abba!*' And now I see it all in a new light, like a new discovery, as with

---

15. *Intimate Notes*, no. 273. (The first part of the Latin quotation is from 2 Samuel 7:9.)

the passage of the years one sees the hand of God, divine Wisdom, divine power. You, Lord, have helped me understand that having the Cross means finding happiness and joy. And the reason, which I now see more clearly than ever, is this: having the Cross means being identified with Christ, being Christ, and therefore being a son or daughter of God."[16]

"London is just too much"

In August 1958—the second week, most likely—Monsignor Escrivá was strolling in London. He felt overwhelmed by that cosmopolitan crossroads of the world— buildings laden with history, incessant traffic, people of all races and languages hurrying through the streets, not looking at each other, wrapped in their own selfish worlds. He was amazed and disconcerted. No trace of God anywhere, everything waiting to be done. He felt discouragement and turned to God in the depth of his heart. "This has slipped through your hands. London is just too much. I can't, Lord, I can't!"

"You can't," came the response, "but I can."

Back in Rome, still deeply moved and impressed, Monsignor Escrivá related what had happened. "Just over a month ago I was in a country I love very much. Sects and heresies are common there, and there is great religious indifference. As I viewed the whole panorama I suddenly felt disconcerted, incompetent, and powerless. 'Josemaría,' I thought, 'you can't do anything here.' That was quite true, because without God I couldn't even pluck a blade of grass from the ground. My whole miserable weakness was so obvious that I almost grew sad—and that is a bad thing. Why should a son of God be sad? He can be weary, because he is pulling a cart like a faithful donkey. But sad? Never! Sadness is evil. Suddenly, in the middle of the street, where people from all corners of the world were crossing paths, I felt within me, in the depth of my heart, the strength of God's power. I felt him reassuring me: 'You can do nothing, but I can do everything. You are weakness, but I am almighty. I shall be with you, and that will have an effect. We shall lead souls to

16. Meditation, April 28, 1963.

happiness, to unity, to the way of salvation. Here, too, we shall sow peace and happiness in abundance!'"[17]

"I was dead"

Another example of God's extraordinary intervention occurred in Rome on April 27, 1954. Monsignor Escrivá, who was suffering from diabetes, went into an anaphylactic shock caused by slow-acting insulin, and was clinically dead for fifteen minutes. Don Alvaro gave him absolution *in articulo mortis*. Monsignor Escrivá was lying unconscious, sprawled across the table in the dining room of Villa Vecchia, as rigid as a corpse. First red, then purple, his face now took on a muddy bluish tinge; his whole body seemed to shrink. He said later that his whole life flashed before him in an instant, he saw the interplay between his human clay and divine grace, and realized he had died. "I was dead," he declared simply, when he referred to this strange occurrence some time later. The most surprising and scientifically inexplicable thing was not that he survived such a serious shock without brain damage, though that was surprising enough, but that he emerged from this near-fatal episode completely cured of diabetes.

It was a certified medical fact, diagnosed and treated, that Monsignor Escrivá had had diabetes since 1944. As yet there was no cure for diabetes. It is also a fact, documented, and verified by several specialists—among them Dr. Carlo Faelli, who had Monsignor Escrivá down as his most seriously ill patient—that on a specific day at a specific time the diabetes disappeared suddenly and permanently.

From then on Monsignor Escrivá would say that he felt liberated, "as if he had come out of jail," but above all he felt indebted.

Two months later, on June 27, talking with his daughters at the Los Rosales Conference Center in Spain, he assured them, "The history of the Work ought to be written kneeling down, because it is the history of God's mercies."[18]

---

17. Meditation, November 2, 1958.
18. Testimony of Mercedes Morado (AGP, HRF T-07902).

10 ✤

Faith with Blood in Its Veins

Life and prayer were never in conflict

In trying to discover what Monsignor Escrivá's interior life was like, we must tread with cautious, respectful steps. From an early age until his last hour, he lived according to his prayer, and prayed according to his life. He did both intensely. For him, prayer was not a thing apart, separated from the working day. It was the breath of life, the driving force, of all his actions. His was a contemplatively active way of being in the world.

Dreaming while he prayed and praying while he dreamed

He managed to charge every instant with prayer, even in his sleep. Waking during the night he realized that he had been praying in his sleep, a special grace.

Monsignor Escrivá was totally natural in the way he worked, ate, thought, studied, went for walks, laughed, and sang, while always conscious of living in God's presence. One day in April 1971, trying without success to strike a match to light a candle in front of the stained glass window in the Galleria della Madonna, his instinctive reaction at the third attempt was to say, "This is just like us, when we resist grace, when we find it hard to give of ourselves, and we have to say *Ure igne Sancti Spiritus*—burn us, Lord with the fire of the Holy Spirit. It only takes a little bit of good will, and it works!"[1]

---

1. Testimony of Helena Serrano (cf. AGP, HRF T-04641), Marlies Kücking, and Mercedes Morado (AGP, HRF T-07902).

From cognac to the Trinity

Once he saw a bottle of Spanish brandy, and noting the name "*103*" on the label, said, "These numbers can be used as a reminder, to help us be united to the Holy Trinity. One God; three Persons in God; and I myself am the zero."[2]

At the beginning of the news on television, when a logo of the globe appeared, he used to pray to Our Lady, *Regina Pacis*, Queen of Peace, for peace in the world.

On one occasion some of his daughters sang a Mexican song to a guitar accompaniment: "I don't know what my life is worth, but here I come to give it to you . . ." Monsignor Escrivá listened, enjoying it, and murmured, "I do know what my life is worth—all the blood of Christ!" Aloud, he said, "Carry on. Carry on singing, my daughters: you have given me a topic for my prayer this afternoon."[3]

A snake at Gagliano Aterno

This continuous consciousness of God's presence did not send him into ecstasies or isolate him. It brought him closer to other people.

During the summer of 1967 he spent three weeks with Don Alvaro and Father Javier Echevarria in a big old house in Gagliano Aterno, in Abruzzi, resting by having a change of work and scenery. On the last day, when they were ready to leave, Father Echevarria took a last look around the room they had been working in to make sure they had not left anything behind. As he was leaving the room, he saw a snake. He took a shovel from the old fireplace, struck it a crushing blow on the head, and left it on the floor, dead. He walked to the car where Monsignor Escrivá and Don Alvaro were waiting, and said proudly, "I've just killed a viper, *heroically!*"

"Are you sure you killed it?"

"Certain, Father! I gave it a heavy blow which left it completely lifeless. It wasn't difficult, because the snake was slithering on the tiled floor and couldn't get out of the way."

---

2. Testimony of Marlies Kücking.
3. Ibid.

Monsignor Escrivá immediately thought about his spiritual daughters, who were staying behind in Gagliano Aterno, tidying up and closing the house.

"Have you warned your sisters?"

"No, Father."

"Well, could you warn them, please? Otherwise, can you imagine the fright they'll get if they go in and find the creature on the floor! And tell them to be careful in case there's another—don't forget how many scorpions we've killed inside the house these past few weeks."[4]

God the spectator, God the guest

He used to speak about the "right kind of divinization." Whether experienced gently or forcefully, the driving passion of his life was the living experience of God. For Monsignor Escrivá, God was so near, so accessible, so intimate that he was both his spectator and his guest.

God was his spectator. Monsignor Escrivá often used to talk about people who may be feeling tired, arid, and cold, and must pray as if acting a farce. "A farce? What an excellent thing, my child! Act out that farce! The Lord is your audience. The Blessed Trinity is contemplating us in those moments when we are 'acting out a farce.' To be God's juggler! How marvelous it is to play one's part for love!"[5]

Monsignor Escrivá felt he was not merely seen and heard, but paid attention to and helped. He went about with a carefree heart, knowing he was watched over lovingly by his God.

God was also the guest of his soul. Monsignor Escrivá's inner life had some stages of dark night, interior loneliness, or spiritual dryness. But those who lived with him realized that he was always involved in conversation with the guest of his soul in grace, and this conversation came naturally to him. He believed and lived in the reality of the indwelling of the Blessed Trinity.

---

4. Written account of Bishop Javier Echevarria.
5. *The Forge*, no. 485.

His powerful allies

There was also the company provided by the Communion of Saints. He had a lively friendship with the angels and saints. Among the saints he found his most effective patrons and intercessors, and among the angels and archangels his most powerful allies.

When Monsignor Escrivá spoke about St. Joseph, the apostles St. Peter, St. Paul, and St. John, St. Nicholas of Bari, St. Thomas More, St. Pius X, St. Catherine of Siena, the Curé of Ars, or the Archangels Raphael, Gabriel, and Michael, he spoke as a friend of theirs. He had a special, personal relationship with every single one of them. He knew their particular strengths, what sort of things to pray to each of them for, what favors he could ask of them.

He did not remember them only in emergencies, but always admired St. Jean-Marie Vianney's priestly zeal, St. Catherine of Siena's ardent love for the Church, St. Thomas More's heroic courage. When he passed by, he stopped to visit Ars, Siena, and Canterbury. Once, in Coimbra, he went to the tomb of St. Elizabeth, Infanta of Aragon and Queen of Portugal, to pay his respects. Tapping on her tomb, he said bluntly: "Hey! Aragonese lady, I'm from your part of the world. Let's see how you treat your fellow countrymen!"[6]

St. Pius X's nephews and nieces presented him with articles from the saint's wardrobe as well as some pieces of furniture. Among them was a simple kneeler, which Monsignor Escrivá used, and a skull cap. When he received the skull cap on January 6, 1971, he kissed it and put it on his head for a few seconds.

"Just putting it on inspires me," he said, "and I ask St. Pius X to give me fortitude: the fortitude of a rock, because I need it."[7]

"That's how my angel used to wake me"

He had a very special relationship with the guardian angels. He asked his own angel for endless favors, from helping him to find a paper he had mislaid, to waking him in the morning. For years he used to call him "my watch-mender," since he did not have a

---

6. Testimony of Mercedes Morado (AGP, HRF T-07902).
7. Ibid.

reliable watch but relied on his angel to wake him on time. One day in Rome, he was reading in the Acts of the Apostles the scene where Peter is in jail and his angel appears to him and wakes him by striking him on the side. Later, Monsignor Escrivá remarked to Don Alvaro and Father Echevarria, "Just like that—with a good prod in the side—that's how my guardian angel used to wake me in the morning, when it was time to get up."

He would often say to one of his daughters, "I saw you in the distance, when you were out yesterday, and I prayed for you to your guardian angel, as I always do when I see one of you."

One day in Villa Tevere he had a visit from the retired Archbishop of Valencia, Marcelino Olaechea, accompanied by a canon, his secretary. They had been good friends for a long time and greeted each other warmly. Monsignor Escrivá inquired playfully, "Marcelino, see if you can guess—whom did I greet first?"

"First? That would be me, I'm sure."

"No, I greeted the dignitary first."

"Come on, Josemaría, explain yourself."

"When a dignitary comes accompanied by someone else, you have to greet the dignitary first, right?"

"And today I've come with my secretary."

"No. You've come with your guardian angel. He's the dignitary! For a long time, maybe forty years, I haven't greeted anyone without greeting their angel first. It helps me so much to live in God's presence!"[8]

"Training" in God's affairs

Monsignor Escrivá's interior life was not a catalog of devotions or a collection of pious practices. There was nothing pietistic about him. The boldness of his spiritual life consisted of 'getting inside' the scenes of the Gospel to take part in them like someone at the scene, 'getting inside' the mysteries of the Rosary like a daring child, 'getting inside' the wounds of Christ crucified—in short, 'getting inside'

---

8. Césare Cavalleri and Alvaro del Portillo, *Immersed in God* (Princeton, NJ: Scepter, 1996), p. 130.

a relationship of love with the three Divine Persons. In time, he discovered a short cut to the Trinity—a personal, family relationship with the 'trinity on earth,' as he called it, Jesus, Mary, and Joseph.

"I feel very much at ease with the 'trinity on earth.' Sometimes I get upset with myself and say, 'Josemaría, you have a formula you don't know how to use. You go from the 'trinity on earth' to the Trinity in heaven with your lips alone. Why don't you go with your heart, all day long, and make yourself a heaven on earth, in the midst of so many disagreeable things?' "[9]

The self-reproach was unjustified. He kept God company continuously in his heart and mind. Mercedes Morado recalled working with him one morning in a conference room when suddenly, between one item of business and another, the Father remarked, "My daughters, during the time I've been here with you I've turned to our Lord lots of times in my heart, to ask him for grace, light, help...and also to say sorry. I do it out of habit. I would like to keep our Lord company physically by spending more time in the oratory. But I can't stay there as long as I'd like to, because I have to work. However, from Don Alvaro's room, where I mostly work, I go to the tabernacle again and again in my imagination, and there I greet our Lord and keep him company in spirit."[10]

At "go again and again," he touched his forehead with his index finger and traced a line in the air as if showing the path his mind took.

Marlies Kücking heard him say something similar during another working session of the governing body of the Work in the same conference room. "Right now I am not alone here with Don Javier and you. I'm praying. I'm in God's presence. And that is no great effort for me: it is like a heartbeat. But in the same way as when the heart stops, death occurs, if I were to lose this contemplative vision for a minute, I would collapse. Therefore, although there are sometimes reasons for losing my calm, I never do so for more than two minutes; it comes back in a jiffy!"[11]

---

9. AGP, HRF 21164, p. 675.
10. Testimony of Mercedes Morado (AGP, HRF T-07902).
11. Testimony of Marlies Kücking.

Although Monsignor Escrivá was a tremendously active man, this habitual state of prayer became second nature to him. It was not a matter of unsought lights or fits of fervor. He worked at keeping up a continuous inner dialogue with God, using simple vocal prayers, aspirations, verses from the psalms, spiritual communions, and acts of love. Every day he adopted one as a "password" that he repeated mentally while working and around the house. Often, encountering someone, he would stop for a moment and murmur, "My son, how many spiritual communions have you made today?" or, "How many aspirations have you said to our Lord so far? I've said thousands!"

Normally he did not wait for an answer. The question was enough. And he asked it early, at the start of the day.

Over the abyss, in Verona

He lived in God's atmosphere. As a result, he did not lose his calm even in tense situations or times of danger. On February 4, 1963, at the time of the Vatican Council, he and Father Echevarria were traveling to Venice with Don Alvaro, who had matters to discuss with Cardinal Urbani, the Patriarch of Venice. The road had patches of black ice, but Javier Cotelo, an architect, who was driving, had not realized the danger. Just past Rovigo, four kilometers from Monselicer, the car suddenly started to slip backwards. There was no way to stop it; it was an old car, and the tires had lost their grip on the road surface. After sliding back a long way, it spun around several times and skidded at high speed until it crashed into the stone barrier, at the edge of a precipice. There it hung, half on the road and half in thin air.

Don Alvaro, sitting in the back beside Monsignor Escrivá, saw that he was very calm, showing no sign of fear or anxiety. From the first moment he had begun saying aspirations and making acts of contrition and love. "I saw him so absorbed in God, with such peaceful trust, that I did the same as him: prayed intensely,"[12] he said afterward.

---

12. AGP, HRF 21170, pp. 208–209; cf. Cavalleri and del Portillo, *Immersed in God.*

Squeezing God's hand

Monsignor Escrivá's piety was not mechanical. Not satisfied with formulas and clichés, he made the words of prayers his own, personalized them, and unearthed new depths of meanings in them. He never tired of meditating on texts of the Bible, sometimes retranslating them in a living way.

"*Ut iumentum factus sum apud te*, I'm like a little donkey before you, *et ego semper tecum*, but you are always with me. That's the presence of God. *Tenuisti manum dexteram meam*. I usually say to him, 'you've taken me by the halter,' *et in voluntate tua deduxisti me*, and you've made me fulfill your will; that is to say, you've made me faithful to my vocation. *Et cum gloria suscepisti me*, and afterwards you'll give me a great big hug."[13]

Other times it was the words of Isaiah, "I have redeemed you and called you by your name: you are mine,"[14] which he said "tasted of honey and honeycomb." He never read Scripture as if reading words from remote times. He saw here a summons by God in the present, whispered in the ear of the soul.

One day he was in the dining room in Villa Vecchia, talking about some aspects of installation and decoration with two of his daughters, Helena Serrano and Montse Amat. There was a lamp on the table with a lampshade of parchment, originally a page in an old choirbook. He started to turn the lamp around slowly, trying to decipher the Latin. Suddenly his face lit up.

"What a lovely thing! Shall I read it to you? 'Jesus, wonderful music to the ear that listens to you, sweetest honey on the lips that name you, delight of the heart that loves you.' What a great truth that is!"[15]

Monsignor Escrivá's radicalism

He called these "reverse distractions,"[16] meaning these homely things should lead us to remember God even more. But this was

---

13. Psalm 72: "I was no better than a beast in your sight, yet I was always in your presence; you were holding me by my right hand. You will guide me by your counsel, and so you will lead me to glory." AGP, HRF 21164, p. 1442.

14. Isaiah 43:1.

15. Testimony of Helena Serrano (cf. AGP, HRF T-04641).

16. Cf. *The Forge*, no. 1014.

spiritual escapism. "Materialize the spiritual life," he used to say. "There is something holy, something divine hidden in the most ordinary situations, and it is up to each one of you to discover it."[17]

One day in the royal hall, you smiled at me

He was moved when a daughter of his, Teresa Tourne, an opera singer, told him how she had vividly experienced God's presence on stage while playing a slave in Puccini's *Turandot* and singing *perchè un dì nella reggia mi hai sorriso* ("because one day in the royal hall, you smiled at me"). She did not lose the thread of what she was doing; her singing was inspired by a higher sensitivity and emotion.

Faith with blood in its veins

Monsignor Escrivá's inner life had love at its heart. He was moved when shown a painted terracotta figure of the Baby Jesus made by Palmira Laguens, a sculptor and a daughter of his. Chus de Meer, Paquita Medina, Cuqui Quiroga, and Mercedes Morado, among others, were in the sitting room of La Montagnola on Christmas Day 1969, and saw Monsignor Escrivá come to the crèche, look at the Baby, smile, pick it up, and lift it high in the air as if playing with a real child. He made a fuss of it and kissed it, saying tender words. "Beauty! My darling! My Baby! I'm going to keep him!"[18]

Where did they chuck you out from?

He did not hide his emotion the day they showed him a beautiful statue of Our Lady discarded by a Swiss church and picked up at an auction. It was a fine carving, life size, in gilded wood, but in need of restoration. It had been temporarily placed in a lecture room in Villa Tevere. Monsignor Escrivá wished to see the statue at once "to welcome her." While still at a distance, he was already breaking into compliments and praises: "My Mother . . . our Mother! What have they done to you! You are so beautiful!" Coming closer, he

---

17. Homily, "Passionately Loving the World," October 8, 1967.
18. Testimony of Helena Serrano (cf. AGP, HRF T-04641) and Mercedes Morado (AGP, HRF T-07902).

looked at the statue's face. He kissed its hands, and continued to talk to Our Lady.

"Maybe you were in a cathedral or in a big church and thousands of souls used to appeal to you in prayer. I have come to welcome you. Welcome to our house, my Mother, our Mother! You'll be treated very well here. We'll try and make up for what people have done to you. My Mother, you know you are Queen of Opus Dei. Yes, you are our Mother, our Queen, our passion, and you know that already!"[19]

From then on there were always fresh flowers at the foot of that particular statue.

The pulse of petition

Monsignor Escrivá did not want his children to copy him. He told them time and again that the only model, the prototype, was Jesus Christ. But he made one exception. "If there is one thing I want you to imitate in me, it is my love for Our Lady." He loved any picture or statue of Mary. In 1924, four years before the foundation of Opus Dei, at a time of great need, he was wandering uncertainly, feeling God was asking him to do something but not knowing what. One of his most fervent prayers was carved with a nail on the base of a column of a tiny statue of Our Lady of the Pillar; a cheap, mass-produced plaster figure. Thirty-six years later, in 1960, through Pily Albas, a relative of his on his mother's side, this statue was located in Saragossa. When Encarnita Ortega and Mercedes Morado showed it to him in Villa Vecchia, Monsignor Escrivá did not recognize it. "What an ugly little statue!" he said.

"It used to be yours, Father," they told him.

"Mine? It can't be! I don't remember ever having bought a statue like that."

"Yes, look at it. You wrote something on it." Mercedes turned the little statue upside down. The carved words were in his unmistakeable writing: *Domina, ut sit! 24/5/1924.*

This had been his urgent prayer at that time. He used to address Jesus Christ in the words of blind Bartimeus: "Lord, that I may see!

---

19. Written and oral testimony of Begoña Alvarez (AGP, HRF T-04861) and AGP HRF 21161, p. 39.

Domine, ut videam!" He prayed in a similar vein to Our Lady, "Lady, may it be! *Domina, ut sit!*" The date, May 24, 1924, made that cheap plaster statue evidence of how Opus Dei had 'happened' to Father Escrivá, who had been praying since 1918 that something he did not know would come to be. "Let it be! What has to be, let it be!" It was a prayer made with his eyes closed.

He contemplated the statue in silence; then, turning to Don Alvaro, said to him, "That it should turn up now is like a caress from God—another testimony, a patent proof of my prayer for many years."[20]

Monsignor Escrivá always stated emphatically that "Our Lady has been our great protector, our refuge, from that October 2, 1928, and even before then."[21] "Like Jesus, we have always kept close to his Mother, Mary, the Mother of God, who has been the Mother of Opus Dei, the Queen of Opus Dei, our beauty. . . ."[22]

He was stating historical fact when he said, "Our Opus Dei was born and has developed under Our Lady's mantle. She has been a good Mother to us, consoling us, smiling at us and encouraging us in all the trying moments of our blessed struggle to bring forth this army of apostles in the world."[23]

The seal of the Work is a cross within a circle that symbolizes the world. It is usually represented with a rose in relief underneath. This is the rose of Rialp—an old, exciting story, told elsewhere, which showed Our Lady's care for Opus Dei.

The camera never lies

Helena Serrano, an expert photographer who lived in Villa Tevere for more than twenty years, took many photographs of Monsignor Escrivá. He rarely posed and only gave in when Don Alvaro suggested. Often he would say to Helena, "My daughter, don't take more photos of me—pray for me." Or, "Go on, Helena, be good! Take photos of your sisters and leave me alone!"

---

20. Testimony of Mercedes Morado (AGP, HRF T-07902) and of Encarnación Ortega (AGP, HRF T-05074).
21. AGP, HRF 20139, p. 9.
22. AGP, HRF 20124, p. 10.
23. AGP, HRF 20127, p. 10.

For years at Mass he allowed pictures to be taken only before the consecration or after communion, but "Never while our Lord is on the altar." But starting in 1967, when under the pretext of liturgical change the Eucharist was being treated without proper respect in many places, he decided that pictures could be also taken at the elevation of the Host or of the chalice, or when the celebrant genuflected or kissed the altar. This was to underline and honor the presence of the Body and Blood of Christ. The pictures were taken to illustrate the internal publications of Opus Dei, *Noticias* and *Cronica*. Even so, Monsignor Escrivá did not enjoy the presence of the camera or the flash, which could distract from the concentration with which he tried to 'live' his Mass.

On the feast of Corpus Christi in 1968 he celebrated Mass in the Pentecost Oratory in Villa Tevere. Ana Lorente and Helena Serrano took a series of pictures, then came nearer the altar to get some close-ups. Monsignor Escrivá whispered earnestly to Father Echevarria, who was serving the Mass, "Not so close! It would be better if they went away. It's one thing to take photos, and quite another to distract me during the Mass. By no means!"

On another occasion, January 6, 1972, the feast of the Epiphany, Helena wanted to capture the moment when he stopped to kiss a little image of Our Lady of Loreto on the landing in La Montagnola. Monsignor Escrivá normally did this whenever he came to spend time there with his daughters. When he saw her with her camera, he asked, "Helena, what are you doing here?"

"I'd like to take a picture of you kissing Our Lady," she replied.

"And so you want me to be a hypocrite, acting out a kiss, so you can take a picture?"

He hesitated, then went on, "I'm not going to be a hypocrite, because I'm going to give her a real kiss!"

Helena Serrano wrote, "We have loads of photos of the Father: celebrating Mass, saying the Angelus or the Rosary, kissing the wooden cross or an image of Our Lady, giving Benediction or making a genuflection when passing in front of the Tabernacle. He is not distracted in a single one of them! The cold, mechanical, inexorable camera does not forgive wrinkles, sneers, or ungraceful, disappointed, inattentive expressions, or bad posture, or being overweight. Even if there were no other witnesses, you would only have to go to the photograph archives to see the Father's piety in his face. The camera 'saw' it, and the camera never lies."[24]

Living continuously in God's presence was not something he improvised. He had a daily plan, doing things at fixed times and not depending on any inclination or reluctance. He observed the norms of Opus Dei spread through the day. He had the same daily plan as any son or daughter of his in the Work, from the *serviam,* "I will serve," said kissing the floor on getting up in the morning to the last thought at night, always dedicated to God.

His norms included two half-hours of mental prayer, Mass, thanksgiving after Communion, reading of the Gospel and some spiritual book, the Rosary, the Angelus or Regina Coeli at midday, a visit to the Blessed Sacrament, reciting the *Preces* or Prayers of the Work, and an intense examination of conscience, focused more on building strength for the struggle than on self-criticism. All of this was accompanied by acts of love, spiritual communions, acts of thanksgiving, short incisive aspirations, acts of atonement, and frequent consideration of the reality of being a child of God. Monsignor Escrivá added to these norms the reading of the breviary as a priest, and, as president general of Opus Dei, the penitential psalm *Miserere,* recited prostrate on the floor before going to bed. In bed, before falling asleep, he turned to God in an unconditional act of acceptance of death: "Lord, whenever you want it, as you want it, and wherever you want it."[25]

There was a different perspective every day. Monday was specially dedicated to the Holy Souls in purgatory. On Tuesday, the guardian angels. On Wednesdays, St. Joseph, patron of the universal Church, patron of the Work, and teacher of the relationship with God. On Thursdays, the Eucharist. Fridays meant an intimate search for Jesus in his Passion and death. Saturdays meant devotion to Our Lady the Virgin. Sundays were a golden feast day in honor of the Blessed Trinity: the Lord's Day was God's recreation, God's glory, God's rest.

---

24. Testimony of Helena Serrano (cf. AGP, HRF T-04641).
25. AGP, HRF 21176, pp. 523–524.

Having pondered and thought it through in prayer, Monsignor Escrivá, as founder of Opus Dei, dared to say he guaranteed eternal happiness to whoever fulfilled these norms of piety every day. "That son or daughter of mine has their perseverance assured: I guarantee heaven for them." This was not dull routine. He lived by these norms and showed how to live by them as joyful "meetings with God our Lord."

One day he was talking with two of his daughters, Colombian and German. Speaking of the norms, he explained they should be "like a firm handshake." To give weight to his words, he shook hands with the priest who was with him. "I can greet him like this, correctly, coldly, out of pure formality, because it is the done thing . . . or I can greet him like this—warmly, affectionately, strongly, with all my heart!"[26]

"The street is our cell"

This inner life allowed him to experience the divine everywhere: the dentist's waiting room, traveling around the city on public transport, enjoying a get-together. He sometimes said in Italian, *nel bel mezzo della strada*—in the middle of the street. "The street is our cell." One day in 1960, when the alterations in Villa Tevere were finished, Salvador Suanzes, nicknamed Pile, asked, "Father, which of the oratories in this house do you like best?"

"The street!"

Pile looked astonished. Monsignor Escrivá smiled. "I love all the oratories in this house. But I prefer the street. 'Our cell is the street' is not just a nice phrase. And you, Pile, my son, and so many sons and daughters of mine, will often have to make your prayer in the street. And it can be done really well there too! Although, whenever we can, we do it in a church or in an oratory, before our Lord who is really present in the tabernacle."[27]

---

26. Testimony of Marlies Kücking.
27. Account of Salvador Suanzes.

A balcony overlooking the infinite

In real unity of life, work and prayer form a working synergy. This could be seen from Monsignor Escrivá's office in Villa Vecchia.

The headquarters of this dynamic mobilization of sanctity and apostolate was a small, narrow room, barely three meters square, with an arched ceiling; light came from a little window on an inner courtyard. One door had an inscription on the lintel: "Oh how little is the here and now; Oh how vast is eternity." The walls were covered with well-thumbed books. There was a crucifix, some drawings of donkeys, and photographs of six of the first people in Opus Dei: Alvaro del Portillo, Jose María Hernandez de Garnica, José Luis Muzquiz, Pedro Casciaro, Ricardo Fernandez-Vallespin, and Francisco Botella. Other decorations were some fishing tackle, a miner's lamp, and a green glass insulator from a telegraph pole, to remind Monsignor Escrivá that he should always be the transmitter of a message. There was also a memento of the Spanish Civil War: the identity disc of a soldier, "E 333171." It hung on an old piece of string with ten small, tight knots, enough to count the Hail Marys while saying the Rosary in the trenches or in combat. There was no filing cabinet, tape recorder, or typewriter.

But this tiny workroom had an outlet. To the left of the table was a panelled door that looked like a built-in cupboard but that opened into a kind of small balcony overlooking an oratory. The tiny balcony had just enough room for a kneeler and one chair. Straight ahead and below was a beautiful altar dedicated to the Blessed Trinity. Here was where Monsignor Escrivá got the apostolic energy demanded of him every day. He did not separate prayer and work.

Monsignor Escrivá was totally consistent, fully a priest of Jesus Christ. He felt he was a man chosen to do what many others could not do, no matter how wise, powerful, or wealthy they were: celebrate Mass. His life was centered on the Mass. It was the essence of his existence. He divided the twenty-four hours of the day: half to prepare for the Mass, the other half to give thanks for it.

He was ever more demanding to discover "any small speck of sin which could have offended you, my God." He would ask Don Alvaro to hear his confession once, twice, or even several times in a week. This was to keep his spiritual faculties and bodily senses in perfect order. He sought to be Christ himself, *ipse Christus*, as worthily as he possibly could when celebrating Mass.

One evening, at the end of a get-together with his sons, Monsignor Escrivá rose and the time of silence, the "night period," began. One of them, Emilio Muñoz, wishing to keep the Father with them a little longer, objected amicably. Already on his way out, Monsignor Escrivá said, "My son, how little you know me—or how little you love me! Don't you realize that at this time of night I am dying to be alone with my Lord, my God?"[28]

If he did not have to travel or go out, Monsignor Escrivá celebrated Mass at midday, after half a day's intense work that began early in the morning. Someone would tell him when there were fifteen minutes left, so that he could prepare by praying alone in the oratory.

"Love me always as you did today"

Once the work he was doing was more complicated and lasted longer than foreseen. Since he did not wear a watch, he was surprised when Father Echevarria said, "Father, we've run out of time, it's time for your Mass." He was irritated at having to hurry, and in this frame of mind he began to vest.

When Mass was over, he spent ten minutes in thanksgiving, as was his custom. Then he called Father Echevarria and Father Ernesto Julia. Both had seen him earlier looking serious, and they were surprised to see him now sparkling with joy. He told them, "I was irritated when I arrived, and when I began to put on the vestments. I was in such a bad temper! But already, on kissing the amice and saying the prayer *Impone Domine, capiti meo galeam salutis*—Place, Lord, upon my head the helm of salvation—I realized that the prayers were coming out really well! And then the whole Mass was wonderful, as if I had been preparing for hours and hours. In the thanksgiving I said to Our Lord: 'I want you to love me always as you did today. Love me always as you've loved me today!'"[29]

---

28. Oral account of Emilio Muñoz.
29. Oral account of Fr. Ernesto Julia.

He was constantly discovering new, more profound meanings in the prayers of the Mass, the rubrics, and even the most apparently insignificant gestures. One day it might be the powerful awareness of God's strength, on saying so often, "Our help is in the name of the Lord," *adiutorium nostrum in nomine Domini.* Another day, joyful conviction that the love of God is eternally young, when at the beginning of Mass he recited, "I shall go to the altar of God, the God who gives joy to my youth." His excited comment was, "I can never grow old while I have this love!" He was past seventy then.

Discoveries

Another time he was amazed by unexpected insights into the Mass as an action of the Blessed Trinity. "I had not appreciated these liturgical endings in all their beauty until today. They are not mere additions, but praise to the three Persons of the Blessed Trinity: 'Through our Lord Jesus Christ your Son'—see how confidently we address God the Father!—'who lives and reigns with you, in the unity of the Holy Spirit, one God, forever and ever.' More and more strongly, I feel the need to relate to the three Divine Persons one by one, singling each of them out, without separating them."[30]

A cosmic encounter: the Mass

Preaching shortly before celebrating Mass, he once said, "In a few minutes I am going to celebrate the Holy Mass; to have a very personal encounter with the love of my soul. . . . I will kiss the altar, with kisses of love. And I will take the Body of my God and the chalice of his Blood and lift them above all things on earth, saying, *Per Ipsum et cum Ipso et in Ipso,* through my Love, with my Love, in my Love!"[31]

Other times he recalled that the Mass is an encounter outside space, with the one sacrifice of Christ. "Join in with the prayer of all Christians who have ever prayed in the past, those praying now, and those who will pray in the centuries to come. More especially with

---

30. Testimony of Fr. Carlos Cardona (AGP, HRF T-06138).
31. Testimony of Begoña Alvarez (AGP, HRF T-04861).

your brothers and sisters; those who are already in heaven, those being purified in purgatory and those spread out over the earth— bravely fighting the big and small battles of peace in their inner lives. In this way, when I celebrate the Holy Mass, as well as being Christ and knowing myself to be surrounded by angels, I will also be surrounded by the clamor of my children's prayer and I will have the strength to demand of our Lord: *Exaudi orationem meam, et clamor meus ad te veniat,* Hear my prayer, and let my cry come unto you!"[32]

Although he did not usually refer to the Sacrifice of the Altar as "an assembly," his experience of the Mass as a great family reunion was very strong. In the Mass he met the Church triumphant, the Church suffering, being purged and purified, and the Church still fighting here on earth. In it he met his own big family, the Work. He reflected silently, "Here we are gathered together on the paten beside the Host, and in the chalice with the Blood of my Lord Jesus Christ!"[33]

One day in January 1973, at the end of an afternoon get-together, Monsignor Escrivá beckoned to Rafael Caamaño, in Rome on a short visit. Strolling through the Galleria del Torrione, they talked. He suddenly remembered something which had happened to him that very morning, and he told Raphael about it casually.

"I really wanted to celebrate the Holy Mass without any distractions. When I was going down to the oratory, a lad from Bilbao who was with me asked: 'Father, what do you want me to pray for?' And I answered, 'Well now, pray that I may celebrate Mass very well.' I began the Mass, and after a bit, a silly thing happened; I don't know why, but my nose began to bleed. And being anxious not to get blood on the altar, I could not concentrate as much as I wanted to."

He pulled a piece of cotton out of his pocket and showed it to Caamaño. "I have it in case my nose starts to bleed again."

Then he added, grinning, "But I was not so distracted as to forget to put all of you on the paten . . . especially the ones who are ill or think they are ill, those who are suffering some problem or think they are . . . there are all kinds among my children!"

32. From the Father, Rome, November 1974.
33. Letter of Bishop Javier Echevarria, August 1989.

Next day he arrived at the Galleria del Fumo, smiling and full of joy, for the usual after-lunch conversation. As soon as he sat down he told them, "I'm so happy. Yesterday something silly happened, something which distracted me during Mass. I was afraid the same thing would happen again today, so I asked our Lord to let me celebrate Mass with total concentration. I asked him for that with all my heart, and I did it! That is why I am so happy!"[34]

Before vesting for Mass, if he saw one of his spiritual sons praying in the oratory, it was not unusual for him to whisper gently in his ear, "My son, will you ask our Lord to show me how to say the Holy Mass better every day?"[35]

To the end of his life he would say, "I am constantly learning how to say the Holy Mass better."[36]

His fingers trembled

Those who saw him celebrate Mass were touched by his concentration, by his obvious and immediate sincerity. There was no routine here. He was obviously concentrating on each genuflection, each kiss bestowed on the altar, each striking of the breast on saying, *mea culpa, mea culpa, mea maxima culpa.* On reciting the Creed, his voice was vibrant with faith. At the mementos of the living and the dead, the urgency and outreach of his priestly prayers were plain to see. Clearly he was intensely moved during the Consecration of the bread and wine. He would sometimes say he wished to "keep alive the emotion he had felt the first time" when, as a deacon in 1924, he had taken the Host in his hands to give Benediction with the Blessed Sacrament. His fingers had trembled.[37]

Forty years later, celebrating Mass one morning in 1964, he went to the right side of the altar for the washing of the hands. The altar server saw that suddenly his hands began to tremble. He looked at his face. It was very serene; he was concentrating totally, deep in prayer. Later, Monsignor Escrivá confided to Don Alvaro, "I recalled

34. Testimony of Fr. Rafael Caamaño (AGP, HRF T-05837).
35. Ibid.
36. Testimony of Monsignor César Ortiz-Echagüe (AGP, HRF T-04694).
37. Testimony of Fr. Carlos Cardona (AGP, HRF T-06138).

that first time, and I said silently, in my heart, 'Lord, don't ever let me take you for granted!' "[38]

After consecrating the bread and wine, he would say in his heart, *Dominus meus et Deus meus!* "My Lord and my God!" Then, *Adauge nobis fidem, spem et caritatem!* "Increase our faith, hope, and charity!" He continued with, "Holy Father, through the Immaculate Heart of Mary, I offer you your beloved Son Jesus, and I offer myself through him with him and in him for all your intentions on behalf of all mankind." Then he made yet another plea, "Lord, give all of us holy purity and *gaudium cum pace,* joy and peace." As he genuflected in adoration, he said a line from St. Thomas Aquinas' hymn, *Adoro te devote, latens Deitas,* "I adore you devoutly, hidden Godhead." His genuflection was profound, slow, and deliberate. Kneeling before his God, Monsignor Escrivá wished time would stand still.

Conscious that he took on "the person of Christ" during the sacrifice of the Mass, he was as if enraptured at relating so closely with the Trinity and knowing himself surrounded by all the angels and saints, "because then," he said, "the altar is a heaven." In the first twenty years of his priesthood he had to make a tremendous effort not to spend longer than he should, out of consideration for the people attending Mass. "The priest is there to serve the faithful," he said, "and should not prolong the Mass for more than half an hour."[39]

The splendor God loves

He had read the Old Testament books of Leviticus and Deuteronomy, where God explains with precise details how he wants man to worship him. Monsignor Escrivá knew God loves splendor if it is accompanied by true love, not ostentation. He wanted oratories, sacred vessels, vestments, and everything directly related to God to be the best possible. "For God, everything is very little," he said countless times. It might be simply putting a few drops of scent in the water where the priest would wash his hands before touching

---

38. AGP, HRF 21165, pp. 147–148.
39. Ibid.

the Eucharistic species; or placing fresh flowers on the altar and leaving them beside the tabernacle in their natural state without water to make them last longer. "Because," he explained, "they're not a decoration but an offering; and we have to do the same with our lives: give everything for our Lord!"[40]

Monsignor Escrivá also tried to procure the finest quality bread and wine for the Eucharistic species. Speaking about this to a group of women of the Work in 1967, he told them, "I have always had a yearning which is a refinement of love: that my daughters should, as soon as possible, not only prepare the hosts and wine for the sacrifice of the Mass, but even grow the wheat and vines themselves, *ut nobis Corpus et Sanguis fiat dilectissimi Filii tui Domini nostri Iesu Christi*, to become for us the Body and Blood of your beloved Son, our Lord Jesus Christ."[41]

He was delighted when a packet containing wine and flour arrived in Villa Tevere in 1975. A daughter of his from Sicily had grown, harvested, and prepared it all herself, and offered it to him for the Mass on the golden jubilee of his ordination. Moved, he said, "This is all about cherishing God who is 'born' in our hands, by preparing the bread and wine with loving care for when he comes down to them."[42]

He often advised his sons who were about to be ordained priests, "In a liturgical ceremony, you need to do everything respectfully and solemnly. And if you make a mistake, don't hurry, don't put it right hastily or abruptly, but solemnly. The mistake is part of the ceremony too."[43]

"Brass"

When the liturgy of the Mass was reformed after the Second Vatican Council, the women who operated the printing press in Villa Tevere printed a special copy of the new texts to make it easier for

40. Testimony of Helena Serrano (cf. AGP, HRF T-04641).
41. Testimony of Mercedes Morado (AGP, HRF T-07902) and Encarnación Ortega (AGP, HRF T-05074).
42. Testimony of Mercedes Morado (AGP, HRF T-07902).
43. Testimony of Fr. Carlos Cardona (AGP, HRF T-06138).

Monsignor Escrivá to celebrate the Eucharist with all the changes in prayers and rubrics. He was very grateful. A few days later, he said to Helena Serrano, "My daughter, I would like to ask you a favor. Make me a small card with the words of the consecration on it in big clear letters. Try to make it dignified, as I want to have it in front of me on the altar while I am celebrating. It pains me to take my eyes off the host and the chalice during the consecration, in order to look at the missal! The trouble is that after all these years of saying the old formula, I can't get the new one by heart . . . and I don't want to make a mistake!"

He started to go, but then added, smiling, "And, please, will you make another one for Don Alvaro while you're at it?"[44]

He wanted the finest materials to be used for divine worship: gold, silver, enamels, precious stones. "Let's never be mean or miserly towards our Lord!" he would say.[45] On big anniversaries or feast days, the people of the Work knew they could make him very happy by presenting him with a set of beautifully embroidered vestments or sacred vessels of well-worked silver or gold encrusted with valuable gems. Everything seemed to him too little for God. Behind those gifts there lay a huge number of small, spontaneous gifts from families and friends.

Normally, however, he celebrated daily Mass with a poor chalice of gilded brass. In a letter dated 1964, he told his spiritual children in Spain, "I was deeply touched by a letter written to me by a miner, which says 'Father, we love you a lot', and adds 'don't get upset, don't worry.' And it reminds me of the poor metal chalice which I normally use to celebrate Mass. It has a fine classic shape and wonderful gilding. So much so that Candida Granda (may she rest in peace) once assured me that it was gold. But then she unscrewed it and we saw that on one of the larger pieces was stamped the word 'brass.'

"Between God, his Blessed Mother and you, my children, I am made to *cut a fine figure*, as they say in Italy: good shape, fine gilding . . . but made of brass: that is what I am. And I thank God for making me see it so clearly."[46]

---

44. Testimony of Helena Serrano (cf. AGP, HRF T-04641).
45. Testimony of Encarnación Ortega (AGP, HRF T-05074).
46. Letter of the Father to Fr. Florencio Sanchez Bella, Rome, 1964.

The toil of the altar

He celebrated Mass with the heart of "a man who knows how to love," as he called himself. Monsignor Escrivá gave of his best in the work of the Mass. God had let him see that the Mass was "God's work," *operatio Dei*, Opus Dei. On October 24, 1966 he explained, "In my sixty-fifth year, I have made a wonderful discovery. I love to celebrate the Holy Mass, but yesterday, I found it really hard work. What an effort it cost me! And I realized that the Mass really is Opus Dei, work, toil, as was Jesus Christ's first Mass: the Cross. I understand that the task of a priest, the celebration of the Holy Mass, is the toil of making the Eucharist; that you experience sorrow, joy, and tiredness. I felt in my own body the exhaustion of a divine work."[47]

Some time later, in Pozoalbero, Jerez, during his 1972 catechesis in Portugal and Spain, an Andalusian asked him, "How does the Father *live* the holy sacrifice of the altar?" After joking about the man's inquisitiveness, Monsignor Escrivá replied, "My Mass is never the same from one day to the next. Every day I linger, in a different way, on this prayer or that offering or that other petition. The Mass, which for me is Opus Dei, wears me out; it exhausts me! I thank God that this is so. It is a wonderful, divine burden, because it is not I but he, God, who carries it. All priests, be we sinners like me, or saints as some are, are never ourselves: it is Christ who renews his sacrifice of Calvary on the altar. I don't 'preside over' anything. I am Christ at the altar! I consecrate *in persona Christi*, in the person of Christ, because I give him my body, my voice, and my poor heart which has so often been stained but which I want him to purify."

Intense silence reigned. The Father sought to locate his questioner in the crowd. At last he found him, and in a strong Aragonese accent he said, "Hey, now you know almost as much as I do!" He stretched out his right hand, palm like a beggar pleading for alms, and added, "Won't you help me to say the Mass, even when I'm not here? Can you understand how it exhausts me?"[48]

---

47. Discourse of Bishop Alvaro del Portillo, Romana, VI, 10, p. 96.
48. AGP, HRF 20761, p. 387.

A wholehearted priest

Monsignor Escrivá made everything center on this "work" that was his and God's. He maintained that the Mass was the "center and root of the interior life." In the evening get-together, at the first stroke of ten, he would jump up and retire in silence. He had in mind the invitation in the words of the prophet: *Praeparare in occursum Dei tui, Israel,* "Prepare, O Israel, to go out to meet your God" (Amos 4:12). He spent the whole night like that, praying even while he slept, and approached the altar steps with intense desire. "I shall go to the altar of God, the God who gives joy to my youth." For this priest, saying Mass was his *raison d'être.*

11

He Was the Father

A visiting card for eternity

Monsignor Escrivá devised his own epitaph. He did not aim to compose an epitaph by which people would remember him, but chose a bare, truthful statement of how he was known to God.

It was October 4, 1957, the feast of St. Francis of Assisi, a day when he had the habit of meditating on the virtue of poverty. He saw poverty as a welcome companion that enabled him to travel light, prepared even to do without basic needs. Going further, he delved into the poverty of his own being. And setting aside all gifts and graces he had received, he saw himself as "a poor sinner, who loves Jesus Christ madly."

Later that day, Monsignor Escrivá and Jesus Alvarez, an architect who lived and worked in Villa Tevere, were considering plans for the crypt beneath the oratory of Our Lady of Peace. Quite naturally, he suggested that Alvarez note down a short text he would dictate "for when you come to bury me," adding, "But when the time comes, you are free to do whatever you think fit."

It was the inscription for his gravestone. After his Christian name and two surnames, a Latin word: *Peccator* (sinner). On the next line, a plea: *Orate pro eo* (pray for him). That was all. Seeing surprise and regret on Alvarez's face, Monsignor Escrivá added with a smile, "If you like, you can add a few more words, *Genuit filios et filias* (he begot sons and daughters)."

When he died, Don Alvaro del Portillo, in agreement with the general council and the central advisory of the Work, decided not to follow the suggestion. It was the first time Don Alvaro had ignored an indication of his, and he did it out of devotion and sense of justice. He was reluctant to put the word "sinner" on the tomb of such a holy man. And even the expression "he begot sons and daughters" did not express how much of a father Monsignor Escrivá was.

Don Alvaro, "expressing everyone's wish," as he said at the time, had just two words placed on the green marble slab that covered the grave: *El Padre* (The Father). These were the most loving and accurate words to describe the man buried there. "The Father" was what people had spontaneously called him, and that was how he would always be remembered.

He was "the Father"

From the moment God planted the seed of the Work in his soul when he was just twenty-six years old, Josemaría Escrivá realized that he was *for* all his children.

He was their Father. In family life with his sons, he treated them with affectionate trust. He knew their comings and goings, how they studied, sang, prayed, played football, and enjoyed themselves. He could tease them, adjust their ties, clean their glasses, tell them jokes, sit with them at breakfast, spread jam on a slice of bread and encourage them to eat it, or go up to their bedrooms with a hot drink when they had a cold.

Toward his daughters, he always maintained the formality, gravity, and distance he had adopted toward all women from the moment he was ordained. But he treated them with still more exquisite courtesy and gentler manners, and put his heart into details of caring for them. He showed a carefully restrained admiration for them, a sort of half-concealed delight, born of the conviction that they were in Opus Dei without his having called, invited, or looked for them. They had come to it, in fact, against his own will and by God's express desire. This "moral and physical" certainty gave a supernatural tone to nearly all his meetings with his daughters. Often he exclaimed,

"Thank God, thank God that you're here!" or "When I see you, I can hardly believe it!"

Their steadfastness and self-denial amazed him. When he had to ask for prayers for some particularly difficult matter, he called on them before anyone else. He entrusted them with any jobs that needed more special care, skill, and patience.

In the 1950s, the artists who were designing a big stained-glass window for the Pentecost Oratory in Villa Tevere prepared a sketch showing the Holy Spirit descending on Our Lady and the disciples. Monsignor Escrivá made them alter the sketch. "You've shown all the disciples as men. I want you to change some of these into women—do you imagine there weren't any women there?"

To the women in Opus Dei, Monsignor Escrivá extended the same love, the same demands, the same spirituality, the same lifestyle as to the men. The Work of God was one and the same and had to be done by all. He put it in very homely terms: "As in all healthy families, I have just one cooking pot; each can take from it what he or she needs."

Sounding the alarm

In times of extraordinary doctrinal confusion and moral collapse, he told his children to be on guard, with precautions they should take against losing their faith, becoming slack morally, letting love of God grow cool, becoming cowardly in the apostolate.[1]

He wrote: "It hurts me deeply to write this, but we have had to endure a stream of impostors who have tried unsuccessfully to mask their heresy by claiming to be prophets of a new age. They are not merely heretics but fanatics; lustful, resentful, and proud. My children, it hurts, but by sounding the alarm in this way, I aim to stir up your consciences so that this tide of hypocrisy does not catch you unawares. . . . We have to respond to this barefaced corruption by being more demanding in our own behavior, and sowing sound doctrine boldly.

---

1. Cf. *Letter*, March 28, 1973.

"My children, don't be lulled into a life of routine. Feel the urgency of doing good, because time is short. Never be afraid to stand up for Jesus Christ. . . . The supreme remedy is piety. . . . Having prayed a lot for a long time and encouraged others to pray, I have given you the directives I deemed prudent in conscience, so that you always have clear guidelines . . . in this time of almost total moral abandonment. . . . Besides, in this way, we will make sure nobody joins the Work in order to cause us harm, because any such person would be unable to keep up the humble self-surrender, struggle, and mature renunciation which we fight to practice."[2]

This Father could enjoy whatever his children liked and found amusing. One day he had to make a real effort not to laugh when he met Olive Mulcahy in Villa Tevere. She had recently arrived from Ireland and addressed him in broken Spanish. "Father, you paint a duck for me . . . and I play for you on the violin . . . yes?"

"Yes, of course! Let's all go to the laundry room; it's right here, my daughter!"

And then and there, with a few rapid strokes, he drew a duck for her on a piece of paper. His daughters loved ducks because they are bold and "learn to swim by swimming." Meanwhile, Olive played a soft Irish melody on her violin.[3] Monsignor Escrivá knew that this was time well spent, not wasted, because moments like this are the spice of family life.

Two violins

One night in September 1949 he stayed up very late waiting for his son Jesus Cagigal, an architectural student from abroad who was to spend several years in Rome helping with the building of Villa Tevere. When he finally arrived, Monsignor Escrivá kissed him on both cheeks and told him to "have something to eat and go to bed, because you must be very tired." Next day he invited him to take a walk around the city "so you can get used to the buildings, and see

2. *Letter,* February 14, 1974, 13–18.
3. Testimony of Helena Serrano (cf. AGP, HRF T-04641).

the colors on Roman houses." At one point he asked, "Have you brought your violin? You haven't? Well, tell the next person who comes here for any reason to bring it with them."

Some time later, Monsignor Escrivá entered the room called "the architects' studio." He noticed two black violin cases on top of a cupboard.

"How come you have two violins?" he asked.

Cagigal explained that another person in the Work, also a music lover, had given him his instrument. "He's not going to continue practicing, and as it's a very good violin, it's important to take care of it and tune it every now and again."

"Oh, no; give it back to him immediately! It's wonderful to develop one's talents; but we also have to practice personal poverty, and you don't need more than one violin."[4]

Monsignor Escrivá wanted all his children to participate in the decoration of the Villa—"all the enthusiasts, the more the better! Even if you only do one brushstroke!" He showed them how to create a patina on an imitation antique carving with talcum powder and vermilion and how to treat an old chest with turpentine to kill the woodworm. He took a close interest in the careful painting of a paneled ceiling in an oratory and made sure the young men working at it stopped for a coffee break. He encouraged Palmira Laguens and Annamaria Notari to work marvels in kiln-fired pottery, as well as papier-mâché. He thought it would do Helena Serrano good to have a free hand to paint whatever she chose, and as soon as he saw a suitable bare wall he told her, "It's all yours! You have a fine space there to paint as you please! What do you think of doing a big world map, and marking all the places where there's a center of women in the Work? There are quite a lot of them already!"[5]

An enterprising artist called Manolo Caballero was finishing a picture of Our Lady as Queen of Opus Dei, done in oils on wood. Monsignor Escrivá wanted it to be a masterpiece. He often would visit the painter and, sitting on a stool or a large fruit basket, stay a while watching him paint.

---

4. Account of Dr. Jesus Cagigal (AGP, HRF T-08244 and AGP HRF 21181, pp. 486–487).
5. Testimony of Helena Serrano (cf. AGP, HRF T-04641).

On one occasion José Luis Pastor, a doctor, was with him. When the artist had gone out to get some solvent and some tubes of paint, Monsignor Escrivá said, "How well this son of mine paints! This is real art!" A few seconds later, he turned to José Luis with an affectionate look and said, "And what about you? You give me my injections with more skill than a champion dart-thrower!"[6]

Monsignor Escrivá received a constant flow of graces and lights from God, to be passed on to his children. He carried a small notebook in his cassock pocket in which to write down quickly and carefully what God gave him. It might be a phrase from his breviary, a line from scripture, which struck him one particular day with new meaning. Convinced that Opus Dei was not his, he acted as a disciple, alert to God's lessons.

A great teacher

He had a real flair for teaching and always expressed himself in contemporary terms. Neither smug nor oratorical, he taught pupils scattered through five continents; yet his teaching always had a direct tone, since he was talking to people in almost every sense who were very close to him. His spiritual children learned the spirit of the Work by seeing how he practiced it. His "lessons" were given in the comings and goings around the house, in get-togethers, on car trips, meditations, comments on the news, or references to something he had read.

Monsignor Escrivá's notebook

One morning, while reading the Gospel he was struck by a familiar passage which he understood in a new light. Later he commented, "'Power came forth from him and healed them all—*Sanabat omnes.'* It filled me with consolation to think that among those *omnes* there must have been all kinds of people: some who loved him and some who didn't. But Jesus made no distinction among them, he did not discriminate between people: *sanabat omnes*, he cured them all!"[8]

---

6. Oral account of Fr. Ernesto Julia.
7. Luke 6:19.
8. Testimony of Monsignor César Ortiz-Echagüe (AGP, HRF T-04694).

Another time he reflected aloud on the theological meaning in two words of the Hail Mary: '*Dominus tecum*, the Lord is with thee.' "I don't know, maybe until now I hadn't realized the theological depth of the phrase 'the Lord is with thee.' It is the Holy Spirit, the whole Trinity. Don't you find a new richness in these words? The Holy Spirit is with you, Mother! How wonderful!"[9]

Other times he used his own inner life to show them he too was made of clay. One day in autumn 1968, when someone spoke to him about "security in the interior life," he answered simply, "My son, I feel very envious of those old ladies who pray with sighs of devotion in the corner of a church. For thirty-eight years it has gone against the grain for me to continue going forward. I've been feeling dry, but doing my prayer by dint of drawing each bucketful of water from the well by hand."[10]

Someone else once asked him how to be more generous towards God and other people. He said, "We each know about that, we realize it when we examine our conscience at night. Often, I have to say to our Lord, 'Josemaría is not pleased with Josemaría today.'"[11]

In answer to a similar question, he said, "You want to know how I did my thanksgiving after Mass today? Well . . . by making our Lord a present of the sorrow I feel at not being able to serve him better."[12]

But in spite of his failings and weaknesses, he used to add that he never felt sadness, melancholy, or loneliness. "I never feel lonely: with the Holy Trinity in my heart, in my soul, how could I? We're never alone. We have no reason to feel lonely or sad or bored, ever! Only those whose lives are empty can be bored."[13]

He made use of the tiniest details. "You see this little scratch on the wall?" he said one day. "Please, my son, make a note of it so it can be given a lick of paint before it gets any worse. It's like a venial sin in the soul—one seems very little on its own, but if after one there comes another and another, the person soon becomes a leper!"[14]

---

9. Testimony of Fr. Fernando Valenciano (AGP, HRF T-05362) and of Marlies Kücking.
10. Testimony of Monsignor César Ortiz-Echagüe (AGP, HRF T-04694).
11. Ibid.
12. Ibid.
13. Ibid.
14. Testimony of Fr. Rafael Caamaño (AGP, HRF T-05837).

Return to Squarciarelli

The song "Arrivederci Roma!" became popular in Italy in the spring of 1956. A young Spanish lawyer, Juan Carlos Beascoechea, was completing a thesis on canon law. He told Monsignor Escrivá in a family gathering one day, "Father, I know a new song. It's very nice and I think you might like it. Shall I sing it for you?"

"Yes, please," Monsignor Escrivá responded. "Sing it for all of us so we can all enjoy it."

Juan Carlos started off in a fine baritone. One verse went "*Si ritrova a pranzo a Squarciarelli, / Fettuccine e vino dei Castelli, / Come ai tempi belli che Pinelli / Immortalo . . . Arrivederci Roma!*" (People meet for lunch at Squarciarelli, / Having fettuccine and the white wine of Castelli, / Like the good old times that Pinelli / Immortalized . . . good-bye, Rome!)

Monsignor Escrivá listened with a smile, tapping his foot in time to the music. When the song was over, he clapped and said to the singer, "My son, before you leave Rome, remind me to take you to Squarciarelli one day, so you can see how beautifully the Italians do things."

Juan Carlos reminded him a couple of times, and he answered, "I can't today, Juan Carlos, but I assure you we will go; it's a promise."

One day Juan Carlos repeated the proposal. Monsignor Escrivá said, "Speaking for myself, I can make it today. What do you have to do this afternoon?"

"Me? Nothing in particular, Father!"

"Well, then, be here at five and we'll go!"

A few minutes before five, Monsignor Escrivá came down the stairs to the Galleria della Campana with Don Alvaro. They got into an old black Lancia, driven by Ramon Labiaga, a chemist from Mexico, who was also a student at the Roman College.

Before leaving Rome, they went past St. Peter's Basilica and said the Creed, as was Monsignor Escrivá's custom. As usual, when he came to "I believe in one, holy, Catholic and apostolic Church," he added "in spite of everything!" to remind himself to beg forgiveness for his sins and other people's. Then they took the road toward Castelgandolfo, passing through Grottaferrata, Rocca di Papa, and Frascati. When they arrived, Monsignor Escrivá pointed to something like a snack-stall, a poor tumbled-down affair with a thatched porch as a dining area. "That's the famous Squarciarelli!" he said.

Juan Carlos' face fell. "Honestly, I had imagined something quite different."

"My son," said Monsignor Escrivá, "that happens with so many things in life. We inject them with poetry in our imaginations, we idealize them, and come to believe they are the epitome of happiness and beauty. But then when we have them in front of us, and see them just as they are, our hearts sink to our boots."

They sat at one of the tables, had some refreshments, and held a lively conversation on all sorts of topics. When Don Alvaro had paid the bill, Monsignor Escrivá took it and tore off the elaborate heading "Squarciarelli–Trattoria." Passing it to Juan Carlos, he said with a wink, "Here, keep it. Maybe some day you will like to look at it."[15]

"And just save myself?"

He was their Father. Already in the 1950s he had warned his children to be careful what they read on subjects connected with faith and morals. "I have to look after the spiritual life and apostolic effectiveness of thousands of people of different languages and cultures in the Work. And so I have to take precautions. We are ordinary people who belong in the world, so we have to do whatever is necessary to avoid going off the rails, to make sure we save our souls; because otherwise, our Lord will be left with fewer instruments he can use."[16]

In 1972, when much was topsy-turvy in the Church itself, Monsignor Escrivá, looking sorrowful but speaking energetically, said, "In these circumstances I can't just say 'Every man for himself!' and save my own life by hanging on to a plank. I have an obligation to save myself and the boat and all my children! If you only knew how it weighs me down!"[17]

---

15. Oral account of Fr. Juan Beascoechea.
16. Testimony of Mercedes Morado (AGP, HRF T-07902).
17. Testimony of Fr. Fernando Valenciano (AGP, HRF T-05362).

Father Carlos Cardona recalled an incident that sheds light on his spirit of freedom. Cardona was an intellectual who would spend hours immersed in books on philosophy, theology, and the history of ideas. One day, Monsignor Escrivá suggested that he do his daily spiritual reading not from the Fathers of the Church or the works of St. Thomas, St. Augustine, or St. Teresa. "Carlitos, how about using *Don Quixote* for your spiritual reading for a time? It will help you keep your feet on the ground and see things in proportion, and above all it will spark your sense of humor."[18]

Like the Good Shepherd in the Gospel, Monsignor Escrivá could say, "I know my own, and my own know me."[19] One day in 1964 he reminded the women who were directors in the central advisory that governing in the Work meant "praying for everyone, worrying about everyone, making oneself understood by everyone, caring for everyone, being kind to everyone: each and every one of them!" This was what he did himself. If one of his spiritual children was having a bad time, he either wrote that person or had someone write on his behalf. He saw to it that the individual was looked after with special care and did not hesitate to invite people in that situation to come to Rome or go elsewhere to have a break.

Replying to an aggressive letter

"Some time ago," he once recalled, "a son of mine wrote me an aggressive letter, a really arrogant one. You could see he was going through a difficult patch. I thought about him a lot, and I prayed a lot for him. Then, with the heart of a father and a mother, I wrote him a letter full of kindness, and in it I called him simply by his name . . . by his *nomignolo*, by his nickname. And that son of mine, when he realized how much he was loved and felt he was being called back with a loving whistle from the shepherd, changed completely. He's out there now, dedicated, absolutely faithful, and very happy!"[20]

---

18. Testimony of Fr. Carlos Cardona (AGP, HRF T-06138).
19. John 10:14.
20. Testimony of Begoña Alvarez (AGP, HRF T-04861).

Respect for souls

God had provided him with the gifts he needed as founder and father to a huge number of children of his spirit. Among them was discernment of spirits, something that went further and deeper than mere psychology and enabled him "to know his own" even without having seen them before.

Generally, Monsignor Escrivá did not give people advice without due consideration or in public. Often, on being asked for it, he gave some general suggestions and then, as if excusing himself, explained, "Here, in front of everyone, I'm not going to say what you ought to do. I'd need to talk to you alone, in the confessional, and ask you a few very direct, specific, personal questions." But sometimes he acted differently, when warned by his supernatural prudence that it was the right moment, even urgent, to say something directly to a particular person. One day in Villa delle Rose, during a get-together, a German daughter of his, a student at the Roman College, asked, "Father, while I'm dedicating myself in a special way to my own personal formation, how can I help the Work in my country from here?"

For a moment he concentrated all his attention on her. Then, as if there was no one else in the room, he began speaking in confidential tones. "My daughter," he began, "what you have to do is follow the timetable of this center. I imagine that, like all good Germans, you always do things on the dot, like clockwork. But above all, follow the timetable for family gatherings. Family life is something wonderful! You can also help by going out for walks and by going on the outings that are organized. Make sure you get the right amount of sleep. Put your studying in its place. Use the time spent in class and in study periods very well, so that they don't take away from the time you need for other things, do you follow me? Of course you do. Take care of all those other things which are just as important as or even more important than studying. Have I explained myself? I know you've understood!"

As soon as he left, she went to see Carmen Ramos, the director of the Roman College. "It's amazing!" she said. "The Father really hit the nail on the head. He used almost the very same words as I've been hearing in my spiritual guidance: to put study in its place, and to spend some of my time sharing with the others, enjoying life with the others. But I'm the only person who knew that. And the Father was able to detect it just as though he'd known me all my life."[21]

Agostino Dona, Roberto Dotta, Firmina Ferreira, Rainer Kiawki, Jose Rodriguez, George Rossman, Francesco Sagliembene, Anna Vettorelli, Giuseppe Zanniello, Cormac Burke, and many others witnessed episodes in which Monsignor Escrivá addressed someone with a spiritual consideration which left the listener dumbfounded "because what the Father is saying is the precise answer to what is worrying me at this moment," though he or she had not even hinted at this concern or problem.[22]

Something like that happened to Umberto Farri, a young Italian who asked for admission to Opus Dei in March 1949, in Rome. A few days later, he went to Villa Tevere to talk to Monsignor Escrivá. He was a little confused, not knowing how to handle the conversation. When he knocked on the door of the room, he thought, "And now what am I going to say to the Father?" He went in, and Monsignor Escrivá got up immediately and came to meet him, beaming. As though reading Umberto's thoughts, he said, "I want you to realize, my son, that you don't have to say anything special to the Father."[23]

"I'm calling from London"

When he was in London in the summer of 1960 he decided to make two long distance telephone calls, one to Osaka and another to Nairobi. Women of the Work were breaking new ground in those cities and having a hard time, without even bare necessities. He knew he and those with him would have to tighten their belts and spend less in London to be able to afford the two calls. But it gave those women a much-needed boost to pick up the phone and hear Monsignor Escrivá. "I'm calling from London, so we'll have to use these minutes very well. I'd like to speak to each of you in turn. Is that possible?" Their Father's warm, cheerful voice raised their spirits and helped them not to feel so far away.[24]

---

21. Oral account of Carmen Ramos.
22. Cf. *Articles of the Postulator*, 1226 and footnote 1394.
23. *Articles of the Postulator*, 1227.
24. Testimony of Encarnación Ortega (AGP, HRF T-05074).

Encarnita Ortega was also staying in the house in London that they rented that summer. She heard the conversations and a few days later read the letters from Japan and Kenya, both saying more or less the same: "The phone call was a totally unexpected surprise, but it came at the very moment we needed it most."

"What's wrong?"

Encarnita recalled a scene years before, in 1943, at the beginning of her vocation. She lived and worked in the domestic administration of La Moncloa residence hall. One afternoon, Monsignor Escrivá came in accompanied by a bishop. Apparently he had just shown him around the students' residence hall and now wanted to show him the kitchen, laundry, and other areas where the domestic staff worked. Encarnita welcomed them "elegantly," as she said afterwards, "and with my best smile." But as he went past her the Father asked in a very low voice, almost a whisper, "What's wrong?" Then he gave her a look of support and encouragement.

"Those few words, 'What's wrong?' and his supportive look were enough. It was just what I needed. At that moment, unknown to anyone, I was having serious doubts about persevering."[25]

"I demand of myself, and make demands on you"

He sometimes confessed, "When I have to reprimand anyone I feel bad about it before, during it, and afterwards; but although it upsets me, I make demands on myself for your benefit."[26] He knew it was easy to be soft and let slip an opportunity of laying down criteria. What was difficult was to correct, to warn someone drifting off course, and to attend to a host of little things. "I love my children more than a mother does," he said, "even when I've never seen them. And I can honestly say that I love each of them as if they were the only one. But if I hadn't shouted at them, the Work wouldn't exist now."[27]

---

25. Ibid.
26. Testimony of Fr. Carlos Cardona (AGP, HRF T-06138).
27. Testimony of Begoña Alvarez (AGP, HRF T-04861).

One warm June morning in 1968 Monsignor Escrivá was walking up and down a courtyard in Villa Tevere with Don Alvaro. They had adopted this habit to be out of the way of the domestic staff and make it easier to clean and tidy the rooms of the old part of the house, Villa Vecchia, where Monsignor Escrivá lived.

Maria Portavella and Helena Serrano were vacuuming and dusting the hall. Monsignor Escrivá opened the door and looked in. He beckoned to Helena to come out and then pointed to the windows on the fifth floor of the office building. Although the sun was blazing, all the lights were on.

"Look," he told her. "Later on, I want you to point out gently to that sister of yours who is cleaning up there that she is wasting electricity."

He continued walking with Don Alvaro, saying the Rosary. After about ten minutes he called Helena again. "My daughter," he said, "not only tell her about it very kindly, but also write a note of experience so that from now on, people will be careful about it."

A few minutes later, Monsignor Escrivá came back into the hall again. He did not look cross, but he was concentrating on keeping patient.

"Look, Helena, when the time comes do everything I told you before. But right now will you please go up there and tell that daughter of mine to turn off the lights? It's an absolute waste and we are really poor!"[28]

The coldness of indifference

He had to keep a keen eye on tiny material details. To him they were not contemptible trifles, but a test of the love of God. This meant being ready to be demanding on others. He explained, "I've never repented of having made demands on people about putting the spirit of the Work into practice. On the other hand, the odd time (admittedly few) that I've been soft on them, I have indeed been sorry afterwards."[29]

---

28. Testimony of Helena Serrano (cf. AGP, HRF T-04641).
29. Testimony of Mercedes Morado (AGP, HRF T-07902).

Monsignor Escrivá taught his children to practice the affectionate custom of fraternal correction that comes from the Gospel itself. He was terrified at the thought that the bitter cold of indifference might ever settle on Opus Dei. "Indifference isn't understanding," he said; "it's demanding and judgmental, but it doesn't correct. On the other hand, affection understands and demands while correcting. In the Work we all have a right to be supported and corrected with love."[30]

"I respect your long hair"

One day he noticed that one of the older people in the Work was wearing clothes more suitable for an adolescent. Calling another of his spiritual sons, he said, "You have to put your heart into God's affairs, into the things that concern the Work, and into what concerns your brothers. The day you live like strangers or stop caring about each other, you'll have destroyed Opus Dei. Find the right moment, speak to that brother of yours, and very kindly and very clearly make him a fraternal correction about it."[31]

The people of Opus Dei were "normal people amongst normal people," "members of the general public." They dressed according to their age, condition, and social status. During a trip to Madrid in 1969, Monsignor Escrivá was talking to a group of students about freedom. One of them had fashionably long, tangled hair. He told him, "I have a profound respect for everything that does not offend God. For everything—including long hair! Besides, in your case, I think your hair looks natural, a sign of sincerity."[32]

He required himself to be demanding on them. One day he severely reprimanded some of his daughters for something quite serious that they had done badly and carelessly, and, as he underlined, "without presence of God." At the door, about to leave, he could hear the silence behind him. Turning back, he saw them crestfallen, and looking at them with immense love, he said, "Do you think that

---

30. Testimony of Encarnación Ortega (AGP, HRF T-05074).
31. Testimony of Monsignor César Ortiz-Echagüe (AGP, HRF T-04694).
32. Ibid.

it doesn't hurt me to say these things? My daughters, if I didn't say them, I wouldn't be your Father but your wicked stepfather!"[33]

The theft of a document

In 1955 the villa at Castelgandolfo that Pius XII had given to the Work had not yet been renovated and transformed into Villa delle Rose. It was being used just as it was for retreats and courses of training and development. Lourdes Toranzo and Gabriella Filippone were asked to go there and conduct a course for married women in Opus Dei.

Before leaving for Castelgandolfo, they went to Villa Tevere, driving an old grey runabout with a canvas top which belonged to Gabriella's parents. They parked the car in Via di Villa Sacchetti, leaving their suitcases and a copy of the *Catechism of the Work* inside. This book had been printed by the monks of Grottaferrata, and the Holy See had several copies. It was not, however, on sale in bookshops, as it was for the use of people of the Work, giving a clear, detailed summary of the spirit of the Work in simple terms. When Lourdes and Gabriella got back to the car, they found that their suitcases and the *Catechism* had been stolen. They immediately told the director of the advisory, Encarnita Ortega, and she told Monsignor Escrivá. He said they should go to Castelgandolfo and look after the course. "Ask Lourdes to come here when it's finished, because I'd like to see her," he added.

Lourdes, who had been in the Work longer, naturally took responsibility for what had happened. When the week-long course was over, she and Encarnita went to see Monsignor Escrivá in the dining room of Villa Vecchia. Not angrily but sadly he said, "I've seen how much you love the Work and your vocation. Don Alvaro and I have been wondering if we should report the robbery to the police. But the only valuable thing that was stolen was the copy of the *Catechism*. We decided it was better not to make a fuss about an internal document. Do you realize what it means to have the *Catechism* stolen like that? Who knows what unscrupulous characters

33. Oral account of Maria Rivero.

may have got their hands on it! My daughter, would you like the love story of your parents, the things that they hold most sacred, to be read aloud in the town square, amidst catcalls, laughs, obscenities, and jeering?"

Lourdes left the room in sorrow. What upset her most was that Monsignor Escrivá did not speak harshly, but more with disillusionment and disappointment than anger or annoyance. The matter was closed, and never mentioned again.

Several months later, Lourdes was living in Villa Sacchetti, next to Villa Tevere, as director of the Roman College of Our Lady, a job she had been appointed to by the Father. One morning, on her way back from giving a class, the house telephone rang just as she got to her office. Picking up the receiver, she heard Monsignor Escrivá's voice.

"*Pax*, my daughter. What have you been doing just now?"

"I've just been giving a class."

"Really? What about?"

"Well . . ."

"Go on, tell me. What was the class about?"

"It was on the love and care we have to have for internal documents, such as, for instance, the *Catechism of the Work.*"

"Thank you very much, my daughter, because I know how much love and conviction you will have put into that class. God bless you!"[34]

"I've learned to wait"

He required himself to wait for the right time to help a son or daughter of his recover after something that might have left them feeling hurt. Encarnita Ortega heard him say, "Souls, like good wine, improve with time. I've learned how to wait—which is a high degree of knowledge!"[35] A man of strong, impetuous character, he sometimes did correct people on the spot, but never by "putting them on the spot." He always took care to show the person concerned some extra sign of care and affection.

---

34. Oral account of Lourdes Toranzo.
35. Testimony of Encarnación Ortega (AGP, HRF T-05074).

"My home is not a barracks"

One warm August evening in 1953 Monsignor Escrivá and Don Alvaro came to Castelgandolfo to spend time with a group of young men of the Work in a course of formation. They set out some benches in the garden in the shade of a magnolia tree. The conversation was lively, with Neapolitan and Mexican songs, stories of the apostolate, and news from other countries. Suddenly there was a silence, the kind that moves some people to say, "an angel is passing by." Monsignor Escrivá said, "Now then, what are you going to tell me?"

Among the group was a naval engineering student, Rafael Caamaño, recently arrived from Madrid. He had some funny stories about La Moncloa residence hall and the jokes played on a particularly gullible student there. He began to tell some of these. Everybody laughed except Monsignor Escrivá, who gradually became more and more serious. From his expression it was obvious that he was not enjoying it. Before Rafael had finished, Monsignor Escrivá interrupted him quite forcefully.

"That's enough. That is not our spirit. We've never played practical jokes on people. Our centers and residences are not army barracks: they're family homes where we try to make life pleasant for each other, and don't treat them rudely or sarcastically or too familiarly either. We treat everyone with extreme tact and courtesy. That's what we've done from the start, and that's what we'll always do."

At the end of the get-together, Monsignor Escrivá went to Rafael, took him by the arm, and walked with him toward the house. "Son, I had to cut you short like that. I want you to understand that I have the obligation, often a hard one, of teaching you—making our spirit and its demands absolutely clear to you. If I hadn't interrupted you to set down the right criteria for living together, everyone, including you yourself, would have thought the Father agreed with all that. You do understand that, my son, don't you?"[36]

On one occasion he was walking through the Galleria del Torrione in Villa Tevere with another priest and noticed that the paint on one wall had been worn away in places, obviously by being rubbed

---

36. Testimony of Fr. Rafael Caamaño (AGP, HRF T-05837).

with a cloth. He pointed this out to Mercedes Morado and Maria Portavella, who were engaged in cleaning that part of the house. He reminded them of the importance of "taking great care of little things," and that "if we neglect the little things, this house, which has been set up to last for centuries, could soon end up as a ruin." Then he said to Mercedes, "My daughter, as the director, you are responsible. This would not have happened if you had specified carefully in the notes on the cleaning how this type of distempered surface should be dusted. Now, kindly tell Helena to touch up the paintwork before it gets any worse!"

Next morning Monsignor Escrivá met Helena and asked, "Do you know where Mercedes is?"

"Right now she should be on the second floor."

"Well, will you do me a favor? Go upstairs and tell her on my behalf that yesterday I told her off for something, and I was wrong. I said that something was not specified in the notes on the cleaning, but in fact it was. I looked it up later. So please go and tell her the Father is very sorry and begs her pardon!"[37]

An order: "Please"

"Please" was how he asked for anything, not just out of good manners but because he detested despotism. He taught that the strongest command in Opus Dei must always be "please," first by practicing it himself. In this way he fostered free, intelligent, voluntary obedience, in which the people concerned could identify with what they were asked to do. Often he said, "The most supernatural reason for obeying is 'because I want to!' "

One day he asked his son Ernesto Julia to do a certain task. Ernesto answered, "I'll do it right away, Father."

"Do you really *want* to do it? Because it shouldn't be a case of my imposing anything on you. I don't want mindless obedience! Where obedience is concerned, I need to be able to depend on you, on your absolutely free will."[38]

---

37. Testimony of Helena Serrano (cf. AGP, HRF T-04641).
38. Testimony of Fr. Ernesto Julia Diaz (AGP, HRF T-06541).

His method was to teach as occasion arose, never missing an opportunity to show the spirit of Opus Dei in deeds. This made the lessons he taught unforgettable.

Sitting on the floor

After lunch one day in the autumn of 1961, Monsignor Escrivá went to the sitting room of the Vicolo part of Villa Tevere with the directors of the general council for a get-together with students of the Roman College. There were not enough seats for everyone, so the youngest men gave up their chairs to the directors and sat on the floor.

A few days later the same thing happened again. This time Monsignor Escrivá took the initiative and to everyone's surprise sat on the floor himself.

"It doesn't matter," he said simply. "In the Work we're all the same."[39]

At this stage his personal struggle took quite a different direction from before. Previously, when he saw something which went against the spirit of Opus Dei, he reasoned, "I can't correct this right now because I'm upset about it. I need to say it calmly so as not to hurt anybody, so that it will be more effective and not offend God. In a few days' time, when I'm calmer, I will say what I have to say."

However, as he got older, he corrected things immediately. His reason was, "If I don't correct this immediately, I'll begin thinking about how I am going to upset a son or a daughter of mine, and I'll get soft. Then there's a risk that I might not say what I ought to."[40]

A time for correction, a time for comfort

It was 1954. Monsignor Escrivá came into the laundry in Villa Sacchetti, calling for the director, Itziar Zumalde. By his tone of voice and frown it was obvious he was angry. Suddenly he noticed another of his daughters, Mirufa Zuloaga, sitting there sewing. He stopped short and his expression changed; he relaxed and smiled. A few days earlier Mirufa's father had died in Spain. When he heard the news,

39. Testimony of Fr. Fernando Valenciano (AGP, HRF T-05362).
40. Get-together with Bishop Alvaro del Portillo, *Noticias*.

he had shown his sympathy in all sorts of ways. Now, meeting her again, he was as kind to her as he could be, asking if she felt more at peace now, if she was less unhappy, how she was getting over it. For a while he forgot other concerns and had nothing but words of affectionate comfort for this daughter.

Then, against his will, he faced up to the duty of the moment. "Has anyone gone to tell Itziar I'm looking for her? Tell her to come quickly, because I have a few things I need to say to her."[41]

One night during the winter of 1956 he noticed that a light had been left on in La Montagnola. He called Encarnita on the house telephone to let her know, adding, "I've made a resolution, a permanent mortification, not to go to bed without correcting everything which I see needs to be corrected. You can't imagine, my daughter, how difficult it is not to let a single thing slip!"[42]

"I've been cross three times"

One afternoon in February 1964 he was talking to some of his daughters in the laundry of Villa Sacchetti, where so many family conversations took place. They talked about different things and then, "Just recently, the act of piety I find that I like best of all is the Act of Contrition. And right now, while I'm talking to you, I'm making one on the inside. Because today I got cross three times! First of all, where certain things are concerned I have not just the right, but the duty to get cross. And the other two times"—here he started to laugh, and had everyone else laughing with him—"of course I get cross too! What did you imagine?"[43]

Easygoing and good humored

But his normal attitude was easygoing good humor, cheerful, expansive, and generous. His normal expression was a mischievous look with the beginnings of a smile that lit up his whole face. He enjoyed being with his children in the Work, and when office work

---

41. Testimony of Helena Serrano (cf. AGP, HRF T-04641).
42. Testimony of Encarnación Ortega (AGP, HRF T-05074).
43. Testimony of Helena Serrano (cf. AGP, HRF T-04641).

prevented him from spending time with them he would call them on the house telephone, exchange a few words, and send an affectionate hug.

One afternoon in October 1954, five students in the Roman College were working in a makeshift study, a bedroom with four bunk beds. One of them, Santi Salord, was teaching Latin. The house phone rang, and one of them answered it. "Yes, Father . . . At the moment? We're in class."

He went back to the others and explained, "It was the Father. He asked me what we were doing, and when I told him we were in class he said, 'Oh, well then, that's that. I was calling to see if you wanted to come out for a walk into Rome with me.'"

"Honestly, couldn't you have told him you had nothing to do?"

Shortly afterward the phone rang again. Another student answered eagerly, "Nothing, Father, I've absolutely nothing to do!"

"Really? That's very wrong! Go and tell the director, so he can give you some work! Don't you realize that in the Work we can't just sit around like gentlemen of leisure?"[44]

Later he told them he did things like that to stir up their sense of humor. "For a son of God it's a serious business to lose one's good humor. Let people who aren't children of God be miserable! Not long ago I was talking to a certain pessimistic prelate, one of those people who see everything overcast. The next day I wrote him a note. Among other things, I said: 'You did my soul a lot of damage yesterday: you made me get sad.'"[45]

Neither bossy nor imposing, he knew how to create a relaxed, easygoing atmosphere so that people enjoyed being with him. Jose Maria Sanabria offers three scenes from among many he witnessed in Villa Tevere in 1959.

"I was hurrying toward the covered walkway in Villa Tevere. I opened the door quickly and it hit the Father, who was coming in the opposite direction at that precise moment. I must have hit him quite hard! I was horrified and didn't know what to do. But immediately the Father opened the door wide, reached out and set

---

44. Testimony of Fr. Carlos Cardona (AGP, HRF T-06138).
45. Ibid.

his hands on my shoulders, saying smilingly, 'My poor son! What a fright the Father gave you hiding behind the door like that!'

"There are some big, low chests in the Galleria della Campana. Some of us used to sit on them while we were waiting to go into the dining room. Then we were told not to use them as seats so as not to spoil them.

"A few days later, when I came home from the university I saw the Father sitting on one of these chests while talking with a group of students from the Roman College. While he was talking the Father was swinging his feet, kicking the chest gently with his heels. It seemed as if he was doing it without thinking, but then he said, 'You've recently been told how it isn't a good idea to sit on these chests, haven't you? There are a lot of us here, and if we all sat on them we'd ruin them in no time. We would be lacking the virtue of poverty. But you know, we don't practice poverty just because we've made it our way of life. We take care of these details for love of Jesus Christ. But if you feel like it one day, after all, it's your home, you sit on it, as I'm doing now, and beat on it with your heels and hands, if that's what amuses you. We're not fanatics of poverty, or order, or little things, my sons. We do everything for the love of God!'

"Another time we were in a get-together with the Father in the Vicolo part of Villa Tevere. At a given moment he took hold of the arm of the person nearest him, Jesus Martinez, looked at his watch, and said, 'Tell me in five minutes, so we can end the get-together.' Then he said, 'I have to make sure myself because you're a set of rogues. I once said, 'I'll go when that fellow finishes his cigarette.' And do you know what your brothers did? When I wasn't looking they replaced the almost finished cigarette with a new one, and then another. . . .'

"The lively conversation went on. After a while the Father took Jesus' arm again to check the time: fifteen minutes had passed, not five. Quick as lightning, Jesus said, 'Don't rely on this watch Father. When it likes, it goes very fast.' The Father roared with laughter at this cheeky remark, tut-tutting and shaking his head, and merely said, 'These sons. . . ! The same spirit!' "[46]

---

46. Testimony of Jose Maria Sanabria (AGP, HRF T-06425).

A bed of nails

Having engendered thousands of sons and daughters of his spirit, he was attentive to their bodies and their souls, and passed on this concern to those who had the job of directing, forming, and caring for the others. "My children," he said, "you have to notice things, you have to be alert. When someone's ill it shows in their face, in their eyes especially, in the reluctant way they go about their duty, in their weariness, in the effort it takes them to do things. It would be unpardonable, and a lack of charity and justice, for you to pay no heed to the physical health of your brothers or sisters who live with you. Well, it would be still more unpardonable if you were to leave them spiritually sick until they died off. You have to be observant! You have to notice when a person is slacking, becoming cold, and gradually drifting away from God and the things of God! And in justice you have the obligation to be demanding on them with fortitude, and take devoted care of them. This means vibrant alertness, in a vigil of love. It isn't easy. I know that very well: I'm always on a bed of nails!"[47]

My heart is on guard

One day in March 1964, on the way out of the village of Albano on the way to Ariccia, Monsignor Escrivá discovered a small statue of Our Lady in one of those little shrines set up by popular devotion at the wayside. He noticed a short Latin inscription beside the statue and read it aloud: *Cor meum vigilat,* "my heart is awake."[48] He repeated it several times. "My heart is awake" stirred him. Soon afterward he said to the women in Villa delle Rose, "My heart is awake. That is how we have to be: with our hearts on guard. We have no right to sleep! Like a mother, like an alert sentry on the night watch, we have to watch, out of love. Love does not sleep . . . and when you really love, you even watch while you're asleep."

---

47. Testimonies of Encarnación Ortega (AGP, HRF T-05074) and of Mercedes Morado (AGP, HRF T-07902).
48. Song of Solomon 5:2.

Then he turned the conversation to the fraternal vigilance that made all in the Work, from the oldest member to the newest, feel and act like *good shepherds* for all the others. "We have to pray for, and help in every possible way, those who are going through a crisis or some difficulty. And if one of your sisters is slack in her struggle or irresolute in her vocation, you have to do all you can to help her forward, while at the same time respecting her freedom. If I wanted to jump out of the window, would you let me? Of course you wouldn't!"

He paused. Drawing himself up, he added in solemn tones, "I don't excuse of sin, sometimes even serious sin, the people who have lived with someone who has lost or thrown overboard her vocation, if they have not provided all possible means to help her."[49]

Another day, at home in the Galleria della Campana, he met a son of his who had just been appointed to the general council of the Work.

"Well, you rascal, when are you coming to sleep in Villa Vecchia?"

Before the man could reply, Monsignor Escrivá corrected himself: "I mean, not to sleep: to keep vigil!"[50]

"I am crying"

Someone was looking for him one day and could not find him. After searching all through Villa Vecchia, he looked into Monsignor Escrivá's private oratory and found him there. He was kneeling in front of the altar with his head in his hands, sobbing bitterly. When Monsignor Escrivá saw the man, he dried his tears with a handkerchief and said, "Yes, I'm crying. Because I'm human like everyone else, and I have a heart. For some time now I've been advising a son of mine not to fight the battle on the main walls of the fortress. He took no notice, and now he's on the point of losing his vocation."[51]

---

49. Testimony of Marlies Kücking.
50. Testimony of Begoña Alvarez (AGP, HRF T-04861).
51. Testimony of Fr. Ernesto Julia (AGP, HRF T-06541).

In Stazione Termini railway station in Rome

He was "the Father." He heard that a Spanish daughter of his, after a period of interior agitation, had reached the point of doubting whether to persevere in Opus Dei. Giving way to a momentary impulse, she had packed her suitcases and left the center where she was living in Milan. "She must be traveling now," they told him, "maybe toward Rome. . . . She hasn't told any of us exactly where she's going."

"What this daughter of mine needs now is to know that, come what may, even though the ground gives way under her feet, she has the Father! Alvaro, will you come with me? Let's go to the Stazione Termini!"

It was late at night when they got back. The person concerned had made up her mind to persevere. At the most difficult moment of her life, she realized that he was the Father.[52]

---

52. Oral account of Gloria Toranzo.

12 ✢

Monsignor at Home

Monsignor Escrivá and his daughters

A car pulled up at the front door of Villa delle Rose, in Castelgandolfo outside Rome, and Monsignor Escrivá got out quickly, eager to see his daughters. He always liked to bring a present when he came to see them. Sometimes he would bring sweets, other times some china ducks or other ornaments for the house. Today, June 17, 1964, it was some records and an antique fan for the collection in their sitting room.

In no time at all, a lively get-together started. Joan McIntosh, an American, asked him why family life was the heart and soul of people's relations in the Work. Monsignor Escrivá smiled. "As a teacher, you know how to explain it perfectly to other people—but you want to hear me say it, don't you? You know we call it 'family life' because the same atmosphere exists in our houses as in Christian families. Our houses aren't schools, or convents, or barracks: they're homes where people with the same parents live. We call God himself Father, and the Mother of God, Mother. What's more, we really love each other."

Monsignor Escrivá made an eloquent gesture, interlacing the fingers of both hands like the weave of a basket. "We really love each other! I don't want anyone in the Work to feel alone!"[1]

---

1. Testimony of Marlies Kücking.

He often said that he was "not a model for anything," but he would make one exception. "If I were an example of anything, it would be that of a man who knows how to love."

Those who lived with him, even for a few hours, could feel that. One of his sons in Opus Dei said, "When you were with the Father you felt looked after, cared for, well treated, and loved. You always received more than you asked for, more than you had realized you needed.

"It wasn't that he had a fabulous memory, so that on seeing you he was reminded of the problem of that friend of yours, or your mother's illness. It wasn't that at all. Your friend's problem and your mother's illness really concerned him: he carried them in his heart, because he had a big heart.

"One fine day I got up with a pimple on the tip of my nose. During the morning I met at least eighteen people who told me one after the other, without fail, that I had a pimple on my nose! At some point the Father passed by the place where I was working, but he said nothing, and shortly afterward someone brought me a tube of ointment 'from the Father, for the pimple.' "[2]

He had a big heart which embraced all his sons. And also his daughters, although he maintained a distance of "5,000" or even "50,000 kilometers" from them. But if it was snowing and he knew two or three of the women from Villa Sacchetti had left early to go to the out-of-town wholesale markets, he would phone to ask whether "those daughters of mine put chains on the wheels of the car." Monsignor Escrivá's way of loving was not angelic or theoretical. It meshed with people's small day-to-day needs.

When the women of the Work went to live permanently in Villa delle Rose, Monsignor Escrivá suggested they get a dog "to guard the house, especially at night time." One morning they found the dog dead. There was no sign of violence, so they concluded it must have been poisoned. That same day they told Monsignor Escrivá.

"Don't worry," he told them, "but get another dog this very day."[3]

In the spring of 1974 the Italian government imposed some fuel restrictions. One was to restrict the use of cars on Sundays and

2. Verbal account of Fr. Ernesto Julia. Cf. also Rafael Gomez Perez, *Working with Blessed Josemaría* (Madrid: Rialp, 1994), pp. 73–74.
3. Ibid.

holidays to those whose plates ended in an odd or an even number, depending on whether the date was odd or even. Monsignor Escrivá immediately talked to Carmen Ramos and Marlies Kücking about it. He was concerned about the women who lived and worked in Albarossa, the catering wing of Cavabianca on the outskirts of Rome, who might find themselves cut off in an emergency since there were many of them and they had only one small van.

"Before Sunday you will need to see to it that these women have another vehicle. Make sure that the plate numbers of the two vehicles are alternate: one odd and the other even. We are poor, but when necessary we spend what we have to."[4]

Around this same time there were demonstrations and disturbances on the streets of Rome, and news of possible attacks by groups of political extremists. Monsignor Escrivá recommended closing windows on the ground floor, having sandbags ready in the garage, and not opening mailboxes.

"I trust our Lord completely, and I know nothing will happen to you. But I think we should use all the available means, humanly speaking, as well."[5]

Force the door open

He adopted security measures for all the centers throughout the world, even to the details of how bars on outside windows and doors could be made decorative.

In Villa Tevere, he ensured that the front door of the women's house, which opened onto Via di Villa Sacchetti, was secured during the day with a heavy chain on the inside and always opened by two people, so that in case of a robbery or attack one would always be able to raise the alarm. He also had a loud bell installed next to the receptionist's desk.

"This bell doesn't need to go off outside but inside the house," he explained, "because if anything happened, we would be the ones to come and help."

---

4. Testimony of Marlies Kücking.
5. Ibid.

All were common sense precautions not intended to make it difficult to go out but get in. Applying this to vocation, Monsignor Escrivá would say "the door is always open" to leave the Work, but to join, "I don't make it easy: you have to push hard—to force the door open."

After the Carnation Revolution

After the popular Carnation Revolution that began in 1974, Portugal went through a period of political turmoil, involving searches, requisitions, and confiscations. Some people of the Work lost their possessions, homes, and jobs. In these times of instability and fear, people were not only afraid but hungry. Monsignor Escrivá, in Venezuela at the time on his last catechetical journey, instructed two of his daughters, Mercedes Morado and Josefina Ranera, to go to Portugal "to help their sisters in need as far as possible, at least with their presence, serenity, morale, and affection." On his return to Europe he stopped in Madrid to get direct news of the people of the Work in Portugal.[6]

In 1955, the women of Villa Tevere took over the operation of the printing press, previously done by men. Monsignor Escrivá made several recommendations about the use of the machines and in particular called attention to the danger of the cutter. "Look, this contraption cuts through a stack of paper two inches thick like butter," he told them. "Martha, please make a notice to warn people of the danger, and put it up where everyone can see it."

He warned about this on several occasions, not ceasing until in 1970 they acquired a high-security cutter with a photo-electric sensor. "What a weight you've taken off my shoulders!" he said. "Thank God, because the hand of a daughter of mine is worth more than the best machine in the world."[7] He was also constantly solicitous that the people who worked with the linotype machines should drink plenty of milk "to neutralize the effects of the lead vapors you breathe in there."[8]

---

6. Verbal account to the author by Josefina Ranera.
7. Testimony of Helena Serrano (AGP, HRF T-04641).
8. Ibid.

One day Palmira Laguens, Annamaria Notari, Jutta Geiger, and other students of the Roman College were decorating the walls with borders in a new area of Villa Tevere called Il Ridotto. Monsignor Escrivá went to encourage them in their work. On leaving, he called two of them aside; he looked serious, rather sad. "My daughters," he said, "sometimes you women are very hard. Don't you have eyes in your heads? You need to have hearts. This sister of yours, Annamaria, is obviously losing weight, she looks like a skeleton, she's very pale, and she has dark circles under her eyes. Is she ill? Has she lost her appetite? What's the matter with her? Tell Chus,[9] or whichever doctor is at home now, to see her immediately and say whether she needs a tonic or she should start having a mid-morning snack. Do whatever is necessary to make this daughter of mine fit and healthy again!"[10]

"What was the matter with Dora?"

Dora del Hoyo was a domestic worker who had been in Opus Dei since the 1940s. She had successfully done all kinds of work, hard and delicate, and was an expert in linens, ironing, and dry cleaning. When a laundry needed to be installed for a large house, be it Villa Sacchetti or Albarossa, Monsignor Escrivá saw to it that her opinion took precedence over the opinions of the architects and engineers. One evening in December 1973, Monsignor Escrivá had guests for dinner and Dora waited at table. Next morning he asked Mercedes Morado, "What was the matter with Dora last night?"

"Dora? Nothing, Father. I don't think anything's the matter with her."

"Look, don't just think: find out and tell me, please. Last night she looked awful. Something was wrong with her. Better not ask her directly, so she doesn't realize I'm worried."

Dora had a toothache. Monsignor Escrivá noticed this in the face of the woman even though he seemed attentive only to his guests.[11]

---

9. Maria Pilar De Meer, known as "Chus."
10. Verbal accounts by Palmira Laguens and Marlies Kücking.
11. Testimony of Mercedes Morado (AGP, HRF T-07902).

Stealing a piece of heaven

He could put himself in other people's shoes. Encarnita Ortega suffered from severe migraine, and Monsignor suffered as if he had migraine himself. On his insistence, Encarnita consulted specialists. After repeated visits to doctors and different methods of treatment with no success, he said finally, "We'll just have to put up with them, and offer them up, my daughter. I think we've done all we could do—all your mother would have done."[12]

He often said, "In Opus Dei the sick are a treasure, for whom we don't begrudge any effort." If necessary, "I'd be capable of stealing a bit of heaven for a child of mind who is suffering, and I'm sure our Lord would not be cross with me!"[13]

In the 1930s, when Josemaría Escrivá put together the points of *The Way*, he wrote the words "Children" and "the Sick" with capital initial letters. He explained, "The reason is that in little Children and in the Sick, a soul in love sees Him."[14]

Once, shortly before Christmas, José Luis Illanes, a talented and lively student from Andalusia, was in bed with a high temperature. Upset that José Luis could not share in the celebrations everyone was enjoying, he asked Marlies and Mercedes to get the catering staff to prepare "a little Christmas tree like the ones we've got in the house, but just a small one, covered with decorations and lots of chocolate figures. The fact is that one of my sons is ill. . . . I've got a tiny figure of Baby Jesus to take to his room. It breaks my heart to think that he has to spend these special family days in bed with a temperature."[15]

In October 1959, Mercedes Morado was told by her doctor that she needed an operation on her gall bladder. When Monsignor Escrivá heard this, he asked her to come to the dining room of Villa Vecchia with Encarnita. Monsignor Escrivá often met his daughters there for personal messages or short conversations.

---

12. Testimony of Encarnación Ortega (AGP, HRF T-05074).
13. Ibid.
14. Cf. *The Way*, no. 419.
15. Testimonies of Mercedes Morado (AGP, HRF T-07902), Marlies Kücking, and Msgr. José Luis Illanes (AGP, HRF T-03390).

"Mercedes," he began, "I don't know what you think. Of course we'll do whatever you say, but I'm going to tell you what I think. What would you say if instead of having the operation here, in a hospital in Rome, you were to go to Madrid to get a second opinion and then, if they say the same, have the operation there?"

"But Father, why?" exclaimed Mercedes. "It would be tremendously expensive—not only the journey, but also more doctors!"

"Well, there are two main reasons. First of all because you don't yet speak Italian properly, and a patient needs to explain to the doctor exactly what the matter is, where it hurts and all the symptoms, as well as understanding what the doctor says. And secondly, your parents live in Segovia, and they'll want to be near you, naturally, during the days following the operation. If you're in Madrid it will be a lot easier for them than if you have the operation here."[16]

At that time the financial situation in Villa Tevere was not very strong. But not only did she have the operation in Spain, she stayed there for months while convalescing.

For Monsignor Escrivá, this generosity was perfectly compatible with avoiding waste like leaving taps dripping or lights on in empty rooms, buying useless "bargains," making lengthy but pointless telephone calls, and so on.

During a meeting one day in the sitting room of La Montagnola in Villa Sacchetti, the phone rang. Someone answered it and, after a couple of brief phrases, hung up. Monsignor Escrivá asked who it was.

"It was from the women's center of the Work in Milan," she replied. "I told them to call back later because we were in a meeting."

"No, my daughter," Monsignor Escrivá told her, "that wasn't right. You can't ignore a long distance call from another city. That's not poverty, it's irresponsible, because they weren't telephoning you for a chat but to tell you something."[17]

---

16. Testimony of Mercedes Morado (AGP, HRF T-07902).
17. Testimony of Marlies Kücking.

Julia herself would never ask for anything

Julia Bustillo had come to Rome with the first group of women when the men were still living in the rented flat of Città Leonina. She was a pleasant, rather forthright woman, a Basque from Baracaldo, who got to know the Work in the 1940s as a cook in the first center of Opus Dei in Bilbao. She was now an elderly lady with a bun at the nape of her neck and never a hair out of place. For everybody in the Work, Julia was a real character, and not just part of the family but part of the very house.

One night in September 1965, Julia did not feel well and had to go to the bathroom. She did not turn the light on so as not to waken anyone. She felt her way along the corridor, but when she reached the stairs she missed a step and fell downstairs, hitting her head and breaking both wrists. A doctor was called, and by dawn she was in the hospital. Monsignor Escrivá was told when it was all over. Extremely concerned, he called a meeting of all the directors of the central advisory and, without mincing words, complained as a father. How could they not have realized that Julia herself would never ask for anything? A woman of nearly seventy should have all she needs in her room and not have to be walking around corridors and staircases at night. Then he asked, "When you called the doctor, did you call the priest too?"

"Well, no, we didn't. We didn't think."

"My daughters, you have to love each other more, you have to love each other better! You worried about her body. Fine. But you didn't worry about her soul."[18]

When the first Japanese women of Opus Dei came to live in Rome, Monsignor Escrivá insisted that as "women are like fragile porcelain there," they should be treated with exquisite delicacy and helped "to adapt to the climate, food, language, and Western customs." Thus: "As they are used to walking on carpets, for the first few days let them use slippers around the house until they get used to our hard floors."[19]

---

18. Testimonies of Begoña Alvarez (AGP, HRF T-04861) and Carmen Sanchez (AGP, HRF T-05132). Cf. *Articles of the Postulator*, 581.
19. Testimony of Carmen Ramos.

Another time he noticed that a European daughter of his who had lived in Africa for several years had prematurely aged skin. He said, "I don't know much about these creams and things, but I'm sure there must be some kind of face cream that will revitalize her skin. Buy her some jars to take back to Nigeria with her."[20]

Bertita was a girl from Ecuador who had just arrived in Rome and was living in Villa Sacchetti, helping with the housework. Monsignor Escrivá knew she had had a deprived childhood, with much hardship and suffering. Now that she was living in a center of the Work, he wanted her to find all the love and joy she had lacked. Whenever a pretty package arrived, he would keep the colored ribbons "for my little daughter from Ecuador." If they received a present of chocolates, he asked the administration to ensure "that Bertita gets one of the biggest ones," even by "cheating" a little if necessary.

One morning Begoña Alvarez answered the house telephone and was surprised to hear Monsignor Escrivá asking about something quite unexpected. "Do you know if Bertita has any woolen vests?"

"Woolen vests? I don't know, Father, I've no idea!"

"Well, find out, please, and tell me."

Begoña lived in La Montagnola with the other directors of the advisory. She asked the person who would know, Blanca Fontan. In point of fact, Bertita did not have woolen vests.

"I thought as much," said Monsignor Escrivá when she reported this. "It's beginning to get cold in Rome, and this daughter of mine must feel it more than anyone else. Will you make sure that she gets herself a couple of woolen vests before the day is out? Nice soft wool that won't scratch."[21]

In the summer of 1955, Encarnita Ortega was away from Rome. Monsignor Escrivá spoke to Helena Serrano and Tere Zumalde. "What do you think of maybe giving Encarnita a surprise by painting and decorating her office while she's away? It's so dark and shabby! Give it a bit of color, brighten it up, hang a few pictures and some other pleasant little surprise. My daughters, this isn't a whim of the Father, it's a small act of justice. When you joined the Work,

---

20. Ibid.
21. Testimony of Begoña Alvarez (AGP, HRF T-04861).

you found almost everything in place, but your older sisters, poor women, have been through all kinds of privations: they have lacked clothes, furniture, and basic comforts; they've suffered hunger and cold; they worked like pack donkeys to get the Work going. Isn't it only fair that they should find something nice now? Will you do it? Of course you will, putting your hearts and souls into it."[22]

That same year he traveled a few times to Germany, where the people of the Work were "lifting the cross from the ground," as they called beginning the apostolate in a new country. On the evening of August 22, Monsignor Escrivá went to Eigelstein, a residence for women students in Cologne, with Don Alvaro and another priest. They were unexpected, and could see the precariousness of the situation and enormous economic difficulties his daughters were having.

Monsignor Escrivá had words of affection and encouragement for each of them: Käthe Retz, Carmen Mouriz, Marlies Kücking, Tasia Alcalde, Pelancho Gaona, and Emilia Llamas. He asked Marlies about her friends, he spoke to Emilia in Italian so she did not forget it, and she told him how she managed to cope in German when they went shopping. He asked Käthe how her parents were, and encouraged Carmen and Pelancho to eat and sleep more, because "you don't look too well, and you must take care of your body, which is the container of the soul." He talked about Burgos, Tasia's hometown. After the conversation, which lasted some time, he took a tour of the residence. At one point he asked, "Where do you wash the sheets and the clothes, yours and the residents'? Don't you have a washing machine?"

There was embarrassed silence. This was something they would have preferred him not to notice. But he insisted on knowing how and where they did the washing, so Tasia explained, "There's a machine provided for the use of everyone in this block."

Monsignor Escrivá made no comment. He went into the oratory again. The walls had been neatly covered with fabric, but not even this embellishment could hide the dire poverty. He said to Don Alvaro, "Alvaro, will you please write to Rome and ask them to paint a nice triptych for the oratory of these daughters of mine."

---

22. Testimony of Helena Serrano (AGP, HRF T-04641).

Before leaving, he gave them a couple of boxes of Swiss choco-lates. "I bet you'd forgotten that such things as chocolates exist!" he said.

At a time when they were counting every lira in Rome, the stu-dents of the Roman College used to walk to their lectures because there was no money for bus fares; meat, wine, and coffee were luxury items, served only on the most solemn feast days. But Monsignor Escrivá was alive to "the small, prosaic needs of his children." The day after his visit, two men from an appliance store arrived at the Eigelstein residence bringing a washing machine, a small spin dryer, and a trolley for transporting the clothes. Don Alvaro had bought these on behalf of Monsignor Escrivá.[23]

A song in the laundry

Occasionally, on special days they showed a film in the main hall of Villa Tevere and Monsignor Escrivá watched it with the students of the Roman College. At other times, he watched films with his daughters. If it was a thriller or a mystery, he used to tease them by giving them false clues or threatening to tell them the ending. Now and again he used the loudspeaker for entertainment. One afternoon in 1954, he used it to call Julia and Rosalia, who were working in the laundry.

"Can you hear me? I have Madrid on the line. If you listen hard you can hear the conversation too."

But what came over the loudspeaker was a song by the singer Agustin Lara. "When you come to Madrid, my darling, I will make you the Empress of Lavapies, / I will carpet the Gran Via with car-nations, / and give you fine sherry to bathe in . . ." They heard Monsignor Escrivá laughing. There was no telephone call at all. "We got this record as a present, and I thought you'd like to hear it!"[24]

"We've eaten three pianos"

During the 1950s, when the one musical instrument in many people's homes was still the old gramophone, Monsignor Escrivá wanted a

---

23. Testimony of Marlies Kücking.
24. Testimony of Helena Serrano (AGP, HRF T-04641).

piano for Villa Tevere so the men in the Roman College could enjoy themselves. Three times, friends gave them the money to buy one, but more urgent needs claimed the money first. Monsignor Escrivá used to say comically, "We've eaten three pianos!" One day the piano finally arrived. He brought his sons together in the sitting room and announced the news. A loud cheer went up. When they calmed down he said, "My sons, I can see you are delighted. I am too. But we were thinking—ahem—that maybe we should give the piano to . . . your sisters in the administration. What do you. . . ?" He did not get to finish the question, as the cheers rose even more loudly.

Later, telling the women in Villa Sacchetti about it, he said, "We had no piano. Then suddenly we got the money for a piano but it turned out we needed it to pay for food . . . and that happened again and again. This is our blessed poverty! In the end we actually got a piano, and my sons have given it up, with enormous joy, without even having seen it. This is true affection in this family of ours!"[25] This was what he had told the American Joan McIntosh— "We are a Christian family and we really love each other!"

From the start, Monsignor Escrivá taught the members of his supernatural family to love God with the same heart with which they loved their parents, and to love their parents with the same heart with which they loved God. He called "Honor your father and mother" "the sweetest commandment" in Opus Dei.

One day in 1964 he called Begoña Mugica and Helena Serrano to the dining room in Villa Vecchia, though their respective jobs had nothing to do with each other.

Monsignor Escrivá showed them an old Castilian oil lamp. "If you get together, there's a job here for both of you," he said. "Begoña, try to clean this metal without destroying the patina on it; and you, Helena, see if you can find a way of changing the silk lining on the lampshades, because it's worn out. An antique is one thing; dirt is quite another!"

That seemed all he wanted. But then he added, "Do you know that you are both going to Spain to do your annual course? Other people will be doing the same in due course, but you two are going to be the first."

---

25. Testimony of Begoña Alvarez (AGP, HRF T-04861).

For people in Opus Dei the "annual course" was a break from ordinary work, a time spent together for three weeks or more, relaxing while studying, or studying while relaxing. In those years of economic hardship, they always did their annual courses near home, to avoid spending money on traveling. Begoña's and Helena's surprise showed in their faces. Monsignor Escrivá made the gesture of sealing his lips. "And now, mum's the word. You don't know a thing."

They realized that exactly four years earlier, in 1960, their fathers had died in Spain, and neither had been able to be with their families then.[26]

Each case was different. That same year, 1960, Mary Rivero's father fell ill: he was an elderly man and was going through a bad time economically. When Monsignor Escrivá heard the circumstances of the case, he weighed what it would mean if Mary were to leave Rome and give up her post as central procurator. "My daughter, you know very well how difficult it is for me—and how it hurts me—to have to do without you here. It would be untrue to say that whoever takes your place will do the work as well as you. But you have to go to Bilbao and take care of your father: that's only fair. We'll be supporting you from here, and I'm sure you'll do it very well! And if you put supernatural outlook and a lot of love into it, you'll be helping us so that the work here won't be weakened by your absence."[27]

He often encouraged his children to write their parents to tell them what they were doing, send them a photograph, and keep them up to date on the Work.

"Count on your parents," he told them. "They have a right to feel that you love them. I love them very much, and I pray for them every day. Bring them closer to God. A good way of doing that is to bring them closer to the Work. How could anything we do be pleasing to God if we neglected the souls of those who have loved us most on earth? You owe them your life, the seed of the faith and an upbringing which has made your vocation possible. Love them and count on them."[28]

---

26. Testimony of Helena Serrano (AGP, HRF T-04641).
27. Testimony of Encarnación Ortega (AGP, HRF T-05074).
28. Testimony of Marlies Kücking.

192 The Man of Villa Tevere

One day, looking at a small picture of St. Raphael in Villa Vecchia, he said to one of his Spanish daughters, "I really love this little picture. Do you know why? Well, because it's the Archangel St. Raphael, it comes from Cordoba, and your mother sent it to us!"[29]

"Our liabilities, which are blessed"

Carlos Cardona's father was very ill, and Carlos, who lived in Villa Tevere, had gone to Gerona in Spain. He wrote to Monsignor Escrivá telling him of his father's death, and in the letter said his parents' house had deteriorated a lot due to dampness and was not very comfortable; the tiny pension his mother was going to receive as a widow would not be enough for her to move. When he got back to Rome, Monsignor Escrivá welcomed him and almost immediately began to speak about his domestic problem. "Carlitos, don't you worry about your mother's house. We'll help her to move as soon as possible."

From then until her death years later Mrs. Cardona received a monthly check to help her manage.[30] Needy or sick parents of some people of the Work, whom Monsignor Escrivá called "our liabilities, which are blessed,"[31] were always looked after.

Monsignor Escrivá said, "When your parents need anything which is not opposed to your vocation, we rush to give it to them, because they are a very beloved part of Opus Dei. . . . I have always impressed upon you that you should love your parents very much and I have stipulated that you should be with them when they are dying. You need to know how to bring them to the warmth of the Work, which is to bring them to God. And whenever necessary the Work will take care of them spiritually and materially too."[32]

Rosalia Lopez, a domestic worker, was one of the women closest to Monsignor Escrivá and served him at table every day at lunch and dinner. She had arrived in Rome in the early days. In 1964 she was going to Spain to spend a few days with her parents, who were

---

29. Testimony of Helena Serrano (AGP, HRF T-04641).
30. Testimony of Fr. Carlos Cardona (AGP, HRF T-06138).
31. Testimony of Msgr. César Ortiz-Echagüe (AGP, HRF T-04694).
32. AGP, HRF 20750, p. 294 and AGP, HRF 20158, p. 402.

shepherds, simple, forthright people in the province of Burgos. A few days before she left, Monsignor Escrivá said to Begoña Alvarez, "You need to prepare Rosalia's trip a little. Apart from her parents' joy at having her visit them, I would like her to take something which they would like and which would be useful at the same time. I thought maybe you could buy a warm jacket for her mother and a shirt for her father. I'm sure they'd enjoy some Italian pasta and an Italian *panettone*. Wrap each gift beautifully, with great care."[33]

Another time it was Martina, an Italian, who was going to spend some days with her family in a little village in Umbria. Her mother was about to give birth to her ninth child, and Monsignor Escrivá wanted Martina to give the family a helping hand. He thought at once of sending a little present: "Some sweets that her little brothers and sisters will enjoy, and maybe a box of biscuits, but not Italian ones—find some foreign ones so it's a novelty for the children."[34]

Small things, but things that showed his love and care.

One day Marichu Arellano, who lived in Villa Sacchetti, got a letter from her family saying that her father was not well. He had not yet been diagnosed, but they feared the worst. Mercedes Morado, director of the central advisory, waited a couple of days before telling Monsignor Escrivá, because he had known this family for years and was very fond of them. When she told him, he asked, "Does Marichu know yet?"

"Yes, Father. She's known for the last two days."

"Two days? And you're only telling me today? Mercedes, you were wrong not to tell me immediately, because something like this, which affects a daughter of mine, affects me too. And all this time she's been suffering, I could have given her a little bit of consolation. What's more, we've lost two days when we could have been praying for them all."[35]

But Monsignor Escrivá did not confuse loving parents with emotional dependency. To the younger people in the Work he said, "It grieves me to say this, but so often it's the family or friends or relatives who thoughtlessly oppose a vocation, because they don't

33. Testimony of Begoña Alvarez (AGP, HRF T-04861).
34. Testimony of Marlies Kücking.
35. Testimony of Mercedes Morado (AGP, HRF T-07902).

understand, or they don't want to understand, or they don't want to receive light from God! They end up opposing all the noble things of a life dedicated to God. They even dare to test the vocation of their child, or of a sister, brother, friend or relative, and end up doing the work, the dirty work, of a procurer. And then they claim to be a Christian family. What a shame!"[36]

Some verses from Cervantes

During his journeys to South America to speak of the teachings of the Church, a young man in the Work spoke to him of the difficulties his mother had raised, arguing that he should first "try other things, see more of life, taste human love so as to be sure, and then make his choice." Monsignor Escrivá answered unhesitatingly. "Some verses by Cervantes come to mind, 'Woman is made of glass, but better not try to see if she will break or not, because everything is possible.' So better not try to see if you will break. Tell her to leave you in peace! Your mom is mistaken here. She ought not to want you to carry out experiments which would be an offense against God. If she doesn't leave you alone, she will lose her own peace of mind, confuse her conscience and put her eternal life in jeopardy. . . . My son, love your mother a lot. Contradict her firmly, but kindly and good-humoredly, because in this she's wrong, poor woman."[37]

On November 2, 1973 he had a visit from parents of a woman who lived in La Montagnola, a member of the central advisory. As soon as they exchanged greetings, the mother said, "Well, I was very curious to meet the person who was more powerful than I was—because I fought hard against my daughter's vocation, but it was no use! You were the stronger, and she and you got your own way."

"I'm sorry to contradict you," Monsignor Escrivá said, "but it is our Lord who was the stronger, not me. If it were for my sake that your daughter were here, she could go whenever, right now if she wanted. Personally, I don't need her at all. Not at all! And I didn't call her: God called her. That is what a vocation is: a grace from

36. AGP, HRF 20147, p. 42.
37. AGP, HRF 20770, p. 664.

God, a divine calling. And it isn't a sacrifice for parents if God calls their children. Nor is it a sacrifice for your children to follow our Lord. On the contrary, it's a huge honor, a great glory, a sign of very special love which God has shown you at a particular moment, but which was in his mind from all eternity. I'd even dare to say this: it's your own 'fault,' because you brought up your daughter in a Christian way. And so our Lord found the spadework done. Your daughter knows she has to be very grateful to you; she's heard me say so hundreds of times, among other reasons because she owes ninety percent of her vocation to you."

Next day, after a work session with the central advisory, Monsignor Escrivá said to the daughter in question, "Look here, I want you to write a letter to your mother on my behalf and ask her to forgive me for saying things so bluntly. Explain to her that I am from Aragon, so I like to speak clearly, face to face, without beating about the bush."[38]

"But Father," she replied, "they were delighted! I could see my mother was pleased, and even *proud.* And my father was so moved when he left you that he asked to speak to a priest. And it's been many, many years since he last received the sacraments."[39]

Appointments are burdens

Opus Dei does not remove anyone from his or her proper place. Members do their jobs according to their capacity, studies, availability, age, health, education, character, and suitability. There are no jobs of greater or less status. Directors are not appointed for life: this is a job they do for a time, then leave to do other things. No one is congratulated on being appointed director, nor does anyone complain when he or she ceases to be one. There will never be such a thing as an "owner-director." Monsignor Escrivá said: "The owner-director does not exist. I have killed him off." It goes without saying there are no grades, levels, social classes, or privileged groups in Opus Dei.

---

38. Testimony of Marlies Kücking. Cf. *The Forge*, no. 17 and 18. AGP, HRF 20156, p. 136.
39. Testimony of Marlies Kücking.

Lawyers are up-to-date in law, doctors study new diagnostic techniques, soldiers perfect their martial skills, cooks their skill in cooking, and business people try to balance their right to legitimate profits with service to society. When some priests of the Work were ordained bishops, Monsignor Escrivá told them, "When you get home, put all your 'jewelry' away in a drawer, because in our family no one is greater than anyone else. It is the same if someone is appointed a governor or a minister in his country: in the Work he continues to be loved as before, but he does not acquire any pre-eminence, nor does he have any special privilege. At home all these honors have no importance whatsoever. Is that quite clear?"[40]

In October 1961 Encarnita Ortega left Rome after holding appointments in the government of the Work for almost twenty years. She returned to Spain, where she worked in other fields of apostolate, as well as working professionally in women's fashion. Monsignor Escrivá's words on parting were, "Your mission, the mission of someone who has been in the Work for a long time, is not to command or impose your opinion, but to keep quiet and let your good example do the shouting."[41]

He impressed on his spiritual children the importance of "humility and service" to prevent directors from falling into the trap of arrogance or complacency. He himself refused to let people help him on with the cardigan he wore at home over his cassock, or carry his suitcase when he was traveling. On going to bed at night, he insisted on carrying his own camomile tea. "I'll carry it myself! What are my hands for?" Often he repeated Christ's words, "I have not come to be served but to serve."[42]

"And the last one for you, boss"

One Sunday morning he called Mercedes Morado and two students from the Roman College who were working on the decoration of Villa Tevere. He wanted to discuss some aspects of their work. On the dining room table in Villa Vecchia was a box of *yemas de San*

---

40. Testimony of Fr. Carlos Cardona (AGP, HRF T-06138).
41. Testimony of Encarnación Ortega (AGP, HRF T-05074).
42. Cf. Matt. 20:28.

Leandro, a sweet from Seville. After making suggestions about ornamental details, he opened the box and shared some sweets. He offered them to Mercedes Morado last, saying, "And the last one for you, boss, because those of us who give the orders should always be last."[43]

He made no distinctions between people or social classes. What made a job important for him was "the love of God with which it is done." On one occasion he said, "If you asked me which I preferred, a daughter who was a professor at the Sorbonne or another who was washing dishes in the latest hospital you've started up out there, I really don't know the answer! It would depend on how they each carried out their work, on the love of God they put into what they were doing. I'd very often envy the one who was washing dishes."[44]

He also said, "All souls are the same, because they are all made in the image and likeness of God. A university vice-chancellor, an ambassador, or a peasant all have the same rank before God. Except that the souls of simple people are often more beautiful, because you learn good manners by being in contact with well-mannered people. So it is that illiterate souls who speak and listen to God the Father, God the Son, and God the Holy Spirit, Our Lady, the Holy Angels, and St. Joseph, can become very delicate souls, really delightful ones. They possess divine knowledge which is the essence of wisdom, and know so many things that the learned of this earth do not know."[45]

Some women in the Work have housework as their profession. It is their responsibility that centers of Opus Dei be cozy, clean, cheerful family homes. Monsignor Escrivá sometimes called them "my little daughters." He felt like "those mothers who are lost in admiration of the child they never expected to have." In 1964 he told some domestic employees in the Work, "You have a special, outstanding place in the heart of this poor founder. I seldom use the word 'founder,' but I am doing so now deliberately. You deserve that special place, because you occupy it in the heart of God."[46]

---

43. Testimony of Mercedes Morado (AGP, HRF T-07902).
44. Testimony of Marlies Kücking.
45. Ibid.
46. Testimonies of Mercedes Morado (AGP, HRF T-07902) and of Marlies Kücking.

Marlies Kücking and Mercedes Morado made a written note of his words. "Though not fully understanding the depth of what I was hearing," Mercedes said, "I clearly realized it was something important in the life of the Work from the Father's attitude and the emphasis he employed in speaking. It seemed to me the Father had just unveiled certain sentiments of his heart."

He paid special attention to his favorite daughters. If the people in Villa Tevere were given some sweets and there were not enough to go around, he sent them to Villa Sacchetti "for the staff." The first rooms to be air conditioned were the kitchen, the server, and the laundry. These rooms also had the most modern equipment. Monsignor Escrivá fostered the setting up of catering schools and colleges in many countries to provide people in the catering profession with scientific and technical knowledge of the highest standard. He also made sure these schools and colleges promoted the image of caterers by giving them education that took in all aspects of the person: spiritual, professional, cultural, aesthetic, social, apostolic, and physical. He also encouraged them to stand up for their rights as citizens.

One day in 1962 in La Montagnola they were installing furniture and putting the finishing touches to the decoration. They wanted Monsignor Escrivá's opinion on a particular ornament to be placed over the door. They needed a small ladder, and two domestic employees brought one in. Monsignor Escrivá thanked them. When they had left, his expression and tone of voice changed, and he said to the women, "Listen carefully. In the Work all of you are servants of each other. You must never let yourselves be served! You, as directors, ought to be the first in coming forward to do the most difficult, demanding, and unpleasant tasks. That's where you have to lead!"[47]

"Today it's my turn to serve"

On March 19, 1959, feast of St. Joseph, the patron of Opus Dei, Monsignor Escrivá came to the servery when the dishes were ready for lunch. Picking one up, he took it into the dining room. Seeing

47. Testimonies of Begoña Alvarez (AGP, HRF T-04861), Marlies Kücking, Helena Serrano (AGP, HRF T-04641), and Mercedes Morado (AGP, HRF T-07902). AGP, HRF 21156, p. 20.

Julia Bustillo, the eldest person there, he went to her and held the dish for her to help herself.

"In the house at Nazareth everyone served each other," he said. "Today it's my turn to serve!"[48]

Some days later he said to the directors in La Montagnola, "In the Work we don't have 'servants.' Different people do different jobs. We each do our own job and all of us serve God, who is our only Lord. It would be a good idea if sometimes (and it doesn't need to be a special day or a feast day, but an ordinary day) you serve at table for those who normally serve you because it's their job."[49]

During her long stay in Rome, Encarnita Ortega visited Cardinal Tedeschini on several occasions and heard him pay tribute to Opus Dei and its founder. He said that of all the people he knew, Monsignor Escrivá was the most attentive to God's plans and carried them out the soonest. "He is the holiest man I know," said the cardinal, "maybe the only saint I know." Then he made another comment: "The biggest miracle achieved by the Father in this Work entrusted to him by God is the vocation of those women who work in the administrations and feel so proud of serving all their lives that they wouldn't change places with a princess."[50] In June 1967, Monsignor Escrivá reminded those who had completed their doctorates at the Roman College of the Holy Cross and were leaving, "We don't create supermen here. You're not going out there to give orders, still less to interfere! You're going to serve. You're going to be the last of all, putting your hearts on the floor as soft carpets for the others to walk on."[51]

The last bedspread

Although people of the Work began to live in Villa Tevere in 1949, they had to share their daily lives with the noise and confusion of builders, plumbers, electricians, and painters for more than ten years. And it was not until 1964 that some details such as bedspreads

48. Testimony of Helena Serrano (AGP, HRF T-04641).
49. Testimony of Mercedes Morado (AGP, HRF T-07902) and Marlies Kücking.
50. Testimony of Encarnación Ortega (AGP, HRF T-05074).
51. Testimony of Msgr. César Ortiz-Echagüe (AGP, HRF T-04694).

were in place. Until then, the beds, of which there were more than 200, were simply covered with blankets. Monsignor Escrivá's blanket was very worn, with a faded green and brown pattern.

In 1956 they received an unexpected donation, and the women thought of using it to buy material for making bedspreads, but in the end the money had to be used for other, more pressing needs. Some years later they proposed to Monsignor Escrivá that they should get the material for bedspreads little by little. Admittedly, they argued, they were nonessential, but they would complete the bedrooms and give them a cozier, more homelike look. Monsignor Escrivá consented but made them reverse the order they had suggested; they should begin with the bedspreads of his daughters on the domestic staff, followed by those of the teachers and students of the Roman College. Next it would be the turn of the members of the general council. And last of all: "Make mine when everyone else has theirs. I want to be the last one."

One Sunday in March 1964 the house telephone rang in Mercedes Morado's office. It was Monsignor Escrivá. "Thank you, my daughter, and God bless you!" he greeted her. "What a surprise I had the other day when I came into my room! I thought I'd gone into the wrong room by mistake. Then I said to myself, 'Long live luxury and its maker! Josemaría, you're getting rich!' Mercedes, my child, when time has gone by and I'm no longer in this world, you will tell your sisters this little story. Why did the Father want to be the last to have a bedspread? For two reasons. First of all, out of the great love I have for my daughters: I wanted you to be first. And secondly, out of poverty. Not having a bedspread simply doesn't matter! The Work is thirty-six years old. And now, for the first time in thirty-six years, I have a bedspread."[52]

To be of use, you must serve

On June 25, 1975, the day before he died, he spoke to Rolf Thomas about service. He referred to passages in the Gospels where Jesus tells his disciples, "he who is first shall be last," "do not seek the first

---

52. Testimony of Mercedes Morado (AGP, HRF T-07902). Verbal account of Begoña Alvarez.

places at table," "I am in the midst of you as one who serves, because I have not come to be served, but to serve." He contrasted this strongly with "the climate of pride which is spread all over nowadays, and which makes people reject anything they consider demeaning." "As a result of your efforts to give life back its Christian meaning," he said, "many people will wonder, with great joy, about whether they can give themselves to a life of service: to serve everyone, for the love of God. And they will see it as what in fact it is: a great privilege! From all parts of the globe the finest souls will come to the Work, the most spiritual and cultured ones, those who wish above all to identify themselves with Jesus Christ, and they'll ask for admission to Opus Dei, with a resolute vocation to serve."[53]

Soon afterward, young women graduates from universities and technical colleges in several countries asked to be admitted to Opus Dei, expressing a preference to dedicate themselves to housekeeping tasks. It was a direct challenge to an individualistic, stony-hearted civilization where nurses, teachers, and housewives were considered anachronisms.

Monsignor Escrivá transmitted a code of conduct: *para servir, servir*—"to be of use, you must serve." To be of service, one had to make oneself available with "the healthy psychological attitude of always thinking about others." And this was service rendered to God himself.

While Monsignor Escrivá regularly recited Psalm 2, which says "serve the Lord with fear" (*servite Domino in timore*), after a time he also began to say to his children a verse from Psalm 99, "serve the Lord with gladness" (*servite Domino in laetitia*). By directing to the Lord what we do for our fellow men, the act of service is done with the gladness of freedom.

Monsignor Escrivá confronts a head of government

In June 1974, Monsignor Escrivá had a get-together with several thousand people in the congress center of General San Martin

---

53. Testimony of Fr. Carlos Cardona (AGP, HRF T-06138). Verbal account of Msgr. Javier Echevarria.

in Buenos Aires, Argentina. A young man spoke up. "I'm in the Work. My mother, who is almost my whole family, because I don't have a father—"

Monsignor Escrivá interrupted. "What do you mean, you don't have a father!" He held up his hands and counted on his fingers. "One, in heaven; another, in heaven; and me: you've got three altogether!"

"Well," said the young man promptly, "as today is Father's Day: congratulations, Father! Anyway, my mother is very happy about my vocation. But sometimes she worries about what will become of me when I'm old. She says I won't have a family. She's here beside me, Father—here she is. I want you to explain to her that we do have a family and love each other a lot."

"Yes," agreed Monsignor Escrivá, "sit down. Once, many years ago, a man in Opus Dei in a certain country was not in agreement with the way the head of government acted, and had written some things in a newspaper which offended this person. And this very powerful person got angry and declared that the Opus Dei man had no family. So I, who do have a family, immediately asked for an audience, and they could not deny me one."

Monsignor Escrivá was referring to an episode that happened in Spain. Rafael Calvo had written an article attacking the Franco regime. The authorities reacted very harshly, and Calvo had to go into exile. Among other insults printed about him was one calling him "a person with no family." Monsignor Escrivá went to Spain immediately and requested an audience with Franco. In it he said Calvo did have a supernatural family, the Work, and Monsignor Escrivá considered himself his father.

Franco inquired, "What if he goes to jail?"

Monsignor Escrivá answered, "I will respect the decisions of the judiciary; but if he goes to jail, no one can stop me from providing my son with all the spiritual and material assistance he might need."

He repeated the same thing to Admiral Carrero Blanco, Franco's right-hand man, who admitted that the founder of Opus Dei was right.

Monsignor Escrivá went on, ". . . And I said to him, '*You* have no family, he has mine! *You* have no home, he has my home!' He said he was sorry."

Under the brush of portrait painter Luis Mosquera at Molinoviejo in September 1966.

The *J.J. Sister*, in which St. Josemaría traveled from Barcelona to Genoa in 1946. Photo taken in the port of Santa Cruz de Tenerife, Canary Islands. The ship was scrapped in 1974.

Above: Buildings at Villa Tevere, Rome, under construction in 1950.

Above right: Aunt Carmen with her boxer, Chato, during Christmas 1956.

Give-and-take with young men in a get-together in Buenos Aires, Argentina in 1974.

Meeting university students and professional women in Rome in the early 1970s.

Relaxing in 1964. In the left foreground, Bernard Villegas, from the Philippines.

With workers and farmers in Jaltepec, Mexico in 1970.

Meeting families at Montefalco, Mexico in 1970.

The best place to live and the best place to die

Monsignor Escrivá then addressed the mother of the boy who had spoken. "Now you know your son has a family and a home, and that he will die surrounded by his brothers, with immense affection. Happy to live and happy to die! Unafraid of life and unafraid of death! Let's see who can say that out there! Unafraid of life and unafraid of death! The best place to live and the best place to die: in Opus Dei!"

He paused, threw his head back slightly and closed his eyes. He took a deep breath and exclaimed with all his heart, "How very well off we are, my children!"[54]

"I would have willingly got down on my hands and knees"

In February 1950, Don Alvaro fell ill with acute appendicitis and liver problems. Doctor Faelli recommended an operation. Monsignor Escrivá tried to cheer him up by telling him cheerful stories. When he saw how bad the pain was, he began to improvise a funny dance. Don Alvaro and another man in the room started to laugh, which was exactly what Monsignor Escrivá wanted: "I had to do what I could to lessen his pain. From a spiritual point of view, although he was offering up everything with great supernatural vision, I thought our Lord would like him to forget about his pain, so I danced. I would have willingly got down on my hands and knees, whatever, moved by the wonderful reality that we are never really alone: God does not abandon us and neither do our brothers and sisters."[55]

One morning in December 1955, Monsignor Escrivá arrived home after praying beside the body of Ignacio Salord, a young student of the Roman College. He paused for a moment to talk with the girls on telephone duty, who saw that his eyes were red and swollen with crying. "He died as he lived," said Monsignor Escrivá. "He knew exactly what was happening, that he was dying. He wished to make a general confession of his whole life. I'd say he didn't need to. Anyway he did!"[56]

54. *Catechesis in America*, 1974, I, pp. 420–422.
55. Cf. *Articles of the Postulator*, 584 and testimony of Raffaele Tomassetti (AGP, HRF T-03359).
56. Testimony of Helena Serrano (AGP, HRF T-04641).

In October 1960 three young people in the Work were killed in a car crash. A few days later Monsignor Escrivá said to one of his sons, Gumersindo Sanchez, "I got the news late, because I was on my way to France. When I heard it, I could not control myself, and I cried like a child—because I'm a mangy donkey and sometimes I drag the cross reluctantly."[57]

In the early hours of December 11, 1961 Armando Serrano died. He had lived and worked close to Monsignor Escrivá for a long time; among other things, he had been the driver on long car journeys. Monsignor Escrivá was so upset he could not eat breakfast but had to leave the dining room in tears and go to the oratory. This was repeated two or three times, and on one of his hasty exits he met two of his daughters. He put his handkerchief in the pocket of his cassock, but could not hide his distress. "This son of mine is dead . . . Armando . . ." he said. "Go and tell the others so they can pray for him."[58]

An accident on the island of Guadeloupe

One morning in March 1968 Monsignor Escrivá had a meeting with the women directors of Opus Dei who had come to Rome from different countries for a special course. He entered the sitting room of La Montagnola at ten sharp. As soon as he sat down, he told them sad news: Vladimiro Vince, a Croatian priest of Opus Dei, had been killed in an air crash on the island of Guadeloupe. Vlado Vince had met the Work as a refugee exiled in Italy during the war. He had translated *The Way* into Croatian.

"I have been to the tabernacle to complain—lovingly, but I did complain—because I find it hard to understand how our Lord, having so few friends in this world, can take those who could serve him, when they are so badly needed! But then, as always, I end up accepting the will of God and saying: *Fiat, adimpleatur*—May the most just and most loveable will of God be done, be fulfilled, be praised and eternally exalted above all things. Amen. Amen."

---

57. Testimony of Gumersindo Sanchez Fernandez (AGP, HRF T-06199). Cf. *Articles of the Postulator*, 605.
58. Testimony of Helena Serrano (AGP, HRF T-04641).

His voice cracked and he swallowed. Standing up suddenly, he apologized: "I can't go on speaking to you . . . Forgive me, my daughters." And he left the room.

At the same time the next day he returned to the sitting room, looking quite different, even happy. He told them what he had just heard: two or three people of the Work, one of them a priest, had flown from Venezuela to Guadeloupe in an aircraft chartered by Air France for relatives and friends of those in the crash. Miguel Angel Madurga had also gone from Rome, sent by Monsignor Escrivá. The crash site was chaotic: bits of the aircraft, dead bodies, luggage strewn about, and the smell of death. The relatives had come to identify the dead, but one by one retreated to their plane, appalled at the scene. The people of Opus Dei kept searching determinedly until they found some personal belongings of Vladimiro. (Later they sent these to Croatia where his mother was still living, together with a photograph album.) While two continued the search, the priest prayed successive responsories for the dead and at a nearby chapel celebrated several Masses for the souls of those killed.

Monsignor Escrivá concluded his account in La Montagnola by saying, "Together with this tremendous sorrow, God has given me the consolation, the joy, of experiencing once again the fact that we are a family and love each other dearly: your brothers have done more for Wlado than husbands did for their wives, more than fathers for their sons. They have done what others, even actual relatives, did not have the courage to do. Always practice that blessed fraternity— heroically, if necessary."[59]

Sofia, Aunt Carmen

In May 1972 Mercedes Morado told Monsignor Escrivá that Sofia Varvaro, a young Italian, had been diagnosed with cancer. The doctors thought she had only a few months to live. Monsignor Escrivá said he wanted to go and see her immediately.

---

59. Testimonies of Begoña Alvarez (AGP, HRF T-04861) and Gloria Toranzo (AGP, HRF T-08033).

"Father, Sofia is living in Villino Prati, in Aunt Carmen's house," they told him. "In fact, she's in the same room Aunt Carmen was in when she died."

"Aunt Carmen" was Carmen Escrivá de Balaguer, Monsignor Escrivá's sister. She had united her whole life and heart to Opus Dei, though she had never actually belonged to the Work. She looked after the domestic administration of centers before there were any women in the Work and put all her affection at the service of Opus Dei. A foundation stone in the history of the Work, after her death on June 20, 1957 she was buried in Villa Tevere in the crypt.

Her little apartment was at 276 Via degli Scipioni. "You know, I said I never wanted to go back to that house again," Monsignor Escrivá said now, "and I've never been back since then. It holds so many memories! But a daughter is more than a sister. I can't let Sofia leave us without going to see her and saying some words of consolation."

A few days later he went to Villino Prati with Father Javier Echevarria. Teresa Acerbis and Itziar Zumalde were waiting for them. He started talking to Sofia before he had even entered her room. "Sofia, *mia figlia!*" When he got to the room, he gave her a holy picture of the Blessed Trinity; on the back he had written a short prayer in big, bold letters.

"Shall I read you what it says?" he asked. "Would you like to say it with me? 'My Lord and my God, into your hands I abandon everything, past, present, and future: big and little, great and small, temporal and eternal.'"

He encouraged her to be cheerful, simple as a child, and let herself be cared for, to take painkillers when she needed them, and to pray for her cure.

"Because there are still very few of you in Italy, and so much apostolate to be done," he explained. "It would be too easy to go to Paradise. There's still a lot of work to be done here! Although for us, the most important work is doing God's will in everything."

"Father," she confided, "when they first told me what I had, my reaction was fear. But not fear of suffering or death—fear because I'm a very ordinary person, worth very little, and I don't want to go to purgatory!"

"How about that! She doesn't want to go to purgatory! You shan't go, my daughter. Don't be afraid, because our Lord is with you. Besides, that's what everybody in Opus Dei is—ordinary! Our Lord has chosen us and he loves us precisely because we're ordinary people. And you have to pray to get better because, just as you are, we need you! You have to help us a lot. Now I feel stronger because I'm relying on you. You can rely on me, and don't be afraid! But if our Lord wants you up there, you'll have to help us even more from heaven."

Monsignor Escrivá followed the progress of Sofia's disease closely. He urged the people looking after her to do all they could for her, with loving care; that they should be "more than a mother or a sister" to her. He told them not to leave her alone, and to help her to say the prayers and fulfill the other norms of piety that everyone in Opus Dei does every day; and to give her painkillers "so this daughter of mine does not suffer unnecessarily."

He went to visit her again at a private hospital in Rome when she had gotten worse. Before going into her room, he said to Teresa and Itziar, "She mustn't realize how we are suffering for her. How long will the doctor let us stay so as not to tire her? Well, when the time is up, if I forget, tell me: I'll only stay as long as the doctor allows."

He went in with Father Javier Echevarria and sat beside the bed. He spoke softly and encouragingly to Sofia about spiritual matters. Because he knew the value of suffering, he asked her to offer up her pain and physical difficulties "for the Church, for priests, and for the Pope."

"Sofia," he asked her, "will you join me in the intentions of my Mass?"

"But, Father, I'm here in bed. I can't go to Mass any more."

"My daughter, now you are a constant Mass! And tomorrow, when I say Mass, I will place you on the paten."

Shortly after this, Sofia said she was getting tired. Monsignor Escrivá made the sign of the cross on her forehead and said good-bye.

On December 24, while chatting with a group of Italian women of the Work, he asked, "How is Sofia doing? Every day when I get to the offertory of the Mass, I place all my sons and daughters who are ill or troubled on the paten."

Sofia was dying. Toward the end, when her caregivers were praying the litany of the Rosary, at the invocation "Gate of heaven," *Ianua coeli,* she smiled and said "That's my one." She died on December 26. Next day, Monsignor Escrivá went to Villa delle Rose in Castelgandolfo as had been planned. As soon as he entered the sitting room he said, "As you know, my daughters, there's been a lot of coming and going recently. Your sisters are starting the Work in Nigeria, a few days ago I blessed another who should arrive in Australia today, and yesterday . . . this other daughter of mine left us to go to heaven."[60]

There was indeed a lot of coming and going. That same month, December 1972, Father José María Hernandez de Garnica, a civil engineer and one of the first three priests of Opus Dei, died in Barcelona. His nickname was Chiqui. Monsignor Escrivá had first met him in the 1930s when setting up the students' residence in Ferraz Street in Madrid. Seeing him come in "dressed like a dandy," Monsignor Escrivá gave him a hammer and nails, saying, "Come on, Chiqui, get up that ladder and help me put these nails in."

How much had happened since then! So many apostolic journeys, so much coming and going, helping to establish the Work in half of Europe! So many loving memories!

In Barcelona in October 1972, at a get-together in the Brafa gymnasium, he confessed to those present that although he was delighted to be there, he had to leave. "A sick person is expecting me," he said. "And I have no right to make a sick person wait—he is always Christ. . . . He needs his father and mother. And I am both father and mother to him."

After visiting Father José María, he said to his sons, "I have been with a brother of yours today. I'm having to make a tremendous effort not to cry, because I love you with all my heart. . . . I hadn't seen him for a few months. And now I think he looks like a corpse already. He has worked hard and with a lot of love. Maybe our Lord has already decided to give him the glory of heaven."[61]

---

60. Testimony of Mercedes Morado (AGP, HRF T-07902). Cf. AGP, HRF 21162, pp. 55 and 208–213.
61. AGP, HRF 20760, pp. 638 and 641.

When Monsignor Escrivá got back to Rome, he had in mind the aspiration *ut in gratiarum semper actione maneamus!* ("that we may always remain in the act of thanksgiving") from an old liturgical prayer. He wrote it in his diary as a "password" for the New Year, 1973, using an exclamation point to emphasize his gratitude, for as he said, echoing St. Paul, "Everything helps to secure the good of those who love God"—*omnia in bonum!*[62]

A box of crystallized fruit

In May 1975, after going to see the construction underway in Torreciudad, then almost completed, Monsignor Escrivá received a visit from the lord mayor and a councillor of Barbastro. After they left, Father Javier Echevarria and Father Florencio Sanchez Bella came in. They had sad news: Salvador Canals, nicknamed "Babo," another of the older people in the Work, had just died. It was he who had gone to Rome with Jose Orlandis to pave the way for setting up the Work there.

Monsignor Escrivá began to cry openly. He prayed a responsory for the dead, interrupted by sobbing. Then, weeping silently, he went to one of the armchairs near the big window overlooking the esplanade of Torreciudad. The others sat around him quietly, respecting his prayerful sorrow. He prayed and remembered. After a while, he said, "I love all of you just the same—all of you—but you have to realize that I've lived through so much with Babo . . . so many years! It's only natural his death should affect me more. It's a hard blow, even though I knew Babo was dying when I left Rome. I even left everything ready—didn't I, Alvaro?—so that his funeral could be celebrated in Tiburtino.

"I went to see him in hospital just a few days before coming here. I wanted to take him some sweets he liked, but I couldn't remember what they were. I asked one of my sons who works in Villa Tevere to find out from the people he'd been living with . . . they said it was crystallized fruit, and bought a small box of them. Afterwards I had a sudden thought, and I called the women in the administration

---

62. Rom. 8:28.

in Villa Sacchetti, and asked them to go to a sweet shop and get a much bigger box, with bigger fruit, and they brought one right away. Alvaro and I went to the hospital. You can't imagine how happy Babo looked to see us. He accepted the box, opened it, and offered us some. Alvaro and I took a small piece each. He looked at the fruits, and chose a really big fat pear. I was delighted! I thought: 'Goodness, what if I'd brought the little box!' Besides, like a mother, when I saw him eating it . . . I got hopeful. But when we left his room, the doctor dashed all our hopes; he said his heart was in a very bad state."

Monsignor Escrivá took out his handkerchief, took his glasses off and dried his eyes. Night had fallen. Everyone was silent. Looking from one solemn face to the next, he stopped at the architect, César Ortiz-Echagüe, and exclaimed, "My son, Opus Dei is the best place to live and the best place to die. I assure you that it's worthwhile!"[63]

---

63. Testimony of Msgr. César Ortiz-Echagüe (AGP, HRF T-04694).

13 ✣

Passion for Freedom

"Did you vote for Kennedy?"

Monsignor Escrivá's voice cut through the atmosphere of the get-together like a knife: "Fernando, that question is out of order!"

It was 1961. Fernando Valenciano had just asked an American, Dick Rieman, if he had voted for John F. Kennedy in the recent American election. Monsignor Escrivá continued, "It's of no interest to any of us here whether Dick voted, or who he voted for. And I would ask everyone in the Work never to bring up such topics of conversation."[1]

In 1958 Irene Rey, a Peruvian, was in a get-together in the Roman College of Our Lady and witnessed an exchange between a girl of the Work and Monsignor Escrivá.

"Father, there are elections in Sicily. I am going to go because I have to vote . . ."

"My daughter, I'm delighted that you're going. But I don't want to know who you're going to vote for. Don't tell me. You know very well you can vote for whomever you like, don't you? Tell me about something else."

People in Opus Dei never speak about politics. Monsignor Escrivá was very clear on this. "If Opus Dei had ever got involved in politics, even for a second, I would have left the Work at that

---

1. Testimony of Fernando Valenciano (AGP, HRF T-05362).

very moment. So don't ever give any credence to anything which tries to link the Work with politics, economics, or temporal issues of any sort. For on the one hand, our means and our aims are always exclusively supernatural, and on the other hand everybody in the Work respects the fact that every single one of us, man or woman, is completely free in secular affairs, and as a logical consequence is personally responsible for his or her actions. Therefore it is impossible for Opus Dei ever to take a hand in any projects other than directly spiritual and apostolic ones, which can have nothing to do with any country's politics."[2]

The radical option of Opus Dei for freedom allows each individual to exercise his or her personal preferences on a wide variety of matters: state in life, job, cultural, sporting, or aesthetic questions. Monsignor Escrivá summed up the inheritance he was leaving in two human characteristics: good humor and love for freedom.

During the 1950s and 1960s in Spain, the presence of some members of Opus Dei in the government, universities, banks, and the media caused some people to imagine a collective "take-over" strategy. There were references to "white masons" and pressure groups. These people did not grasp that personal holiness is individual, self-determined, responsible, and free, a project in which each person maps out his or her own destiny.

"The oddity of not being odd"

The Second Vatican Council had not yet proclaimed the "universal call to sanctity" so it is understandable that many Christians at that time still thought good lay people should be a sort of appendix or "long arm" of the clergy, reaching out to the world on the orders of the clergy; they did not realize that lay people should act in the world on their own initiative. This was the novelty of Opus Dei from the start, but there was also "the oddity of *not* being odd," which made some people regard members of the Work with suspicion.

---

2. AGP, HRF 21159.

"We could never be a pressure group"

One day in 1964 Monsignor Escrivá was chatting with a group of his daughters about these matters. "I never talk about politics. I respect all political opinions when they are not contrary to the Church, the faith, and the teachings of Jesus Christ. Moreover, I respect and obey the authorities of whichever country I am in. But I love freedom, because without freedom we could not serve God. Without freedom we would be wretched. Catholics must be taught to live as Catholics; not just to call themselves Catholics, but to be citizens who take personal responsibility for their free actions. Not long ago I wrote to a very important person—you can imagine it was whoever you choose, I don't mind—that God's children in Opus Dei live *in spite of being Catholics*."

He may have been referring to a long letter he had written from Paris on August 15 of the same year to Cardinal Angelo Dell'Acqua, the secretary of state of the Vatican, aware that it would get to Pope Paul VI's desk.[3]

He went on, "It isn't true that we go around like a flock of sheep. It simply isn't true! Nor are we a pressure group. People who say so are wrong. I have a great many children of all sorts, from all over the world, of every race, and speaking many different languages. I'm not boasting, since I have to practice collective humility. If I were to try to use coercion in a temporal matter, everyone would leave. They'd say, 'Who does he think he is!' We have to be totally free in everything."[4]

In some ecclesiastical and political circles people feared that Opus Dei was a power bloc or pressure group. In others, both ecclesiastical and political, people were trying to turn Opus Dei into precisely that: an organized infiltrator of 'moles' programmed to invade the structures of society. There were even those who imagined that thousands upon thousands of people of Opus Dei could be manipulated and sent into action at one stroke.

False ideas of the Work led some to suggest, "Why don't all the people in Opus Dei standardize their political aims, and become, if

3. *The Canonical Path of Opus Dei*, Appendix 1, 49, HRF, EF-640815T-2.
4. AGP, HRF 21131, p. 37.

not a party, at least an effective social power with a religiously ori-
ented vote?"

Monsignor Escrivá himself time and again said no. "In the Work
we never give directives on how people should exercise their rights
and duties as citizens. Each individual acts according to his or her
conscience. No one is told to go for one option or another. If there
is something to be said regarding public life in a particular country,
that's the domain of the Church hierarchy, the bishops, and not
ours. We defend our own personal freedom and everybody else's."[5]

He also said, "Even if everything people say were true ten times
over in the field of economics, we could still never be a pressure
group because of the real freedom we enjoy in Opus Dei. As soon as
anyone tried to impose their own opinion about a temporal matter,
the other people of the Work who think differently would have the
duty to rebel."[6]

To a group of students of the Roman College he said in 1967,
"My sons, we love everyone, including those who don't understand
or don't want to understand our free, personal actions as simple
Christians. They can't get it into their heads that you are as free as
birds. We are completely free, and have the right to think and act as
we please. We each do as we please in temporal affairs, as long as it is
not contrary to the Catholic faith. There is a wide range of opinions
to choose from. No one will ever say anything against your exercising this noble freedom, and that has been true since 1928.

"There were certain people who wanted us to be a political
party so as to be able to manipulate us; but Opus Dei is not that.
Opus Dei is the holy freedom of the children of God. There are
some things—not many—that we all agree on: the faith and the
teachings of Jesus Christ, and the spirit of the Work. In everything
else you are completely free. We live in a world of disguised or
open tyranny, and this marvelous individual freedom of ours, with
its corresponding personal responsibility, is beyond some people's
understanding—they find it hard to imagine such a beautiful thing
can exist!"[7]

---

5. AGP, HRF 21123, p. 38.
6. AGP, HRF 21123, p. 9.
7. AGP, HRF 20156, p. 1115.

No politics here

José Luis Muzquiz, a civil engineer who was one of the first three priests of Opus Dei, together with Don Alvaro and Jose María Hernandez de Garnica, in 1975 recorded some of his personal experiences as one of the first people to join the Work. In part his story reads:

> In forty years I don't recall ever having been asked about my political opinions. On the other hand, when I was in the United States, I do remember going to vote with another person of the Work, and even though we didn't talk about it, I was sure he had voted differently from me. The Father had spoken to me right at the beginning about freedom in these matters of opinion. This has always been practiced in Opus Dei, in every country and in all circumstances.

He also recalled his first encounter with Father Escrivá. The meeting took place in 1935, in the DYA Academy. DYA was an acronym for *Derecho y Arquitectura* (Law and Architecture), but to the people of the Work it also meant *Dios y Audacia*—God and Daring.

"I went to 50 Ferraz Street in the afternoon—I am nearly sure it was four o'clock—to visit the Father. I was curious to know what this priest would think about the situation in Spain, the political parties and the political leaders of the day. At that turbulent time in the prewar years, all the priests discussed politics.

"The Father spoke to me right from the start in a supernatural, apostolic tone. 'I'm very pleased you've come,' he said. 'I've been looking forward to meeting you, and I've been praying for you a lot.' No priest had ever spoken to me like that. Later, the Father told me, 'There's no greater love than Love itself. Other loves are petty by comparison. . . .' I said I had a certain interest in the political field: in fact I asked the Father what he thought of one of those public figures—I think I mentioned Gil Robles, for whom I had a certain liking. The Father answered straightaway: 'Look, people here will never talk to you about politics. Young people from every background come here: Carlists, Popular Action, monarchists of the Spanish Renewal party, and so on. Why, yesterday the president and the secretary of the National Association of Basque Students were here.' Then the Father added, 'On the other hand, you will be asked many other 'awkward' questions. You'll be asked if you pray, if you make good use of your time, if you are trying to please your parents, and if you study, because for a student, studying is a serious obligation.' I was left in no doubt whatsoever about freedom in political matters."[8]

Ullastres and Lopez-Rodo

One morning in February 1957 Monsignor Escrivá spent some time with the students at the Roman College. One of the younger lads, thinking to give Monsignor Escrivá a big piece of news, told him the Italian press that day had reported that a Spanish politician had just been appointed a minister in Franco's government. That referred to Alberto Ullastres, who was in Opus Dei.

Monsignor Escrivá responded that he personally did not care. What did interest him, he said, was whether that son of his was fulfilling his plan of life and doing his job, no matter what it was, honestly. He added humorously, "I'd be more concerned if they told me that that son of mine had a boil on his back."[9]

A few days later, a cardinal who was a friend of his telephoned from the Vatican to congratulate him on the appointment. Monsignor Escrivá's answer was similar: "Why congratulate me? I don't care one way or the other! This matter concerns Alberto Ullastres' professional and political life. As a father, I'm pleased about the professional success of all my children, but nothing more! What I'm really interested in is Alberto's sanctity and health. For the rest, I don't care whether he's a minister or a road sweeper, so long as he sanctifies himself in his work."[10]

These words and others in the same vein were not for mere outward show. Alberto Ullastres himself wrote some notes of a meeting with Monsignor Escrivá following his ministerial appointment. "When I was appointed Minister for Commerce in February 1957 I asked the Father for advice: what norms of action should I follow to live my vocation better in this new experience in my life? The Father

---

8. Written testimony of Fr. José Luis Muzquiz (AGP, HRF T-04678).
9. Testimony of Giorgio del Lungo (AGP, HRF T-07700).
10. Testimony of Juan Portavella (AGP, HRF T-7584). Cf. *Articles of the Postulator*, 802.

answered 'Just this: Do the norms and love freedom.' I could tell that he didn't want to say any more."[11]

During that same period Laureano Lopez-Rodo, also in Opus Dei, began to stand out in the Franco regime. He was to become Minister of the Development Plan and then Foreign Minister. He met Monsignor Escrivá in Lourdes on November 20, 1957. In his pocket diary he noted down that same day, "The Father told me a series of things:

> You have total political freedom: this is no joke!
>
> Serve your country loyally.
>
> Try to unite people, bring them closer together; always work with a plus sign (he traced out a cross), which is the sign of charity.
>
> Work serenely.
>
> When you leave the job, do so cheerfully. It shouldn't matter a fig to you. Not even half a fig!
>
> If your work prevents you from doing your norms of piety, you have to realize that that work is not Opus Dei but *opus diaboli*— the work of the devil.
>
> Always aim for holiness.

"Each of these recommendations was just exactly what I needed."[12]

"Don't be fanatical about anything!"

Four years later, on November 27, 1961, Lopez-Rodo had another conversation with Monsignor Escrivá in Rome. Monsignor Escrivá insisted on the same things: charity and freedom. He told Lopez-Rodo that "serving one's country for love of God is more praiseworthy than serving a human being. No one is worthy of this service: only God." Then he stressed, "In the Work we are completely free: the directors will never give you an order or make a suggestion. Like all Catholics, we follow the indications given by the Church through the hierarchy. We accept all the opinions the Church accepts and we accept all political parties except totalitarian ones."

---

11. Testimony of Prof. Alberto Ullastres (AGP, HRF T-05409).
12. Testimony of Dr. Laureano Lopez-Rodo (AGP, HRF T-04696).

Even though he was talking to a minister of a country ruled by a military dictatorship, or maybe precisely because of that, Monsignor Escrivá dwelt on the question of freedom, taking a view above political questions. "With the passing of time," he explained, "I've come to love freedom more and more. We have to respect other people's freedom and be understanding; accept that others have their reasons for thinking differently; and admit that we ourselves may be in the wrong. Let's never be fanatics. There's nothing in this world worth being fanatical about. The only things we stick to unreservedly are the truths of the faith, but everything else—*everything*—is a matter of opinion. And if this or that person thinks differently, so what! He's not offending me, so I don't take offense!"[13]

Lopez-Bravo with Monsignor Escrivá

On another occasion Gregorio Lopez-Bravo, also a minister for a while in Franco's government, took advantage of an official trip to Rome to visit Monsignor Escrivá. He said later, "Every time I tried to talk to Monsignor Escrivá about the difficulties I met with in my work, he always reacted by reminding me that his mission was not political but priestly, and all he could do was remind me of Catholic doctrine. He told me repeatedly that Christians were not second-class citizens, unmindful of, or detached from, the problems of our time: we had to be out there 'where history is being made.' . . . Whenever I tried to get a more precise idea of his ideas on freedom and responsibility in civil life, he would answer that 'our behavior as ordinary Christians has no other limits than those marked out by the Church,' and that 'each individual should study the problems in the light of the Church's teaching and seek concrete solutions with an upright conscience and with full personal freedom.' . . . Every time we spoke together, he insisted that I should avoid thinking that I was in possession of the truth in matters of opinion like politics. 'Get rid of all kinds of intolerance and fanaticism: you cannot treat anyone coldly or with indifference just because they think differently from you,' he recommended."[14]

---

13. Ibid., and testimony of Rafael Caamaño (AGP, HRF T-05837).
14. Testimony of Gregorio Lopez-Bravo (AGP, HRF T-03214).

Thomas More would have been in Opus Dei

Lopez-Bravo was married and had a big family. In January 1970, when he was at home in Madrid, he received a photocopy of an old engraving of St. Thomas More, who died by order of Henry VIII, for opposing the King's divorce. On the back of the print was a note from Monsignor Escrivá. "St. Thomas More knew how to love his family, his country, the Holy Church of God, and the Roman Pontiff. If he had lived today he would have been a supernumerary of Opus Dei."[15]

Vicente Mortes was also married, in Opus Dei, and a minister of the Spanish Government. After a meeting with Monsignor Escrivá in Rome in September 1963, Mortes made some notes of their conversation. "I'm pleased that you're serving your country. Your job demands a lot of sacrifices and dedication, and so it can be a good way to sanctity. In any case, I couldn't say which job is more important: yours or the person who shows in the visitors. The most important job is always the one which is done with the greatest love of God."

In October 1967, when Monsignor Escrivá was in Pamplona, Vicente Mortes had another conversation with him. "Don't worry, you zealous politician," said Monsignor Escrivá. "I'm not a politician at all. I have my arms wide open to everybody, do you see that? Look, I have no right to have any political opinions. I myself defend the 'freedom of consciences,' and they call me a heretic for it; but not 'freedom of conscience' which means everybody doing just what they like."

Mortes saw him again on February 11, 1968 in Villa Tevere. "In politics as in everything else," Monsignor Escrivá told him, "use the plus sign, which is in the shape of a cross and means addition. In earthly matters there are many ways of achieving an end, and a lot of these are equally good. A politician who rejects people who think differently from him is a bad politician. Don't ill-treat anyone, not even those who are on the wrong road: talk to them and listen

---

15. Ibid., p. 3. Supernumeraries are a majority in Opus Dei. They live in their own homes. They are married or may marry in the future. They have the same vocation as everyone else in the Work, and participate in the apostolates of Opus Dei as far as their family, professional, and social duties permit.

to them, to bring them to God! Respect other people's freedom. Remember the plus sign: Add! Add! Don't divide! . . . Those of you who have a vocation to serve your fellow citizens deserve all my respect. What's more, you're completely free, as long as you don't offend God. But I won't go any further than this general criterion. I won't say a word more! I've never put spokes in the wheels of anyone's personal work, in anyone's work for society, because you're citizens like everyone else."[16]

"You've come to the wrong place"

Vicente Mortes had met Father Escrivá in 1940 in the students' hall of residence in Jenner Street in Madrid. At the time he was a young man from the provinces who was just beginning his civil engineering studies. Thirty-five years later he remembered that first meeting clearly. "My father and I had come to Madrid from Valencia to look for accommodation. Father Eladio España, an exemplary priest, rector of Corpus Christi, had often spoken to me about Father Josemaría Escrivá, the author of *The Way*, who had established a students' residence in Madrid.

"We arrived at number six Jenner Street and went up to the first floor. We waited in a small reception room with a balcony looking onto the street, until a few minutes later a young priest appeared before us, with a robust, cordial appearance: it was the Father. We tried to kiss his hand as was the custom then, but he gently pulled it away. We sat down and my father started talking to him about me. He explained that I was an only child and was going to be living away from my family for the first time. He was afraid I would be 'lost' in the big city. So he really wanted to leave me in a safe place where my comings and goings could be checked; where, in other words, I would be watched.

"As my father spoke, Father Josemaría Escrivá's face changed; he became serious, very serious. Then he interrupted my father, saying, 'You've come to the wrong place. In this residence we don't keep a watch on anybody. We try to help the residents to be good Christians

---

16. Testimony of Vicente Mortes (AGP, HRF T-04203).

and good citizens, free men who make up their own minds and shoulder responsibility for their own actions. In this house we love freedom very much, and anyone who is not capable of handling it and respecting other people's freedom has no place here.'

"Fortunately, my father understood that Father Josemaría was right: without a sense of personal responsibility, supervision would be useless, less than useless, because it would not make people into free men. In the end, the Father said that as far as he was concerned, I could stay.

" 'Go up to the third floor,' he told us, 'and speak to the director, Justo Marti, who's a law graduate. He'll tell you if there's a room available and how much it costs. That's not my business. My job as a priest is the spiritual guidance of the residents.'

"He said good-bye to us very warmly. I've never forgotten his words, which at the time, in Spain in 1940, sounded extremely harsh to me. One did not often hear people talk about freedom. Later, over the years, how often I heard the Father use this word! Without any doubt it was much more for him than an aspiration or an ideal: it was the air he needed to breathe."[17]

Among the many memories Vicente Mortes wrote down, one clearly outlines the freedom which has always been exercised in the Work in public and political decisions. "On coming to Madrid to begin my third level studies, I joined the Sindicato Español Universitario (Spanish Student Union), whose national president at the time was Jose Miguel Guitarte.

"In the Jenner Residence, I met some fine people, responsible students with good standing among their classmates. I thought the SEU would receive a great boost if these men joined and became leaders: they'd be excellent delegates who would attract others. I spoke to Guitarte about it and he thought it was a splendid idea. I went happily off to see the director of the center. He listened to me carefully, and when I had finished, he very gently pointed out my mistake. 'Look, Vicente,' he said, 'I can't talk to any of the residents here about politics. They are each completely free to think and act as they think fit in matters of opinion—which means almost everything,

---

17. Ibid.

because there are very few dogmas of faith laid down by the Church. But it doesn't concern me, and it isn't my role to encourage or discourage anyone over this or that political initiative. It would be meddling in other people's freedom.' It was very clear that once again I'd come to the wrong door."[18]

A letter to the Abbot of Montserrat

Respect for people's actions and personal opinions in Opus Dei are the fruit of a deep-rooted passion for *responsible freedom*.

Certain churchmen were not able to understand the freedom that people of the Work enjoyed in their professional work and activity in society. Monsignor Escrivá wrote to Dom Aurelio M. Escarre, Abbot of Montserrat, on March 25, 1958: "The last paragraph of your letter amused me because I too 'criticize' my children in public when I think 'their free, personal actions in society' call for it; although in many activities in this same sphere they deserve praise, which we ought not to begrudge either."

He went on to say that this personal freedom was well known to all in Opus Dei. "And as a consequence it brings with it *responsibility*, which is also *personal and exclusive*, whether for successes or failures. So, logically, the Work can on the one hand never be held liable for the professional, social, and other activities of the individuals who belong to it, and on the other hand it can never obstruct their personal freedom, as long as they act conscientiously within the ambit permitted by the faith and the Church's teaching. I know full well that Your Reverence will not hesitate to point this out at the opportune moment. I also know that people will be grateful to you and will understand, because all decent people who are capable of respecting the freedom of others all over the world do understand this."

"Neither ultra-conservative nor progressive"

Freedom in all matters of opinion also applies to philosophy and theology. One day in March 1964 Monsignor Escrivá reminded a

---

18. Ibid.

group of women of the Work in Rome, "In matters of faith we follow the doctrine defined by the Church. In all other matters left by God to the free will of human beings, we each think as we please, including on theological matters. That is why I absolutely forbid particular schools of thought or doctrine to be held in common by people of Opus Dei in matters of opinion, because in philosophical and theological matters we are also free."[19]

In the same conversation he said, "Those who call us ultra-conservative are mistaken. The same goes for those who say we are progressive. We are free, *qua libertate Christus nos liberavit*—with the freedom in which Christ set us free. . . . Love freedom then, within the limits of our vocation. However, as the world is drowning in tyranny, there may be people who don't understand us. Being tyrants themselves, they can't understand souls who live *in libertatem gloriae filiorum Dei*, in the freedom of the children of God. We have to be champions of holy freedom."[20]

Schools of tyranny

He often warned his children to struggle "against every kind of tyranny, and in case of doubt, always go for freedom."[21]

One day in the autumn of 1967, while strolling in the gardens of Lariz, a house in Elorrio in northern Spain, he told those with him he had compiled a fat file of notes on tyranny. "A tyrant normally has two or three taboo areas which no one but himself is allowed to touch. To ensure this, he allows those around him to tyrannize others in their turn about everything else. And so the practice of tyranny becomes a real school of tyrants."[22]

As he defended the freedom of consciences, he advised, "Don't straitjacket your piety . . . all you need to do is tone it up from time to time. . . . In the contemplative life one can't give general guidelines on the basis of a few people's experience, as some mystical writers have done. God acts in souls, in each soul, in the most varied ways."[23]

---

19. Testimony of Marlies Kücking. Cf. AGP, HRF 21123, p. 35.
20. Ibid.
21. Testimony of Msgr. César Ortiz-Echagüe (AGP, HRF T-04694).
22. Testimony of Rafael Caamaño (AGP, HRF T-05837).
23. Testimony of Msgr. César Ortiz-Echagüe (AGP, HRF T-04694).

Monsignor Escrivá wanted freedom to reign supreme in the inner life, where man meets God one-to-one. He encouraged his children "not to tie themselves to any particular system in the interior life" and to "do your own prayer in freedom, to put something personal of your own into your relationship with our Lord. There is—there needs to be—a lot of self-determination in the spiritual life."[24]

"Even along the hard shoulder"

He used to compare the Work to a wide avenue, with plenty of walking space, where each person goes at his own pace. "The road of the Work is very wide," he said. "You can go along it on the right or the left, on horseback, cycling, on your knees, crawling like little children, or even along the hard shoulder, so long as you don't leave the road."[25]

In advocating freedom Monsignor Escrivá fostered diversity. Thus he said, "Within the general vocation to Opus Dei, which is to sanctify one's work in the midst of society, God gives each person a particular way of achieving it. We're not all cut out from the same template, like an insole. Our spirit is so ample that what is common to all of us is not destroyed by legitimate personal diversity, by healthy pluralism. In Opus Dei we don't put souls into a mold and press them; we don't want to straitjacket anyone. There is only one common denominator: our desire to reach our final goal, that's all."[26]

"In Opus Dei," he said, "the more we differ from each other the better, always provided the small common denominator remains intact. We respect everybody and defend their freedom; I'm not fanatical, not even about Opus Dei, and I beg you for the love of God not to be fanatical about anything. Have generous hearts."[27]

When Opus Dei began to spread over the world, Monsignor Escrivá established guidelines for asking people to go abroad. The new post should be proposed, not imposed; they should be given time

---

24. AGP, HRF 21156, p. 411.
25. AGP, HRF 21159.
26. AGP, HRF 21159.
27. AGP, HRF 21160.

to make up their minds; if they accepted, they should then be asked if they were going of their own free will; and because of this freedom, they should know that it was not a sign of bad will to acknowledge they were incapable of doing such a job in such a place.

"I have just one vote"

From the beginning, he established team management of the Work, to avoid any trace of authoritarianism. All matters, whether great or small, were to be studied in detail by several people. He himself governed with the help of a team of men, the general council, and of women, the central advisory.

When some matter required discussion, he called on two or three people more directly involved to solve it together. He listened to their reasoning, and only then, last of all, gave his own opinion.

When explaining how Opus Dei was run he always said it was collegially. "I have just one vote."

On the other hand, as founder of the Work, he did not delegate making rules or establishing criteria in anything that affected its essence. Only he had the grace, the *charism*, and therefore the responsibility for the decision.

He often spoke of his temper, commenting that our Lord wished to use it for Opus Dei. "You can't use a straw as a crowbar," he said.

"You're not here as a decoration"

At the beginning of the 1950s he gave Javier Echevarria, then a young law student and a student at the Roman College, the job of keeping an eye on the refurbishment of one part of Villa Vecchia. Javier, from the Chamberi district of Madrid, was the youngest of eight children in a middle-class family. His father had died three years previously. Although no one suggested it to him, he had come to Rome on an impulse to be near Monsignor Escrivá.

One day a supplier arrived at the house. Javier let him in. At that moment Monsignor Escrivá came down the stairs and, meeting the man on his way in, said good morning. He asked Javier, "Do you know the man who's just come in?"

"No, Father, I don't."

"Don't you? Well, my son, you're not here as an item of decoration. You're here to see how the building work is going, how the work is being done, what the men need, and who comes and goes. And the obvious thing to do if anyone you don't know comes in is to ask him: 'Who are you?' because this is *your* house. Yours! And if you don't bother to look after it, if you're not interested in who comes in here to work, it means you have very little sense of responsibility."

Javier went pale. Monsignor Escrivá grasped him by the shoulders, shaking him affectionately while saying, "Don't you realize, Javi, my son, that it isn't I, or any other person, who gave you this job at this moment, but God our Lord himself? So you have to put your heart and soul into it, all your sense of responsibility."[28]

"Will you be my secretary?"

Javier Echevarria recalled another event: "During those times of building alterations in Villa Tevere, on one occasion we had to move the contents of the Father's office to another area, to leave the room free for the workmen. The Father asked all of us then in the Roman College, about eighteen of us, to help so the job could be done very quickly.

"The Father said to us before we began, 'I have complete trust in each of you here. So I am not going to worry about how you do it. I am sure you are going to respect all the material: I know you won't touch a thing, or take anything, or sneak a look at anything. The Father trusts his sons implicitly.' We organized a chain, passing things from one to another. Suddenly I saw that in one of the cupboards we were carrying there was an open box containing the Father's visiting cards. I didn't think it would matter to take one of these cards, because they just had the Father's name and address printed on them, nothing handwritten. So I took one card and kept it. I was glad to have it, and I mentioned it to someone a few days later, not attaching any importance to it. When the Father heard about it, he asked to see me alone. He said in all simplicity, directly

---

28. Verbal account given to the author by Bishop Javier Echevarria.

and emphatically, 'My son, if you behave like that, I'll never be able to trust you.'

"I was shattered to hear these words. For an instant I thought the Father was magnifying a simple matter of a visiting card out of all proportion, but as he went on I understood the depth of his reprimand. 'Before you started moving the office, I told you all clearly that you should not touch anything. But it seems that that didn't matter to you. If you go on like this, Javier, I shall never be able to trust you or rely on you. You need to change a lot.'"

The sequel came not much later. "One day in 1952 or 1953—I was twenty at the time—the Father asked me if I would be his secretary. I said 'yes' immediately. Among the first instructions he gave me, I remember, he said, 'You can look freely into all the cupboards and desks in the office where I work and the room where I sleep. Open all the drawers, because I won't be keeping anything secret from you.'

"I could not help thinking of the visiting card episode. From the Father's correction I had learned that if I did not carry out an instruction, he could not count on me. I knew for a fact that at no time had the Father withdrawn his trust. And now that he was asking me to be his secretary I had the most palpable proof that the Father trusted his children and relied on them totally, with no restrictions whatsoever, without abusing their freedom, like a good father, but at the same time demanding responsibility, like a good director."[29]

From then on Monsignor Escrivá had Javier Echevarria by his side as his secretary. In 1956, when he chose two guardians, *custodes*, to help him in all his personal needs, both spiritual and material, he designated Don Alvaro del Portillo and Father Javier Echevarria.

Respect for freedom in work

Helena Serrano, head of the printing press in Villa Tevere, relates an incident that speaks volumes about Monsignor Escrivá's respect for his children's freedom in their work.

"Several times during the Second Vatican Council, Don Alvaro asked us to print various conclusions of the council. He was the

---

29. Ibid.

secretary of the commission which wrote the decree *Presbyterorum Ordinis.* I remember that each time Don Alvaro had to explain something regarding the lettering of the text he wanted us to do, the Father simply and discreetly moved away to the other side of the room, or actually left the room, waiting on the other side of the half-open door, but not listening. He was aware that Don Alvaro's personal work at the Vatican was none of his business."[30]

When Villa delle Rose was being set up in Castelgandolfo, some material with specific characteristics was needed. They searched high and low for it without success. One day Monsignor Escrivá said at a get-together, "We're going crazy because your sisters say it has to be that specific kind of material and no other!" An Italian timidly suggested, "Father, I could ask my family if you like, because we have a textiles mill."

"But my son, why didn't you tell us this before?"

"The fact is . . . well . . . it didn't seem right for me to obtain clients for my father from here."

"My son, sometimes I find you a bit too 'rigorous'! But do you know what I say? Very good! Excellent!"[31]

A courageous freedom

He often said Christians needed "holy shamelessness" to become involved in other people's lives, "just as God got involved in mine, without asking for my permission first." But they should do this without trampling on privacy, and with extreme delicacy. "One has to enter souls on one's knees."

On April 9, 1971, in Villa Tevere, he had a visit from a group of students and young professional women from Holland, Germany, Italy, and Austria. One of them, a German Protestant, asked him, "I see a tremendous gulf between my religion and Catholicism, in spite of our common faith in Christ. How can this abyss be overcome?"

"My daughter," he responded, "there is indeed a lack of unity among Christians. I respect other people's beliefs, so much so that I

---

30. Testimony of Helena Serrano (AGP, HRF T-04641).
31. Ibid.

would not speak to you about the truths of the Catholic faith unless you asked me to. But all of you, Christians and non-Christians alike, can count on my loyal, selfless, cheerful, priestly, *divine* friendship. When I meet people who aren't Catholic, as I'm not a hypocrite, thank God, I usually say to them, 'I'm a Catholic and I know that I have the truth.'" Then he went on, "You have another faith and I respect you with all my heart, with all my soul! To such an extent that I would do anything to defend the freedom of consciences; but my conscience does not allow me to say you hold the truth."[32]

Three years later in Lima, in response to Keiko Watanabe, a young Japanese wife and mother who was a Buddhist and wished to learn about Catholicism, he said, "With my personal ecumenism, because I can't do anything else without compromising my faith, I will tell you that I have the truth. However, I want you to know I respect your faith and your beliefs. And with God's help I'd lay down my life to defend the freedom of your conscience."[33]

When people of other religions heard him speak of the Catholic faith with such assurance, they did not detect any arrogance or animosity. Here was a priest with arms wide open, faithful to revealed truth but not brandishing doctrine like a club. He always looked for what united people.

Two Swiss brothers, Calvinists, visited him in Villa Tevere on Easter Sunday, 1970. As usual, he told them he had the whole truth and they did not, but he would give his life to defend the freedom of their consciences. His charm and open-mindedness, and the supernatural turn he gave the conversation, disarmed these men. After the visit they said, "We've seen the joy of the Resurrection today. This has been the best Easter Sunday of our lives."[34]

"I thought they were trying to catch me"

The Cremades were a large family from Saragossa in Spain. The parents, Juan Antonio and Pilar, had ten children, several of whom belonged to Opus Dei. In 1964 they all went to Rome together for an

32. Testimony of Marlies Kücking.
33. Testimony of Irene Rey (AGP, HRF T-05955-3).
34. Written account of Bishop Javier Echevarria given to the author.

audience with Paul VI and to meet Monsignor Escrivá. Juan Antonio and Pilar were celebrating their silver wedding anniversary.

Monsignor Escrivá said Mass for them in the Holy Family oratory in Villa Tevere and invited them to stay for breakfast. At one point he talked about freedom. He encouraged Juan Antonio and Pilar to be friends of their children and allow them to practice personal freedom; they should not try to make their family a "minor seminary" or aim for "all their children to join the Work." Looking at each of the ten children, he said, "Let each traveler go his own way!"

At the time one of the Cremades boys, Javier, was antagonistic toward anything having to do with Opus Dei. He felt his family or his friends in Miraflores (a center in Saragossa) might be setting out a trap to catch him. However, he did decide to study medicine at the University of Navarre. Soon after arriving there, he telephoned his parents, urging them to come see him. "Come as soon as you can," he said, "I've got something important to tell you."

When they arrived, he blurted out, "I've asked to join the Work."

His father, dumbfounded, asked how the change had come about. Javier explained, "I was convinced they were out to catch me. I thought the Miraflores lot were after me. But when we were in Rome in March, and heard the Father speak about freedom so forcefully, saying how we were completely free and asking you not to coerce us morally, I said to myself: 'Javier, no one's pushing you, no one's putting pressure on you. You're alone and it's up to you to decide for yourself. Do whatever you choose.' And in that sense of freedom, I decided to write to the Father asking to join Opus Dei."[35]

"Why am I wearing this black cassock?"

One day Monsignor Escrivá was speaking to some of his sons about holy steadfastness, not yielding, "as I am convinced of the truth of my ideal." He spoke about holy shamelessness, "disregarding what people might say," and about holy forcefulness "to bring souls to God by calm, fearless apostolate." Some present felt this holy forcefulness

---

35. Testimony of Juan Antonio Cremades (AGP, HRF T-05846).

or holy coercion should have immediate effect "as the word of God is always fruitful and cannot fail."

Monsignor Escrivá called their attention to the mysterious interplay of freedom and grace. "Not everybody has to be in the Work. It's a vocation, and God gives it to whomever he pleases. My children, we have to really love freedom. . . . The only kind of 'holy coercion' we have is prayer, setting a good example, and being a good friend. You may think that'll take a long time! But I say to you that grace is far quicker than we are. The conversion from Saul to Paul was the work of a moment! And then he thought it over for three long days.

"Nobody, not even at their darkest times, ought to feel they are in the Work because they were pushed to come in. They have to have said yes freely, absolutely freely! *Because I really want to!* That's the most supernatural reason."

He plucked at his cassock, adding, "If I am wearing this black umbrella-cover, it's because that's what I want to do! I said to God one day: I surrender my freedom. And with his grace, I've kept my promise."[36]

"My yoke is . . . freedom"

He continued speaking of this passionate union between freedom and grace, freedom and self-giving for the sake of love, and willing service. "And when, on occasions, the devil makes us feel the weight of this yoke we have taken on freely, we have to hear the words of the Lord: *iugum enim meum suave est, et onus meum leve,* 'because my yoke is sweet and my burden is light,' which I like to translate freely as: my yoke is freedom! My yoke is love! My yoke is unity! My yoke is life!"

---

36. Testimony of Msgr. César Ortiz-Echagüe (AGP, HRF T-04694). Cf. AGP, HRF 21119, p. 15.

14 ✤

The Flight of the Peregrine Falcon

When showing people around the old house of Molinoviejo in Spain, at the end of a long corridor with dark wooden beams and reddish tiles the guide may point to one wall, and say, "That's the wall-hanging with the quotation '*I flew so high*'; it was made very early on, on the Father's instructions." It is a kind of tapestry done in old ochre- and gold-colored cloth, showing a peregrine falcon in the middle. Around the edge are the words: "I flew so high, so high, that I overtook the prey"—a quotation from the *Spiritual Canticle* of St. John of the Cross. The complete verse is this:

I went out seeking love
And with unfaltering hope
I flew so high, so high,
That I overtook the prey.

The image of the falcon inspired St. John to write verses and notes loaded with symbolism about the contemplative life. Monsignor Escrivá found the simile of the falcon and other birds who dare to soar high enormously inspiring in reference to the interior life.

Monsignor Escrivá on one occasion spoke about "the shared solitude" of the priest. "We are never alone. Some say priests are people without love, but it isn't true. We *are* in love: in love with our Lord. A priest has no need for any other love. People also say 'they're all alone.' It isn't so! We have a closer companion than anyone, and are in better company, because our Lord never leaves us. We are in love with Love, the Creator of Love! . . . Every morning we lift up the Sacred Host, we raise the Chalice above the altar and say *per Ipsum, et cum Ipso, et in Ipso,* through my Love, with my Love and in my Love. We are in love!"[1]

Like a thief: "You are mine"

He described his decision to become a priest like the decision of someone falling in love. He was a teenager and had other dreams and ambitions. In 1917 or 1918, walking in the snow on the streets of Logroño, he was strangely and deeply moved to see the prints of bare feet. Someone was walking barefoot in spite of the cold for love of Jesus Christ.

"I had no thought of becoming a priest, but Jesus came into my soul as love comes: *sicut fur,* like a thief, at the most unexpected moment. He said: Now you are mine, *meus es tu!* He made me feel the cry of Isaiah: *ego redemi te, et vocavi te nomine tuo, meus es tu!* I have redeemed you, I have called you by your name, you are mine. They were the inklings of Love!"[2]

Many years had gone by since he was ordained a priest in 1925. One day in February 1960, talking with philosophers and theologians who were in the Work, about freedom as an aid to knowledge, he offered this reflection: "The heart always reaches farther than the head. Intelligence falls behind. Some of you philosophers might say, 'what about the maxim *nihil volitum nisi praecognitum—* you cannot want something you do not know?' Well, even then! If not, how can you explain love at first sight, between people who've never met before?"[3]

Another time, at a get-together with students from several parts of the world who had come to Rome to spend Easter with the Pope, a girl from Argentina took the microphone and told him how the previous night she had clearly seen her vocation to total self-surrender, and had asked to be admitted to the Work. She asked, "Father, how can I be 'the last in everything, but the first in love'?"

---

1. Testimony of Marlies Kücking. Cf. *The Forge,* no. 38.
2. AGP, HRF 20771, p. 540.
3. Testimony of Fr. Carlos Cardona (AGP, HRF T-06138).

Monsignor Escrivá recognized the words as his own from *The Way*. Beaming, he exclaimed, "My daughter! Is it true? Is it true that our Lord is giving you the grace to go unnoticed, willing to serve everybody, to be the last in everything? Is it true, my daughter? Well, as from last night you have a love which satisfies without cloying, which fulfils totally. I have known it for many years. You and I are going to be first in love! No one is going to outdo us!"[4]

Toward the end of the 1960s Monsignor Escrivá had a visit one morning from a young couple in Rome on their honeymoon. Afterward, the woman said to Mercedes Morado, "I told the Father that at first I didn't love the man who's now my husband. I fell in love with him gradually by getting to know him. And now I'm crazy about him!"

Mercedes and Marlies Kücking had a work session later with Monsignor Escrivá. Referring to the young couple, he said, "Did you see those lovebirds? What a lesson for us! What a lesson for our relationship with Jesus! We have to look at him as those two look at each other; we have to speak to him as those two speak to each other and love him as they love each other. They've made me feel a holy envy!"[5]

Over seventy, he seemed inflamed with youthful ardor. "Begin with aspirations; later on contemplation will come, you can't imagine how. Like people in love, who repeat untiringly, 'I love you very much.' . . . Then, time goes by, and maybe their love grows cold. But our Love is always young. It never fades. See if you can find a man of my age who talks about his love as I do! Maybe you won't find many.

"It is a love forged out of renunciation and immense joy, out of unexpected blows and calumnies, out of a darkness that is filled with light, and out of unshakable trust. So what! When I stop to think, I just have to accept the truth of what I wrote so many years ago when I was young, and did not love more than I do now: Love . . . is well worth any love!"[6]

"I could never grow old with this Love," he said hundreds of times.

---

4. Testimony of Begoña Alvarez (AGP, HRF T-04861).
5. Testimony of Marlies Kücking.
6. Testimony of Begoña Alvarez (AGP, HRF T-04861). *The Way*, no. 171.

The truth about Monsignor Escrivá's age

One day in January 1965 he was getting ready to bless the first linotype press in the little print room in Villa Tevere. While Father Javier Echevarría helped him to put on the surplice, he said to those around him, "The Father is old. I am sixty-three!"

The next second he corrected himself vehemently. "No! I'm young! I am only a little over thirty years old, which is the time I have spent serving our Lord Jesus Christ."[7]

When he was a young priest in his twenties, Father Escrivá asked God to grant him the prudence and gravity of an eighty-year-old to carry out his task. He felt too inexpert and immature to be 'another Christ.'

In his *Intimate Notes* of 1931, only twenty-nine at the time, he was already writing with remarkable confidence, "Jesus, help me live our Mass, help me celebrate the Holy Sacrifice with the calm gravity and composure of a venerable priest. Even if I were to experience *the dark night*, may I not lack light when I am another Christ."[8]

Much later, he would joke with his children about calculating "how old the Father really is." On February 6, 1967 he said to a group of women, "I'm far older than you imagine." They had celebrated his sixty-fifth birthday less than a month before. Monsignor Escrivá smiled.

"Shall we work it out? Let's see, I need a pen and paper. Have you a piece of paper?"

Mary offered her pocket diary, and Monsignor Escrivá made quick notes. "Eighty years: how I pleaded with Our Lord to grant them to me! Sixty-five years on the outside. Two thousand more or less, we can round it up, as *alter Christus*, because we are all of us other Christs. We all have to be, ought to be, saints . . . all of us."[9]

This was what he wrote on the diary page:

on the inside: 80
on the outside: 65
Alter Christus: 2,000
Total: 2,145
6–2–67

---

7. Testimony of Helena Serrano (AGP, HRF T-04641).
8. *Intimate Notes*, no. 317, October 11, 1931.
9. AGP, HRF 21156, p. 518. Cf. testimony of Begoña Alvarez (AGP, HRF T-04861).

Monsignor Escrivá and women

"The gravity of an eighty-year-old." In this naturally spontaneous and friendly man, gifted at communication, gravity became an acquired reserve, a studied kindness and distance, when dealing with women. He had decided on this when young. "God gave me to understand this," he explained.

He did not write to women or attend a social function where he might have to converse with a woman alone. He was never alone with any woman, old or young. To hear women's confessions, he used a confessional with a grille as partition, and if he had to hear a sick woman's confession, he left the door of the room open. When visiting his daughters in Opus Dei, he always asked another priest to accompany him.

"'Twixt holy man and holy maid. . . ."

One day he told a big group of his daughters that he loved them "with the love of a father and a mother." To the two priests with him, he explained afterward, "The unlimited, fatherly love I have for my daughters is something real, and I tell them so when they are all together. But it would never occur to me to repeat those words to one of them individually, so as not to give rise to any stirrings of sentimentality on my side or on the side of the woman concerned."[10]

He made his own the maxim of St. Teresa of Avila: "Twixt holy man and holy maid, a wall of solid stone be laid!" Precisely because he had the feelings of a normal man, he kept his heart locked "with seven locks." This did not make him loveless. Priestly celibacy for him was not an imposition that crushed his virility or a form of sublimation; it was a joyful reality—"a joyful affirmation of love," he used to say, explaining that a chaste heart was full to overflowing with "a Love that satisfies without cloying."

He spoke of celibacy as "the most precious jewel in the crown of the Church." For him, celibacy meant not merely remaining single and without ties, but a commitment of passionate surrender to a

---

10. Written account by Bishop Javier Echevarria.

God who is "a jealous lover who is not satisfied with sharing," who wants to be loved *ex toto corde*: wholeheartedly.

"I can see, but I don't look"

One day in 1971 Luigi Tirelli was talking to him after lunch about "Checco," who was also in the Work, lived in Verona, and had many friends who were priests. Monsignor Escrivá listened with great interest. Suddenly he exclaimed, "Tell those priests they have a Friend— and the friends of that Friend! That way they'll never be alone."[11]

Love led him to be vigilant regarding his senses and faculties. He used to say, "I can see, but I do not look at what I ought not to look at." And, "At my age"—he had just turned fifty—"I have to make a real effort not to turn around every time I see a good-looking woman pass by."[12]

The marchioness's eyebrows

One day during a get-together, Jim, who lived in Kenya, spoke of a certain Kenyan teacher who, along with black skin and hair, had blond eyebrows. Then Monsignor Escrivá told about a married couple he knew well at the beginning of the 1930s in Spain, the Marquis and Marchioness De Guevara. He gave them spiritual guidance, and sometimes had lunch with them. A young painter did a portrait of the marchioness, and remarked that she had "each eyebrow of a different color," something highly unusual. When he heard this, Monsignor Escrivá realized that he had never noticed it. "I had not noticed it," he said "because I had never looked into her eyes."

They went on talking about other things. A Mexican mentioned an image of Christ venerated in Montefalco, in Morelos State. Monsignor Escrivá said, "Pray to him, looking at his face, looking . . . at his *eyebrows*, as one looks at a person one loves."[13]

---

11. Testimony of Msgr. César Ortiz-Echagüe (AGP, HRF T-04694).
12. Testimony of Encarnación Ortega (AGP, HRF T-05074).
13. Testimony of Msgr. César Ortiz-Echagüe (AGP, HRF T-04694).

The good kind of anticlericalism

Although he was a priest through and through, twenty-four hours a day, he instinctively rejected clericalism and surprised many people by announcing that he was anticlerical—but with "the good kind of anticlericalism."

He taught his sons who were priests, and practiced it himself, that clergymen should not "meddle" or seek to be waited upon or retain privileges or organize the apostolate of the laity or intrude on the laity's civil, professional, or social activities or aim to be "the sauce in every dish." Nor should they use their priesthood to avoid civic duties or obtain benefices, sinecures, or other comforts; or allow cliques of followers or admirers to grow up around themselves. They should not set themselves up as leaders of anything or anybody or make themselves indispensable in any job, anywhere.

He insisted on two attitudes that others could see in him: "I have not come to be served, but to serve,"[14] and "Do and disappear: that only Jesus may shine forth!"[15] He also warned priests against the temptation of feeling they were "proprietors" of the souls they attended spiritually.

"Treat him well for me!"

Like all those from Aragon, Monsignor Escrivá used "me" in all sorts of ways to express paternal devotion: "Do the norms for me," "Sleep the right amount of time for me," "Be faithful for me!" and "Take care of that daughter for me!" He began letters to his children with "May Jesus take care of you for me" or, if it was a general letter to everyone in the Work, "May Jesus watch over my daughters and sons for me." Referring to Jesus Christ in the Eucharist, he told his sons who were priests: "Treat him well for me!"

He often told his children, "Be faithful for me!" Rather than a demand to be faithful to him, this was a call to fidelity to their vocation.

Father Carlos Cardona recalled how one day, between 1955 and 1957, Monsignor Escrivá spoke about fidelity. "He told us he

14. Matt. 20:28.
15. Cf. *Articles of the Postulator*, 993.

had received a letter from someone who did not want to persevere, and was asking to leave the Work. In the letter this person said that in spite of his decision he loved the Father very much. The Father observed, with an expression of deep sorrow, 'It would have been better for him to love me less and Jesus a bit more!' "[16]

In 1954, Monsignor Escrivá went to see the finishing touches on the oratory dedicated to the Heart of Mary in Villa Tevere. Happy at how well the holy water font had turned out, he said to his daughters who were with him, "Give a good bonus to the workman who did this, and tell him he's a real artist!"

They did. The brick-layer, surprised, said, "Oh, I would do anything for Monsignor!" They repeated this to him, expecting him to be pleased. But his reaction was different. "What a pity! How very sad that he should do it for me and not for God!"[17]

Offering holy water

A Spanish couple, Luis and Flora Ibarra, met Monsignor Escrivá in Villa delle Rose. Entering the oratory to pay his respects to the Lord in the Blessed Sacrament, as was his custom, Monsignor Escrivá dipped his fingers into the holy water font and politely held out his hand for Flora to take the water from his fingers. With hand still outstretched, he said, "I've never done that to any woman before, apart from my mother."[18]

He did not like having his hand kissed and would hide it in the folds of his cassock whenever he could. Once as he was going along the Galleria della Madonna in Villa Tevere, several women from Villa Sacchetti approached, and one of them, Carmen Maria Segovia, said, "Father, I want to kiss your hand."

"Well," he answered, "you can kiss the hand of God our Lord!" Taking a small crucifix from his pocket, he kissed the hands nailed to the cross. "See how easy it is? I often do it. You do it too!"[19]

16. Testimony of Fr. Carlos Cardona (AGP, HRF T-06138).
17. Testimony of Helena Serrano (AGP, HRF T-04641).
18. Testimony of Begoña Alvarez (AGP, HRF T-04861).
19. Testimony of Helena Serrano (AGP, HRF T-04641).

"No one should become attached to me"

This slightly aloof attitude was his response to a powerful inner inspiration given him many years before. In 1939, at the end of the Spanish Civil War, Father Escrivá was among the first priests, perhaps the very first, to enter Madrid, riding in an army truck, and wearing his cassock. People were in the streets cheering and applauding, and when they saw a priest, they swamped him, seeking to kiss his hands. He was moved by this palpable demonstration of hunger for God but determined that no one should be ensnared by him personally. "I understood very clearly," he said later, "that no one ought to become attached to me! I pulled a big crucifix from my pocket—my 'weapon' I called it—and I offered it to people, so they could kiss Jesus Christ and not my hands. This rectitude of intention is essential for the apostolate: leading souls to God, and never consenting to their becoming entangled or diverted to us. Anything else would be sacrilegious robbery."[20]

However, on March 28, 1974, anniversary of his ordination, Monsignor Escrivá called on his spiritual daughters in La Montagnola, and conscious of the dignity of the priesthood, held out his hands, palms upward, for them to kiss. "Today is indeed a day for kissing the palms of hands which have received priestly consecration," he told them.[21]

Confession: with sealed lips

Another aspect of the priesthood on which he laid great stress was the faculty to forgive sins, including the seal of confession. Notes taken by Bishop Javier Echevarria, who lived with Monsignor Escrivá in Rome for twenty-five years, refer to the importance of the seal, which he called *onus et honor*, a burden and an honor.

In August 1955 he said, "We've all experienced the immense joy of being able to unburden our souls of some big problem that was worrying us to a reliable friend who listens to us sympathetically and gives us advice. We trust that person, secure in the knowledge that

---

20. Testimony of Begoña Alvarez (AGP, HRF T-04861).
21. Testimony of Mercedes Morado (AGP, HRF T-07902).

he won't tell anyone else about our problem, because we've opened our souls to him. Besides, as it's a person of sound doctrine, he knows he's obliged to keep this natural secret.

"Well, if this happens with good friends on earth, imagine the peace and the joy we feel on confiding in our Friend in confession! Because Jesus understands us, helps us, solves our problems and, what's more, he forgives us. And the secret of what we say in confession is even more absolute: it is strictly between Jesus and the person speaking. May the seal of confession be blessed a thousand times! I assure you that all the priests in the world keep it zealously and love it because God ordains it. . . . It is good to know that the very severe penalties imposed by the Church on those who violate it are very just. These penalties, rather than instilling fear in me, actually lead me to take more care of everything referring to confession. They make me realize how careful our Lord has wished us to be, never even to hint at what we have heard in confession."[22]

The following dates from 1964: "The Holy See imposes an oath of silence on people who work in particular congregations, on certain matters. It is so serious that they cannot show in any way that they know anything of the subject they have been dealing with, not even *ictu oculi*, with a movement of the eyes! It is obvious really, because otherwise they could cause great damage to the Church or to souls.

"Well, even more serious, absolutely so, must be the secret we priests keep of what we have heard in confession. What a joy for priests to know they are trustees of Christ's forgiveness! And how wonderful it is, to realize the great peace they give to souls by their total silence! When you forgive sins in the confessional, think about the total silence with which Christ takes the weight of the sins of all humanity; a silence which is continued in the sacramental seal, a proof of God's mercy. Everything that is said in confession is covered forever under the safe, unbreakable slab of God's forgiveness!"[23]

In 1970, speaking to a group of his sons who were priests, he said, "God has wished the priest to keep the secret zealously, and the Church commands it. The priest doesn't speak about what he has

22. Notes made by Bishop Javier Echevarria.
23. Ibid., 1964.

heard, even indirectly; he doesn't think over what we have told him. Let us love the seal of confession with all our might, as something which even protects the penitent psychologically!"[24]

On other occasions, referring to "the ruling passion for hearing confessions and guiding souls," that together with "preaching, and teaching sound doctrine" ought to fill the heart of every priest, he pondered the absolute guarantee of the seal of confession. "What peace and joy the soul experiences! I would even dare to say that God's mercy is something tangible, because of the inviolable seal of confession, which is a confirmation that Our Lord has said to us, 'I have forgiven you; your sin is totally forgotten.' "[25]

"Your Highness, kneel down"

One day a very important person, related to royalty, visited Monsignor Escrivá in Rome. At one point in the conversation, the visitor put on a serious air, and, lowering his voice, said in confidential tones, "I want to tell you something secret . . ."

Monsignor Escrivá interrupted him gently but firmly. "Your Highness, kneel down and speak to me in Confession, which is the utmost secrecy you could ask for. In any case, you are speaking to a priest, a man of honor, and that ought to be enough for you. I assure you whatever you say to me in confidence, I will keep reserved in my soul, in accordance with Christian teaching. I don't find it hard to do so, because besides being my duty, it is demanded by simple honor, which is what I always try to live by."[26]

24. Ibid., 1970.
25. Ibid., 1972.
26. Ibid. Cf. *Articles of the Postulator,* 732.

15 ✢

Traveling Light

From early on, Monsignor Escrivá experienced poverty as a resolve not to *possess* things even if he *had* them. This kind of poverty set him free. When he spoke to people who wanted to be apostles of Christ, he stressed that chastity and poverty were essential. They make war on the tyrant everyone carries in himself and bring the guarantee of eternal happiness. In a point in his book *The Forge*, he expressed his desire "to live and die in poverty, even though I may have millions at my disposal."[1] He was being realistic here, because he had to act as one who did own things: money, buildings, household goods, and all kinds of things needed to do Opus Dei and spread it over the world.

Yet for a long time he had had practically nothing: desperately short of food, clothing, shoes, books, and cash, with no house of his own. Moreover, people who have gone to begin the Work in a new country have always suffered an almost total lack of resources, "shamefully poor" and deprived of every comfort. But these are, and ought to be, temporary situations. The people of the Work earn their own living. So Monsignor Escrivá himself, and his children in the Work, would always have sufficient means to live "a simple and temperate life."[2]

This defined the poverty practiced in Opus Dei—a voluntary poverty, never imposed by force. It does not mean not having things,

---

1. *The Forge*, no. 46.
2. *The Way*, no. 631.

but being detached from them, using things without considering them one's own, doing without superfluous things, not complaining when something necessary is lacking, choosing the worst for oneself, not acquiring habits of self-indulgence, not being ruled by whims.

In March 1950, for the silver jubilee of his ordination to the priesthood, Monsignor Escrivá was given a watch as a present. He liked it, and was delighted to wear it at first, but after a short time he stopped.

"I liked it so much I was getting attached to it, so I've handed it in. Out of sight, out of mind."[3]

He did not normally carry a pen, but used the one in the room where he worked, which belonged there. Whenever he was somewhere else and needed to write something, he had to borrow a pen.[4] His handwriting was bold and emphatic, and not every pen suited him. Adapting his writing to the pen he was using was a way of "living in poverty" without being noticed.

Santiago's walkie-talkie

He practiced constant small acts of detachment. One day his brother Santiago, after spending time thinking of a present that would be really useful, gave him a walkie-talkie. It was indeed a practical idea, enabling him to contact people anywhere in Villa Tevere. He accepted it gratefully and spent time learning how it worked; he appeared delighted with it. Santiago went off satisfied at finding something his brother would use every day. But that same day, the walkie-talkie went to the women of the Work in La Montagnola.[5] That was what he did with all his presents; he never kept them.

Full time and no watch

In Italy, Christmas presents are given at Epiphany, "*la befana.*" Monsignor Escrivá's present every year was a small pocket diary, and every time he was as pleased as if it were a real surprise.

---

3. Testimony of Encarnación Ortega (AGP, HRF T-05074). Cf. *Articles of the Postulator*, 1068.
4. Ibid.
5. Testimony of Marlies Kücking.

For Christmas 1974 (which was to be his last Christmas), the women in Villa Sacchetti and La Montagnola wanted to give him a triple picture frame holding photographs of Don Jose Escrivá and Doña Dolores, his parents—"the grandparents," as the people in the Work called them. The central picture would be one of Our Lady of Torreciudad, to whom Monsignor Escrivá owed his miraculous cure at the age of two.

At that point, however, Don Alvaro told them not to go ahead. "The Father has heard about it," he explained, "and asks you not to bother with this present. He says, 'If my children don't have photographs of their families in their rooms, neither will I.' "[6]

He always found a good reason for turning down presents. On different occasions he declined a brush and comb set on the grounds that "that's too good for me,"[7] a pair of slippers because "the ones I have are still in good shape," a wool cardigan because "this one I'm wearing has a lot of life in it yet . . . or do you want me to give up practicing poverty?" His German daughters sent him a color television set in 1975. He did not keep that either. "The Father is much happier knowing that his daughters in Rome are enjoying it."[8]

In fact there was a gentle, ongoing tug-of-war, with the women trying to guess what the Father would like and Monsignor Escrivá off-loading the gift without offending them. After a long time, they realized he would only accept things which could be used in divine worship somewhere: chasubles, embroidered palls, chalices, ciboria, and so on. On that sort of thing, expense seemed to matter little to him.

The men solved the problem by giving him a new diary every year, with a pencil or red ballpoint pen as an "added extra." But the women persisted in looking for something new. Occasionally they overcame his resistance, or so it seemed. In 1974, having failed with the triple photograph frame, they decided to give him a clock for his desk, to replace the one he had, which was a cheap one that had come free with something else. Having heard that on his catechetical

---

6. Ibid.
7. Ibid.
8. Ibid.

travels through Europe and Central and South America, he would often ask "What time is it in Rome now?" and "What will those children of mine be doing now?" they decided his Christmas gift would be a "universal clock" showing time zones and the local times in the different cities around the world where people of the Work lived.

The clock was duly placed on the desk in Don Alvaro's office, where Monsignor Escrivá used to work because it was a bright room and did not need an electric light on all day as his did. Within a week, Father Javier Echevarria called Carmen Ramos and Marlies Kücking, and handed them a box they recognized as the one the clock had come in. Dismayed and thinking at first that Don Javier had made a mistake, they exclaimed, "But Don Javier, this is the clock we gave the Father!"

"Yes, I know," he answered. "But what can I do? The Father is giving up everything he particularly likes. And he liked this a lot."[9]

His room

Monsignor Escrivá had only the essentials in his room, and these were of very modest quality. The room itself was really a passageway, with a door at each end; it had no window, and the floor was of diamond-shaped blue and white tiles. There was a plain wooden chair and a varnished cane wastebasket. At the foot of the bed was a little maroon mat stitched and restitched whenever it started to fray. One Epiphany, his daughters in the Work gave him a small, good-quality fur rug. When Monsignor Escrivá saw it, he thanked them gratefully, but then said, "Don't be upset, but I'm never going to use it. Good things have to be for Our Lord. The mat I already have is more than enough for me."[10]

A stub of red candle

In December 1967 he spent several days in Castelgandolfo in the "Lake House," a building next to Villa delle Rose. Just before returning to Rome, he dropped in to see those in Villa delle Rose itself.

---

9. Ibid. Testimony of Carmen Ramos.
10. Testimony of Helena Serrano (AGP, HRF T-04641).

They had already put up the Christmas decorations, and from one of the ornaments in the corridor he took a red candle stub with a little sprig of holly, saying with a mischievous expression, "I'm going to take this." When he got to Villa Tevere, he placed the little ornament on his desk and kept it there for several days. One morning, after working through a pile of papers, he went to the Galleria del Fumo, where there was a crèche in the sitting room. Candle stub and holly in hand, he bent over the little figures of the Mother and Child and put the ornament in the crèche, saying softly, "My Mother, here you are . . . I've brought you all I have."[11]

A heap of many small efforts

He took care of things as if he only had them on loan and had to pass them to the next generation exactly as received. He never underlined passages in books, he took care of his clothes, and he opened and closed doors as carefully as if in someone else's home. His reason above all was his love for little things. As he said in *The Way*, "*Great* holiness consists in carrying out the *little* duties of each moment."[12] In the course of his day he kept track of "many small things" that involved being very much "in God's presence." He saw that only rarely would ordinary Christians play a heroic role in life; but little things, "without splendor and of no value,"[13] were always within reach. "You have mistaken the way if you scorn the little things;"[14] and "Perseverance in little things for love is heroism."[15] Here was the raw material for transforming "the daily prose into epic verse."

God doesn't ask any more of us

One brilliant day in June 1956, Monsignor Escrivá was walking up and down a corridor on the third floor in Villa Vecchia with Carlos Cardona, giving him the outline of a forthcoming article on the

---

11. Testimony of Mercedes Morado (AGP, HRF T-07902).
12. *The Way*, no. 818.
13. Cf. *The Way*, no. 178.
14. Ibid., no. 816.
15. Ibid., no. 813.

doctrine of work as the hinge of the call to holiness in Opus Dei. Cardona was taking rapid notes in shorthand. Suddenly Monsignor Escrivá stopped and pointed to some windows through which the sun was streaming. "Those shutters ought to be closed," he said. "The sun could damage everything in there."

Cardona hurried to pull down the blinds, without stopping to secure the shutters properly, running the risk of damaging the walls. Monsignor Escrivá quickly held them, preventing them from banging against the walls. Then with the same seriousness and interest as when he was dictating the article, he said, suiting the action to the words, "Carlos, before opening the window you have to fasten the shutters. You do it as a little mortification, you say an aspiration silently, and that is all God asks us for! He doesn't ask any more of us!"[16]

Many of his children learned from him the simple "art" of closing a door properly, "saying a few silent words of love to our Lord!" Often he pointed out a crooked picture or that a lightbulb had burned out; or that care should be taken not to scrape the skirting board when using the floor polishing machine. This was taking care of little things. He had a lively awareness of "God waiting for us there, in those little things."[17] More than once, after pointing out some little detail, he said, "Forgive me for having such a sharp eye!"[18]

He would say, "If there are doors, why are they open? If they are to be left open, what do we need doors for?" So many young people went through Villa Tevere year after year that he had to explain time and again that "doors are for opening when necessary and then closing again. Doors are meant to be closed; otherwise we'd have put archways all over the house, which would have been much cheaper."[19]

One day in 1972 Monsignor Escrivá went to the print room with two priests from England and Ireland. They were on their way to a large gallery lined with glass cases containing liturgical vestments

16. Testimony of Fr. Carlos Cardona (AGP, HRF T-06138).
17. Testimonies of Helena Serrano (AGP, HRF T-04641) and of Marlies Kücking.
18. Testimony of Helena Serrano (AGP, HRF T-04641).
19. Ibid.

valuable either because of the quality of the embroidery or the antiquity of the material. He asked Helena Serrano to turn on the lights in the cases, adding, "Then you can go—we'll turn them off."

Helena switched on all the lights and went out, closing the door so quickly that the catch did not engage. Monsignor Escrivá called her back, and said softly so that no one else could hear, "If you had closed the door for love of God, you would surely have done it properly."[20]

No voice to say "I am poor"

The poverty Monsignor Escrivá practiced and taught had two other notable characteristics. In the first place, it was the secular poverty of ordinary people. It had to be practiced with dignity, in keeping with each individual's social and professional life, observing fashion and technical progress, as well as having a certain elegance. In Monsignor Escrivá's words, it was "the kind of poverty which has no voice to say 'I am poor.'"

Second, it was not collective poverty but decidedly personal. Each individual was to gauge his or her own needs, acquire and use the things needed, take care of them to make them last longer, keep an account of expenses, and try to earn enough not only to support himself but also to contribute to Opus Dei's apostolic works. Each also had to keep a check on his dependence on or detachment from the things he used. All of this was summed up by Monsignor Escrivá, "You should act like the father or mother of a large and poor family." He explained, "Fathers or mothers who have many children and not much money practice poverty unostentatiously. They work out how to save money on this, that or the other thing. When summer's coming, they may decide, 'If I spend any money on that, we might not be able to afford a holiday, or to get the children new shoes,' and so on."[21] He taught his children a thousand ways of saving money by using up leftover food, or reusing wrapping paper and twine. He taught how to make a fine wall hanging with scraps

---

20. Ibid.
21. Testimony of Mercedes Morado (AGP, HRF T-07902).

of old fabric; how to buy things wholesale or direct from the factory; and how, for a few lira at the Roman flea markets, to buy an old piece of furniture that, cleaned and repainted, would be useful and decorative.

He noticed small details of domestic economy. Once when he was staying in Paris, his daughters there served him a foreign brand of mineral water. He told them afterward, "From now on, try to buy local products, because they're cheaper. What's more, it means you can return the empties and save some francs that way too!"[22]

Another time, in Cologne, he had written several postcards to different places. He wanted everyone in Eigelstein to sign the one for his daughters in Rome, which he would then send in an envelope. The card already had stamp on it, so he tried to remove the stamp. Turning to Giorgio, a son in the Work and a priest, he joked, "Come on, you're a doctor: finish off this operation for me!"[23]

Another time, passing through the dining room which had just been vacated by the residents of the Casa del Vicolo in Rome, he noticed that many glasses had a bit of wine left and there was unstirred sugar in the coffee-cups. He remarked to the people with him, "Tell those lads only to serve themselves the amount they intend to eat or drink. It is a real lack of poverty to have to throw out all that wine and waste all that sugar."[24]

He saved the most unlikely things. He had a green box on his desk where he kept small rectangular bits of paper—pieces of used envelopes that he used for notes or writing down phrases for later on in preaching or writing. He said, "Yes, I do use paper well: I write on both sides—and I don't write on the edge because I can't."[25]

But he insisted that people who worked in centers of the Work be paid promptly and generously. On special feast days, they also got a little treat for themselves and their families; and sometimes a bonus, "even though we ourselves have to do without."

22. Testimony of Marlies Kücking.
23. Ibid.
24. Ibid.
25. Testimonies of Encarnación Ortega (AGP, HRF T-05074) and Helena Serrano (AGP, HRF T-04641).

A workman is robbed

At the end of the 1940s, at the height of postwar scarcity, he received a letter from Ramon Montalat, a son in the Work who was taking care of the building work at Molinoviejo conference center in Spain. Ramon told him what had happened to one of the workmen: "He had been saving hard for some time to pay for his wife to give birth in a hospital, and to buy a crib and outfit for the baby. When he heard that the birth was imminent, he went back to Madrid, and when he got there he couldn't resist the temptation of going to his local pub to meet his friends and show off the fortune he had accumulated by effort and hardship. On leaving the pub, he was robbed."

A few days later the painter Fernando Delapuente arrived in Madrid from Rome. He was in charge of overseeing the work in Molinoviejo and Villa Tevere at the same time. He had a message for Ramon Montalat and Jesus Alberto Cagigal, who were directly responsible for Molinoviejo: Monsignor Escrivá wanted the worker who had been robbed to be reimbursed all the money he had lost and a bit over—as much as they could manage—as a present for the birth of his child.[26]

Though generous to the point of extravagance to bring cheer to people's lives, he never allowed any avoidable waste. "We are very much in favor of clean air and clean water, and we have no use for darkness: we do things in the light of day. But put love of God into turning off taps properly and turning off lights that aren't needed. In these big houses, if everyone were to leave the light on five minutes more than necessary, added together it would pay the electricity bill of an average family for a month."[27] Crossing a landing, he would often turn to whoever was there, point to the lighted lamps, and say, "Either the lights on the stairs or the ones on the landing, but not both!"[28]

Yet he insisted on surrounding our Lord in the Blessed Sacrament with light; making the oratories radiant during liturgical actions; switching on all lights in corridors and rooms which a

---

26. Testimony of Ramon Montalat (AGP, HRF T-04690). Cf. *Articles of the Postulator*, 1101.
27. Testimonies of Marlies Kücking and of Helena Serrano (AGP, HRF T-04641).
28. Testimony of Helena Serrano (AGP, HRF T-04641).

priest was to pass through while carrying Communion to a sick person's room. And he said, "Feast days stand out because the worship is extra rich, people put on their best clothes, the meals are especially well prepared and presented, and there is a cheerful atmosphere everywhere."

In the spring of 1955, recalling the economic difficulties of Opus Dei in its early years, he said to his sons, "On many occasions during the past twenty-six years I found myself destitute, in the most total want and with absolutely nothing on the horizon. We lacked even the essentials. But we lived through all that with such joy! Because, since we were seeking the Kingdom of God and his justice, we knew that all other things would be given to us, multiplied many times over. My children should be cheerful if they ever lack something vital, while at the same time they should do their best to make sure they don't lack anything."[29]

An ink bottle and a razor

For many years Monsignor Escrivá himself had almost nothing at all. "He never had anything. He would travel with an ink bottle full of holy water and a razor," Regina Quiroga declared. She was a Franciscan tertiary who first met Father Escrivá in 1938 when he was preaching a retreat for priests in Vitoria. She, Maria Loyola, and Maria Elvira Vergara testified that "he only had half a cup of white coffee for breakfast every day," and "he only had one cassock, and on one occasion he gave it to us to mend; it was in tatters, but we did our best to fix it for him as quickly as possible, as he was waiting in his room for us to finish it."[30]

In someone else's shoes

In the 1930s, Pedro Casciaro was impressed by the "smartness, cleanliness, even elegance" of Father Escrivá's appearance. "Later on," he

---

29. Testimonies of Archbishop Julian Herranz and Fr. José Luis Soria (AGP, HRF T-07920). Cf. *Articles of the Postulator*, 1072.

30. *Articles of the Postulator*, 1077. Testimonies of Sister Maria Loyola Larrañaga and Sister Maria Elvira Vergara (AGP, HRF T-04388).

said, "I began to realize he always wore the same cassock, keeping it well brushed and very clean indeed. I also noticed how, when celebrating Mass, he not only genuflected slowly and with tremendous concentration, but in such a way that his right foot was always concealed under his cassock and alb; in the most natural way, he was careful not to show the soles of his shoes. The fact is that although they were perfectly clean and shiny, they were in dire need of new soles or, even better, of being thrown away. It was not surprising he wore out his shoes, considering the long walks he had to do. He hardly ever took the tram, but walked from one end of Madrid to the other: from St. Elizabeth Street to Ferraz Street, from the Salamanca district to Vallecas."[31] What he did not say was that the old shoes Father Escrivá wore had been thrown out by the university students at the Ferraz Residence.

A priest who did not charge

During the Spanish Civil War, undernourished, with no money, and only the clothes he wore, sometimes running a temperature, Father Escrivá traveled all over the country to give spiritual help to his sons scattered on different battlefronts and military hospitals.[32]

One time in Utrera in the south of Spain, after going to see someone who needed spiritual help, he went to the ticket office in the station, put all his money down on the counter, and said to the ticket clerk, "I want to get to Burgos. How far will this get me?"

"Let me see. . . . You only have enough here to get as far as Salamanca."

With no money left to buy anything to eat, he finished the journey as best he could. Recalling this episode and others like it, he said years later, "We have not flinched at anything when a soul was at stake—neither affection, nor sacrifice, nor money. And I don't think our Lord will blame us for that; on the contrary, he'll put it in the scales on the good side, and it will become pure gold, weighing as heavy as lead, because it represents the tremendous value of charity."[33]

---

31. Testimony of Fr. Pedro Casciaro (AGP, HRF T-04197). Cf. *Articles of the Postulator*, 1092.
32. EF-380419-2 (Letters to his sons in Burgos). *Articles of the Postulator*, 1075.
33. Ibid., 1076.

At the time of greatest penury, "with absolutely nothing on the horizon," when he had to choose between having lunch or dinner, and, in the middle of winter, the four of them in Burgos had just one sweater to share between them, the words of a psalm suddenly occurred to him: *iacta super Dominum curam tuam, et ipse te enutriet,* "Cast thy care upon the Lord, and he shall sustain thee."[34] He decided to forfeit the only income he might get: stipends for saying Mass and preaching. That was in 1938. For the rest of his life he would not accept money for exercising his priestly ministry.[35]

Live with the problem or live with the mystery

By experience he found that when he forfeited something that appeared to offer a solution to his problems, he was transferring the problem to God, and God "can always do more!" This hopeful, trusting abandonment of a child gave him peace, joy, and relief from all worry, and enabled him to live in each present moment with a wonderful freedom of spirit. Years later, during a get-together with his children in Barcelona in 1973, he said, "We had nothing. Sometimes I found just the amount we needed at that moment, down to the last peseta; I did not understand then but I do now, and I realize it was a clear sign of the working of God's Providence. If the Work of God had been done with the money of men, it wouldn't have been much of a Work of God!"[36]

Encarnación Ortega recalled that "from 1942 to 1944 he would come to the house in Jorge Manrique Street, and later to the Zurbaran Residence in Madrid, and when the time came for him to go home he would ask us for a peseta, as he had no money to get the tram home."[37]

---

34. Ps. 54.
35. *Articles of the Postulator,* 1078. Testimonies of Fr. Pedro Casciaro (AGP, HRF T-04197) and Fr. Francisco Botella (AGP, HRF T-00159).
36. *Articles of the Postulator,* 1090. Cf. Testimonies of Fr. Florencio Sanchez (AGP, HRF T-08250) and of Dr. Alejandro Cantero (AGP, HRF T-06308).
37. Testimony of Encarnacion Ortega (AGP, HRF T-05074).

Shades of black on a cassock

Even when the Work was spreading throughout the world, he had only the bare minimum for himself: an old cassock, finally thrown away in 1964 after he had worn it every day for twenty years; and a newer, more presentable one, for going out or receiving visitors. The old cassock "had so many patches it was difficult to tell which piece was the original cloth."[38] Seeing him arrive in Portugal in this worn-out garment, a son of his exclaimed, "But Father, this cassock has several shades!"

Monsignor Escrivá was amused. "I wore it for the journey. But don't you worry, my son, I will get changed in a minute and look really smart."[39]

He took care to keep his threadbare cassock brushed, sewed buttons back on as soon as they fell off, and gave it to the domestic staff to clean and iron, so that it looked relatively neat. One day he asked one of his daughters for a favor: he showed her a book of matches and said, "See if you can make us a little book just this size, with leaves of felt. My mother had one to keep needles and pins in when traveling, and it's a very practical idea. We would like to do our own mending while we're away."[40]

His outward appearance was always very correct and proper. He used to say, "Poverty isn't the same as not being clean; there's no reason why you shouldn't have more than one shower a day when the weather is hot, out of consideration for others; or even use some of the lighter, clean-smelling eau-de-colognes, because the best smell for a man is not to smell of anything."[41]

Monsignor Escrivá combined hard work at home with a high-profile social life. Although he did not attend cocktail parties or receptions, as president general of Opus Dei he did receive visits and guests every day, and naturally he dressed properly. Having only had the minimum of clothes, he had to change several times a day.

---

38. Ibid.
39. Cf. Hugo Azevedo, *Uma luz no mundo* (Lisboa: Ediçoes Prumo, Lda.).
40. Testimony of Helena Serrano (AGP, HRF T-04641).
41. Written account by Bishop Javier Echevarria.

Helena Serrano, who had a photographer's sharp eye for detail, noticed his care on this point. "I saw the Father going through the hall of Villa Vecchia, wearing his old cassock. Half an hour later I needed to ask his advice about a problem in the print room. I called the map room on the house telephone and Father Ernesto Julia answered it, and told me, 'The Father has just gone to change, as he's expecting visitors any minute. Go to the entrance of the sitting room of La Montagnola and you'll catch him as he passes by, and can ask him whatever you need." So I did, and the Father came along wearing his good cassock, the Roman-style one. He said he would get back to me when the visit was over, as he wanted to deal with the matter properly. Less than half an hour later he called us to the dining room of the Villa. Two of us went, taking the material we were having problems with. When we got there, I realized the Father had changed his cassock again: he was wearing his old one once more, the one he used around the house."[42]

Monsignor's wardrobe

Monsignor Escrivá sometimes declared he could tell the state of soul of one of his children in the Work by looking at the inside of his or her wardrobe. He always kept his own wardrobe unlocked so his daughters in the Work could put away his laundered clothes.

After he died, Carmen Ramos and another woman of the Work went to clear out his wardrobe. Hanging were his cassock, a woolen cardigan, an old woolen cape he had gotten years before from an army friend, and the trousers he wore under his cassock; shoes, underclothes, a few pairs of socks, a few collarless shirts, and a black woolen scarf. Several sets of cuffs, some white Roman collars and some handkerchiefs were folded up very neatly in boxes. There was also a leather whip which he used for self-discipline, the little sewing box for sewing on buttons, and nothing more.[43] Five or six minutes was all it took to pack it all up.

42. Testimony of Helena Serrano (AGP, HRF T-04641).
43. Testimony of Carmen Ramos.

Three untouchables

Deliberate detachment from owning and using things is hard and meritorious. But higher and deeper still is the poverty of one who surrenders his privacy, time, and future plans. These features of poverty of spirit were part of Monsignor Escrivá's daily life, practiced in such a natural way that they went unnoticed.

First, privacy. Monsignor Escrivá lived among people whom he met constantly in the corridors, in get-togethers, on walks, at talks and meditations; he celebrated their birthdays and feast days with them and shared their troubles; he prayed in the oratory or watched a film with the rest. He led formational activities, went for walks around the city with groups of them, or sat with one for long periods if he was ill. Anyone who lived under the same roof with him could easily find out where the Father was and what he was doing at any given moment. He had no time to himself and no place to be alone in; he knew that he was constantly observed as an example for others.

At the much deeper level of conscience, he placed his inner life in the hands of his confessor and confidant, Don Alvaro. Everything material, great and small, he placed in the hands of Father Javier Echevarria; from saying the synovitis he suffered from was causing pain in his elbows or he had not been able to sleep all night, to asking for a glass of water when his diabetes provoked raging thirst.

In the same way he surrendered his time. Monsignor Escrivá summed it up simply: "Do your duty *now*, without looking back on yesterday, which has already passed, or worrying over tomorrow, which may never come for you."[44] He encouraged people to live intensely in the *hodie et nunc*, today and now. *Nunc coepi!*—"I am beginning now!"—was the language of his spiritual struggle.

Monsignor Escrivá used time voraciously, making the most of each "hour of sixty minutes and each minute of sixty seconds." He did not need a watch because, as he explained, "after one job I do another; after attending to one matter I attend to the next one," wishing to die "squeezed out like a lemon."

---

44. *The Way*, no. 253.

His struggle to overcome his defects and acquire virtues was intense, consisting of short-term objectives, skirmishes, exact accounting, and a daily examination of conscience, checking it on waking in the morning, at midday, toward evening, and last thing at night. He had only "today" to win "this beautiful battle of love," *hoc pulcherrimum caritatis bellum.*

One spring day in 1960, talking to a group of his sons, he said, "I have no time to think about myself. I'm always thinking about others and about Jesus; and through him, about others and about myself. My midday examination of conscience is: 'Jesus, I love you!' And then I aim to advance on some small particular point. I haven't time for anything else! When night comes, it's: 'Lord, I haven't thought about myself all day!'"[45] He worked for today, solved problems today, prayed today, and loved today. "Tomorrow" was "the adverb of the defeated."[46]

On one occasion some young men in the Work wished to present him with a planner of the kind that fits into a diary and unfolds to show the whole year. Monsignor Escrivá declined the gift. "My children, I don't need a planner: my life is in God's hands. I can't go around calculating and scheming, like a strategist. I live here and now, and I know that *tempus breve est*: time is short, the time for loving God is short."[47]

Cruel doubts

Finally there was the surrender of his plans for the future.

Monsignor Escrivá was even detached from the vocation and mission entrusted to him by God on October 2, 1928: to do Opus Dei on earth. On at least two occasions—June 22, 1933, the eve of the feast of the Sacred Heart, in the Church of Perpetual Succor in Madrid, and again on September 25, 1941 in the Collegiate Church of La Granja at San Ildefonso in Segovia—he had the temptation or "cruel doubt" that the Work might after all be his invention about which he was deceiving others. Both times he reacted in the same

---

45. Testimony of Fr. Carlos Cardona (AGP, HRF T-06138).

46. *The Way*, no. 251.

47. Verbal account by Maria Jose Monterde to the author.

way. "Lord, if the Work is not here to serve you and to serve your Church, destroy it! Destroy it immediately!"[48] Both times the immediate response was peace and joy.

From then on he had an unshakable conviction: "Heaven is bent on the Work being fulfilled." The Work would flourish as God willed. His task was to put his whole heart and soul into the effort, without being worried about anything. He did not consider himself the maker or manager of the Work, still less its proprietor. He did not even consider himself its founder. "I'm not the founder of anything!" he would say, adding each time that he was just "a deaf and clumsy instrument." This was not just assumed humility. The Work existed by an initiative on God's part. He would never have guaranteed the success of something he invented; but knowing God to be the guarantor, he had a powerful sense of assurance.

Dr. Carlo Faelli was Monsignor Escrivá's doctor from 1946 until his death in 1975. Afterward he wrote a signed testimony: "He spoke little about himself and when he did it was only as God's instrument to do His Work. He never attached any importance to his own things. He gently passed over them. He was not interested in them. He never made a show of his position (as founder and president general of Opus Dei). He would say jokingly, 'I'm just a priest.' I told him he had no need to humble himself in front of me, but I think he took no notice. I can state as a fact that he had a keen sense of humor."[49]

Having emptied himself and become poor and free, Monsignor Escrivá never worried about tomorrow. "I'm not worried but occupied," he often said.

---

48. AGP, HRF 21502, note 134 and AGP, HRF 20165, p. 200.
49. Testimony of Dr. Carlo Faelli (AGP, HRF T-15734).

16 ✣

Clay and Grace

n 1942 Father Escrivá was the target of many accusations, insults, and calumnies. The attacks he called "the opposition from good people" had begun. One night, in the student residence hall on Diego de Leon Street, he went to the oratory. Alone on his knees beside the tabernacle, he sobbed. But after a while he said, "Lord, if you don't need my good name, what do I want it for?"

Later he confessed, "It was hard, it was very hard because I'm very proud, and huge tears were running down my face . . . but from that day on, I couldn't care less about anything!"[1]

Sixty brays, a line drawn, and a burst of laughter

He often repeated a kind of litany of lowliness: "I am worth nothing, I have nothing, I can do nothing, I know nothing, I am nothing . . . nothing!"[2] When his children in the Work wished him a happy sixtieth birthday, his response was, "Sixty years, Josemaría: sixty brays!"[3] And again: "I've drawn a line under all these years, and they add up to a burst of laughter!"[4]

---

1. *Articles of the Postulator*, 1034. Cf. Testimonies of Msgr. Javier de Ayala (AGP, HRF T-15712) and Fr. Pedro Casciaro (AGP, HRF T-04197).
2. *Articles of the Postulator*, 964.
3. Ibid., 977.
4. Bishop Alvaro del Portillo, January 9, 1976. AGP, HRF 21165.

A mangy donkey

In his *Intimate Notes* from the '30s, referring to matters of conscience, the letters '*b s*' (for *burrito sarnoso*, "mangy donkey") often appeared. That was how he saw himself before God: covered with mange, but wanting to be a humble, hard-working donkey.

On occasions he recalled an inner locution he had heard: "A donkey was my throne of glory in Jerusalem." He said, "Can't you see? Jesus is satisfied with a poor animal as a throne. I don't know about you, but it doesn't humiliate me to recognize that I'm a donkey in our Lord's eyes."[5]

Canon Joaquin Mestre, secretary to Bishop Marcelino Olaechea of Valencia for years, one day asked Monsignor Escrivá for a picture of himself.

"Certainly, certainly!" replied Monsignor Escrivá. "I'll get you one right away." He went into the next room and returned carrying a small wrought iron donkey. "There you are, there's your picture of me. That's me: a little donkey. And I hope I'll always be a little donkey before God, his beast of burden, bringing peace."[6]

In May 1975, the last time he went to Torreciudad, he beamed with delight on discovering a picture of a donkey in a small oratory. It was in a picture of the Flight into Egypt. He went to it and kissed it, saying, "Hello, brother!"[7]

In his office in Rome he also had a simple, roughly carved statue of St. Anthony, patron saint of domestic animals. Half-joking, yet wholly in earnest, he celebrated St. Anthony's feast day every year as if he were his own patron saint.

Toward the end of his life, during a brief stay in Madrid, while he was chatting with three or four of his sons, one of them, Francisco Garcia, several times heard Monsignor Escrivá quietly murmur words from Psalm 72: "*ut iumentum factus sum apud te!*—I have become like a donkey before you!"[8]

---

5. *Articles of the Postulator*, 974.
6. Ibid., 975.
7. Ibid., testimony of Don Joaquin Mestre (AGP, HRF T-00181).
8. Testimonies of Msgr. César Ortiz-Echagüe (AGP, HRF T-04694) and of Fr. Florencio Sanchez Bella (AGP, HRF T-08250).

A superiority complex

In Rome one day in 1968 an Italian university student asked him, "Father, how can we reconcile humility with the aplomb and superiority complex which Christians need in order to stir the world?"

"Look, my daughter, I have three doctorates and I'm an old man, so I must know something; but when I come before God I recognize that I'm just a donkey. Before God I know nothing, I'm worth nothing, I can do nothing. On the other hand he is wisdom and omnipotence—and he is my Father! Without him I have a great inferiority complex, but with him, with his help, I can do everything! I'm his son, and I have the resources of his wisdom, his power. And I say with St. Paul: *omnia possum in eo qui me confortat*, 'I can do everything in him who comforts me.'"

"I have this 'superiority complex' in order to serve, to serve others without their noticing this service, this work; to do it for love of God. The 'superiority complex' is a clear manifestation of humility: without God I can do nothing, with him I can do everything that is beautiful, bright, and great!"[9]

"I am a beginner . . . a babbling child"

He considered himself to be "a deaf, blind, and clumsy instrument," "a sinner who lives among saints," "a big fool who has not yet learned the lessons God tries to teach him," "a beginner," "a babbling child," "a zero," "nothing . . . nothingness!"

One night in 1957 he saw a famous scientist on television presenting a large number of books, the fruit of many years' work. Next day Monsignor Escrivá said to some of his children, "When I saw that old man, looking so natural and straightforward, I felt very ashamed in God's sight, because after so many years of vocation I can't say the same—I can't present this or that completed work. I've done nothing. I know nothing. I'm still learning the alphabet in the spiritual life. I feel like a beginner."[10]

---

9. Testimony of Fr. Francisco Garcia (AGP, HRF T-06386).
10. Testimony of Jose Miguel Ibañez (AGP, HRF T-07015). Cf. *Articles of the Postulator*, 970.

"Ah, ah, ah . . . I cannot speak"

One day in Madrid in 1941, Jose Ramon Madurga came upon Father Escrivá reading and making notes in a notebook. Father Escrivá showed him what he had been writing: a phrase from Jeremiah (1:6) where the prophet argued with God that he did not know how to preach, that he was like a child, awkward at expressing himself. "Look, read this," he said. "'Ah, ah, ah, Lord God, I do not know how to speak, for I am only a child!' I often use these words as a prayer, an aspiration, when I'm preparing to preach or give a talk."[11]

Seeing himself as an instrument for contact between others and God, he tried not to distract people or get in their way. In 1948 he preached a retreat for professional men in Molinoviejo. Aware that the people attending were fired up with enthusiasm and when the retreat was over there could be an explosion of praise for him, he organized a quick getaway. The director of the retreat was a law professor, Amadeo de Fuenmayor; Monsignor Escrivá told him, "Amadeo, when the last talk is finished, stay in the oratory with all of them. Give me a few minutes to get into the car and set off for Madrid. Don't say the final aspiration until you hear the engine start!"[12]

In 1964, after a stay in Pamplona during which he preached to many people, he said how ashamed he felt at the demonstrations of affection he received. "They carried me around like a statue in a procession!" He added, "Later on I heard that there had been many conversions, lapsed Catholics going to confession . . . and I remembered the clay our Lord used to open the eyes of the blind man in the Gospel."[13]

A Rhodesian journalist, Lynden Parry, insisted on thanking him for her conversion to Catholicism and the discovery of her vocation to Opus Dei. Without hesitation, he said, "All of us have so much to thank our Lord for! Don't thank me. God writes a letter and puts it in an envelope. You take the letter out of the envelope and throw the envelope away."[14]

---

11. Testimony of Jose Ramon Madurga (AGP, HRF T-05848). Cf. *Articles of the Postulator*, 982.

12. Testimony of Msgr. Amadeo de Fuenmayor (AGP, HRF T-02769). *Articles of the Postulator*, 1003.

13. Testimony of Jose Antonio Fernandez (AGP, HRF T-06521). Cf. *Articles of the Postulator*, 984.

14. Testimony of Lynden Parry (AGP, HRF T-06521). *Articles of the Postulator*, 981.

On countless occasions he said that in the Work he was "a disproportionate instrument" God had chosen "so people can see that the Work is his." On October 2, 1971, doing his prayer aloud with the general council of Opus Dei in Rome in the light of a stained glass window depicting the descent of the Holy Spirit on a group of early Christian men and women, he turned slightly toward the altar and said, "Thank you, Lord, for your continuous protection and for having intervened, sometimes very obviously—I didn't ask for it, I don't deserve it!—so there could be no doubt that the Work is Yours, only Yours, totally Yours."[15]

"A filthy rag, trash"

At other times he put it more bluntly: "I am a filthy rag, I am trash, and God has chosen me so everyone can see that the Work is his."[16] When his children wished him a happy feast day on any October 2, he would turn their praise back on themselves, in the words of an Italian proverb: *Il sangue del soldato fa grande il capitano!*—"The soldier's blood makes the captain great!"

Told some visitors had gone away comforted and strengthened by their conversation with him, he said, "Of course! They are excellent people and whatever you give them, they turn into good wine. On the other hand, if they were bad, they would turn even the good wine of the wedding feast of Cana into vinegar."[17]

After receiving visitors, he was often visibly moved. "What good people!" he would say. "Our Lord is constantly teaching me lessons! I'm always learning!" One day he had had more than the usual number of visitors. Far from showing any sign of tiredness, he displayed admiration and gratitude. "Those who come are so good, and it's so difficult to be good! To be even half-good requires such an effort! I see myself as very small indeed, a mere pigmy, beside them."[18]

One evening in Villa Sacchetti, Giuseppina Bertolucci read aloud a letter from her family telling how happy they all were after

15. *Articles of the Postulator*, 999.
16. Ibid.
17. Testimony of Marlies Kücking.
18. Testimony of Oscar Fernandez (AGP, HRF T-06531). *Articles of the Postulator*, 972.

being in Rome with the Father. She started reading some words of praise—"every time they remember him, their eyes shine"—but Monsignor Escrivá would hear no more. "All right, all right. 'With my fondest love,' and let's go on to something else!"[19]

Another of his daughters started to tell him how she had been to see Cardinal Casariego, and the cardinal said, "Pray for me, so that I may be half the saint Monsignor Escrivá is."

"No, my daughter! Don't take any notice of what he said on that point!"[20]

A conversation with Paul VI

Returning from the Vatican after what was to be his last meeting with Pope Paul VI, Monsignor Escrivá looked very serious, even upset. Only later did he say what had happened. In the middle of their conversation, Paul VI had suddenly stopped and exclaimed, "You are a saint!" Monsignor Escrivá's spontaneous answer was, "Here on earth there is only one saint: the Holy Father. All the rest of us are sinners."[21]

"Our Lord is my general"

He always felt very far from the total identification with God to which he aspired. He knew he was struggling in a constant state of beginning anew—*nunc coepi*, he said. But he never felt complacent.

An army general and his wife came to visit Monsignor Escrivá in Villa Tevere in October 1964. Monsignor Escrivá confided, "From the little balcony of my office I can see the tabernacle in the oratory. And there, in the evening, I often say to our Lord, who is my general: 'I am a soldier, your little soldier in this war of peace. And as a soldier, although I have fought hard today, Josemaría is not pleased with Josemaría.'"[22]

---

19. Testimony of Marlies Kücking.
20. Ibid.
21. Account by Bishop Alvaro del Portillo, Get-together, *Noticias*.
22. Testimony of Mercedes Morado (AGP, HRF T-07902).

Neither a saint nor a devil

Attacks did not overwhelm him, and praise did not make him vain. He had an exact sense of who he was. In July 1950, speaking of good and bad stories circulating about him for some time, he declared, "Some people have said that I'm a saint, and it isn't true: I'm a sinner. Others have said that I'm a devil; and they're not right either, because I'm a son of God."[23]

On February 25, 1947, when he and some of his children were living in the Città Leonina apartment, Vatican Radio broadcast news of the *Decretum Laudis*, the first solemn approval of the Holy See for Opus Dei. Father Escrivá borrowed a radio, wishing to listen to the news with his daughters: Encarnita Ortega, Julia Bustillo, Rosalia Lopez, Dora Calvo, and Dora del Hoyo, the only women of Opus Dei then living in Rome. The speaker praised the founder of Opus Dei and his work to the skies. Father Escrivá had not expected that. He became withdrawn and silent, standing with head bowed and eyes half-closed. He was praying intensely.[24]

The following year in Madrid, at the opening of the beatification process of Isidoro Zorzano—an Argentinian engineer, one of the first people of the Work—Father Escrivá sat among the public; Bishop Leopoldo Eijo y Garay, Bishop of Madrid, had to urge him to sit beside him on the podium.[25] Also in 1948 at the ordination ceremony of several men of Opus Dei in the Church of the Holy Spirit in Madrid, Monsignor Escrivá, wearing dark glasses, came in discreetly by a side door and took a place in a corner of the chancel.[26]

The doctorate . . . for the donkey

Professor Carlos Sanchez del Rio recalled when Monsignor Escrivá was awarded an honorary doctorate by the University of Saragossa in 1960. "He was very humble. I saw how moved he was when we gave him his honorary doctorate. He was grateful for the affection,

---

23. Cf. Testimonies of Fr. Francisco Botella (AGP, HRF T-00159), Fr. Ernesto Julia (AGP, HRF T-06541), and of Mercedes Morado (AGP, HRF T-07902). *Articles of the Postulator*, 969.

24. Testimony of Rosalia Lopez (AGP, HRF T-07918). *Articles of the Postulator*, 966.

25. Testimony of Aurora Bel (AGP, HRF T-04888). *Articles of the Postulator*, 967.

26. Verbal account by Mercedes Morado to the author.

but at the same time he listened to the glowing homage which we read about him as if against his will—as if he was not being given it for any merits of his own."[27] Returning to Rome, Monsignor Escrivá took the ring he had been given during the ceremony and hung it on the ear of one of the small ornamental donkeys in his office.

In October 1960, when the University of Navarre, founded by Monsignor Escrivá himself, was formally constituted, several public functions were held. A journalist, Joaquin Esteban Perruca, observed him closely. He recalled how by popular demand Monsignor Escrivá had to appear on the balcony of the town hall. People were cheering and applauding. The journalist wrote, "The Father remained deeply recollected all the time, as if the applause were not for him."[28]

With his forehead on the floor

One day in Rome in 1955, two women of the Work visited a prelate called Father Pedro Altabella. He made a prediction: "I assure you, the day will come when the name of Josemaría Escrivá de Balaguer will be known in the farthest corner of the world." Back at Villa Tevere, they told Monsignor Escrivá what was said. He commented, "It is true; Father Pedro is not mistaken. It will happen. . . . That's why I pray Psalm 50, the *Miserere*, every day prostrate on the ground, with my forehead touching the floor."[29]

"Go unnoticed and disappear"

In Madrid in April 1970, he stayed in the center of the Work on Diego de Leon Street. One morning he came into the dining room for breakfast with his sons and noticed some of the decorations. He recalled how the lamp had been bought in the early 1940s. "It came from a billiard room, and as it's made of bronze, it is very heavy; every time my mother saw it she was afraid it would fall on someone." Then he noticed some small gilded wooden pedestals that had been

---

27. Testimony of Carlos Sanchez (AGP, HRF T-02853). *Articles of the Postulator*, 1018.
28. Testimony of Joaquin Esteban (AGP, HRF T-01887). *Articles of the Postulator*, 1019.
29. Verbal accounts by Mercedes Morado and Gloria Toranzo to the author and testimony of Begoña Alvarez (AGP, HRF T-04861).

placed under a clock and under a set of ornamental candlesticks on the mantelpiece. He had suggested this touch on an earlier trip. "You've done it very nicely," he observed. "That makes them stand out more. In civil life, people also need a kind of pedestal so that their worth can be seen. On the other hand, I've always preferred to go unnoticed and disappear. . . . 'He must increase and I must decrease.' And even then. . . !"[30]

In a letter from the 1930s he told the vicar general of the Madrid diocese, "I see more and more clearly that God's will is for me to go unnoticed and disappear."[31] More than forty years later, he expressed the same idea in almost the same words, on the eve of March 28, 1975, the golden jubilee of his ordination to the priesthood: "I wish to spend this jubilee in my usual way: to go unnoticed and disappear is my part, so that only Jesus shines forth."

Every year Opus Dei ordains a new batch of priests. Generally speaking, Monsignor Escrivá did not attend the ordination ceremonies, but stayed at home and prayed. When people asked why he was not there, he answered firmly, "My way is to go unnoticed and disappear."

At the beginnings of Opus Dei, well-meaning people advised him to take a university professorship or some honorary post so as to have more influence and make himself heard, and not be just "a plain priest." Invariably he answered, "If I limit myself to being a priest 100 percent, there will be many other 100 percent priests, and there will be many good Catholics who will be professors, employees, or peasants, who will faithfully serve the Church as 100 percent Christians."[32] In those first years in Madrid, a priest outside his own diocese, he wanted a way of being incardinated into the Madrid diocese. It was arranged for him to meet Father Pedro Poveda, founder of the Teresian Institute and secretary to the Patriarch of the Indies, someone very well situated who could help solve his problem. When they met, Father Poveda suggested, "Maybe you could think about the post of honorary Palace chaplain."

30. Testimony of Msgr. César Ortiz-Echagüe (AGP, HRF T-04694).
31. This mode of conduct appears in the *Intimate Notes* at least from 1932.
32. Testimonies of Joaquin Mestre (AGP, HRF T-00181), Fr. Pedro Casciaro (AGP, HRF T-04197), and Fr. José Luis Muzquiz (AGP, HRF T-04678). Cf. *Articles of the Postulator*, 1004.

"And what's that?" asked Father Escrivá.

"Well, now, you would dress more or less like me, and you would get a benefice."

"But, Father Pedro, would that give me the right to be incardinated in the Madrid diocese?"

"No, it wouldn't."

"Then I'm not interested."[33]

Father Poveda was surprised and impressed. To be part of the clergy attached to the Royal Household was a much sought after honor; but Father Escrivá turned it down because it was not what he needed to carry out his mission. From that point on, a deep friendship developed between Father Poveda and Father Escrivá.

Around the same time, Bishop Cruz Laplana of Cuenca, a relative of Father Escrivá, offered him a canonry in Cuenca Cathedral. Father Escrivá rejected the offer. Leaving Madrid and moving to Cuenca when Opus Dei had just begun growing would place obstacles in the mission to which God had called him.[34]

"I don't want to be a bishop"

In the same way, on February 11, 1933, he rejected an interesting proposition made by Father Angel Herrera, recently appointed president of Catholic Action in Spain. Father Herrera offered to appoint him director of the house of the counsellor of Catholic Action, where he was planning "to bring together the most outstanding of the secular Spanish clergy." Besides apostolic influence on these priests, it was clear that this post could be a springboard to the episcopate.

"Think it over, Father Josemaría," urged Father Herrera. "I'll be bringing the best priests in Spain together in this house, and what I'm proposing is for you to be their director."

"No, indeed," he replied. "I'm very grateful, but I cannot accept. I have to follow the path chosen for me by God. Besides, I can't accept for the very reason you yourself give: because the best priests

---

33. *Articles of the Postulator*, 1014.
34. Testimony of Joaquin Mestre (AGP, HRF T-00181). *Articles of the Postulator*, 1015.

in Spain will be gathered here, and I'm obviously not capable of directing them."[35]

It has been said, without foundation, that Father Escrivá wanted to be a bishop. But actually he took steps to avoid the possibility. After the Spanish Civil War he spent a great deal of his time preaching retreats to bishops, and his standing and reputation grew. No doubt he heard comments about the possibility of being made a bishop, so he asked his confessor (at the time, Father José María García) for permission to "make a vow never to accept the burden or dignity of being made a bishop." Father Garciá responded that without the permission of the Bishop of Madrid, he could not allow such a vow. Father Escrivá then presented the problem to Bishop Leopoldo Eijo y Garay of Madrid, on March 19, 1941. Among his notes is: "The Bishop has not given me permission. I am really upset."[36]

During the 1950s he was awarded a civil decoration. At a get-together, one of his sons, an army man, congratulated him. Monsignor Escrivá smiled and said, "For you military people this business of getting medals is an important affair, but not for me. I—and you, too, at the bottom of your heart—am only interested in one cross: the Holy Cross."[37]

He explained that the worst thing that could happen to anyone was to receive nothing but praise. He was grateful when people corrected him, and took note of the corrections to improve. He had to struggle with the Holy See not to be deprived of "fraternal correction," a fundamental means of formation in Opus Dei. The Vatican notified him that according to traditional custom, "a superior cannot be corrected by his subordinates." But Monsignor Escrivá insisted that he not be deprived of this help. In the end, approval was given to his having two *custodes*, guardians or aides, to live close to him and advise and correct him. Don Alvaro and Father Javier Echevarria had this job for years.

---

35. Ibid. Fr. Angel Herrera, lawyer, founder of "*Accion Nacional*," a political party, and editor of the newspaper *El Debate*. He was ordained a priest in 1940. He was made a cardinal by Pope Paul VI in 1965.

36. Cf. Césare Cavalleri, *Immersed in God, An Interview with Alvaro del Portillo on the Founder of Opus Dei* (Princeton, NJ: Scepter, 1996), p. 205.

37. Cf. *Articles of the Postulator*, 1017.

"Alvaro does not let me get away with a single thing!"

He was grateful to them for pointing out things to improve on or make amends for. He said this one day to a group of women of the Work. "They point out things to me too, and I receive them with my head bowed down. If ever I think they're wrong, I stop and correct myself—and I see that the one who's wrong is myself."[38]

He was chatting one day while the construction at Villa Tevere was going on with several of his daughters, showing them how the work was progressing. Don Alvaro was there. Monsignor Escrivá, leaning on a bar of the scaffolding, confided, "Don Alvaro corrected me today. It was hard to accept. So much so that I went to the oratory for a moment. Once there, I said, 'Lord, Alvaro's right and I'm wrong.' But after a second, I said, 'No, Lord, this time I am right. Alvaro doesn't let me get away with a single thing, and that doesn't seem like affection but cruelty.' And then I said, 'Thank you, Lord, for placing my son Alvaro near me, who is so fond of me that he doesn't let me get away with a single thing!'" He turned toward Don Alvaro, who had been listening in silence, smiled at him, and said, "God bless you, Alvaro, my son!"[39]

"I'm not a river which can never turn back"

Encarnita Ortega recalled hearing him say he found it hard to be corrected, "especially when what they tell me is true," but "on feeling an inner resistance, if I'm alone I say aloud, 'They're always right! They're always right!'"[40]

He corrected himself quickly. He said once, "I'm not a river, which can never turn back. It would be foolish and stubborn not to change your mind when you have new data."[41] And he said, "I assure you that correcting yourself rids your soul of bitterness."[42]

---

38. Testimonies of Maria Luisa Sanchez (AGP, HRF T-05134) and of Fr. Ernesto Julia (AGP, HRF T-06541). Cf. *Articles of the Postulator*, 1058.
39. Verbal account of Lourdes Toranzo to the author.
40. Testimony of Encarnación Ortega (AGP, HRF T-05074).
41. Testimony of Marlies Kücking.
42. Cf. *Articles of the Postulator*, 1059.

"I've come to say sorry"

One day in Madrid in 1946, he went into the catering department of the Diego de Leon residence in mid-morning. It looked a mess: a cupboard door half open, another cupboard untidy inside, groceries and supplies not put away but still in baskets and bags, and a pile of dirty dishes in the sink. Much upset, Father Escrivá called for the director, but she was not in. Flor Cano, another woman of the Work, came instead and received the full flood of protest. "This can't be allowed! It just can't! Where is your presence of God while you're working? You have to do things with much more sense of responsibility!"

Without realizing it, he had been raising and hardening his voice. Suddenly he stopped. Then, in a completely different tone, he said, "Lord . . . forgive me! And you, my daughter, forgive me too."

"Father—please—you're absolutely right!" said Flor.

"Yes, I am, because what I'm saying is true," he responded. "But I ought not to have said it in that tone of voice. So please forgive me!"[43]

On another occasion in Rome he reprimanded Ernesto Julia over the intercom for neglecting an important job. Ernesto did not protest or make excuses. Shortly afterward, someone informed Monsignor Escrivá that Ernesto had not known about the matter because he had not been asked to do it. Without delaying a second, Monsignor Escrivá picked up the intercom and asked Ernesto to come to where the two buildings, Casa del Vicolo and Villa Vecchia, met. When Ernesto got there, he found Monsignor Escrivá waiting for him with arms wide open. With an engaging, affectionate smile, he said, "My son, I'm sorry. I beg your forgiveness and restore your good name to you!"[44]

He was quick and generous whenever he needed to put something right or ask forgiveness. One day in January 1955, while students of the Roman College were chatting with him in a corridor in Villa Tevere, Fernando Acaso came by. Monsignor Escrivá asked if he had collected some furniture which was to be placed near

43. Testimony of Florentina Cano (AGP, HRF T-04913). *Articles of the Postulator*, 1055.
44. Verbal account by Fr. Ernesto Julia.

some stairs. Fernando gave an evasive reply without making it clear whether the furniture was in the house. Monsignor Escrivá interrupted: "But have you brought it home, or not?"

"No, Father," said Fernando. Monsignor Escrivá then told all of them there always to be "sincere and direct, unafraid of anything or anybody" and "without making excuses, because no one's accusing you!"

At that moment Don Alvaro came along, looking for Fernando Acaso. "Fernando, you can pick up the furniture whenever you like; there's money in the bank for it now." Here was the reason for Fernando's evasive explanation. In front of everyone, he apologized. "Forgive me, my son, for not listening to your reasons. I can see that it wasn't your fault. With your attitude you've given me a splendid lesson in humility. God bless you!"[45]

In the summer of that same year, 1955, Monsignor Escrivá was in Spain and spent a day in Molinoviejo with a big group of his sons who were doing a course there and having a rest. Among them was Rafael Caamaño, who had just come back from Italy where he had taken a three-year course in naval engineering. Monsignor Escrivá beckoned him and Javier Echevarria over to a stone fountain among the trees. "Rafael, I have to beg your pardon for maybe having scandalized you that time by not giving money to the beggar. I needed to tell you that that's not my spirit. Although I never carry any money, I could have—I ought to have—asked one of you to give some coins to that poor man. Now you know: the Father did wrong and begs your forgiveness."

Rafael said nothing. Only much later he managed to recall the event. Months back, he had gone with Monsignor Escrivá and two other people on a drive in the outskirts of Rome. They stopped to have a coffee in one of the *castelli*. A beggar came up asking for alms, and they gave him to understand they had no money for him. Caamaño realized that this commonplace event had touched Monsignor Escrivá.[46]

---

45. Testimony of Fr. Antonio Linares (AGP, HRF T-04559). Cf. Césare Cavalleri, *Immersed in God*, p. 83.
46. Testimony of Fr. Rafael Caamaño (AGP, HRF T-05837).

One day in Villa Tevere Monsignor Escrivá went into the office of the secretary general of the Work and corrected some errors which two or three of the people working there had introduced into a document that misrepresented the spirituality of Opus Dei. Having made plain the far-reaching consequences such mistakes could have, he left. After a while he came back, looking peaceful and joyous. "My sons," he said, "I've just been to confession to Don Alvaro, because what I said to you before was something I had to say, but I shouldn't have said it the way I did. So I went to our Lord to ask him to forgive me, and now I've come to say sorry to you."[47]

Another time he was hurrying along a corridor when one of his daughters tried to stop him with a question for which it was neither the time nor the place. Hardly slowing, he shrugged and said, "How should I know? Ask Don Alvaro!" Later that day the same girl was tidying things in the hall of Villa Vecchia as Monsignor Escrivá and Don Alvaro passed. Monsignor Escrivá said, "I'm sorry, my daughter, for having answered you as I did earlier on. Those of you who live with me have so much to put up with!"[48]

In his pocket diary he copied a phrase from St. John's Gospel every year: *Numquid lex nostra iudicat hominem, nisi prius audierit ab ipso?* "Does our law judge any man without first giving him a hearing?" (John 7:51). He meditated on that, put it into practice, and recommended it to others.[49]

He also corrected himself or changed his mind if he could do someone a service. In 1970 Monsignor Escrivá was making a stopover at the Madrid airport on his way from Rome to Mexico. There was a big group of media in the international departure area, hoping to get photographs of the founder of Opus Dei, and the photographer of the newspaper *Nuevo Diario*, Eduardo Caliz, could not get a shot. A big, heavy man, he pushed through the crowd to Monsignor Escrivá and said, "Let us have a few photos!"

Monsignor Escrivá answered cheerfully, "Look, I'm not Concha Piquer" [a famous singer], "I'm only a poor man!"

---

47. Verbal account by Fr. Ernesto Julia.
48. Testimony of Helena Serrano (AGP, HRF T-04641).
49. Testimonies of Begoña Alvarez (AGP, HRF T-04861) and Encarnación Ortega (AGP, HRF T-05074).

The journalist replied, "I don't care at all for myself, but I have to do my job. This is my children's bread and butter."

At that he stopped short and, turning toward Eduardo Caliz, looked him in the eye and smiled. "If you have to do your job, and earn your children's bread and butter, I'll stay here and pose until you tell me to stop!"[50]

Monsignor Escrivá's "guardians"

A part of Monsignor Escrivá's humility less generally known was his voluntary submission, in apparently insignificant things, to Don Alvaro, who was, for want of a better word, the "guardian" of his soul. Although Monsignor Escrivá ranked above Don Alvaro there is evidence that in questions of a personal nature, he obeyed him unhesitatingly, determined to seek "a golden opportunity to be able to obey."

One day in the print room he was examining type fonts and lay-out options for a certain text. Instead of deciding there and then, he specified, "This is fine, but don't do it yet: wait till Don Alvaro comes back and see what he thinks. He's out right now."[51]

His breakfast was always a roll and a cup of lukewarm white coffee, without sugar. One day, he saw some fried eggs on a dish all ready for him and Don Alvaro. He asked that they be taken away "so that someone else can have them, because we're not going to." But Rosalia, waiting at table, told him "Don Alvaro asked for them," and he accepted them immediately.[52]

On January 9, 1968, his birthday, he had a short get-together in the morning with the women in La Montagnola; Don Alvaro was there. They chatted animatedly. Suddenly Monsignor Escrivá looked searchingly at all of them and said confidentially, "My daughters, I'm going to tell you something, because you are all grown up here, so you can pray for something for me."

There was an expectant silence. Monsignor Escrivá turned to Don Alvaro and asked, "Alvaro, shall I tell them?"

---

50. Witnessed by the author, Barajas Airport, Madrid, 1970.
51. Testimony of Helena Serrano (AGP, HRF T-04641).
52. Testimony of Encarnación Ortega (AGP, HRF T-05074).

"Father, better not," replied Don Alvaro.

"Shan't I tell them?"

"I think not, Father."

"Well, my daughters," said Monsignor Escrivá, "there's nothing more to say. You'll find out about it in due time. And now you can offer up this little curiosity to our Lord."[53]

Although especially in his last few years he woke up before dawn, he remained in bed until Father Javier Echevarria, his other "guardian," said it was time to get up, because he had been told to rest more. If at a get-together Father Echevarria told him it was time to finish because he had work waiting for him, he always got up without delay, no matter how interesting the conversation was.

One day in 1961 at Christmas, Monsignor Escrivá had been talking with some of his daughters in the laundry of Villa Sacchetti. On his way through the Galleria della Madonna, Helena Serrano said, "Father, now that you're here, why not come and see the crèche we've set up in the print room?"

Monsignor Escrivá turned toward Don Alvaro and Father Echevarria. "Shall I go?"

When both assented, he smiled happily and said, "Let's go."[54]

"Doctor, do whatever you have to do"

He practiced this docility also toward doctors and dentists, to the point of voluntarily suppressing the slightest complaint when he put himself into the doctor's hands. His dentist, Dr. Kurzio Hruska, a Protestant, was very impressed. He often treated Monsignor Escrivá in his office at 10 Via Carducci, in Rome.

"Whenever possible," recounted Dr. Hruska, "he preferred to have an appointment early in the morning so he could work without interruption afterward, even though he knew that after the treatment he would not be feeling well.

"He always arrived early for his appointment. And if I was running late and kept him waiting, he would enter the examination

---

53. Testimony of Mercedes Morado (AGP, HRF T-07902).
54. Testimony of Helena Serrano (AGP, HRF T-04641).

room with the same good humor. He did not like making people wait for him because, he said, 'I respect your work very much.'

"As a patient Monsignor Escrivá was a very disciplined, humble person. I was amazed, because it's not often one finds people like that: he was humble in all his gestures. Humble, in spite of his tremendous energy and dynamism. It was strange: first of all he looked at you, he looked into your very soul. You could almost say that he X-rayed you! And then straight away he became a docile patient. Whatever I said or did was fine by him. This was an added difficulty for me, given his delicate dental situation. Sometimes I'd say, 'Tell me if this hurts.' And as he did not complain, I would interrupt the operation in some surprise and say, 'I'd prefer you to tell me everything and not just put up with the pain, because it isn't possible that I'm not hurting you right now.'

"My medical treatment was not always 'friendly.' Sometimes I'd say, 'I'll have to give you an injection.' And he would reply, 'Doctor, do whatever you have to do!' So I did. I had to do a lot of hard, painful work on his mouth. And I asked him, 'How can you stand it?' 'Man has to get used to everything,' he said. Even if I'd nailed a spike into his gums, he would have accepted it. I think I would have been able to crucify him and he would have put up with it. As a man and as a patient he was very humble; but it was not a mean-spirited or offensive humility. The fact is, he was always content, balanced, cheerful and serene. He felt himself to be a son of God. 'God will cure me,' he used to say, and this made him unconcerned about his body, and any physical discomforts or illness."[55]

Marquis of Peralta

Sometimes it is easier to give way than exercise rights. Monsignor Escrivá experienced this when, in 1968, he decided to revive the title of Marquis of Peralta, which had belonged to his ancestors centuries before. He wanted to be able to pass it on to his younger brother Santiago and his descendants, in compensation for supporting the development of the Work from the beginning at the cost of a small family inheritance.

---

55. Testimony of Dr. Kurzio Hruska (AGP, HRF T-15732).

Although he had no intention of making use of the title himself, he knew he would be criticized by people who would see his action as proof of worldly vanity and snobbishness. He thought it over carefully in his prayer and consulted several people within and outside the Work—Cardinal Dell'Acqua, Cardinal Marella, Cardinal Larraona, Cardinal Antoniutti, Cardinal Bueno y Monreal, and the Archbishop of Madrid Casimiro Morcillo. All agreed. On the civil side, he had the favorable report of the Council of State and the Deputation of Grandees of Spain. Some, like Cardinal Larraona, a famous canon lawyer, argued that from the viewpoint of lay mentality it was not only a right but an obligation. "It's your duty. You have always taught your children to fulfill their civil obligations and to exercise their rights as citizens. Therefore if you did not do so, you would be setting them a bad example."[56]

He was not mistaken in thinking this would be a new opportunity for people to insult him. The affair stirred up a controversy in the press. At one point, alone with Don Alvaro, Monsignor Escrivá declared, "My son, it is often much more difficult to exercise a right than to carry out a duty!"[57] He never used the title himself, but in the shortest possible time transferred it to his brother, who became the Marquis of Peralta.

On one occasion he was given an antique tapestry of red velvet. In the center was the heraldic shield of the family who had owned it. Someone suggested replacing the emblem with Monsignor Escrivá's family crest. He refused, and proposed the inscription *Iesus Christus, Deus, Homo*—"Jesus Christ, God, Man." "It makes me so happy to put those words there!"[58]

The tomb of the unknown soldier

In April 1969, on a trip to Madrid, he visited the crypt in the Diego de Leon residence for the first time. In two sarcophagi on either side of the altar lay the mortal remains of his parents, Jose Escrivá

---

56. Cf. AGP, HRF 21165, pp. 1010–1012. Cf. Césare Cavalleri, *Immersed in God*, pp. 15–21.
57. Ibid.
58. Testimony of Mercedes Morado (AGP, HRF T-07902).

and Dolores Albas. Monsignor Escrivá explained to those with him, "I have allowed you to bring my parents' bodies here to represent all your parents. They fulfill the role of the 'unknown soldier' who lies buried in so many monuments to the war dead." And he added, "The first thing I did on coming into the crypt was to pray for all the parents of the people of the Work, living and dead."[59]

"A founder without foundation"

How did he cope with being the founder and still stay humble?

While still a young priest, Father Escrivá had accepted being called "the Father" in the most natural way, but he was reluctant to be called "the founder." This unsought charism, far from conferring a privilege, obliged him to have a greater sense of responsibility. In molding and forming the spirit of Opus Dei, his word was not just decisive but was the only one divinely authorized. He did not share this work or delegate, but carried the load alone. He alone had *seen* the Work, whole and entire, and he responded with the faithfulness of an instrument who had received a command.

In some aspects, including the juridical form of the Work, which did not depend exclusively on him, he was capable of waiting as long as necessary and putting up with red tape, rather than take a false step. When people called him "the founder," he responded, "Well, my children call me the founder of Opus Dei, and indeed I am; but I am *a founder without foundation*. The foundation is Christ alone. When he comes for me it will be seen straight away that I'm not at all indispensable. I am a founder who is not needed."[60]

An old yellowing piece of paper

At times he spoke of himself as "a hindrance." On a piece of paper, yellowed with age, undated, written in his own handwriting

---

59. Testimony of Msgr. César Ortiz-Echagüe, No. 12, 3.

60. Testimony of Fr. Joaquin Mestre (AGP, HRF T-00181), Isabel Cipriani (AGP, HRF T-05778), and John Debicki (AGP, HRF T-07591). Cf. *Articles of the Postulator*, 971.

and signed Mariano—one of his Christian names which he began using during the Spanish Civil War—the following confession can still be read:

> In a Work of God I am nothing more than a hindrance. Mariano.

A postscript adds: "Then just imagine my role! Alvaro."[61]

On September 24, 1968, at an evening get-together in Rome, after recalling episodes from the early days of Opus Dei, Monsignor Escrivá explained, "It was very hard in the beginning. With you men, things worked out at the first attempt: however, there were some people who came to the Work and then left without even saying good-bye. And I spent many hours praying in front of the tabernacle. Now I pray everywhere, but then I thought that I was not praying unless I was in front of the tabernacle. Anyway, when I go to Spain now, and see the marvelous development of the Work, I have palpable proof that it is God who has done everything, because he made me see how powerless I was."[62]

Another day in the spring of 1967 in Pozoalbero, Spain, Manuel Pedreño told him an amusing story about a boy from Seville who said: "When I'm big I want to be one of the men in Opus Dei so I can live in a house of the Work."

Monsignor Escrivá then told how on October 2, 1928, the day the Work was founded, he had thought that everyone would live in their own homes, as the Work was for ordinary Christians who had to be saints in their own circumstances. Soon afterward God showed him the need for some to live together to attend to formation and corporate works of apostolate. He said, "Our Lord works in the same way as a good teacher: first of all he gives a general impression, an overall view. Later on he fills in the details. You will find out about fifty percent of these things here; the other fifty percent you will find out in heaven. It's all God's doing, nothing is mine. You have to realize that God has even spoken through a donkey! Remember Balaam's donkey?"[63]

61. Cf. Testimony of Begoña Alvarez (AGP, HRF T-04861).
62. Testimony of Fr. Fernando Valenciano (AGP, RHF T-05362).
63. Testimony of Msgr. César Ortiz-Echagüe (AGP, HRF T-04694).

"As a notary, I testify . . ."

A month before his death in May 1975 he went to visit the almost completed shrine of Torreciudad. During the tour of the shrine, they went past an open-air altar where there was a bell with historic significance: it was one of the bells that had pealed in the belfry of the Church of Our Lady of the Angels in Bravo Murillo Street in Madrid on October 2, 1928. Father Escrivá had heard those bells in Garcia de Paredes Street at the moment he saw the Work.

Don Alvaro went to look at the plaque on the wall, translating the first few sentences from Latin aloud.

"On the morning of 2nd October 1928 while this bell and the others of the belfry of the Madrid Church of Our Lady of the Angels were ringing and the peals of praise were going up to heaven, Monsignor Josemaría Escrivá de Balaguer received the seed of Opus Dei in his heart and mind . . ."

Monsignor Escrivá had been listening carefully in silence. Now he turned to the people around him and said firmly but without raising his voice, "I'm called Escrivá, which means scribe or notary. Very well then, as a 'notary' I testify to what you have just heard."[64]

"Will you carry on with the Work?"

He knew he was only the receiver and transmitter of a message "as old and as new as the Gospel," the universal call to holiness for all men and women in all circumstances at all times and everywhere. From early on he understood that everyone in the Work ought to "do Opus Dei in the world, by being Opus Dei yourself." In 1931, when he was twenty-nine and the Work was still very young, he was ready to hand over the baton to others. With violent religious persecution gathering strength in Spain, Father Escrivá asked a seventeen-year-old boy who had recently joined Opus Dei, "If I am killed, will you carry on with the Work?" In 1936, shortly before the outbreak of the Civil War, Father Escrivá summoned a few young men into the dining room of the Ferraz Street residence in Madrid,

---

64. Ibid.

and said, "If I were to die now, for whatever reason, will you carry on with the Work?"

"Yes, Father," each responded.

"Will you swear it?"

"Yes, Father. With all my love, I swear it."

Don Alvaro remembered this vividly forty years later. He was one of those young men.[65]

But Monsignor Escrivá was well aware that he had received the charism of founder and gave himself to it wholeheartedly. He had to remain "attentive" in case God wanted to make him aware of new details. In a get-together in the Roman College on April 23, 1959, he said, "I'm still alive, which means that the Work is young and there are still many things, customs, small points to be brought out. You will have to help me. The foundational stage will be closed when you bury me. Until then all of you are co-founders. Everything is complete, and the spirit of the Work is not just sketched out but sculpted! But the foundation will be closed only when you have the kindness and compassion to bury my body. Maybe you'll have to wait another twenty-four years and you'll be taking me out in the sun in a wheelchair; or I might even die tonight—and may God receive me in his mercy and love."[66]

Monsignor Escrivá did not consider himself spiritually remarkable or a model, much less a saint. When referring to himself, expressions such as "a poor man," "a filthy rag," "a ragamuffin," and "a poor sinner who lives among saints" were constantly on his lips.

Speaking to his spiritual sons in Rome, he said once, "I adorn myself with the jewels of your daily self-surrender, and like that I have enough confidence to talk with our Lord. That's my strength: your self-surrender! . . . My dear sons, I don't know how I have the nerve to call myself the father of such children, who have given themselves so completely to God. For years I've had the impression that I'm living among saints. Lord, what sons you have given me, although I'm just a sinner!"[67]

65. Verbal account by Bishop Alvaro del Portillo: AGP, HRF 21164, pp. 1467–1468 and 1491–1492.

66. Testimony of Fr. Carlos Cardona (AGP, HRF T-06138).

67. Cf. Testimonies of Fr. Carlos Cardona (AGP, HRF T-06138) and Salvador Suanzes (AGP, HRF T-06378).

On March 27, 1975, eve of his golden jubilee as a priest, he admitted while praying aloud that he saw himself as small, awkward, and clumsy. "Fifty years have gone by, and I'm still like a faltering child. I'm just beginning, beginning again, as I do every day in my interior life. And that's how it will be till the end of my days: always beginning anew. Our Lord wants it that way, so that none of us may ever have any reason for pride or foolish vanity."[68]

Next day he spent some time talking with his daughters. "Be really convinced there is no one in the world as happy as we are, and that we invent almost all the difficulties we meet—they are never of any real importance. I can tell you so after drawing a line under these past fifty years, adding up the sum and bursting out laughing: a laugh which means I forgive everything and ask God for forgiveness myself. I forgive everything, and I ask God for forgiveness!"[69]

In 1940, he again asked some of his sons if they would carry on with the Work if he died. Finally he said, "I should hope so! It would be a poor show if instead of following our Lord, you had merely been following a poor man like me!" He stressed over and over again, "I'm not aiming for you to love me, but for you to love God and be faithful to him."[70]

Referring to his successor, he often said to the members of the general council: "You will have to love and venerate in a very special way whoever comes after me." He also told them, "When I hear in this blessed Rome, how some institutions suffer a kind of earthquake when the founder or foundress dies . . . I assure you there will be no such earthquake in the Work. Of that I am certain." Later he added, "You have to love him already, because he will govern better than I do."[71] On December 27, 1973, he said sincerely, "I don't want to be a despot. What I want is that on the day I die, everything should carry on as if I were still here. Otherwise I've been wasting my time."[72] On March 19, 1975, he said, "I'm not necessary. I'll be able to help you more from heaven. You'll be able to do things better than I do. I'm not needed."[73]

---

68. AGP, HRF 21164, p. 747.
69. Ibid.
70. Cf. Testimony of Fr. Jose Orlandis (AGP, HRF T-00184). *Articles of the Postulator*, 985.
71. *Articles of the Postulator*, 988 and 989.
72. *Articles of the Postulator*, 991.
73. *Articles of the Postulator*, 992.

Another angle on Monsignor Escrivá's humility was this theme of "beginning and beginning again" which made him see himself as "a faltering child." It was the opposite of bitterness, resentment or any kind of mischief-making and intrigue. Monsignor Escrivá had the dynamism of a child who was always enthusiastically beginning to read the first page of a new book, linked to a continuous act of returning to cleanness of soul. He made this act of returning like "the prodigal son returning to his father's house," along the paths of contrition and confession—humble, well-trodden paths which he often used.

He called acts of contrition, sorrow, and atonement "staples," like the metal staples sometimes used to hold pieces of broken pottery together. He compared himself to an old clay vessel, "any old cheap earthenware," cracked and needing to be held together with clips.

Monsignor Escrivá's confessors

From the beginning Father Escrivá did his best to go to confession to the same priest for as long as circumstances permitted. When he was fifteen in Logroño, he turned to Father Jose Miguel, a Carmelite friar, for spiritual guidance. It was Father Miguel who made those footprints in the snow, and he suggested to Josemaría that he too should become a discalced Carmelite. Young Josemaría, having pondered the matter in prayer, understood that this was not what God wanted of him. But to be available for the vocation he could not yet see clearly, he decided to become a priest.

His father put him in touch with the Abbot of the collegiate church in Logroño, Father Antolin Oñate, and with Father Albino Pajares, an army chaplain, who prepared him to enter the seminary with academic and spiritual teaching. However, Josemaría received his spiritual guidance during this time from Father Ciriaco Garrido, canon of the collegiate church.

During the years in the seminary in Saragossa, he received help from the rector, Father Jose Lopez, Monsignor Miguel de los Santos Diaz, Father Antonio Moreno, and Cardinal Soldevila himself. Soon after his ordination, from 1926 on, he was guided by Father Jose Pou de Foxa, whom he always remembered as a loyal man and good friend.

When he moved to Madrid, he went to the Jesuit Father Valentin Sanchez for spiritual guidance. This began in 1930, and was twice interrupted for reasons beyond his control. The first time was in 1932, when the Republican government ordered the expulsion of the Jesuits; Father Escrivá then went to confession to Father Postius, a Claretian. The second time was during the Civil War, which forced priests to go into hiding or flee the Republican zone. Father Escrivá took refuge in the Honduran legation, which had diplomatic immunity, and went to confession every week to Father Recaredo Ventosa, who was also being sheltered there. After crossing the Pyrenees in 1937 to the Nationalist zone, he took Father Angel Sagarminaga as his confessor during his stay in Vitoria; and in 1938, while in Burgos until the end of the war, he first chose Father Saturnino Martinez as spiritual director, a very devout priest; but Father Martinez's health was precarious and so he could not attend to him regularly. Then Father Escrivá went to the Claretian Father Francisco de Borja Lopez, whom he always remembered with gratitude. In the early 1940s, when Father Lopez came to see him in the Diego de Leon residence in Madrid during the great scarcity of the postwar years, Father Escrivá gave him a warm cape, the only one he had.

From April 1939, living in Madrid again, he sought out his old confessor, the Jesuit Father Valentin Sanchez. It was Father Sanchez who had one day asked Father Escrivá, "How is that Work of God getting on?" Without knowing it, he had conferred the name Opus Dei on an undertaking that did not have a name. He continued to receive spiritual guidance from Father Sanchez until the autumn of 1940, when he felt he was morally obliged to stop. The key factor—trust—had failed.

Don Alvaro, a witness of the last two meetings between Father Escrivá and Father Sanchez, offered the following account. "In 1940, the Father had prepared the documents for the diocesan approval of the Work at the insistence of the Bishop of Madrid (Bishop Leopoldo Eijo y Garay). Since part of it related to the spirit of Opus Dei and was no more than an account of the ascetic way our Lord was taking him, that is to say, his own interior life, it seemed opportune to show these documents to Father Sanchez too. The Father always distinguished between what referred to the foundation of Opus Dei, which did not involve his spiritual directors, and what affected his own spiritual life. So his intention was not to ask Father Sanchez for his opinion about Opus Dei, but about his own spiritual life. I seem to remember the meeting when he gave him the documents took place in September 1940.

"A few weeks later I went with the Father to visit his spiritual director. Father Sanchez, who had always encouraged him to be faithful to his foundational charism, told him this time, in very different tones, that the Holy See would never approve the Work. And he cited the numbers of several canons of Church law to corroborate this statement. He returned the documents to him and dismissed him.

"The Father really suffered a lot in that meeting but did not lose his peace of mind. He repeated his conviction that as the Work was God's, He would be responsible for bringing it to a safe harbor. He also added clearly and submissively that he could not continue to go to confession to Father Sanchez because he no longer trusted him.

"It was evident that Father Sanchez was being strongly influenced, almost coerced, by others. Such a sudden and radical change is otherwise inexplicable. It was a time when a violent persecution was raging against the Work.

"I made a note of the canon numbers mentioned by Father Sanchez. As soon as we got home, I checked them out with the Father, and discovered that the numbers had been quoted at random and had nothing to do with the issues at hand."[74]

Despite everything, Father Sanchez and Father Escrivá parted amicably; the founder of Opus Dei was grateful for all the good done to his soul in the past. Father Escrivá used to go to see him at a center of formation run by the Jesuits in the Chamartin district, in the north of Madrid and a long way from Atocha, the district he lived in; despite the distance, he used to walk there. Not once but several times Father Sanchez had kept him waiting a long time, sometimes hours, before receiving him. Many years later, when Monsignor Escrivá was living in Rome and was having lunch with Father Arrupe, general of the Society of Jesus, at the Jesuit headquarters in

---

74. Cf. Césare Cavalleri, *Immersed in God*, pp. 100–105.

Borgo Santo Spirito, the founder of Opus Dei paid grateful tribute to the memory of Father Valentin Sanchez, who had died by then. He recalled the long walk from Santa Isabel to Chamartin and how sometimes after getting there and waiting, a lay brother would come out and tell him, "Father Sanchez cannot see you today." His recollection was good humored. "I have always considered it a good way to form my soul," he said. "Like that, I learned to adapt myself to other people's circumstances and to control my impatience, not getting upset about anything."

At this, the old lay brother serving table said unexpectedly, "Well, I know all about that! I was the one who had to give the disagreeable message, after you had been waiting for an hour or two! I remember perfectly well that it wasn't just once or twice, but several times that this happened."[75]

From that autumn 1940 when he stopped going to Father Valentin Sanchez, Father Escrivá took Father José Mariá Garciá, spiritual director of the Madrid seminary, as his confessor. From the first he made it clear he intended to go to confession to a priest of the Work "as soon as the first priests are ordained." And so he did, four years later on June 26, 1944, the day after the ordinations of the civil engineers Alvaro del Portillo, José Luis Muzquiz and José María Hernandez de Garnica. Father Escrivá, living in the Diego de Leon residence, went to the center of the Work in Villanueva Street, and there found Don Alvaro.

"Alvaro, my son, have you heard anyone's confession yet?" he asked.

"No, Father."

"Well, you're about to hear mine, because I want to make a general confession to you! Let's go to the oratory."

From then until the end of his life he went to confession to Don Alvaro every Sunday, and often during the week as well. Sometimes, on a big feast day, he would say to his sons, "I've already celebrated today. Would you like to know how? I asked Don Alvaro to come, and I went to confession. It's a good way to celebrate!"[76]

---

75. Written account by Bishop Javier Echevarria to the author.
76. Testimony of Fr. Carlos Cardona (AGP, HRF T-06138).

On his last visit to Torreciudad, not yet open for public worship, he asked the architect César Ortiz-Echagüe, "César, are the confessionals in the crypt finished?"

"Yes, Father," answered César. "Would you like to come and see them now?"

When they got there, Monsignor Escrivá said, "There will be many confessions here. That's what I'm hoping for from Our Lady: abundant grace to move many souls to a profound conversion. And as I've always liked to set people a good example, as tomorrow is my day for going to confession, if one of the confessionals is ready I'd be very happy to be the first to use it!"

Thus Torreciudad was inaugurated, with a man on his knees confessing his sins.[77]

He often said he was "always returning," like the prodigal son. "That way, my sins don't take me away from God, but rather turn me to him like a son."[78] Like a refrain, he repeated in Latin or Spanish short phrases from Scripture: "Lord, you know all things: you know that I love you"; "I am a poor, humble servant"; "a humbled, contrite heart you will not spurn." They were acts of contrition "with which even lost battles are not lost."[79] These "staples" of the soul did not humiliate Monsignor Escrivá because "in God's eyes they shine like medals."[80]

A soul put together with staples; earthenware clay

Manuel Caballero, an artist, was modeling an image of Christ crucified that was to be installed in the Galleria degli Offici of Villa Tevere. Monsignor Escrivá told him, "My son, every morning before starting work you should say the Creed and ask our Lord to arouse at least an aspiration in the heart of everyone who looks at it; and pray that the Father, whenever he sees it, will be able to say with his whole heart, *Domine, Tu omnia nosti, Tu scis quia amo te*, 'Lord, you know all things, you know that I love you.' "[81]

---

77. Testimony of Msgr. César Ortiz-Echagüe (AGP, HRF T-04694).
78. Testimony of Fr. Carlos Cardona (AGP, HRF T-06138).
79. Ibid.
80. Ibid.
81. Written account by Bishop Javier Echevarria to the author.

In 1972 his children in Portugal presented him with an old china soup tureen, held together with staples. Monsignor Escrivá was moved by it. Later, speaking of the soup tureen, he waxed lyrical. "It's an ordinary thing but I loved it, because you could see it was well used. It had been broken—it must have belonged to a big family—and they had mended it with staples so as to go on using it. What's more, it had been decorated with the words *amo te, amo te, amo te* before firing. I felt very akin to that soup tureen. I prayed about that old bowl, because I see myself like that too: like the broken clay tureen, stapled together, and I like to say to our Lord that, stapled together as I am, I love him so much! We can love our Lord, my children, even when we are broken."[82]

Although he saw himself like that, at the same time he said, "It is obvious that God helps needy souls like mine to mature as wine matures. I say to him at Mass: 'Lord, let yourself be seen through my wretchedness.' "[83]

The last Holy Thursday of his life, March 27, 1975, Monsignor Escrivá made his personal prayer aloud. "I adore the Father, the Son, the Holy Spirit, one God. I don't understand this marvel of the Blessed Trinity, but you have placed in my soul a yearning, a hunger to believe. I do believe! I want to believe like the best. I hope! I want to hope like the best. I love! I want to love like the best.

"You are what you are: perfect goodness. I am what I am: the filthiest rag in this rotten world. And yet, you look at me . . . and you seek me . . . and you love me. . . . And when I see how little I understand of your wonder, of your goodness, of your wisdom, of your power, of your beauty . . . when I see I understand so little, I'm not disheartened. I'm glad that you are so great that you don't fit inside my poor heart, inside my wretched head. My God! My God! If I can think of nothing else to say to you, this will suffice. My God!"[84]

Realizing that a group of his sons were present, he said, "We must be in heaven and on earth, all the time. Not between heaven and earth, because we are of the world. In the world and in paradise

---

82. Cf. Testimony of Dr. Alejandro Cantero (AGP, HRF T-06308) and *Articles of the Postulator*, 1024.
83. Cf. *Articles of the Postulator*, 1027.
84. AGP, HRF 21164, p. 750 (90).

at the same time! . . . In heaven and on earth, divinized, but knowing that we are of the world and made of clay: an earthenware pot which our Lord has chosen to use in his service. And whenever it has got broken, we have stapled the bits together again, saying like the prodigal son, 'I have sinned against heaven and against you.' . . . God has chosen to deposit a very rich treasure in us. Am I exaggerating? No, I've said very little! . . . God our Lord, with all his greatness, dwells within us. Heaven dwells habitually within our hearts. I'm not going to say any more." [85]

85. AGP, HRF 21164, p. 752.

17

Working Summers

Whenever Cardinal Pizzardo met Monsignor Escrivá, he would take Escrivá's head between his hands and give him a loud kiss on the nape of the neck, exclaiming, "Thank you for teaching me how to relax!" And if he saw that people were surprised, he would go on, "I used to be one of those people who think that in this life, when you're not working you're wasting time. But he gave me a new, wonderful idea: resting does not mean doing nothing, it's not laziness or idleness, but changing one's occupation, turning to a different, useful, relaxing activity for a while."[1] Pizzardo was secretary of the Holy Office and prefect of the Congregation for Seminaries and Universities. He knew what it was to work hard, but he had to learn relaxation.

For many years, Monsignor Escrivá would answer those who insisted he slow down, "I'll rest when they say 'may he rest in peace.'" As time passed, however, he realized that he was wrong, and explained, "You cannot keep your head and your body under constant stress; if you do, you'll collapse."

---

1. This chapter could only have been written with the help of someone who had lived closely with Monsignor Escrivá. The author is grateful to Monsignor Javier Echevarría for his accounts, both written and taped, and also for generously taking the time to recall events and put them into writing in reply to demanding questions from the author. Thanks to his help, it has been possible to reconstruct nine stretches of time, unpublished until now, in the life of Monsignor Escrivá: the nine summers from 1965 to 1973.

"This man has an absolute atom bomb in his mind"

From 1958 on Monsignor Escrivá began to leave Rome and spend his summers in Great Britain, Ireland, France, or Spain, staying in houses that were rented or lent to him. In 1958, 1959, and 1960 he spent some weeks in July and August in Woodlands, a rented house at the end of Courtenay Avenue, toward the north of Hampstead Heath in London. The owners were a quaint couple: he was in the film business, while she practiced palmistry and spiritualism. In 1961 and 1962 Monsignor Escrivá returned to the same area of London but stayed in another house, 21 West Heath Road, rented out by a Mr. Hoskin, a war tribunal judge of Russian-Jewish origin. In those summers he combined rest and study, as well as giving impetus to the people of Opus Dei not only in Britain and Ireland but also in continental Europe: he traveled to different cities in France, Spain, and Germany in 1960, and in 1962 he went to Austria, Switzerland, and France.

In the summer of 1963 he spent some time in a house called Reparacea in Navarre in northern Spain, between San Sebastian and Pamplona, and in 1964 he went to Elorrio, a town near Bilbao. He asked Don Alvaro and Father Javier Echevarria to suggest plans and programs for work on other matters than their usual ones during the holiday period. When he left Rome he deliberately disconnected from his regular work and delegated as much of the task of governing as he could. But his mind kept working.

Viktor Frankl, a Viennese psychiatrist who was a disciple of Freud and Jewish like him, said after visiting Monsignor Escrivá in Villa Tevere, "This man has an absolute atom bomb in his mind." During those summers, as well as reading, studying, and writing, he conceived numerous initiatives that he either noted down himself or had someone else note down.

Traveling on foot

He barely had time to learn any sport other than walking, but he had done a great deal of that in his life from sheer necessity: unable to afford a bus or trolley, he had pounded the streets doing a dawn-to-dusk apostolate. When quite old, he could walk three hours in the morning and, if necessary, another three in the afternoon. As a newly ordained curate in Perdiguera, while the village was taking its siesta he would go out into the open countryside to pray alone or teach the sacristan's son his catechism. Later on, traveling all over Europe and preparing the ground in countries where Opus Dei was to come, he always went around the cities on foot so that he really got to know them and could pray for them. As a result, his legs were strong and muscular, though his arms were so thin it was difficult to give him an intramuscular injection.

"Father, that's cheating!"

From 1965 on Monsignor Escrivá spent August outside Rome, though still in Italy. He took up a cheap sport, *le bocce,* an Italian bowling game requiring more skill than strength. Played on bare earth in the open country, it raised great clouds of dust, so Monsignor Escrivá always changed all his clothes to play, taking off his cassock, wearing an old shirt, old trousers, and black tennis shoes.

He was not particularly good at it, but it was a game for four people, two on a side, which gave it the excitement of competition. Monsignor Escrivá usually played with Javier Cotelo, an architect who normally drove Monsignor Escrivá's car, against Don Alvaro and Father Javier Echevarria, who always won. Monsignor Escrivá did his best to handicap these habitual winners. Sometimes, when it was their turn to bowl, he nudged them a little to put them off balance.

"That's not fair, Father! That's cheating!" one would protest.

"But, Alvaro, that's part of the game! Don't you pride yourself on how well you can do it? Well, you have to have some handicap!"

Other times, if his ball was so far from the premium ball that it hadn't a chance, he would pick it up and, making a "magic pass," say, "You thought the ball was there? Well, it isn't. It's . . . here!" And he moved it nearer. Often the two Javiers would keep playing while Monsignor Escrivá and Don Alvaro followed the game from the sidelines. Monsignor Escrivá cheered for Cotelo like a fan, precisely because he was not gifted and nearly always lost. When now and then he did win, Monsignor Escrivá would tease Father Javier, "You're no good, Javi! You're past it!"

One day the two pairs had been playing a long time. Only one ball was left—Monsignor Escrivá's. With a bit of luck, he could reach maximum score. He threw. To everyone's surprise, especially his own, the ball landed beside the premium ball. With a guilty expression he declared, "I'll never do that again—that was worse than my usual cheating. Shall I tell you what I did?"

The other three looked at him. Monsignor Escrivá lowered his voice, as if ashamed of what he was going to say. "Before throwing the ball, I prayed earnestly to my guardian angel for a good strike. But now I realize it's wrong to involve my angel in a game that has not the slightest importance."

1965: Castelletto del Trebbio

In 1965 a friend of Don Alvaro's called Signor Scaretti gave them the use of a house on a farming estate in Castelletto del Trebbio, about twenty kilometers from Florence, on condition they left before mid-August when he was planning to go there with his family.

The house was old, dilapidated, and far from comfortable. It had no telephone or television. It was reached by a rough, unpaved track up a steep hill and surrounded on all sides by fields full of crops. Like most of Tuscany, the area had a continental climate, very cold in winter and very hot in summer.

Monsignor Escrivá, Don Alvaro, Father Javier, and Javier Cotelo spent several weeks of July and August there. Four women of the Work, Marga Barturen, Victoria Postigo, Dora del Hoyo, and Rosalia Lopez, had gone ahead to take care of the domestic arrangements and turn the ramshackle house into a cheerful home. Signor Scaretti had noted that there were some beautiful pieces of Capodimonte porcelain, valued at forty million lira (about US $30,000) in the dining room. As soon as he arrived, Monsignor Escrivá asked the others to wrap them up carefully and put them away to avoid the risk of breaking them.

A stranger in another person's home

Conscious he was using a building, furniture, and fittings not his own, he took great care to avoid any damage. If they moved any of the furniture to facilitate their work or study, he would ask Javier Cotelo to "make a drawing of the room as we find it, so as to be able to put everything back in the same places when we leave." He was careful that furniture did not mark walls and replaced the lightbulbs as necessary.

He did not mind feeling like a stranger in another person's home, since it helped him live detachment and poverty, and he took care of other people's things as if they were his own. One summer in London he had found a column of ants going from the garden into the sitting room and out over the balcony on the other side. Asking Dora and Rosalia for the vacuum cleaner, with the help of Father Javier Echevarria he exterminated the "troops." Years later, during a summer in Premeno in the north of Italy, he helped in a similar operation, armed with a big stick while Father Javier Echevarria and Javier Cotelo burned the ant hill after first pouring gasoline on it.

A scorpion hunt

In Castelletto del Trebbio the enemies were scorpions with a nest near Father Javier Echevarria's room. Monsignor Escrivá joked, "Javito, your heart is obviously made of stone, because scorpions always go straight to where you are." When Father Javier Echevarria one day told him he had just killed one, Monsignor Escrivá assumed an air of deep concern and said, "Look, I don't know if it's true, but I've heard that scorpions always go in pairs. That's a popular saying. So let's go to your room for a moment to look for the other one. We don't want you to be stung. Not that it would sting you out of revenge, but they do come in twos."

They found the second scorpion. Monsignor Escrivá was delighted. "You see, I told you so. The trouble is that you city lads simply don't know about the adventures of country life."

For those weeks Monsignor Escrivá organized a schedule, with time to pray, work, and play sports, as well as go for walks and excursions. He was working on revising a text called *The St. Gabriel Instruction* that he had written about supernumeraries in Opus Dei and the apostolate with married people. He began writing it in May 1935 and finished in September 1950. There were no photocopiers then, only a poor-quality cyclostyle, which was a sort of stenciling machine, and the printing press in Villa Tevere did not yet exist. So they had made typewritten copies to distribute where the Work was being established. Some of the typists had made errors and even dropped some words. The same thing had happened with the *St. Raphael Instruction* about the apostolate with young people and the *St. Michael Instruction* concerning the numeraries and associates. Monsignor Escrivá had the whole set recalled while preparing just one text that would be printed.

Monsignor Escrivá spoke with Don Alvaro and Father Javier Echevarria about the need to "be self-critical, and do our work really well because we cannot offer up shoddy work to our Lord." He insisted a lot during those days on "the asceticism of little things." He was taking notes on his reading for a proposed book on the contemplative life, to be called *Dialogue*. It was well along, but he never finished it.

He also studied the documents of the Second Vatican Council and prayed about the big themes still to be debated— the priesthood and consecrated life. He was grateful for the document *Lumen Gentium,* some of whose points echoed the spirit of Opus Dei, which thus became part of the solemn teaching of the Church. Monsignor Escrivá spent much time in the little oratory they had set up in Castelletto del Trebbio, thanking God for the Church's stamp of approval on what for so long was criticized, misunderstood, or rejected.

As there was no television set and the daily paper arrived late, every day on returning from their walk Monsignor Escrivá asked Don Alvaro's permission to turn on the radio so they could listen to the one o'clock news. He wanted to keep up with world affairs, nearly always making some comment of a spiritual kind and encouraging whoever was with him to pray for such and such a country or situation or person.

We'd prefer to go to confession to a priest of the Work

After nearly a week in Castelletto del Trebbio, Monsignor Escrivá asked to see Marga Barturen, director of the little housekeeping team. Father Javier Echevarria was present during the conversation.

Monsignor Escrivá reminded her of the advisability of going to weekly confession and said, "You're free to go to the parish priest of the nearest village, or if you prefer you can go to a church in Florence."

Later that day Marga came back and said, "Father, we've been thinking it over, and we've come to the conclusion that we'd prefer to go to confession to a priest of the Work."

"But who?" asked Monsignor Escrivá. "The only ones here are Don Alvaro, Don Javier, and myself. And as you know, the Father does not hear the confessions of any of his children except in case of necessity.[2] As for Don Alvaro and Don Javier, they are on the general council and hold posts of government, and I don't wish them to exercise this pastoral mission with people of the Work.[3] So I repeat, you have all the freedom in the world to go to confession to whomever you like."

"Yes, Father," persisted Marga. "We know that the grace of the sacrament comes to us no matter whom we go to. But to care for our interior life, we'd prefer to bare our consciences to someone who is practicing the same spirituality as ourselves, without having to go into long explanations."

"That's very true," replied Monsignor Escrivá. "But I insist you can go to any priest around here or in Florence. And without wanting to make you conceited, I should tell you that with your life of piety, you will do a lot of good to whoever hears your confessions."

Marga stood her ground. "Father, we'd rather go to a priest of Opus Dei."

"Well . . ." said Monsignor Escrivá finally, "as there isn't a center of the Work around here, we'll have to see what we can do."

As soon as she left the room, Monsignor Escrivá said to Father Javier Echevarria, "You'll have to organize things so as to be able to hear your sisters' confessions. This very important task is one of the ruling passions which priests in Opus Dei should have. To carry it

---

2. Monsignor Escrivá never wished to hear the confessions of people of the Work, "so as not to tie my hands," as he said. By this he meant that the sacramental seal of confession would have reduced his freedom to express himself when directing Opus Dei, when preaching, when giving indications for governing, etc., when the decisions affected those whose inner lives he had heard about in confession.

3. Following the same criterion as the founder, priests who occupy positions of government in the Work do not normally hear the confessions of those directly subject to their authority.

out as God wills, invoke the Holy Spirit, and try to serve each soul generously, knowing it is worth all the blood of Christ." From then until the end of their stay, he never made the slightest reference to the subject, illustrating the extreme care with which the sacramental seal and the seal of spiritual guidance should be treated.

The sun was oppressive, sometimes even hotter than in Rome. But Monsignor Escrivá did not complain, even though he wore a black cassock all the time.[4] Once a week they went down to Florence, city of the Medicis and Savonarola, on the Arno River. Monsignor Escrivá loved art, but they did not go to the museums or walk about the city looking at the splendid buildings. They spent most of the time praying in the Church of Santa Maria Novella or the Church of the Holy Cross, beside Dante's monument. Santa Maria Novella was the principal church of the Dominicans in Florence and the Holy Cross of the Franciscans. At this stage of the Second Vatican Council, the spiritual needs of these ancient religious families were uppermost in his mind.

After some weeks in Castelletto del Trebbio, they went to Piancastagnaio, an estate near Orte that had no telephone or television either. It was up for sale, and the owner let them have it for a few days.

Monsignor Escrivá was keen to find a house with some land for the students of the Roman College of the Holy Cross to have during the holidays. For some years they had gone to the estate of Salto di Fondi, on the coast near Terracina. But what had once been a quiet beach was now invaded by tourists and not an ideal place for spiritual formation and relaxation.

As soon as they arrived at Piancastagnaio, they realized that they were near sulphur springs that gave off a disagreeable smell. Monsignor Escrivá made no reference to the smell, but when the time was up, he said, "After having been there for just a few days, I realize it's not the place we're looking for."

---

4. Monsignor Alvaro del Portillo said in an interview with Césare Cavalleri (op. cit.): "He never stayed in bed beyond the prescribed time, and never took a siesta" (p. 36). "He never had any use for the siesta; in fact, he directed that people of the Work should not sleep in the early afternoon, except on doctor's orders" (p. 41).

Summer 1966

In the summer of 1966 they returned to Castelletto del Trebbio. As before, Monsignor Escrivá reminded his daughters of their freedom to go to confession wherever they wished. Instead of Marga Barturen, now living in America, Blanca Fontan headed the housekeeping team. The response was unanimous; they preferred to receive spiritual guidance from a priest of the Work. Father Javier Echevarria again was entrusted with this task. "Be punctual," Monsignor Escrivá said, "and be available whenever they ask for confessions: don't fail them."

Monsignor Escrivá spent much time in the oratory. He wished to ponder the best way of putting into effect the conclusions of the recent general congress of Opus Dei. But above all he was concerned about the Church and the authority of the Pope in this postconciliar time of tension, conflict, abusive interpretations, and biased articles.

The Council had opened the door to an appropriate canonical formulation for Opus Dei as a personal prelature. Though new in itself, this extended a form already known and used in the Church: personal jurisdictions. In 1929 Monsignor Escrivá had already seen this as the key to Opus Dei's situation, as he wrote in his *Intimate Notes*; he mentioned this to Pedro Casciaro in 1936.[5] Now he was asking God for guidance to be able to present a sound, well-documented petition to the Holy See to become the personal prelature of Opus Dei. It would have to be at the opportune time, when the dust had settled. On his walks with Don Alvaro and Father Javier Echevarria, he said more than once, "I offer my life to God so we can achieve a definitive solution, although I may not live to see it if our Lord asks me for that sacrifice."

In ecclesiastical circles and the media, the word postconciliar was much abused at the time, used to represent whatever was novel, modern, progressive, and, above all, the opposite of what had been. In those conversations on the grounds of Castelletto del Trebbio, Monsignor Escrivá said, "We have been in a 'postconciliar period'

---

5. Monsignor Alvaro del Portillo, *Letter*, November 28, 1982, 28. See Chapter 6.

since the first century, since the Council of Jerusalem. The 'postcon-ciliar period' is an imprecise and incorrect term to use in reference to Vatican II, because this last Council has continued and ratified all the previous ones. There can be no discontinuity between the previous ecumenical assemblies of the Church and the one which ended last year." Years later he would say the same in front of thousands of people. In the summer of 1966 these were the first reflections of a man who refused to bow to fashion.

Monsignor Escrivá made use of all possible means to pray for the Church. For August 4, feast of St. Dominic Guzman, he organized a trip to Bologna to celebrate Mass in the Church of St. Dominic, where the holy founder of the Dominicans was buried. On the way there and back, he urged his three companions to pray a lot for the religious. "The religious state has been and continues to be absolutely necessary in the Church," he said.

Father Javier Echevarria normally helped Monsignor Escrivá when he celebrated Mass. The Mass at St. Dominic's made such a deep impression on him that years later he wrote, "I remember vividly how devoutly he celebrated that Mass. I say this because, while every one of his Masses was a jolt for those present, in that Church of St. Dominic we could *feel* our Father praying in a very special way for the religious, lovingly and gratefully and, I would say, with special affection."

Abrainville, France

A few days after August 15, they left Castelletto del Trebbio by car and went to Abrainville, a town near Etampes, where the people of Opus Dei in France had found them a house in the countryside. The last time Monsignor Escrivá had been in France, he had drunk no wine but only mineral water; when someone asked him if he disliked French wine, he answered, "Even though French wines are very good, the only thing I'm interested in, here in France, are souls."

After lunch every day they went from Abrainville to Paris. There, in a center of the Work called Dufrenois, he spent a while with his sons. He made an occasional visit to an antique market and a second-hand clothes market, and not much more.

On August 30, he went to Couvrelles near Soissons. Couvrelles is a fine old house, not very big but well proportioned, with a seventeenth-century façade, surrounded by woods and with a small lake at the back. It was to be an international conference center for cultural discussions, lectures, intensive courses of doctrinal formation, retreats, and short courses. The housekeeping staff would run a catering school and hold activities for married people.

Monsignor Escrivá consecrated the altars at Couvrelles. Sitting on stone steps leading up to the house, sons of his from France, Germany, Belgium, Holland, Switzerland, Italy, and Spain listened to him say, "No one can keep the treasure of the faith or the treasure of a vocation for himself alone!"

1967: Three weeks in Gagliano Aterno

In 1967 they found some land for sale near Rome in the Via Flaminia area called Saxa Rubra, meaning "red rocks." The permanent campus of the Roman College of the Holy Cross, Cavabianca, would be built there with space for 200 people, sports facilities, and gardens. There would be an independent residential annex for the housekeeping staff called Albarossa. The financing and construction of these buildings was one of Monsignor Escrivá's "last three acts of madness."

The spread of the Work all over the world and the growth in the number of vocations meant a greater number of students at the Roman College every year. They were living on top of each other in Villa Tevere, which needed to be used for the purpose for which it had been built, as the center for the government of the Work, the general council for men and the central advisory for women.

In April that year Monsignor Escrivá went to Lourdes, and from there to Pamplona, Molinoviejo (near Segovia), Pozoalbero in Jerez, Lisbon, and Fatima. The crisis in the Church had become more acute, as Pope Paul VI said during his visit to Fatima.[6] Monsignor Escrivá embarked on a round of prayer and preaching that would occupy him unceasingly until his death.

---

6. Pope Paul VI, Homily in Fatima (Portugal), May 13, 1967.

He had never liked to receive media attention, but now he gave interviews to some major newspapers and magazines: *Time, Le Figaro, The New York Times, L'Osservatore della Domenica*, and others.

Huge gatherings were planned for early October in Pamplona, when Monsignor Escrivá would meet with the Friends of the University of Navarre in open-air get-togethers of over 35,000 people on the university campus. Meanwhile he spent three weeks in August in Gagliano Aterno in the Abruzzi region of Italy.

The house, lent by a Baroness Lazzaroni, had a family oratory, with a commemorative stone saying St. Francis of Assisi had been there. Monsignor Escrivá read the text but made no comment. Shortly afterwards he arranged to meet two of his spiritual sons, members of the general council, in Gagliano Aterno. One was Giuseppe Molteni, a layman with a doctorate in chemistry and another in theology, who was general administrator of Opus Dei at the time; Monsignor Escrivá called him Peppino. As they were getting ready to go out Monsignor Escrivá took him into the oratory and showed him the inscription; later he joked, "Peppino, my son, it's impossible to find anywhere in Italy, even the remotest corner, where either St. Francis of Assisi or Garibaldi hasn't been. You can't deny that you Italians are a bit over the top with these memorials!"

"*Certo, certo*," responded Peppino. "It's a custom we have all over Italy, and we do it to make each different place into somewhere special: Leonardo da Vinci was here, Torcuato Tasso was here, or Dante, or Garibaldi. . . . *Così facciamo patria!*—that's how we make our homeland!"

Monsignor Escrivá burst out laughing.

Life in that old house was restricted, as there was hardly any space to stroll. Now and then they went out for a drive. As they approached the closed gate, near the gatehouse where the caretakers lived, Monsignor Escrivá would ask one of the Javiers to open and close the gate. He explained, "We're giving them enough bother with attending to the upkeep of the house. As an act of charity, and so that they can see we don't want to give them any more work, every time we go out I want one of the two of you to get there first. That way we'll leave this couple and their children in peace."

He always said a few words of greeting to the caretakers, with the car stopped, while the gate was being opened or closed.

"How are you? How's the work going? Sorry to give you extra work these days we are here. But I remember you every day in the Holy Mass, I pray for your family and for whatever your concerns are."

To begin with, the caretakers were somewhat reserved, but Monsignor Escrivá won them over. Gradually they began the conversation themselves.

In the village of San Felice d'Ocre in the Abruzzi region there is a conference center of Opus Dei called Tor d'Aveia. The students of the Roman College were spending their holidays there for the first time. Monsignor Escrivá went there several times to visit them and his daughters who were doing the cooking and housekeeping.

One day he spoke to Blanca Nieto: "Director, you need to have a tremendous apostolic spirit! In this village, yes, this very one, you have to make friends with all the women and all their daughters, big and little. And try to give them a deep understanding of Christianity. I want this center to be a focus of apostolate for the whole village. And then the whole area will benefit. If you're apostolic, you'll find that the rivalries between one village and another, which are so typical of Latin countries, will cease. With your charity, your service, and the interest you take in everyone here, you'll reach out to the neighboring villages, after leaving a deep impression on the women who live here in the village of San Felice d'Ocre."

After spending time with the women, he went to see his sons. It was around this time that male fashions were beginning to be more colorful. Monsignor Escrivá joked with a young American wearing a loud orange shirt with green check trousers, "But my son, are you going to a fairground?"

Even though he thought football was an "almighty chaos," he encouraged them to organize matches to let off steam. Some days later, however, he found one with his arm in a splint and another on crutches. He clutched his head in astonishment and cried, "Lord help us! What have you done? I told you to exercise and do sport, but you've gone too far! I don't say that these things can't happen, a dislocation or something like that, and I'm not telling off this lad, who looks very noble with his arm in a sling. But I do say you shouldn't take more risks than necessary, especially if you see you aren't strong enough, or you can't reach, or it's too difficult. Be prudent for me, including when you're doing sport. If not, the Father, who is father and mother to each of you, will be far more worried about you than you could imagine."

Afterward he said privately, "How tough they are! I'm delighted to see them so healthy and so strong!"

English people's reserve

Later on they had a sing-along with guitars and maracas. He asked them for apostolic news from their different countries. He encouraged the South Americans to develop and deepen their education and cultural background, saying gently, "What I'm about to say is not criticism, but sadly, in your countries, sometimes, the secondary schooling is not very thorough and your university studies are a bit weak. . . . Do I make myself clear?"

He urged the English to have "the daring to get into other people's souls." He told them, "You've been brought up to have a tremendous respect for other people's privacy, and that's a very praiseworthy virtue, but, my children, that respect must not be used as an excuse for not offering the help which we are obliged to give to others as Christians. While still being very English, you have to get into other people's lives fearlessly, going against the grain if necessary. In that way your country, which has given such great service to humanity, can continue to give that service through the real Christian spirit you are called to spread. Don't forget, my English children, that your country is a crossroads, and from it you can do great good or great evil. You can't fall into the mistake of neglecting your own countrymen. If you don't care for the people you live with, how much less will you care for those who live in other countries, which you used to call the colonies. And you've an obligation to continue helping those people!"

The days in Gagliano Aterno passed quickly. Monsignor Escrivá was working on what would later be the statutes of Opus Dei. What he did not suspect was that within two years he would have to call an extraordinary congress to debate and approve the statutes he was now drawing up. In that summer of 1967 no one could have guessed that a very grave threat was taking shape against the Work.

1968: Sant'Ambrogio Olona

A year later, in mid-July 1968, Monsignor Escrivá and Father Javier Echevarria went to say good-bye to his friend Cardinal Angelo Dell'Acqua, the Pope's vicar for the diocese of Rome. They were going to the north of Italy for a few weeks, having been lent a house near Varese outside a village called Sant'Ambrogio Olona. The cardinal was pleased. "That's wonderful! I'm from Sesto Calende, which is very close to Sant'Ambrogio, and I expect to be there for some days' holiday in August. I'll come and see you without fail."

As they left, Cardinal Dell'Acqua spoke to Father Javier, who had been waiting outside. Taking advantage of the fact that Monsignor Escrivá was a little distance ahead, the cardinal said, "Take good care of him for me! It does me so much good to talk to him! Each of my conversations with Monsignor Escrivá is a real tonic for my soul. *Arrivederci!*"

The villa in Sant'Ambrogio Olona had three stories. There was a French garden with rose bushes in geometric flowerbeds lined by boxhedges with narrow paths between them. On many afternoons Monsignor Escrivá spent a while on the esplanade in front of the house in conversation with his daughters who were looking after the running of the house, Begoña Mugica, Dora del Hoyo, Rosalia Lopez, and Maria Jose Monterde.

As soon as they arrived on July 18, Monsignor Escrivá asked, "Have you thought about a schedule?"

"If it's okay with you," Maria Jose said, "we thought we could follow more or less the same as in Rome."

"Whatever suits you best. You sort it out, and let us have a written copy."

Maria Jose soon gave him a sheet of paper with the times of breakfast, lunch, afternoon tea, and dinner, when the housekeeping staff needed to do the cleaning, and when the staff could use the oratory.

Monsignor Escrivá read the page carefully. Then he asked for a pen and wrote, "Don't kill yourselves cleaning the house!"

A cigarette holder for Don Alvaro

In conversations in Sant'Ambrogio Olona, Monsignor Escrivá kept coming back to two subjects: work well done and faithfulness to the Church.

One day Don Alvaro, Father Javier Echevarria, and Javier Cotelo went to Varese to do some shopping, while Monsignor Escrivá stayed home to work. In the afternoon, he saw Maria Jose and Begoña and told them, "The others have gone to Varese to get a cigarette holder for Don Alvaro. This son of mine practices poverty to such an extreme that his cigarette holder was all scratched and burned—it looked horrible! So with that excuse I sent them off to enjoy themselves."

It was the feast of St. Mary Magdalene, a saint he felt great admiration for because she was "madly in love" with Jesus Christ.[7] "Who knows what she was really like!" he said. "Compared with some of today's women, she might well pass for a good person. . . . We also are full of sin—indeed we are. We mustn't be discouraged, but rather turn to God our Lord at once. We ask him for help and he forgives us—he always forgives us!"

Two days after his arrival he had asked for a bigger table than the one in his room. Finding a table-tennis table in the cellar, they covered one half neatly with wrapping paper and set it up in his room on its own legs. He wrote an important doctrinal document on this improvised table, in the form of a letter that began "*Fortes in fide*—strong in the Faith." It was a powerful letter putting everyone in Opus Dei on guard at this time of desertions, rebellion against authority, fraudulent theology, deceptive morality, within the Church itself.

"I neither can nor want to, nor am I going to write it"

On this table Monsignor Escrivá also worked on his notebooks of "*Intimate Notes*" that began in 1930 and were something like a diary.

---

7. Cf. Josemaría Escrivá, *Holy Rosary* (Scepter Publishers, 2003).

After each date, he had written spiritual reflections, details about his interior life, and even supernatural experiences.

These notes had begun in 1926, but later on he burned the first notebook covering the time immediately before and after October 2, 1928. When Don Alvaro or Father Javier asked why, without going into details he called those years "the history of God's mercies." As to the first notebook, he said, "At the time God did wonderful things through a poor instrument," and he thought that "in later years, anyone who read about those things would think that the priest to whom such immense favors had been granted must have been a very holy person or someone of very deep spirituality. And I know myself very well, although not completely. I know what I am: a poor man, a sinner who loves Jesus Christ madly: but a very great sinner."

Don Alvaro and Father Javier insisted that he should rewrite that notebook during the summer. "Even if you only write what has stayed vividly in your memory, Father," they said, "it would mean such a lot for all of us later on; it would be something of great value to us."

He stood firm. "No and no. If I refuse to rewrite it, it's not because the very many favors of God, which really took place, have been wiped from my memory. Indeed not. It's because I would be afraid I might add a bit of my own human interpretation and deviate even minimally from the truth of exactly how things happened."

This was a recurrent theme of their conversations in Sant'Ambrogio Olona. But he said, "It's useless for you to go on. I've said clearly that I neither can nor want to, nor am I going to write it." Concerning the first moment, the "zero plus one," of Opus Dei, Monsignor Escrivá always said the absolute minimum, as if modesty kept him from lifting the veil on certain graces.

The Prague Spring

That summer of 1968 saw the crushing of the "Prague Spring." Soviet tanks destroyed the beginnings of freedom in Czechoslovakia. Monsignor Escrivá followed the situation hour by hour, listening to news bulletins on the radio. He was visibly shattered for the Czechoslovakian people. After Mass, even before breakfast, he wondered aloud, "What will have happened, what will be happening now in Czechoslovakia?" The night before he might have been up praying "for that country which is suffering the brutal onslaught of Communist tyranny. . . . Let's hope that everything ends without bloodshed!"

Later, when he was calmer, he said, "It is a real shame that so many countries are shrugging their shoulders and say nothing, in spite of the clear abuse of power by the Soviet Union. I don't understand it. I can't understand how the West can be so passive when another sovereign nation is invaded in the name of ideology. I understand that we're in a 'cold war' situation and a certain strategic balance has to be maintained, a certain give and take. But this tolerance seems to me to be simply a farce. What makes it even worse is that the aggressor state sits on the Security Council of the United Nations with a right of veto and with a vote accepted by other countries."

What mattered for him were truth, freedom, justice, and the dignity of man. "This omission, this public washing of hands, this nonintervention in something which goes against the mind and conscience of everyone who loves freedom, perhaps will later be used to justify a certain sort of colonization within what we call the 'free world.' Under the banner of economic might, this is a colonization of underdeveloped countries who are offered, and in fact given, help and material assistance. But in exchange, conditions are imposed which go against authentic development, against the true progress of the people. And above all, they go against the natural law and the most basic moral law."

Even when the press, radio and television, in condemning the invasion of Czechoslovakia, extolled the spirit of the Prague Spring, Monsignor Escrivá was not deceived. "The uprising of Dubcek and all the Czechoslovaks who follow him may be a good indication, a crack in the Soviet bloc. But we need to pray a lot, because those who lead this movement still call themselves Marxists. So even if they did break the umbilical cord with Moscow, there wouldn't be real freedom in the new order they built either. There cannot be real freedom where Marxism exists."

Turning to Our Lady under the title "Star of the East," *Stella Orientis*, he entrusted these people to her care, "and all the people behind the Iron Curtain, where the Christian faith is harassed and persecuted, so that the sun of true freedom may shine once again and they may recover the rights they are deprived of, rights that are part of human dignity."

One morning, walking with Don Alvaro and Father Javier Echevarria, he said, "These days I'm praying a lot for Czechoslovakia. I'm remembering the bishops and priests of that country in a special way because they're more at risk in the terrible persecution which communism has always wrought. Maybe it's being done in a more refined, subtle way now, without making any martyrs, but it's deliberately undermining and destroying the personality of Catholics. The lay people who declare themselves Catholic must be suffering the same harassment and hostility. I'm praying a lot for them. The discrimination they're subjected to at work or in their pay or in their social life will have an impact on their families, and that's very sad. I've no objection to your asking permission in spiritual guidance to offer special mortifications for these people. They've been suffering for years, but now they're undergoing even more, and with greater violence."

One day Maria Jose Monterde drove into the village of Sant'Ambrogio to buy some fruit. Returning, she saw the car Monsignor Escrivá used parked with him, Don Alvaro, Father Javier, and Javier Cotelo inside, windows down because of the heat. She could hear the voice of the radio newscaster. A few days before the house radio had broken down, so now they were using the car radio to hear the news.

Father Javier's jigsaw puzzle

Monsignor Escrivá wanted to pay a quick visit to Switzerland to see the people of the Work there. A few days later they went, but not to see his children. As the feast of the Assumption drew near, he suggested a pilgrimage to the shrine of Our Lady at Einsiedeln.

Some days before traveling, he gave Father Javier Echevarria some written papers to put in order. After a few seconds, Father Javier returned. "Father, there's a page missing. It must be somewhere here."

"No, it isn't. It's not here. Look for it, because I've given them all to you."

Father Javier went over the papers again and verified that a page was missing. He returned to Monsignor Escrivá.

"Father, I've searched for it and that page is missing."

"Well, it isn't here. You must have it. You'll have dropped it on the way."

Father Javier looked at the wastepaper basket beside Monsignor Escrivá's desk, which was full to the brim. "Mightn't it be in the bin? Maybe you tore it up by mistake."

Monsignor Escrivá continued writing and did not answer. Father Javier picked up the basket and took it into the room he was using as his office. In a few minutes Monsignor Escrivá came in and found him putting together a jigsaw puzzle of bits of paper that little by little revealed the lost page.

"Javi, my son, I'm sorry!" exclaimed Monsignor Escrivá. "You were right. And to crown it, look at all the extra work I'm giving you. I'm the one who should have searched more thoroughly; you've taught me a lesson so that next time I won't be so sure of myself."

And there he stayed, almost timidly helping Father Javier by cutting pieces of adhesive tape to stick the pieces of paper together. "And besides forgiving me," he added, "I want you to offer up this nuisance for me. You can see how much I need you to help me to work and improve!"

The trip to Einsiedeln was very short, thirty-two hours there and back. He said, "I can't deny it: we've really been through the mill. But we went to see Our Lady, so it was worth it!"

As summer passed, Monsignor Escrivá remarked, "I wonder whether Cardinal Angelo Dell'Acqua is in his house at Sesto Calende by now? It's odd that by this time in August he hasn't shown any signs of life."

At the end of August they left the house in Sant'Ambrogio Olona. A few days later, a postcard mailed in Sant'Ambrogio arrived at Villa Tevere. It was from Cardinal Dell'Acqua, explaining that he had had to postpone his holidays due to work, but that as soon as he arrived he had gone to visit them, hoping to have a long conversation with his friend Josemaría. He added that Monsignor Escrivá had become as elusive as an *uccel di bosco,* a woodcock, notoriously difficult to locate.

1969: Villa Gallabresi, Premeno

For the summer of 1969 they rented a small house in the country, also in the north of Italy, in Premeno near Milan. This was a small village in the Intra district, less than a kilometer from Lake Maggiore.

The house, Villa Gallabresi, was surrounded by a strip of garden with tall pines. As the house was a little isolated and unprotected, before going there Monsignor Escrivá asked that the oratory be installed on the second floor, for greater security. There would be four bedrooms on that same floor: his own, Don Alvaro's, and the rooms of Father Javier Echevarria and Javier Cotelo.

The sitting room, dining room (which also served as a common workroom), kitchen, and laundry were on the ground floor. Maria Jose Monterde, Begoña Mugica, Dora del Hoyo, and Ines Cherubini, who were doing the housekeeping, lived on the top floor. A central staircase joined the different levels. The fact that the staircase was very steep and the steps rather high enabled Father Javier Echevarria to make a discovery about Monsignor Escrivá's interior life. After a few days in the house, he noticed that Monsignor Escrivá was going up and down the stairs very often. Father Javier soon discovered why: Monsignor Escrivá was practicing his habit of "escaping" for brief moments to the tabernacle.

The area was very humid. Each day dawned with the house shrouded in mist and fog, and each brought a few hours of rain. Sometimes the fog was so dense that nothing could be seen beyond the pine trees in the garden. When the fog lifted after two or three hours, Lake Maggiore appeared in the distance, a beautiful blue. This dampness affected Monsignor Escrivá: his knees became swollen, and his shoulders, elbows, wrists, and knees were all painful. In spite of this he did not lessen his brief, frequent visits to Jesus Christ in the tabernacle.

The summer of 1969 was filled with intense work and prayer. Monsignor Escrivá, Don Alvaro, and Father Javier were preparing the material for the extraordinary congress of Opus Dei announced in June. The basic text was the statutes of the Work. Many people thought that this congress of Opus Dei was to carry out the indications of Vatican II that every ecclesial institution should revise its constitutions and regulations. Monsignor Escrivá had this faculty already in his own right as founder.[8]

His motive for convoking this congress arose from definite proof of a new, severe attack against the very structure of Opus Dei and its setting in the Church. The extraordinary congress was to study and safeguard the juridical path of the Work.

Back in 1960 and in 1962 he had taken "official" steps in the Vatican, clarifying that Opus Dei was not in fact a secular institute, even though it was one in Church law; and that the juridical framework that best suited it was a prelature. There was now a new attack. A commission had been set up to review the juridical status of Opus Dei. It included several people "notoriously hostile to the Work." Monsignor Escrivá presented a petition to the Holy See naming these people and giving examples of their "manifestations of belligerent prejudice." He rejected the authority of the commission for this reason. Pope Paul VI himself took the responsibility for dismantling it.

A witch hunt

Even so, the activities of those two or three churchmen antagonistic to Opus Dei had created a climate of distrust against the Work in some Vatican circles. One of those clerics, a man of considerable influence, embarked on a witch hunt, seeing Opus Dei behind everything that happened. Monsignor Escrivá's trips up and down the creaky stairs of Villa Gallabresi were understandable.

As in previous summers, they played the Italian bowling game and went for walks on the outskirts of villages near Lake Maggiore: Intra, Arona, Lantino, and Stresa. Sometimes they stopped at bric-a-brac stalls. Monsignor Escrivá liked to pick up knick-knacks that could be used for a joke or present. In Arona he found a little wooden Alpine soldier costing 220 lira, or about twenty cents.

---

8. In 1950 the Holy See granted Monsignor Escrivá—as founder of Opus Dei—the faculty to change the statutes of the Work to adapt them to the needs arising in the practical life of the institution.

"Look!" he said. "Shall we get it for Umberto as a joke? I'm sure he'll like it a lot!" Umberto Farri, a lawyer, had had an enthusiasm for military life since he was a child.

Another day they found a little hunting dog which moved its head and had a pheasant in its mouth. Monsignor Escrivá said, "This could be for Paco Vives—he's so keen on the hunting of the good old days."

He picked up a yellow rubber duck and burst out laughing. "There you have our Peppino's duckling!" He used the Italian word for duckling, *anatroccolo,* pronouncing it in imitation of the Lombardy accent and Milanese intonation of Giuseppe Molteni, "Peppino."

In this relaxed way, in day to day life, Monsignor Escrivá taught them to be always thinking of others, to love each other like a real family and also to save some lira by buying these little figures in advance, and much more cheaply than they could in Rome.

One day he chatted with the housekeepers and some women visiting from Milan. Don Alvaro joined them as Monsignor Escrivá was asking them to pray for the Church. He recalled having recently read the expression "a social priest" in a newspaper. His comment was, "When you qualify the word 'gold' or 'silver' with another word, it's usually because they are not pure gold or pure silver. A priest is a priest and that's that. His mission is exclusively spiritual: the care of souls. And as soon as he goes beyond that, it's a bad business."[9]

Monsignor Escrivá was heartbroken at the desertion of so many priests who were abandoning their calling. "You have to pray more, because there are priests who don't want to pray, or to guard their senses or to make an examination of conscience . . . and disaster strikes! In the Work, everyone, young and not so young, *everyone* has to pray, guard their senses, and do their examination of conscience, because otherwise we would be courting disaster!"[10]

The optimum viewpoint

Monsignor Escrivá suffered an alarming loss of vision that summer, especially in his right eye. At first he thought it was temporary and

---

9. Oral account of Maria Jose Monterde to the author.
10. Ibid.

did not say anything about it, but as the problem continued, he mentioned it to Don Alvaro and Father Javier. "I'm finding it difficult to read because I can hardly see. Quite often my sight becomes quite blurred, like a fog. Celebrating Holy Mass is when I notice it most. I think I need to get it seen to, don't you? Maybe I should see an optician. And in the meantime I'll try and be patient and cheerful! For the moment, I'll try to keep on working and reading, and the day I find I can't, I'll offer up the limitation, the annoyance, to our Lord."

They went to Milan on July 28 with Calogero Crocchiolo, a medical doctor who was in the Work, driving, and there he visited an optician called Professor Romagnoli, who did a thorough examination. He concluded that Monsignor Escrivá was developing cataracts.

"I could only relax if I could forget about the Work"

A few days later, July 31, they returned to Milan on business, taking a car ferry across Lake Maggiore.

It was already quite late when they got back, but Monsignor Escrivá wanted to see his daughters because he had bought some sweets for them. He also wanted to tell them that he was going to Einsiedeln as he had the year before.

Maria Jose and Begoña noticed that he was not looking very well. They said, "Father, you look quite tired."

"We've been working in Milan," he explained briefly. "But anyway, I relax more when I'm working than when I'm not. Not working wears me out."

"Even so, Father, you haven't stopped since you came from Rome. What can we do to help you rest?"

"I'd only be able to relax if I could forget about the Work. But I don't want to forget about the Work! Or about God! Well, I can't forget about God, because I'd die."[11]

He did not talk about the work on his desk during those days: the final juridical formula of Opus Dei. But those around him could easily detect his concern. It was his "special intention." He told his daughters, "So you want to know about the special intention? We'll only achieve it by prayer—a lot of prayer. We don't want to have

---

11. Ibid.

to make vows. How will a person join the Work? By entering into a civil contract. It's true, my daughters, don't look so surprised; they'll make a civil contract. I love freedom. I don't want anyone to be forced. The sense of honor of my daughters and sons is enough for me to have complete trust in your self-giving. We'll return to the founder's original idea. We've had to do things another way, but the time will come when our own way will be opened up for us."[12]

On August 4 they set out on a pilgrimage to the shrine of Our Lady of Einsiedeln. The little group returned to Villa Gallabresi on August 6. Monsignor Escrivá was radiant, as he always was when, as he said, he had "been to see Our Lady."

"I haven't brought you any chocolate from Switzerland this time," he said. "But we've brought you a surprise, which I think you're going to like. At least it will last longer than chocolate." The surprise was a piece of costume jewelry for each of them.[13]

That summer he got a message from Villa Tevere saying Pope Paul VI had sent him a telegram and a gold-plated bronze medal, as a token of affection and congratulations on the twenty-fifth anniversary of the first ordinations to the priesthood of men of Opus Dei: the engineers Alvaro del Portillo, José María Hernandez de Garnica, and José Luis Muzquiz. This kind gesture from the Pope brought tears of gratitude to his eyes. Recently he had been weeping a lot, though he tried not to let anyone see him.

On August 26, just before leaving Villa Gallabresi, Father Javier Echevarria went into Monsignor Escrivá's room. Maria Jose and Dora were tidying up, and he turned to leave. But then he said from the doorway, "The Father is suffering a lot, for reasons we can't go into now. We know very little, but I'm telling you this so you pray more—even more!"[14]

"I laugh because I have God's presence"

Monsignor Escrivá was indeed suffering. Two years later in Rome, on March 25, 1971, he told a small group in a get-together, "I laugh, I even laugh out loud all by myself, because I have God's presence.

---

12. Ibid.
13. Ibid.
14. Ibid.

If I didn't—the things I could say! But two years ago I wept a lot. You can't imagine how consoling those tears during Mass were, even though they hurt my eyes. My serenity now, like my tears then, are all God's doing."[15]

1970: Villa Gallabresi again

The year 1970 was a difficult one for Monsignor Escrivá. The hostility and mistrust in ecclesiastical circles were like a cold cloud. Monsignor Escrivá was overwhelmed with anguish. On May 1, he suddenly decided to cross the Atlantic to Mexico, to prostrate himself at the feet of Our Lady of Guadalupe. There he prayed for nine days, until he had moral certainty that Our Lady had heard his plea and was obtaining the solution. Kneeling in a little balcony high up in the Basilica of Guadalupe, or down below, gripping the iron railing, Monsignor Escrivá asked for specific, very important things for the Church and Opus Dei.

Clama, ne cesses!

That summer, back in Premeno, his work for those weeks in August consisted of studying in depth the conclusions of the extraordinary congress held in Rome the previous year.

On the morning of August 6, just before vesting for Mass, he said to Father Javier Echevarria, "This very morning, something has happened to me, and I want you to know about it. A while ago in my room, before coming to the oratory, while I was begging our Lord in my head and in my heart to enable the Work to fulfill its mission with souls as he intends it to do on this earth, I felt the Lord putting in my mind some words of Scripture. These words have filled me with confidence and given me a new impetus to increase my prayer of petition, to persevere in prayer, and to encourage my children never to stop praying—not even for an instant! Prayer is the only weapon Opus Dei has. What I heard within me was *Clama, ne cesses!* 'Cry aloud, spare not!' These words

---

15. Testimony of Fr. Fernando Valenciano (AGP, RHF T-05362).

came to me without my having thought of or sought them. I don't know . . . I'm very moved. . . . I feel in my soul just as I did at the beginning of the Work."

Celebrating Mass that day, he joined his palms together and rested his forehead on his fingertips, closing his eyes and becoming totally absorbed. He did the consecration very slowly, speaking the words one syllable at a time over the host and the wine. He genuflected, kissed the altar, and recited the texts with singular devotion.

Clama, ne cesses! was from the prophecy of Isaiah: "Cry aloud, spare not, lift up your voice like a trumpet; declare to my people their transgression, to the house of Jacob their sins."[16]

Three months earlier, on May 8, after deciding to make the long pilgrimage to the shrine of Our Lady of Guadalupe, he had another unexpected locution: *Si Deus nobiscum, quis contra nos?* "If God is with us, who can be against us?" These words were of St. Paul's Letter to the Romans. But not quite. The Letter to the Romans read, *Si Deus pro nobis, quis contra nos?* (Romans 8:31) "If God is for us, who is against us?" But he had heard *Si Deus nobiscum, quis contra nos?* "If God is *with* us . . ."

And now *Clama, ne cesses!* God was taking him by the hand, and whispering to him what he had to do.

Contraband tobacco?

They made several excursions from Villa Gallabresi to Castello d'Urio, a conference center of Opus Dei near Lake Como. Monsignor Escrivá had several get-togethers and conversations with his children in Castello d'Urio.

They also went to Switzerland. As soon as they could see Switzerland on the horizon, at Il Ticino, they prayed for the apostolates of the Work there. On the way back, as Don Alvaro and Father Javier both smoked, Monsignor Escrivá suggested they buy cigarettes, "because it will be cheaper here than in Italy." Father Javier went into a tobacconist, where he was told that border controls restricted cigarettes to one carton per person. "Well, as there are four of us,

---

16. Is. 58:1.

buy four," said Monsignor Escrivá. When they got to the border crossing, the *carabinieri* asked "Excuse me, *signori*, have you anything to declare?"

"I don't think so; we've got no more than the allowance."

"But what exactly have you got?"

"Four cartons of cigarettes."

"I'm sorry, that's too many. You can't take a quantity like that."

There followed an exasperating argument with the youngest, most inquisitive *carabiniero*, who seemed to enjoy the idea of catching three clergymen red-handed. At this stage Monsignor Escrivá, quiet until then, intervened, saying to Father Javier Echevarria, "Leave it, Javi. If he says we can't take four cartons, let's go back to where you bought them, even though it's a waste of time and possibly a surrender of your rights. But at least we will avoid upsetting this *carabiniero*, and we won't have to stay here arguing about a few packets of cigarettes."

Back at Villa Gallabresi, Monsignor Escrivá told Father Javier, "Look here, Javier, I don't mind being a laughingstock to defend a just, worthwhile cause. But when it's an insignificant matter, we need to act prudently so as not to leave priests in a bad light, as happened today at the frontier. Anyone who witnessed the whole business could have got the wrong impression that we were trying to smuggle something, breaking the law and not fulfilling our duty. Someone could have been scandalized by that false impression. In the future, try and be more prudent, especially when some action, no matter how innocent or correct it is, might be misconstrued; even if it's just one person and they're mistaken anyway."

They went to Milan several times, as they had the previous summer. On one trip they visited the cathedral, a jewel in stone with a Gothic façade, 130 pinnacles, and 2,300 statues decorating the exterior columns. As soon as they went in, Monsignor Escrivá asked an attendant, "Excuse me, *Signore*, can you tell me where the Blessed Sacrament chapel is?"

"What?"

"Where's the Blessed Sacrament chapel?"

"I'm sorry, but I don't know. First it was here, then they moved it somewhere else, and now I don't know where it is."

Monsignor Escrivá tried to conceal the sorrow this reply caused him. He could not comprehend that anyone could be working in a cathedral without knowing where "the Master of the house" was. They made a quick tour of the cathedral to find the Blessed Sacrament chapel. Monsignor Escrivá went straight toward the altar and fell to his knees, close to the tabernacle, saying, "Lord, I'm no better than anyone else, but I need to tell you, with all my strength, that I love you! I love you for all the people who come here and don't tell you so. I love you for everyone who will come in the future and won't say so."[17]

He stayed kneeling on the cold stone floor and praying until Don Alvaro tapped him on the shoulder.

August 23, 1971: Caglio

Caglio was a small mountain village near Lake Como and about eighty kilometers from Castello d'Urio. There they rented a small house called Villa Sant'Agostino, for several weeks of July and August in 1971. As usual, they installed the oratory in the best of the upstairs rooms for security reasons. The bedrooms were on the same floor. Downstairs there was a dining room, kitchen, and sitting room that doubled as a work room.

Monsignor Escrivá and Don Alvaro were exhausted when they arrived. It had been a year of very demanding work during which certain "good people" of the Vatican, one especially, had continued to fuel an atmosphere of mistrust against the Work. In the worst moments, Monsignor Escrivá constantly repeated a prayer he wrote to leave everything in God's hands. "My Lord and my God, into your hands I abandon everything past, present and future: big and little, great and small, temporal and eternal." It was the prayer he taught Sofia Vavaro on her deathbed the following year (see Chapter 12).

Monsignor Escrivá's relaxation was to plunge into intimacy with God. The only work he had brought with him to study was the five books of the Pentateuch. The day they arrived, they watched the

---

17. Testimony of Begoña Alvarez (AGP, RHF T-04861), to whom Monsignor Escrivá related this in Rome.

news on television after dinner. Father Javier Echevarria told them, "On this channel there's a film next: 'The Song of Bernadette,' starring Jennifer Jones. It's a very old film—I saw it years ago—but as far as I can remember it was sensitively done." They started to watch it, but after three quarters of an hour, just when, as Javier Cotelo said, "We had really got into it," there was a violent storm and the electricity was cut off. With a cigarette lighter, Father Javier went in search of candles, and they chatted by candlelight for a while. Don Alvaro went to the window to see if there was light in the gatehouse, but darkness reigned, and he reported, "There's no sign of this being fixed." Monsignor Escrivá was talking about the film, but when he heard Don Alvaro's remark, he said, "All right, let's wait a few minutes more. And if the electricity doesn't come back on, we'll do our examination of conscience and offer up this little setback for the apostolates of the Work. It's nothing much, but the spiritual life, like human life, is made up of little things like this."

That summer he again went to see his Italian daughters and sons in Castello d'Urio. Other outings were more utilitarian in character: they visited furniture factories in the area, where Monsignor Escrivá noted prices, types of furniture, transport costs, and so on, and asked for catalogs and business cards. Cavabianca, the final premises of the Roman College of the Holy Cross, was under construction at the time, and he was thinking of its furniture and fittings. When the time came to acquire the furniture, he gave the catalogs and addresses he had collected to Helen Monfort and the interior decoration team, so that they could "buy good-quality things at factory prices, with plenty of choice."

Monsignor Escrivá and his companions usually went for walks around the city of Como. They always went into the cathedral to spend a while there: Monsignor Escrivá wanted to keep Jesus Christ company in the tabernacle. Afterwards they would sit on a bench in the nave and, rather than walking around like sightseers, would observe the marvelous works of art: the tapestries from Ferrara, Florence, and Antwerp; the *Sacra Conversazione* by Luini; the Chapel of the Crucified Christ; the "Wedding of the Blessed Virgin Mary"; the domed cover on the baptismal font; and the decoration of the transept dedicated to the Assumption. Now and then Monsignor Escrivá noticed an ornamental detail such as the paneled ceiling that could be copied for an oratory of the Work. Then he would say to Javier Cotelo, "See those panels? Make a quick sketch so we remember the combination of gold and colors later on."

Four years later, with César Ortiz-Echagüe and other architects in Rome, he was trying to settle on the best position for an organ, and the matter was becoming quite complicated. Monsignor Escrivá suggested, "How about putting it at the front and to one side, near the altar?" He had seen this solution in the cathedral in Como, where there were two fine sixteenth-century organ cases, one on each side at the front of the central nave.

The watermelon seller

One morning before going down the hill into Como, they stopped at some roadside fruit stalls—not a market but a few country people who set up their rustic stalls on a few planks. Monsignor Escrivá took particular notice of a man selling watermelons. He was a rough-looking man, short, lean, and swarthy, who advertised his merchandise on a crude placard: *Cocomeri, 100 lire per kilo.*

"Shall we buy a watermelon and take it to your sisters? That will save them having to go and buy it themselves. Go on, Javi, although you're such a townsman, see if you can get a nice ripe one."

Monsignor Escrivá was always amused by Father Javier's seriousness and used to provoke him on purpose or put him into unusual situations like this, with everybody around looking on. Father Javier got out of the car, went over to the stall, and began talking, not to the salesman but to his son, a plump little boy.

"Hello, sonny!" he said. "Since you're the expert, can you pick me out a nice ripe watermelon?"

The boy's father pointed, saying, "Take that one." The child trotted round, picked up the watermelon, and gave it to Father Javier without a word.

"Do you think it's ripe?" Father Javier asked.

"My father said so."

While the man was weighing the watermelon, Father Javier continued talking very simply to the child. "Excuse me saying so, but you look a little plump—do you eat nothing but watermelons?"

"Oh, no, I eat pasta and pizza as well."

"Well, you certainly have a good time here, learning from your father. You have to love him a lot and help him so he doesn't get so tired."

"Right."

"At the same time, offer up everything you do to Baby Jesus."

"Yes."

That same evening, when Monsignor Escrivá was alone with Father Javier, he said, "Javi, the next time we stop to buy something at this watermelon stall, be a bit more affectionate towards that little boy, not just tossing him a few sentences on your way out. You have to realize that maybe that child will never have any Christian example or teaching given him in his whole life. Maybe you're the only priest who will ever even speak to him about right and wrong, or about God and Our Lady. And besides, his father's there too and will hear what you say to his son, so you can awaken an interest for the things of God in him too. If you put your mind to it in those few minutes of conversation, you can find a way into his life, and leave the imprint of God on his soul."

A few days later they stopped by the stall again. Monsignor Escrivá winked at Father Javier, saying, "Go on, as you were successful the first time, you try again. See what you can do!"

Monsignor Escrivá was passionate about God, and everything, no matter how trivial, led him to God. The caretakers at the Caglio house were a married couple with three children. One morning, while walking in the gardens around Villa Sant'Agostino, Monsignor Escrivá saw the man working in the garden, with his youngest son, about four, clinging to his trouser leg. Monsignor Escrivá looked at the child, seeing his eyes round with admiration, not missing any of his father's movements. Later, he commented, "I was moved by that child's eyes; I felt a holy envy of him. And I asked our Lord for that same sense of sonship for us, so that we always wish to be like that, contemplating our Father God with admiration, sure that he does things 'divinely,' because, in his providence, he takes care of the whole field we have to work in."

1972: Civenna, and a pair of heavy boots

For the summers of 1972 and 1973 they found a house in Civenna, a mountain village in the north of Italy near the city of Lecco, in the lakes region and near the Swiss border. In 1972 Monsignor Escrivá took a lot of work with him: he continued to revise the statutes of Opus Dei and prepared two books of homilies which would be published under the titles of *Christ Is Passing By* and *Friends of God. Friends of God* was published posthumously, as were *The Way of the Cross, Furrow,* and *The Forge.* The day after they arrived, they went out for a walk on an uphill mountain track. They had hardly gone 100 meters when Monsignor Escrivá called a halt. "With these city shoes we won't get very far. We'd better go back, get the car, and go to the nearest place where we can buy proper walking boots."

"The nearest place is Lecco, and that's about twenty kilometers away."

"Well then, let's go to Lecco!"

When they got there Monsignor Escrivá suggested going to the market before going to a shoe shop. "There must be boots for the locals there, and it will be much cheaper than buying them in a proper shop."

He was right, and each bought a pair of boots for 10,000 lira, about $7. Amid the shouting and bustle of the market, as if it were the most natural thing in the world, Monsignor Escrivá sat down on an empty wooden fruit-box, took off his shoes, tried on the boots, walked about a bit, stamped, and said to the stall holder with a beaming smile, "They're a perfect fit! I'm going to keep them on."

One day the housekeeping team threw away two of Don Alvaro's vests because they were very worn. While walking around Como, they spotted a sale in a shop offering "four vests for 3,000 lira." Monsignor Escrivá urged them to take advantage of the offer. He also asked Father Javier Echevarria to buy candy for his daughters in the Work. When he saw him coming out of the candy shop carrying a very small bag, he teased him. "But Javi, my son, haven't you overdone it a bit? Your sisters are going to think you're an absolute Scrooge! Next time, try and be a bit more magnanimous."

"Alvaro, will you treat us?"

Except on really long car trips, Monsignor Escrivá and his companions seldom stopped for refreshments away from home. So unusual was it that when it did happen, Father Javier Echevarria noted it in his diary. One hot August morning, around midday, after a long walk around Lecco, they came across a kiosk selling *granita di caffè*, a delicious drink of iced coffee. Javier Cotelo remarked that Monsignor Escrivá's sister—Aunt Carmen to everyone in the Work—used to treat her "nephews" or "nieces" to a *granita di caffè* when they went shopping in Rome in hot weather. On behalf of everyone Monsignor Escrivá addressed Don Alvaro, "Alvaro, will you treat us to a *granita di caffè*, just this once?"

This particular part of Brianza was generally cool and damp, with frequent rain, fog, and storms. One day Giuseppe Molteni drove from Milan to Civenna with Carlos Cardona to work on some of the homilies Monsignor Escrivá had been revising. It was pouring rain and storms swept across the whole region. During the drive, Guiseppe, enamoured with his Brianza, kept repeating like a salesman, "And yet, Carlos, behind those clouds the sun is shining!"

Carlos told Monsignor Escrivá about this as soon as they arrived. "So that I wouldn't lose heart every time there was a thunderclap, Peppino would say, 'And yet, Carlos, behind those clouds the sun is shining.' And I would answer: 'Well, if you say so, it must be so. But, lord, how it hides!'"

Monsignor Escrivá roared with laughter. "Peppino, you're a scream! But you'd better reach an agreement with your fellow countrymen, because they keep saying the rain and fog are the region's wealth. Anyway, in praising your country you've stated a notable truth that can be applied to the spiritual life. There are times when we fail to see the light, maybe through our own failure to correspond to grace. On other occasions, our Lord permits this darkness to try our faith and loyalty. Years ago I said that on the road to God, once we have seen our vocation with the light of grace, we have to go forward with faith and fortitude, maybe leaving shreds of clothes, or even skin, on the thorns of the wayside briars. But we have to carry on in the certainty that God is the same as always and cannot fail. If we are faithful to him, after the darkness and the storm comes the calm, and a marvelous sun will shine still more brightly for us. My children, having heard the voice of God you cannot look back."

As Civenna was just over four kilometers from the Swiss border, and less as the crow flies, they could get Swiss television channels. Their house had a color television set, and the first time they turned it on Monsignor Escrivá was as surprised as everyone else. "Isn't it good?" he exclaimed. "I had no idea the image would be so clear and the color so natural. The color's so attractive that you're captivated no matter what program is on."

After the television set had been turned off, he reflected aloud, "All this progress, great and small, has to bring us to give great glory to God. All noble human work, done well and used properly, is a fabulous instrument for serving society and sanctifying ourselves. I suppose the same thing happened to you as to me a moment ago when we were watching television: it was easy to raise one's heart to God, thanking him for the technical perfection of the image and the color. And then there's an idea which is always going around my head. I thought of the good and the evil which can be done with television and with all the media. Good? Yes, because it's a wonderful vehicle for reaching out to so many people, capturing their attention in such an attractive way. Bad? It's that too, because images and words can be used to spread bad doctrine and false morals. And people swallow these errors and falsehoods without realizing it, they welcome it like pure gold. That's why I insist so much that the apostolate through the media will always be very important. And Catholics who have a professional vocation to the media, journalists, people working in the press, radio, and television, have to be present and active: to be absent would be a shameful act of desertion."

One morning the telephone rang early. It was Giuseppe Molteni, asking to speak to Don Alvaro.

"Hello, is something the matter, Peppino?"

"Yes, Don Alvaro, I'm sorry for calling so early, but Cardinal Dell'Acqua is dead."

"Good Lord! Where? What happened?"

"It was quite sudden. He was in Lourdes. We haven't heard many details. But as I know how much the Father loves—loved—him, I thought it was better for me to telephone and give you the news rather than your hearing it suddenly on the radio or seeing it in the paper."

"Thank you very much for telling us, Peppino. You've really given me a shock. It's going to be a terrible blow for the Father, because they were very fond of each other. I'll tell him right now so we can begin to pray for his soul."

It was indeed an unexpected and heavy blow for Monsignor Escrivá. In the following days his sorrow could be seen in his face. Cardinal Angelo Dell'Acqua had been a good friend of his and a great ally in the Roman Curia. He said, "I feel as if a brother had died. He was like a brother to me. But it hurts even more because he was a loyal servant of the Pope and the Church, and God our Lord doesn't have many of them. I know how much he suffered at the hands of certain people who did not understand his self-giving and self-denial, or his fidelity to the authority of the Church. He will have found his reward in heaven. From now on I will appeal to him as an intercessor."

A lonely death for a Pope

He returned to the subject when they were talking together in the sitting room or walking around Lecco. He recalled how the cardinal had told him of Pope John XXIII's long death agony, riddled with cancer and in great pain. Pope John had known Cardinal Dell'Acqua as a young priest and affectionately called him "Angelino." When the cardinal went to visit the Pope, now old and sick, the Pope's face would light up. The Pontiff would confide, "Angelino, I'm suffering so much. . . . I'm offering it all to the Lord for the Church, and especially for the Second Vatican Council." Amid the comings and goings of doctors, secretaries, camerlengos, and monsignors, it was dreadful to see the Pope's loneliness, on the human plane, in his last hours.

"Come here, Angelino, come nearer," the Pope asked. Dell'Acqua approached his bed. The Pope took his hand and pressed it. "Like that I feel better! Like that it's easier to bear the pain which is sometimes so bad that it wears me out. . . . I'm in terrible pain. I think of God our Lord, I think of the Church and the Council, and I offer all my sufferings for its fruits." When it was time to say good-bye, John XXIII kept his friend a little longer, like a child afraid of being left alone. "Angelino, Angelino *mio*, don't leave me! Stay with me a little longer!"

Monsignor Escrivá recalled his many warm conversations with Cardinal Dell'Acqua. "He often said to me, 'If I were asked to testify at the beatification process of Pope Pius XII or Pope John XXIII, I would necessarily have to speak of the great affection they both had for Opus Dei. Each of them told me so explicitly, and I consider it a debt in conscience to ensure that their affection should be recorded in history.'"

In the autumn of 1972, Monsignor Escrivá set out on the first of his catechetical journeys throughout Spain and Portugal, going to Navarre, Biscay, Madrid, Andalusia, Valencia, Catalonia, Lisbon, Oporto, and Fatima. This was a novel way of preaching, combining mass communication, to reach thousands of people at a time, with the atmosphere of a family get-together. He made three exhausting forays to Central and South America not long afterwards, in 1974 and 1975, so his last summer holiday was in 1973.

1973: Monsignor Escrivá consoles Pope Paul VI

The situation in the Church was so serious that Pope Paul VI decided to move forward the Holy Year Jubilee of 1975, declaring it open on June 10, 1973. This was an attempt to stir the consciences of Catholics. On June 22, before the cardinals of the Roman Curia, the Pope decried "the doctrinal confusion and lack of discipline which are overshadowing the shining beauty of the Spouse of Christ, the Church."[18] The Pope was distraught at the deterioration, deviation, and anarchy. Monsignor Escrivá thought it was time for him to visit the Holy Father and offer him consolation. On the 25th of that month, he went to see him in a private audience that lasted an hour and a quarter, well beyond the time set by Vatican protocol.

---

18. Pope Paul VI, Address, June 20, 1973.

As soon as Monsignor Escrivá came into the Pope's presence, he dropped to his knees on the marble floor. Paul VI reached out and raised him. When both were seated, Monsignor Escrivá took out his pocket diary, in which he had made some notes of what he wanted to say. He had encouraging news about the perseverance of thousands of men and women in the Work and about the apostolates thriving in so many countries and areas of social life. As for vocations to the priesthood, that year like every year since 1944 a new batch of laymen—each with two doctorates, civil and ecclesiastical—were to be ordained.

In July Monsignor Escrivá and his companions returned to Civenna, staying in the same house as the year before. One morning, though the day had dawned cold and bleak, with heavy dark clouds and squally showers, they went to Lecco to walk there. Monsignor Escrivá walked for two or two and a half hours, but Don Alvaro less. He sat on a bench to wait for them. When Monsignor Escrivá joined him, he found him very pale, with dark shadows under his eyes, and shivering with cold.

"Alvaro, you don't look well! What's the matter?"

"I had a bad night," replied Don Alvaro, "and now I'm feeling really cold. As the Grandmother would say, I'm a bit under the weather."

"Let's go. We'll go home at once!"

On the way to the car, Monsignor Escrivá told Father Javier, "Javi as soon as we get back, could you telephone Castello d'Urio for José Luis Pastor to come and see your brother, please? Tell him to come as soon as he can, but without alarming him."

Driving home, he scolded Don Alvaro. "Why didn't you say something before coming out? I get upset when you do things like that. I know you were thinking of the rest of us, and we're grateful, but you ought to have told me you weren't feeling well, and we'd have been quite happy to stay at home. Alvaro, my son, don't ever do it again!"

"I thought it was just a passing indisposition, because I was tossing and turning all night. But don't worry, Father, I don't think it's anything serious."

Don Alvaro had a somewhat weak constitution, and had had several major operations. He worked full time and hard at two jobs: in Villa Tevere to serve the Work, and in the Vatican to serve the Holy See. What kept him going was his spirit.

Don Alvaro's "passing indisposition" did indeed get worse. He ran an intermittent high fever for weeks. It made him perspire profusely, soaking sheets and mattress so that the bed linen had to be changed several times a day and during the night as well. Monsignor Escrivá and the two Javiers took turns staying with him. José Luis Pastor, the doctor, diagnosed a serious kidney infection and suggested going to Spain and consulting Dr. Gil Vernet from Barcelona to see if an operation was needed.

When Don Alvaro recovered a little, they decided to make the trip. Before they left they had to be vaccinated at the airport since there had been an outbreak of cholera in Italy and a vaccination certificate was required to leave the country. On September 1, the day before they intended to travel, the four of them went to Milan airport. There was a long line of people all waiting for the same thing. One of the medical staff recognized Monsignor Escrivá and approached him courteously, saying, "*Monsignore*, forgive us! Come this way please, and you will go through immediately, you won't have to wait."

Monsignor Escrivá refused. "No, thank you. I'm very grateful, but I'd rather stay here and wait for my turn."

As the official kept insisting, Monsignor Escrivá explained, "I'm really very grateful to you, but I don't wish to take anyone else's place—they're not here just for the fun of it. They must have other things to do, maybe even more urgent ones than mine."

Next day, when the airplane took off and flew over Milan and Brianza, Monsignor Escrivá "stormed" the tabernacles of churches he could see from above. He sensed that he might never return.

It was the last holiday he took.

18 ✢

Rome, How You Shine!

The flat roof of Villa Vecchia, rising above all the other buildings of Villa Tevere, affords a view over the Cimino, Mario, and Sabine hills around Rome. Monsignor Escrivá had a plaque set there with a Latin inscription: *O quam luces Roma, quam amoeno hinc rides prospectu! Quantis excellis antiquitatis monumentis! Sed nobilior tua gemma atque purior Christi Vicarius, de quo una cive gloriaris!—MDCCCCLI.* This can be rendered, "O Rome, how you shine! How beautiful you look from here, in splendid panorama! How you stand out with your many monuments of antiquity! But your noblest and purest jewel is the Vicar of Christ, in whom you alone glory! 1951."

The date carved at the end of the inscription, 1951, was when Monsignor Escrivá felt so uneasy—"like a roaring lion," as he put it—with forebodings of hostility on the part of people with power to influence opinion in very high places, even reaching Pope Pius XII himself. They were plotting to expel the founder, divide the men and women of the Work into two separate institutions, and break up Opus Dei. This plaque, with the passing of the years, became a sort of testimonial to unshakable fidelity.

Monsignor Escrivá also said, "I feel completely Roman, since Roman means universal, catholic, and because it leads me to have a tender love for the Pope, *il dolce Christo in terra,* the sweet Christ on earth, as St. Catherine of Siena, whom I count as a most beloved friend, liked to repeat. . . . Being Roman does not mean being narrow, it means being genuinely ecumenical: it implies a desire to enlarge one's heart, to open it to everyone."[1]

He had wanted to 'Romanize' Opus Dei from very early on and so, even without money to do it, set out to establish the headquarters in Rome. He also set up the Roman College of Our Lady near Rome, in Castelgandolfo, and the Roman College of the Holy Cross at Cavabianca. Men and women of the Work would come to acquire degrees in the humanities, canon law, and theology, as well as for all sorts of courses. Yearly at Easter time, crowds of university students—in the early years in the hundreds, now in the thousands—gather as pilgrims to see Peter, *videre Petrum*, and to have a get-together with the prelate of Opus Dei.

"This is where the Pope's hand rests"

Whenever a daughter or a son of his in the Work came to Rome, whether for a few days or to stay and work, Monsignor Escrivá inquired, "Have you been to St. Peter's yet? You haven't? Well, ask someone to take you as soon as possible. Shall I tell you the route I usually take? First of all I go to the chapel of the Blessed Sacrament and make a visit there, and a spiritual communion. Then I greet Our Lady at the altar of Our Lady of Perpetual Succor. Then, beside the Altar of the Confession, I kneel down and say the Creed. Maybe everyone else is standing, but I find I have more devotion when I say it on my knees. By the way, before you leave write a postcard to your parents. They'll be delighted to get one with a Vatican postmark."[2]

Monsignor Escrivá wanted everyone in the Work to be imbued with the spirit of Rome, which he interpreted as catholicity of soul, a universal mentality, and, above all, loyal affection for the Pope, "no matter who he is."

Ubi Petrus, ibi Ecclesia, ibi Deus—"Where Peter is, there is the Church, and there is God," he used to say, to show the double reason, theological and human, for his love for the Pope. "We want to be with Peter because the Church is where he is and God is with him;

---

1. Josemaría Escrivá, *Loyalty to the Church*, Homily, June 4, 1972.
2. Testimonies of Encarnación Ortega (AGP, HRF T-05074), Begoña Alvarez (AGP HRF T-04861), Marlies Kücking, and Mercedes Morado (AGP HRF T-07902).

God is not present where the Pope is absent. This is why I wanted the Work to be in Rome. Love the Holy Father very much. Pray a lot for the Pope. Have a lot of affection for him. He needs the affection of his children. And I can understand that very well. I know it from experience because I am made of flesh and blood, not stone. So I like the Pope to know that we love him, that we will always love him for this one reason: because he is the sweet Christ on earth."[3]

On July 11, 1949 a young man in Opus Dei called Miguel Angel Madurga arrived in Rome. Monsignor Escrivá took him and another man to visit the four main Roman basilicas. At St. Peter's, cutting through corridors and rooms that he seemed to know well, they came to the throne room and the balcony from which the Pope would give his blessing to the people. Monsignor Escrivá made some affectionate remarks about Pius XII. He approached the papal throne and pointed to the right arm. "This is where the Pope's hand rests," he whispered. Then he bent and kissed it.[4]

With that kind of warmth, he encouraged others. "Our greatest love, our highest esteem, our deepest veneration, our fullest obedience and our warmest affection must also be for the Vicar of God on earth, the Pope. Keep very close to the Roman Pontiff, *il dolce Christo in terra!* Follow his teachings, pray about them, and defend them both in speech and writing."[5]

Monsignor Escrivá's lifetime covered seven papacies: those of Leo XIII, Pius X, Benedict XV, Pius XI, Pius XII, John XXIII, and Paul VI. He knew the last three personally, and all three received him in audience several times.

Each of these occasions was a singular event, celebrated as a special day by those at Villa Tevere. At these meetings, which he prepared for well in advance in his prayers, Monsignor Escrivá spoke simply and sincerely like a son to his father. But far from getting used to them, he could not help becoming emotional. Tears filled his eyes, he got a lump in his throat, and his voice trembled in the presence of the Vicar of Christ. Don Alvaro went with him on some of these visits and was surprised that this man who governed Opus

3. AGP, HRF 21158, pp. 216–217. Testimony of Begoña Alvarez (AGP HRF T-04861).

4. Testimony of Miguel Angel Madurga (AGP, HRF T- 03340). Cf. *Articles of the Postulator,* 643.

5. Josemaría Escrivá, *Letters,* January 9, 1932, October 20 and 24, 1965, 73.

Dei with a firm hand and could dominate huge mixed crowds from a stage was so moved. "He was always so deeply moved that he found it hard to speak."[6] Monsignor Escrivá himself explained the reason while telling a group of his sons about the visit Pope Paul VI had made the day before to the ELIS Center, directed by people of Opus Dei in Tiburtino, a working-class district of Rome. "I was deeply affected yesterday. I always get moved, whether it was Pius XII, John XXIII or Paul VI, because I have faith."[7]

Pope Pius XII

Pius XII bestowed the *Decretum Laudis* or "Decree of Praise" on Opus Dei and gave it his pontifical approval. In 1949 he temporarily turned over to the Work an old house and some land near Lake Albano in Castelgandolfo that had been used by a Countess Campello for works of mercy. The garden had run to seed and the house was infested with vermin. To make the place habitable the first thing needed was a thorough cleaning and disinfecting. In 1957 Pius XII appointed Monsignor Escrivá a consultor of the Congregation of Seminaries and Universities and member of the Pontifical Academy of Theology. That same year he entrusted the prelature of Yauyos in Peru to Opus Dei.

"Wherever no one else wants to go, we will go"

Yauyos and Huarochiri formed a vast, rugged territory in the Andes, with a scattered population of illiterate, impoverished Indians. Under the leadership of Monsignor Ignacio de Orbegozo, a priest of Opus Dei, a handful of people of the Work developed a bold social and educational project. The mule and two-way radio were their means of communication and teaching in these remote areas over 15,000 feet above sea level.

Years later, Monsignor Escrivá, speaking about Yauyos to two young Peruvians visiting Rome, told them, "In a few years' time you'll have many native priests, who will be very well trained and

---

6. Bishop Alvaro del Portillo speaking in a get-together, AGP, HRF 21165, p. 852.
7. AGP, HRF 20577, pp. 47–55. *Articles of the Postulator*, 647.

educated and will do a wonderful job. But 'missions' are not normally our thing. Our vocation is actually to stay in the middle of the world, in the heart of society. Taking responsibility for Yauyos was something I agreed to when the Vatican suggested it, so that no one could ever say I had denied the Holy Father anything. They showed me a map with better situations in other countries, for me to choose from. I said, 'Wherever no one else wants to go, we will go.' That's how we chose Yauyos."[8]

Pope John XXIII

At the death of Pius XII on October 9, 1958, Monsignor Escrivá mourned for him and prayed and got others to pray for the conclave that was to elect a new Pope. He told his children, "You know the love we have for the Pope . . . no matter who he is. We already love the next Pope. We are ready to serve him with all our hearts, *ex toto corde tuo, ex tota anima tua*; and we are going to love the new Pope like that."[9]

After five o'clock on October 28, Monsignor Escrivá, watching television, was disconcerted to see smoke from the chimney of the Sistine Chapel in a strange grey plume. A few seconds later, white smoke appeared clearly. He dropped to his knees, praying devoutly and intensely, "*Oremus pro Beatissimo Papa nostro* . . . let us pray for our blessed Pope. May the Lord preserve him and give him life and make him happy on earth, and not let him fall into the hands of his enemies." Then he gave the joyous news to his daughters and sons over the intercom: "*Habemus Papam!* We have a Pope!" Everyone in the house was to celebrate the event as a big feast day, he said.

Cardinal Angelo Giuseppe Roncalli, who took the name of John XXIII, had already met the Work. In 1954 he had visited two centers in Spain, La Estila in Santiago de Compostela and Miraflores in Saragossa. In his diary for July 23, 1954, he called Opus Dei "an interesting and edifying institution which is new to me."

---

8. A get-together with ISSA students. AGP, HRF 21154, p. 86.
9. AGP, HRF 20057, p. 65.

The Vatican "head-hunts" Don Alvaro

Pope John's pontificate was notable for the calling and setting up the Second Vatican Council. He would have liked Monsignor Escrivá to participate, but he understood that the president general of Opus Dei could not neglect the governance of the Work for years. Instead, he entrusted several posts to Don Alvaro del Portillo, in the preparatory stages as well as during the council itself, appointing him consultor of the Sacred Congregation of the Council, judge and censor of the Supreme Congregation of the Holy Office, president of the ante-preparatory Commission for the Laity, member of four other commissions, and a council adviser. While Vatican II was in progress, from 1962 to 1965, Don Alvaro was additionally appointed secretary of the Commission on the Discipline of the Clergy and Christians, and consultor on commissions regarding bishops, religious, doctrine, the Code of Canon Law, and other matters.

From 1959 on, for practically the whole of Pope John XXIII's pontificate and a good part of that of Pope Paul VI, Don Alvaro had to divide his time between his duties in the Work and those entrusted to him directly by the Holy See. He spent almost more time at the Vatican than in Villa Tevere. Monsignor Escrivá never protested. "That's all right," he said. "That's what the Holy Father has decided. We have to serve the Church as the Church wants to be served."[10] While conscientiously respecting whatever was confidential, they talked almost daily about Vatican II.

Three other people in Opus Dei were council Fathers: Monsignor Ignacio de Orbegozo, prelate of Yauyos, Monsignor Luis Sanchez-Moreno, auxiliary bishop of Chiclayo, also in Peru, and Monsignor Cosme do Amaral, auxiliary bishop of Oporto, Portugal. In addition, a large number of bishops, experts, theologians, and canon lawyers from all over the world involved in the work of the council came to Villa Tevere to visit Monsignor Escrivá and seek his opinion on matters under debate.

From his backwater in Villa Vecchia, Monsignor Escrivá followed the progress of the council very closely. He prayed hard and got

---

10. *Articles of the Postulator*, 209.

others to pray. In July 1962 he wrote a letter encouraging everyone in Opus Dei to offer up their daily work, "for the happy outcome of this great enterprise, the Second Vatican Ecumenical Council. I know that this is our Holy Father's main intention, and I want us too to contribute from our patch, with our prayer, penance, and work, which we sanctify and which sanctifies us. . . . These are our great weapons, and the only means Opus Dei has."[11]

One afternoon Don Alvaro had a high temperature. The commission he was working in had to reach some important decisions, and his presence was needed. However, he was close to collapse and should undoubtedly have been in bed. Monsignor Escrivá looked at him, worried and hesitant. If he listened to his heart he would say, "Go to bed at once," but in the circumstances he told him, "Dear Alvaro, I think you should go, my son."

When Alvaro had left, he turned to Francesco Angelicchio and said, "You think I have no compassion for the man, don't you? But there are some things which have to be done even though they shorten our lives. I fear for his health. I need him. We need him. The Work needs him."[12] Among the things that had to be done, in his view, was "serving the Church as she wishes to be served."

ELIS Center

Pope John XXIII appointed Monsignor Escrivá a consultor of the Commission for the Authentic Interpretation of the Code of Canon Law, turned over the land at Castelgandolfo to the Work in perpetuity, raised the school at Pamplona to the rank of university, and asked Opus Dei to undertake a social project in the Roman district of Tiburtino, with funds raised by a worldwide collection for Pius XII's eightieth birthday. This project was the ELIS Center (*Educazione, Lavoro, Istituzione, Sport*—Education, Work, Training, Sport) for young people.

---

11. AGP, HRF, EF-620712-1.
12. Testimony of Francesco Angelicchio (AGP, HRF T-3322).

"It is destined to open up hitherto unknown horizons"

On March 5, 1960 Monsignor Escrivá went to the Vatican for an audience with Pope John. During the conversation, the Pope said, "The first time I heard about Opus Dei, I was told that it was an impressive institution which was doing a lot of good. The second time I heard about it, I was told that it was a *very* impressive institution which was doing a *terrific* amount of good. The words entered my ears, but love for Opus Dei lodged in my heart."[13]

Monsignor Escrivá told the Pope about the delays that lasted twenty years until the Holy See gave its approval for Opus Dei to have non-Catholics and non-Christians as "cooperators." "Everyone, Catholic or not, has always found a warm welcome in our Work. As you can see, I have not learned ecumenism from Your Holiness but from the Gospel," he said.[14]

In a second audience, on June 27, 1962, Pope John said, "Monsignor, the Work opens up before my eyes infinite horizons which I had not discovered before."[15] Monsignor Escrivá in a letter to his children reported, "I have stored every detail of this meeting between a son and his father in my mind and heart. . . . My mind keeps going back to that audience, and I can recall every little detail of it: not only the day and time it took place, but also the paternal benevolence and attentiveness in the Pope's eyes, the slightest gesture of his hands, the affectionate warmth of his voice, the deep, serene joy that shone in his face. . . . He holds all of us in his heart. He knows us and understands us perfectly."[16]

While Pope John XXIII was dying Monsignor Escrivá prayed for him intensely. He altered his timetable during those days, saying Mass first thing in the morning to offer it up for the Pope if he was

---

13. AGP, HRF, 21075, pp. 18–19; 20162, pp. 385–386.
14. AGP, HRF, 21503, Note 266. Op. cit. *Conversations*, 46. Interview with Jacques Guillaume-Brulon, in *Le Figaro*, Paris, April 16, 1966. Also in *Conversations*, 22. Interview with Pedro Rodriguez in *Palabra*, Madrid, October 1967. Cf. *Opus Dei*, Peter Berglar, p. 246, and Ana Sastre, *Tiempo de Caminar* (Madrid: Rialp, 1989), p. 457.
15. Testimony of Carmen Mazzucchelli, Countess of Ruidoms (AGP, HRF T-05052).
16. AGP, HRF, EF-620712-1.

still alive or as immediate intercession for his soul if he had died in the night.[17]

When the Pope died, whenever Monsignor Escrivá met one of his sons in his comings and goings around the house he would remind him by way of greeting, "Pray for the conclave!" or "Are you praying a lot for the new Pope?"

Pope Paul VI's immediate circle

The task awaiting the new Pope was not an easy one. Pope Paul VI did not always find among his immediate collaborators the understanding and courage needed to support him in his delicate task. At one point during Paul VI's pontificate, Monsignor Escrivá told some of his older sons, "The trouble is within . . . within and high up."[18]

He remembered Pope Paul VI, when he was still Monsignor Montini, as "the first friendly hand I found here in Rome; the first affectionate word for the Work which I heard in Rome was spoken by him."[19] As Pope, he received Monsignor Escrivá in protracted, affectionate audiences on several occasions. During one he presented him with a chalice with the pontifical emblem embossed in ivory, identical to one he had given Patriarch Athenagoras of Constantinople a few weeks previously. He came to Tiburtino for the solemn inauguration of the ELIS Center, now in operation with a big residence hall, a catering school, and a parish church nearby, also entrusted to priests of the Work.

When Monsignor Escrivá asked Pope Paul to bless everyone there in the new buildings, the Pope replied, "*Benediciamo insieme*" (Let's give the blessing together). Monsignor Escrivá was so moved he dropped to his knees and bowed his head. As Paul VI was leaving, Monsignor Escrivá knelt again outside the door on the wet ground—it had been raining—to kiss his ring. The Pope took hold of his elbows, raised him firmly, and embraced him, saying, "*Tutto, tutto qui è Opus Dei!*" (Everything here is Opus Dei!)

---

17. Testimony of Marlies Kücking.
18. Testimony of Monsignor César Ortiz-Echagüe (AGP, HRF T-04694).
19. AGP, HRF 20115, p. 47.

"No authority on earth . . ."

Monsignor Escrivá had for years been importuning the Holy See for a clear canonical formulation, based on the ordinary law of the Church and not on privilege, that would guarantee the lay nature of Opus Dei, including the right of people in the Work to do any honest job and hold and express their own ideas in social, political, cultural, artistic, and all other matters.

On May 25, 1962 he wrote a long letter to those who held positions in the governance of Opus Dei. "In my view . . . it is not just a question of faithfulness to God's will but also of justice towards all of you. . . . So that your decision might be a conscious and free one, before being admitted to the Work, each of you was told as a matter of justice that you were not going to be religious, nor similar to religious. You were told that you would retain your own personality and your state as ordinary lay people . . . ; and that on coming to Opus Dei you would not change your state in life, but would continue in your current one. You were told, finally, that your professional vocation and your social duties would continue to be an integral part of the divine vocation you had received.

"How could I now commit the crime of obliging you to follow a different vocation? There is no way I could require this of you, nor could I employ disloyal arguments which would violate your freedom of conscience, to ask you to renew your commitment to the Work by embracing a vocation different from the one we have received from God.

"I cannot do this to you, and nor can anyone do it to me. . . . Besides being a wicked action on the human plane, it would be a grave fault against Christian morality, divine positive law, and even natural law. . . . I love and revere St. Francis, St. Dominic, and St. Ignatius to the depths of my soul, but nobody in the world can force me to become a Franciscan, a Dominican, or a Jesuit, any more than anyone can oblige me to get married. . . . In the spiritual life it is God's grace, his will, that counts; his desire is what points out a way and a mission. . . . Who could ever modify a God-given vocation?"[20]

---

20. Josemaría Escrivá, *Letter*, May 25, 1962, 33–35.

Urged on by "a grave commitment to defend the integrity of our spirituality, our secular vocation and our condition as ordinary Christians,"[21] Monsignor Escrivá repeated these and other arguments to Cardinal Angelo Dell'Acqua, acting secretary of state, in writing from Paris[22] and face to face in Rome, asking him to pass his words on to the Pope. Seeing the danger that members of secular institutes could be equated with religious in the Second Vatican Council, he said, "There is no authority on earth that can oblige me to be a religious or to get married, because it would be an attack on the freedom that the Church defends in Canon Law, and would be severely punished. According to Canon Law any decision of that sort, apart from being punishable with excommunication, would be absolutely invalid."[23]

On October 10, 1964 during an audience, Paul VI gave Monsignor Escrivá to understand that the canonical solution for the Work would be published soon in one of the council documents; and so it was. In the Decree on Priests, *Presbyterorum Ordinis*, of December 8, 1965, "personal prelatures" for "specific pastoral works" were authorized. This was the appropriate form for Opus Dei, although it was another seventeen years before Pope John Paul II was to establish Opus Dei as a personal prelature.

An unexpected proposal from Father Arrupe

A little-known incident on January 18, 1966 highlights the cordial relations between Monsignor Escrivá and Father Arrupe, the general of the Society of Jesus, and shows how difficult it was for some religious to understand the secularity of people of the Work. Father Arrupe had visited Villa Tevere twice, and each time Monsignor Escrivá visited Borgo Santo Spirito, the headquarters of the Jesuits, in return. The visits included a long lunch and lasted some time.[24]

---

21. Ibid., 26.
22. Monsignor Escrivá wrote a long, detailed letter to Cardinal Dell'Acqua, acting secretary of state, asking once again for an appropriate canonical form for Opus Dei. The letter was written in Paris and dated August 15, 1964. HRF, EF-640815 T-2.
23. Written account by Bishop Javier Echevarria to the author.
24. Someone imaginatively attributed to Fr. Arrupe the remark: "Yes, they say the founder of Opus Dei lives in Rome," meaning he had not seen him personally. In 1965 Fr. Arrupe was

On this occasion the party included Father Bajot and Father Iparraguirre, with Father Arrupe, and Don Alvaro and Father Javier Echevarria, with Monsignor Escrivá. At a certain point Father Arrupe said to Monsignor Escrivá, "Monsignor, I believe we could organize an apostolic activity together, between the Jesuits and Opus Dei."

There was a sudden silence in the little dining room. Nearly forty years of misunderstandings and jealousies originating with a few energetic Jesuits were dissolved. Monsignor Escrivá smiled at Father Arrupe and then spoke very slowly.

"Father Arrupe," he said, "I'm truly grateful to you for the suggestion, but it's not possible, because you have to practice a discipline and follow norms that have nothing to do with the lives of people of Opus Dei. If we were to start an initiative of that kind, it would most probably damage both institutions, as each would see its own spirit diminished: on Opus Dei's side by having to adapt to the religious way of life, and on yours, by having to adapt to the secular activity of people who, though not worldly, live and work in the world, busying themselves with temporal affairs. I think we can both work in the service of the Church, closely united by the Communion of Saints." Promising Father Arrupe "a lot of support: mine, and that of all the people in the Work, who will always pray and make sacrifices for the Society of Jesus," he concluded: "I think you will understand it perfectly if I tell you we are like two brothers who have different professions: one a doctor and the other a lawyer. They cannot set up a joint practice together, because one job has nothing whatsoever to do with the other."[25]

Vatican II concluded on December 7, 1965. The many deviations that followed betrayed the letter of the council's documents and produced widespread damage. Priests and religious who abandoned their calling caused much harm. But even more harmful were the many priests and religious whose minds were no longer Catholic but who stayed on within the Church, under the passive gaze of certain

elected father general of the Society of Jesus. From that time until 1970, twelve long meetings took place between the two men, most of them over lunch: in Villa Tevere, September 12, 1965; December 8, 1965; December 22, 1966; February 28, 1968; and March 27, 1969. In Borgo Santo Spirito, October 10, 1965; January 28, 1966; November 23, 1966; November 11, 1967; December 14, 1968; January 19, 1970; and March 16, 1970.
25. Written account by Bishop Javier Echevarria to the author.

intimidated and weak superiors and pastors who preferred to say nothing rather than provoke disobedience.

"This Pope and the next one"

"A flock is healthy when the shepherds take care of the sheep," Monsignor Escrivá said to a group of his daughters, "when they set the dogs on the wolf; when they don't drive the flock to places where there are poisonous plants, but places where the sheep can feed on good pasture. It's the same with souls. They need shepherds who are not dumb dogs, because dogs that don't bark are useless: they have to bark and raise the alarm.

"I beg you to pray very much for the Church, for the present Pope and for the next one, who will be a martyr from the start. Pray for the Christian people to have some defense against all these heresies and errors."[26]

As rebellion moved on to questioning what the Pope said, Monsignor Escrivá sent a long letter to his children in the Work, urging them "to defend the authority of the Pope from all possible attack, as his authority can only be conditioned by God."[27]

Vatican II: A pat on the back for Opus Dei

His realistic vision did not mean he was opposed to or disagreed with the council. Its documents set the stamp of approval on what he had been teaching since 1928: the universal call to holiness, the sanctifying value of work, the apostolate of lay people, the freedom of the laity in temporal affairs, and unity of life.

During an audience with Paul VI, Monsignor Escrivá reminded him, "Your Holiness has spoken recently about sanctified and sanctifying work . . ."

"Yes, I did," responded the Pope.

"Well, Holy Father, for saying the same thing, years ago, I was reported to the Holy Office."[28]

---

26. Josemaría Escrivá, *Letter*, February 14, 1964.
27. Testimony of Marlies Kücking.
28. AGP, HRF 21503.

When the council ended, Monsignor Escrivá told his children, "Thirty years ago, some people accused me of being a heretic for preaching some aspects of our spirit . . . it's now clear that we were ahead of the times, and it has become clear because you've prayed a lot."[29] Pope Paul VI himself said to him one day, "God has given you the charism of placing the fullness of the Church out there *in the street.*"[30] Among the Church authorities who pointed him out as a man ahead of his time were Cardinals Ugo Poletti, Joseph Frings, Franz König, Giacomo Lercaro, Sebastiano Baggio, Sergio Pignedoli, Marcelo Gonzalez Martin, Mario Casariego, and others.[31]

"The traitors are within"

But these were stormy times in the Church. On November 25, 1970 Monsignor Escrivá told the directors of the general council of the Work, "I am suffering desperately, my sons. We are living through a time of madness. Millions of souls are confused. There is a great danger that in practice all the sacraments are being emptied of their content—all of them, even baptism; and the very commandments of the law of God are losing their meaning in people's consciences."[32]

Three years later, at a work session with the directors of the central advisory, he said, "Pray for the Church, my daughters. The situation is very serious. It's as if our mother were at the point of death. Although you know the Church cannot die, because our Lord has promised it cannot, and his word is infallible. Even so, I have to tell you that things are very bad and I would not be a good father or a good shepherd if I didn't say so. I often prefer not to make you

29. AGP, HRF 21144, p. 73.
30. Testimony of Bishop Enrique Pelach i Peliu (AGP, HRF T-07678).
31. Op.cit., among others: Cardinal J. Frings, *Für die Menschen bestellt,* Erinnerungen des Alterzbischofs von Köln, J.P. Bachem Berlag, Köln, 1973, pp. 149–150; Cardinal Sebastiano Baggio, *Avvenire,* Milan, July 26, 1975; Cardinal Sergio Pignedoli, *Il Veltro,* Rome XIX (1975), 3–4; Cardinal Marcelo Gonzalez Martin, *Los domingos de ABC,* Madrid, August 24, 1975; Cardinal Franz König, *Corriere della Sera,* Milan, November 9, 1975; Cardinal Mario Casariego, homily given in the church of Montealegre, Barcelona, and reproduced in *L'Osservatore Romano,* Vatican City, July 14–15, 1975; Cardinal Poletti, "Decree of Introduction for the Cause of Beatification and Canonization of Josemaría Escrivá de Balaguer," Introductory Decree, *Rivista Diocesana di Roma,* March–April, 1981.
32. *Articles of the Postulator,* 217.

suffer and keep such painful things to myself."[33] And a month later, again speaking with his daughters: "My daughters, I feel anguish deep in my soul for the Church, this good mother of ours who is being treated so badly. The traitors are within her."[34]

"Pray for the Church, which is sick"

He increased his prayer and mortification and asked everyone for prayers for "the Church, which is sick," as well as total fidelity to the Pope. "Love the Holy Father, the present one and the next one, who will find everything shattered to bits. Love him and support him in everything he says whenever it is about universal doctrine."[35]

He ordered thousands of rosaries and distributed them to his visitors, asking them to "wear them out" praying for the Church. He set out to travel around Europe, making penitential pilgrimages to shrines of Our Lady. These were uncomfortable journeys by car, with his health already failing.

Monsignor Escrivá on stage: Christianity and dynamism

The diabetes he had suffered from, which was suddenly cured in 1954, had led to subsequent complications: kidney insufficiency and heart trouble that caused poor circulation. He had synovitis in his elbows and knees, cataracts in both eyes and double vision. Yet he embarked on three separate rounds of public catechesis involving long journeys: in 1970 to Mexico, in 1972 to Spain and Portugal, and the third, divided between 1974 and 1975, to Central and South America. Each was exhausting. He came with no notes, no prepared text, no rehearsal. He called it "jumping into the bull-ring without a cape." Leaving his self-imposed enclosure in Rome, he traveled the world talking about God and only about God. He

33. Testimony of Begoña Alvarez (AGP HRF T-04861). Testimonies of Marlies Kücking and Mercedes Morado (AGP HRF T-07902).
34. Testimonies of Marlies Kücking and Mercedes Morado (AGP HRF T-07902).
35. AGP, HRF 21162.

did not preach sermons. In these get-togethers Monsignor Escrivá answered questions. People raised doctrinal and moral dilemmas, yet it was a family conversation.

Monsignor Escrivá's combination of Christianity and dynamism engaged people, moved consciences, and initiated conversions.

"And a thousand lives if I had them"

Often he cried out, "I'm suffering over souls!"[36] In March 1975, three months before his death, he said to his sons, "When I became a priest, the Church seemed to be as solid as a rock, without a single crack. Its unity was clearly visible: it was a block of enormous strength. Now, looking at it from a human point of view it looks like a building in ruins, a heap of sand which is melting away, being stamped upon, scattered, and destroyed. The Pope has said more than once that it's destroying itself. Hard words, terrible words! But that cannot really happen because Jesus promised that the Holy Spirit would be with the Church always, until the end of time. What can we do about it? Pray. We can pray."[37]

For years, and with increasing intensity, Monsignor Escrivá had offered his life to God (often adding "and a thousand lives if I had them") "so that the time of trial may be shortened" in the Church. He renewed this as his conscious intention every morning when he celebrated Mass.

A message for the Pope's doctor

At 9:25 on the morning of his death, before leaving for Villa delle Rose in Castelgandolfo by car, he sent for two of his sons who were members of the general council: Giuseppe Molteni and Father Francisco Vives. He informed them that Dr. Ugo Piazza, a medical doctor and friend of the Pope, wished to talk to someone in the Work, as he had just been diagnosed as having an incurable cancer and given only a few months to live. Monsignor Escrivá sent

---

36. Testimony of Marlies Kücking.
37. AGP, HRF 21164, March 28.

them to offer Dr. Piazza whatever service they could give him, and entrusted them with a specific message for him to give Pope Paul if he should see him or speak to him: Dr. Piazza was to tell the Pope "that every day, for years, I have been offering the Holy Mass for the Church and the Pope. You can assure him—because you have heard me say so many times—that I've offered my life for the Pope, no matter who he is. We keep quiet and try to work hard and peacefully, even though there are some people in the Church who don't look on us kindly."[38]

After they left, he spoke to the central secretary, Carmen Ramos, on the house telephone and gave her the same message, asking her to pass it on to Dr. Piazza's daughter.[39] This was not his usual behavior. When he wished to say something to the Pope, he either wrote him or asked for an audience. Perhaps he just wanted to send the consolation of a friendly, supportive message to a Pope who was suffering. In any case, when he celebrated his last Mass at 7:53, he had made a heroic offering of his life and his death for the Pope and the Church.

Tears that burn

His pain for the havoc in the Church was even more intense while he was celebrating Mass. Disregarding the presence of Father Javier Echevarria, who used to serve his Mass, he would often cry openly, even sobbing aloud. "At a certain age," he commented on one occasion, "a man's tears burn his cheeks."[40]

Sometimes at breakfast he would lay aside the newspaper, hold his head in his hands, and start praying, asking God for pardon. He felt responsible for the infidelity of so many ecclesiastics and the disorientation of so many Christian, "because I don't pray or mortify myself enough."[41] Privately he insisted that Don Alvaro should give him permission to do twice as much corporal mortification as before.

---

38. Bishop Alvaro del Portillo, *Letter*, June 29, 1975, p. 35. Written account by Bishop Javier Echevarria to the author.
39. Testimony of Carmen Ramos.
40. AGP, HRF 21166, pp. 155–159.
41. Testimony of Begoña Alvarez (AGP HRF T-04861).

One day, preaching a meditation to the general council, he said, "I am constantly in Gethsemane, in the agony in the garden."[42]

"Josemaría, you used to be so jovial!"

On New Year's Day, 1971, he met with some of the directors of the Work. He spoke about his deep concern for the Church. And then: "Pray too for me to be good, faithful, and cheerful—and that I may be able to smile! For the last two years, I've found it very hard to smile. Now, when I'm shaving, I look at myself in the mirror and I hardly recognize myself. I say to myself: 'Josemaría, you're not the man you were. You used to be so jovial!' They've taken away my smile. I've never been a depressed or sullen sort of person. But, my daughters, you can't imagine how hard it is! It hurts so much when there are people whom you love but at the same time you sometimes find repellent! You can't imagine what it is to feel love and repugnance in your heart at the same time. Pray, keep on praying for the Church!"[43]

In the spring of 1971, speaking once again of the Church, he declared to a small group of women in the Work, "I don't mind telling you that I'm very peaceful now, but some years ago, when you could see this catastrophe falling on the Holy Church, I could not go up the altar steps without bursting into tears like a baby. My eyes got inflamed and I had to go to the optician. I've never been one for crying, but they were sweet tears, although they hurt my eyes: God sent them to me." Then, quoting the words of the locution *clama, ne cesses*—"cry aloud, spare not"—that he had heard the year before in Premeno, but without describing what had happened, he added, "I don't cry any more, but I have clamored ceaselessly since August 6, 1970, in the absolute conviction that God wants it. And I say the same to you: Cry out, pray, plead from the bottom of your heart!"[44]

---

42. Testimony of Fr. Carlos Cardona (AGP, HRF T-06138).
43. Testimonies of Mercedes Morado (AGP HRF T-07902) and Marlies Kücking. Cf. Testimony of Fr. Carlos Cardona (AGP, HRF T-06138).
44. Testimony of Begoña Alvarez (AGP HRF T-04861).

"This psalm will end in glory"

But he felt sure that "the end of all these sufferings of the Church is in sight: after the night comes the dawn, and the splendid light of the sun."[45] Sometimes, as if scrutinizing the future, he said, "This psalm will end in glory—yes, in glory."[46]

---

45. Ibid.
46. Testimony of Marlies Kücking.

19 ❖

A Luminous Twilight

You will sing it for me, without tears

t was an early afternoon in March 1957. Ten or twelve young men were having coffee and chatting in the Galleria del Fumo with Monsignor Escrivá. They had had lunch and were having a brief get-together before starting work again. Someone had drawn one of the blue canvas curtains to shade the room a little from the brilliant sunlight streaming through the windows, and someone else, or perhaps the same person, had put on a record, a song by Nila Pizzi that had won at the San Remo Festival. It was a lively, catchy number, and Monsignor Escrivá loved it.

> *Aprite le finestre al nuovo sole:*
> *è primavera, è primavera,*
> *Lasciate entrare un poco d'aria pura . . .*
>
> *Open the windows to the new sun:*
> *Spring is here! Spring is here!*
> *Let in a little fresh air,*
> *with the fragrance of gardens and meadows in flower.*
> *Spring is here, it's the feast of Love!*

Then Monsignor Escrivá surprised them all. "I'd like to hear that song when I'm dying," he said.

When he spoke of his own death, he did not appear to imagine it as something quick that would take him by surprise, but as a long drawn-out process, a difficult ordeal. He imagined death as a violent tearing apart of body and soul, a final combat for which he was always prepared. "It's all about winning the last battle," he said.

Sitting in an armchair with his back to the sliding window of the gallery, he listened to the song and now and again joined in, singing in Italian:

> *The first red rose has bloomed.*
> *Spring is here, spring is here!*
> *The first swallow has returned*
> *And glides through the clear sky,*
> *Bringing good weather.*
> *Boys and girls in love,*
> *Open the windows to the new sun,*
> *To hope and joy—*
> *Spring is here, it's the feast of love!*

He scanned the faces of the people there in the Galleria del Fumo: Don Alvaro, Father Javier Echevarria, Father Joaquin Alonso, Father Julian Herranz, Giuseppe Molteni, Juan Cox, Dick Rieman, Bernardo Fernandez, Father Severino Monzo. And there he stopped. Father Severino was a tall, robust young man, a priest with a doctorate in economics and canon law, and also a very good singer. Monsignor Escrivá gave him a mischievous smile and, like someone making an appointment, said, "You'll sing it for me—without tears."[1]

Not so much as a black tie

He had told his sons more than once that after his death he did not want "so much as a black tie" around.[2] Pizzi's springtime tune fitted in with his idea of death: the impassioned meeting of two people in love. He once said, "Recently, while I was saying good-bye to a young

---

1. Verbal account of Fr. Severino Monzo to the author. Cf. HRF T-07823.
2. Testimony of Marlies Kücking.

married couple, some words came to my lips: 'Pray for me to be a good son of God and to be cheerful until death . . . though dying, for us, is like getting married.' We ought not to wish for death, but when we are told *ecce sponsus venit, exite obviam ei!*—'Come on out, the Bridegroom's here for you!' we will ask Our Lady to intercede for us at that very difficult time when the body is separated from the soul—which is extremely painful, because the soul was made to be united to the body—and we'll go out joyfully to meet him who has been the love of our life!"[3]

Monsignor Escrivá clearly had a nuptial idea of death. He was fond of singing "human love songs with a divine meaning," and he must have prayed more than once taking these lines as his starting point. They were admittedly trite, but they were astonishingly similar to the greatest love song ever written, the Canticle of Canticles.

There are instantaneous deaths, but not sudden ones

In August 1941 Father Escrivá preached a retreat to a group of young women in the oratory of the Diego de Leon students' residence in Madrid. Encarnita Ortega and Nisa Gonzalez were among them. More than thirty years later Encarnita remembered fragments of a meditation that had surprised her. "Death for a Christian, for a person of Opus Dei, is never sudden," said Father Escrivá. "Something you don't expect is sudden, and we are constantly looking for and expecting God. For us, a sudden death is as if our Lord surprised us from behind, and we turned round and fell into his arms."[4]

One day in December 1965 he went with Don Alvaro to see a set of liturgical vestments for Masses for the Dead which Mercedes Angles was embroidering. She had transferred onto a new piece of black silk the multi-colored flowers of an old Manila shawl. Monsignor Escrivá joked about the vestments being "so flowery and festive" despite being for Masses for the dead. Then he added, "It's

3. AGP, HRF 21156, pp. 51–52.
4. Testimony of Encarnación Ortega (AGP, HRF T-05074).

very pretty. Besides, it's right for it to be as joyful as that. For us, death isn't sad."[5]

When the workmen were still building what was to be the crypt, an oratory with space for several burial niches, Monsignor Escrivá asked to have it decorated "in a cheerful style, with nothing frightening!" He suggested symbols of peace, joy, fertility, and immortality, in soft tones with touches of gold to lighten the atmosphere of the room so that people could pray there happily. He kept repeating, "We Christians don't die, we just move house."

One day he went down to the crypt. In the center of the floor was a rectangular space with a cover on it; this was to be his tomb. He came close to it, then gathered up his cassock and started jumping on the cement cover, saying, "You might as well make the most of the opportunity now! Later on when I'm in there, you won't be allowed to do this! I'll jump and skip on it too, while I can—after all, I'll have plenty of time to keep still!"[6]

On December 5, 1968 Monsignor Escrivá went to visit Marisa Tordella, a young married Italian woman with two very small children. She was gravely ill, and had asked to be admitted into Opus Dei just a few months previously. Marisa said, "Father, I'm at peace. I trust our Lord to help me right up to the last minute. I think a lot about my children, because they're so small! But I've asked Our Lady to take care of them when I'm gone."

Those outside could hear the murmur of a lively conversation and even laughter.

Marisa's husband joined him as soon as he came out. "You must be wondering what your wife and I were talking about to make us laugh so much," said Monsignor Escrivá. "Shall I tell you? We were talking about death!"[7]

Over one of the doors where he worked was an inscription in old Spanish which reminded him of the tension between time and eternity: *Oh cuán poco lo de acá. Oh cuán mucho lo de allá*—"How little what is here. How great what is there."

---

5. Testimony of Marlies Kücking.
6. Verbal account by Prof. José Luis Illanes to the author. Testimony of Encarnacion Ortega (AGP, HRF T-05074).
7. Testimony of Marlies Kücking.

In bed at night he used to say a prayer he had composed. "Lord, how often you've forgiven me! Lord, I appeal not to your justice but your mercy. You've forgiven me so often! Grant me a happy death: whenever you want, as you want and wherever you want; right now if you like! But, if possible, give me *spatium verae poenitentiae*, a time for true contrition: may I have a little more time to love you more! Grant that I may get rid of the residue of evil from my life. May I be able to wipe out the last traces of it with more love of God."[8]

"A little more time to love you more." He often told his children, "It's uneconomical to die young."

"I live because I do not live"

On October 12, 1968 he was in the Zurbaran Residence in Madrid with about 200 women university students. One of them said passionately, "For people, one must be prepared to do whatever is necessary, to give of oneself completely, to give up one's life!" On the stage of the auditorium, Monsignor Escrivá turned rapidly in the direction of the voice, then replied, "Give up one's life? No, indeed! We have to live, and go on living! I don't agree that death is the answer. I'm quite old but I don't wish to die—although whenever God wants, I'll be delighted to go to that encounter: *in domum Domini ibimus!* With his mercy we will go to God's house."

Then, softening his tone, he went on. "Pray for me to be cheerful, even when I am dying. May those around me see me smile as I have always seen my children smile at the hour of their death, knowing that *vita mutatur, non tollitur*, life is changed, not taken away; that it's nothing more than moving house, leaving behind the things of this world to go and meet love: a love which doesn't ever betray us, which satisfies without cloying, which is light, total harmony, delight, the love of loves.

"You'll say, 'Then do you wish to die, Father?' Absolutely not! That would be against the spirit of Opus Dei. I've been preaching for forty years that we don't desire death. Wishing for death is mere cowardice. We have to desire to live, to work for our Lord and love

8. AGP, HRF 21175, pp. 523–534.

all souls deeply. In the time of St. Teresa of Avila, people in love—the mystics as well as those who sang about human love—to demonstrate the intensity of their love, used to cry 'I die because I do not die.' There's a famous poem which goes

Come, death, so furtively
that I do not feel you coming
lest the pleasure of dying
should bring me back to life again.

"I disagree with that way of thinking, and I say the opposite: 'I live because it is not I who live; it is Christ who lives in me.' May Christ live in me, my daughters. If you want to do something for me, ask God our Lord that Christ may live in me. Even though I'm so old, I'd want to live for many more years, to be able to love all souls, everyone, and show with deeds that I'll never bear a grudge against anybody. Living and working! Age doesn't matter: we're always young!"[9]

A house of cards

In the years 1902–1913, in the peaceful rural backwater of Barbastro and Fonz where Josemaría Escrivá spent his childhood, the norm was for a child to live happily unaware of suffering and sorrow. Yet his three younger sisters died in the space of four years. Rosario on July 11, 1910, aged nine months, when Josemaría was eight, Lolita on July 10, 1912, at the age of five, when Josemaría was ten, and on October 6, 1913, Asuncion, nicknamed Chon, who was eight.

His sisters had died from the youngest upwards, as if death were ascending a ladder. With the logic of children, he told his mother one day, "It's my turn next." The conviction did not make him gloomy, but it did make him grow up faster. One afternoon his sister Carmen was playing cards with friends. The game over, they built a tall house of cards. They were keeping very quiet and holding their breaths, when Josemaría walked in. He came up to the table and with a sweep of his hand brought down the house of cards.

---

9. AGP, HRF 21157, pp. 1092–1094.

"Why did you do that?" the girls exclaimed. Josemaría hesitated a moment, then said, "That's what God does with people: you build up a castle and when it's almost finished, God knocks it down."[10]

Seeing with God's eyes

Did he have an intuition that his end was near? It seems he did. Speaking to his daughters in the Work, he began to make references to his death. "Years ago I did not say these things, but now it pleases God that I speak like this. I have to be ready, so as to hear him when he calls me."[11]

On one occasion he told his sons, "I'm no longer needed. I'll be able to help you better from heaven. You'll do things better than I. You don't need me."[12]

Often he endorsed the person who was to succeed him. "When I die, my children, I want you to love the Father very much, no matter who he is, even though it could pass through your mind that he's not intelligent enough or holy enough, or a thousand other things that might occur to you and which you have to reject immediately, because they are evil. Love him very much, my children: it's very hard to carry this burden!"[13] And again, "In this blessed Rome, I sometimes hear that the founder of a particular institution has died and the institution then undergoes a tremendous upheaval. I assure you that in the Work there will be no such thing. Of that I'm certain."[14]

"I want to see you face to face"

During the last years of his life, Carmen Ramos was central secretary for the women of Opus Dei worldwide, and often discussed matters of governance with Monsignor Escrivá. She regularly took notes of what he said. From October 1974 to June 1975 she recorded his exact words.

10. Testimony of Maria del Carmen Otal, Baroness of Valdolivos (AGP, HRF T-05080).
11. Testimony of Mercedes Morado (AGP, HRF T-07902).
12. *Articles of the Postulator*, 992.
13. Bishop Alvaro del Portillo, *Letter*, September 30, 1975, 36.
14. *Articles of the Postulator*, 989.

Later Carmen realized that in those last nine months he consistently added a few words on a more personal note. He asked for prayers for the Church; he inquired after people, and he said what he never normally said face to face: "I love all of you so much, my daughter!" He felt an urge to "thank you for the way you look after me." And before hanging up, he would say good-bye in cheerful, warm tones: "God bless you, my daughter!"[15]

On January 1, 1975, the year he died, he spent a while with his sons on the general council in the Commissions Room in Villa Tevere. He asked for champagne to be brought in to toast the New Year. "This year which is beginning now, I will be much closer to our Lord than ever," he said.[16]

On January 29, he left for Venezuela to embark on his third catechetical journey in South America. He was exhausted. For some time his sight had been failing, and with his right eye he could barely distinguish shapes and found light very bothersome. Very few people knew because he did not complain. He walked briskly, wore dark glasses in sunny places and around the house, and going up or down stairs made sure that Father Javier was in front and Don Alvaro behind.

As they were about to leave on this third preaching trip to Latin America, word came from the airport that the flight was delayed because of fog. Monsignor Escrivá was in the dining room of Villa Vecchia with Don Alvaro. He asked to see Carmen Ramos and Marlies Kücking, and chatted with them for a while. In a voice that cracked and was faint, he confided, "My daughters, I'm not keen, I have no desire to go on this journey. I'm going to South America again because it is the express will of God that I should go. But I myself don't have the strength. I'm also going because I love my children, and I make God's will my own; but if it were not so, I wouldn't be making this journey."

He held a glass of water in which a tablet was dissolving. Holding it out to Don Alvaro, he said, "Alvaro, look and see if it's dissolved yet, I can't see it."

---

15. Testimony of Carmen Ramos.
16. Bishop Alvaro del Portillo, cf. AGP, HRF, 21165, pp. 36–37 and 39. cf. testimony of Marlies Kücking.

"It's a cloudy day, Father, and quite dark in here . . . but no, it hasn't dissolved yet."[17]

The problem was the cataracts diagnosed in Milan by Dr. Romagnoli. Monsignor Escrivá had chosen as a sort of leitmotif for his prayer this year the words of the Gospel: *Domine, ut videam!* "Lord, that I may see!" Occasionally in the oratory, gaze fixed on the crucifix on the altar, he would say sadly: "I can't see you! I can't see you, my Jesus!"[18] From Psalm 26 he took the words *vultum tuum, Domine, requiram*—"thy face, Lord, do I seek," and repeated them constantly, from at least December 1973 on. Sometimes, even during a meal, he would exclaim, "Lord, I want to give you a hug."[19]

"People in love try to see each other," he said. "They only have eyes for their love. Isn't it only natural for this to be so? The human heart feels this urge. I cannot honestly deny that I'm moved by a desire to contemplate the face of Christ. *Vultum tuum, Domine, requiram.* I will seek your face, O Lord. I like to close my eyes and think how the time will come, whenever God wills, when I will be able to see him, *not as in a glass darkly . . . but face to face.*"[20]

Another time he told some of his sons, "I simply can't stop learning. I'm dying to see Jesus, to know his face. I hunger to meet my God. Yesterday I wrote down something I'd read, and I recited it over and over again: *ostende faciem tuam et salvi erimus*—'show us your face, and we shall be saved.' Grant me to see your face, and then I'll be in heaven, I'll be saved, I'll be safe!"[21] He once said, "When I'm doing the prayer on my own, I often shout it out, even though I'm doing mental prayer! I hunger to see the face of Jesus Christ! But let it be. The time will come."[22]

The final folly

Several times during his catechetical tour of Spain and Portugal in 1972 he said he still had "three follies to accomplish." But he only

17. Testimony of Carmen Ramos.
18. Verbal account by Fr. Ernesto Julia.
19. Bishop Alvaro del Portillo, AGP, HRF 2115, p. 37.
20. AGP, HRF 21164, pp. 673–674.
21. Ibid.
22. Ibid.

mentioned two: Cavabianca, the site of the Roman College of the Holy Cross, and the Shrine of Our Lady of Torreciudad near the Pyrenees in Huesca in northern Spain. One day in Portugal a son of his asked, "What's the third one?"

Monsignor Escrivá smiled broadly. "To die in time!" he answered. "Because the time will come when I will just be a nuisance here."[23] And one day in 1966 he had said, "I beg of God that I may be able to dress myself right up to the last day. It's more reasonable, and more in keeping with the spirit of Opus Dei, that I should die peacefully in bed, like a bourgeois. But if I had my way I would like to die with even my shoes on!"[24]

And he did. He died in his office, with his shoes on.

"Having done his prayer, he set off"

On that last day, June 26, 1975, he got up very early, as he always did, and put on his new cassock because he was going out. He did half an hour of prayer as usual.

He celebrated a Mass in honor of Our Lady in his oratory at 7:53 a.m. The oratory had a beautiful reredos in Carrara marble representing the Holy Trinity. Father Javier Echevarria served the Mass. After his thanksgiving, he had a frugal breakfast with Don Alvaro and Father Javier while looking through the newspaper. He spoke to two of his sons in Opus Dei, Father Francisco Vives and Giuseppe Molteni, and asked them to pay a visit to Dr. Ugo Piazza, Paul VI's doctor (see Chapter 18). At 9:35, with Don Alvaro and Father Javier, he left for Castelgandolfo; Javier Cotelo was driving. The heat was already oppressive. They said a part of the Rosary, then chatted. Cotelo told about some nephews of his who had visited Rome.

The sitting room decorated with fans

They arrived at Villa delle Rose in Castelgandolfo at 10:30 a.m. Monsignor Escrivá wanted to say good-bye to his daughters in

23. AGP, HRF 20166, p. 213.
24. Testimony of Fr. Carlos Cardona (AGP, HRF T-06138).

Opus Dei—graduates from all over the world who were doing further studies in the Roman College of Our Lady—because he planned to travel to Asturias in northern Spain in a couple of days. As soon as he met them, he said, "I was very keen to come and see you. We're spending these last few hours in Rome trying to finish off all the work in hand, so I'm really not at home to anyone except you."

He spoke about how all the baptized should have "a priestly soul": taking God to people and people to God. He also insisted on love and loyalty to the Church and the Pope, "no matter who he is." Then he asked them for news. Several talked about the apostolate of Opus Dei in their countries.

"I always say the same thing," was his comment. "You have lots of work ahead of you!"

After about twenty minutes, Monsignor Escrivá began to feel unwell. He went down to the priest's room, a small office, with Don Alvaro and Father Javier, and rested a while; when he felt a little better he got up to leave. They urged him to stay and rest longer, but he refused.

On his way out, he pointed out to Chus de Meer and Elisa Luque some details that could be improved in the priest's office. Then he went to the oratory for a moment to bid our Lord farewell. Chus, Elisa, Conchita, and Vale went down to the garage to see him off, and he said, "Forgive me, my daughters, for being a nuisance!"

Javier Cotelo drove fast. Monsignor Escrivá had asked to be taken home by the shortest route. He seemed tired but peaceful, and his expression was contented, even cheerful. He said little, and the others conversed sporadically. Most likely he was continuing his thanksgiving for the Mass he had celebrated that morning, as was his custom; from midday on he would begin to prepare for the Mass of the following day.

It was three minutes before twelve when the car stopped in the garage of Villa Tevere. They went directly to greet our Lord in the Blessed Trinity oratory. Monsignor Escrivá genuflected on his right knee in a profound gesture of adoration. He looked at the tabernacle, which was in the shape of a Eucharistic dove.

"Javi, I don't feel well"

They went up in the wooden elevator to Don Alvaro's office, where Monsignor Escrivá worked. As soon as he entered the room he called out, "Javi!" Father Javier Echevarria was out on the landing, closing the door of the elevator. Monsignor Escrivá summoned all his strength to call again: "Javi! . . . I don't feel well." Then he collapsed. The midday sun was pouring in through the windows, and the Angelus bells were ringing.

"Ego te absolvo—I absolve you."

Don Alvaro, realizing the gravity of the situation, gave him absolution while holding him in his arms. As he made the sign of the cross over him he recalled how exactly thirty-one years before, on June 26, 1944, as a newly ordained priest he had heard Father Escrivá's confession and given him absolution for the first time. Since then, how often had he made that same gesture, saying *ego te absolvo a peccatis tuis*—"I absolve you from your sins"!

Soon afterward he administered the Anointing of the Sick. Monsignor Escrivá had often begged him forcefully, "When I'm dying, don't deprive me of that treasure!"[25] For an hour and a half a titanic struggle took place in Don Alvaro's office, with cardiac massage, artificial respiration, injections, oxygen, and electrocardiograms. Several of his spiritual sons, Father Dan Cummings, Fernando Valenciano, Umberto Farri, Giuseppe Molteni (Peppino) as well as Doctors José Luis Soria (Joe) and Juan Manuel Verdaguer took turns applying these remedies as Monsignor Escrivá de Balaguer lay on the floor.

Father Javier Echevarria came in and out bringing medical assistance as needed, then stood back a bit. Catching Don Alvaro's eye, he burst into inconsolable tears.

Kneeling on the floor beside Monsignor Escrivá's body, Joe Soria bent down until he was touching his face. He lifted one eyelid and then the other. Monsignor Escrivá's pupils were completely dilated.

---

25. Cf. Césare Cavalleri, *Immersed in God,* p. 198.

There was no contraction, no reaction to the stimulus of light. He whispered, "No pupil reflex."

He kept on scrutinizing the eyes for some sign of life. "It was like diving into the Father's interior,"[26] he said later.

As they tried to keep Monsignor Escrivá's heart beating, Don Alvaro telephoned Carmen Ramos and asked her to get everyone in La Montagnola and Villa Sacchetti to go to the different oratories in the house and pray "for a very urgent intention." But from a human point of view, there was nothing to be done. Monsignor Escrivá's heart had stopped.

Now there were other things to do. The Pope was informed via Cardinal Villot, the secretary of state, of Monsignor Escrivá's death. Others got a board on which to carry Monsignor Escrivá's body to the oratory of Our Lady of Peace. Don Alvaro removed the relic of the *lignum crucis*, the True Cross, which Monsignor Escrivá was wearing round his neck. "I will wear this *lignum crucis* until we elect a successor to the Father," he told those present.

As he took off Monsignor Escrivá's shoes, he was unable to hold back his tears.

Father Javier Echevarria emptied the pockets of his cassock: his small pocket diary, crucifix, rosary beads, a handkerchief, and a whistle which a girls' club had sent him. Father Carlos Cardona, Father Julian Herranz, and Father Javier Echevarria then dressed him in liturgical vestments: the amice, lace alb, cincture, stole, and chasuble. Meanwhile Jesus Alvarez had ordered a coffin, prepared the grave in the crypt for burial, and called a friend who was a sculptor to come and make a death mask of Monsignor Escrivá's face and hands.

When all these tasks were finished, everyone left except Don Alvaro and Father Javier. Several women came into the oratory and cleaned Monsignor Escrivá's face, removing the bits of plaster left by the mask, and combed his hair. They used a set of combs and brushes he had been given years before, but which he had given to his daughters with the same excuse as always: "I don't need them, and what would I be doing with these luxuries?"[27] They decorated

26. The author heard this said by Fr. José Luis Soria in El Brezo (Palencia), in August 1975.
27. Verbal account by Marlies Kücking to the author.

the oratory with fresh gladioli and red roses. Monsignor Escrivá's body was laid out on a white sheet and a funeral pall on the floor, in the style of the nobility who in death refused to be lifted up on a platform or catafalque. At once priests started saying requiem Masses *de corpore insepulto* (before the burial), one after the other all afternoon, evening, night, and the following day up to the funeral Mass itself.

As soon as Vatican Radio officially announced the death of the founder of Opus Dei, a constant, peaceful flow of people began to pass through Villa Tevere to pray. The news traveled fast by radio, telephone, cable, and telex. Those in France, Germany, and Spain heard quickly, but delays on the telephone lines meant that Ireland, Australia, Argentina, Uruguay, and Paraguay heard the news several hours later. Since the people of Opus Dei in Spain were the "first-born" in the Work, the counselor of Opus Dei there, Father Florencio Sanchez Bella, received a call early from Don Alvaro.

Don Alvaro's tribute

From dawn next day Don Alvaro stayed near the body of Monsignor Escrivá as it lay in the chapel, moving only to greet cardinals and bishops who had come to pray.[28] At mid-morning he rose from the side bench, went to the center of the nave, knelt beside Monsignor Escrivá's head, and bent down as if to kiss him, but he did not: he rested his forehead on the forehead of Monsignor Escrivá. He stayed in that position for several seconds, asking "to be a faithful executor of his wishes" and "that I may be capable of caring for the Work as you would" in this period of mourning and appointing a successor.

---

28. According to the account of Bishop Alvaro del Portillo to Césare Cavalleri (*Immersed in God*), Archbishop Benelli, representing Paul VI, Cardinals Wright, Ottaviani, Rossi, Seper, Baggio, Garrone, Philippe, Oddi, Guerri, Palazzini, Traglia, Violardo, Casariego, and Carboni, among others were present at the lying in state. He also mentioned Archbishop Travia and the Polish Bishop Deskur. Some of these and Cardinals Fürstenberg and Aponte, "as well as many other bishops, prelates, priests, and superiors of the different orders and congregations" attended the Requiem Mass celebrated in the Church of St. Eugene in Rome on June 28. The Father general of the Society of Jesus and "many nuns and religious, some of whom had relations in the Work, were among those at the funeral."

Rising, he took three red roses from one of the bouquets and placed them at Monsignor Escrivá's feet. Words of St. Paul came to his lips—a tribute he could never have expressed in the lifetime of Monsignor Escrivá, because he would not have allowed it: *Quam speciosi pedes evangelizantium pacem, evangelizantium bonum!* "How beautiful are the feet of those who preach the Gospel of peace, of those who bring glad tidings of good things!"[29]

Don Alvaro knelt there beside Monsignor Escrivá's body, repeating his tribute interiorly. He recalled Psalm 18: *et ipse tamquam sponsus procedens de talamo suo,* "he comes forth like a bridegroom leaving his chamber."[30] Death for him meant the culmination of love.

And he will rise up like a giant

The same psalm goes on: *Exsultavit ut gigas ad currendam viam,* "like a giant he rejoiced to run his course."[31] Don Alvaro remembered how Monsignor Escrivá had enjoyed this verse and how vigorously he used to recite it. This was how he had always seen him, as a giant, *ut gigas.*

He saw him again now, still a giant. Monsignor Escrivá reposed peacefully like a warrior who had bravely fought his last battle. But there was something disconcerting in this stillness. Monsignor Escrivá was not made to lie inert. He was one of those who live and die on their feet, since they have no time for resting.

Don Alvaro raised his eyes, and caught Father Javier's glance. His eyes were swollen and red from crying. He gave the younger man a faint smile, conveying confidence. "Nothing will happen in the Work. Nothing at all. There will be no disquiet, no orphanhood, no vacuum . . . because the Father, like the patriarchs of ongoing families, not only 'engendered sons and daughters' but engendered sons capable of being Fathers. And so he will always be the Father of all the children and the Father of all the fathers."

29. Rom. 10:15.
30. Ps. 18:6.
31. Ibid.

CHRONOLOGY

DATE	EVENT
1902	January 9: Josemaría Escrivá born in Barbastro, the second child of José Escrivá and Dolores Albas who were married in Barbastro on September 19, 1898. His older sister Carmen was born on July 16, 1899. His father had a textile business and a chocolate factory. He was from Fonz and his family came from Balaguer. His mother was from Barbastro, and her family came from the highlands of Aragon. January 13: He is baptized in the parish cathedral of the Assumption and given the names of Jose, María, Julian, and Mariano. Years later he will join the first two names together as a sign of his love for Our Lady and St. Joseph. He will use his fourth name, Mariano, quite often in his correspondence during the Spanish Civil war. April 23: Josemaría receives Confirmation.
1904	Josemaría becomes seriously ill and doctors give up on treatment, but he unexpectedly recovers. His parents attribute his cure to the intercession of Our Lady of Torreciudad, and take him on a pilgrimage of thanksgiving to the shrine where the ancient image of Our Lady of Torreciudad is venerated.
1906	Josemaría begins nursery school at the Daughters of Charity school in Barbastro.

1908	Josemaría Escrivá starts school with the Piarist Brothers in Barbastro.
1910	Josemaría's youngest sister Rosario dies aged nine months.
1912	On April 23, Josemaría Escrivá makes his First Communion, a little younger than is usual at the time, in accordance with the new decree of Pius X. On June 11 he sits the common entrance for the baccalaureate in the Huesca Institute. His sister Dolores ("Lolita") dies at the age of five.
1913	Death of Josemaría's sister Asuncion or "Chon," aged eight.
1912–15	Josemaría sits exams of his first three years of baccalaureate in Lerida.
1915	His father's business collapses. The whole family moves to Logroño where Mr. José Escrivá gets a job in a textile store.
1917–18	Josemaría goes to San Antonio school and finishes his baccalaureate in the Logroño Institute. He has the first inklings of his vocation. At the end of 1917 some footprints in the snow of a Discalced Carmelite arouse in him a strong desire to love God. Forgoing the study of architecture he decides to become a priest so as to be more available for whatever God wills for him.
1918	Young Josemaría Escrivá begins his studies of theology in the seminary of Logroño as a day pupil.
1919	Josemaría's brother Santiago born. Josemaría realizes that God has heard his prayer: on deciding to become a priest he prayed for his parents to have another son to take his place at home.
1920	Josemaría moves to Saragossa to further his study of theology at the Pontifical University. He lodges in the St. Francis of Paola seminary.

1922	Cardinal Soldevila, archbishop of Saragossa, appoints Josemaría Escrivá to the post of seminary inspector of St. Francis of Paola and confers on him the tonsure and minor orders.
1923	Escrivá begins to study law at the University of Saragossa. He combines ecclesiastic and civil studies up to June 1924.
1924	June 14: Josemaría ordained sub-deacon. November 27: His father José Escrivá dies suddenly in Logroño. December 20: Josemaría is ordained deacon.
1925	March 28: Josemaría Escrivá is ordained priest in the church of the San Carlos seminary where he has spent so many hours in prayer—sometimes spending the whole night there alone during his years as a seminarian. He celebrates his first Mass in the chapel of Our Lady of the Pillar on March 30 for the repose of his father's soul. The next day he takes up his first pastoral mission, as a locum priest in the parish of Perdiguera, a small town of 870 inhabitants in the province of Aragon at the foot of the Alcubierre mountain range. He will always remember fondly his first "cure of souls" as a priest. Returning to Saragossa on May 18, he takes charge of the chaplaincy of the Church of St. Peter Nolasco. He carries on with his law studies. To support his family—his mother, his sister Carmen, and brother Santiago—he gives private classes and teaches at the Amado Institute.
1927	Father Escrivá takes his law degree in January. He works in Fombuena parish from April 1–17. April 19: he moves to Madrid. From June 1 he is Chaplain of the Foundation for the Sick in Madrid and carries out a tireless apostolate: he prepares thousands of children for confession and communion; visits the sick and the disabled in their homes or in hospitals; administers the sacraments to many souls who are dying; and performs works of mercy in the poorest areas of Madrid. Besides all this, he teaches Roman law and canon law in the Cicuendez Academy. He begins writing his *Intimate Notes*.

1928	On October 2 Father Escrivá is on retreat in the head-quarters of the Pauline Fathers (Garcia de Paredes Street, Madrid). When sorting some notes in his room, he sees Opus Dei, a way to holiness in ordinary work and the fulfilment of Christian duties. From that moment onward, he redoubles his prayer and mortification, intensifies his apostolate, and begins to look for people who can understand and practice this ideal that God has made clear to him.
1930	February 14: While Father Josemaría Escrivá is celebrating Mass in the private oratory of the Marchioness of Onteiro (Alcala Galiano Street, Madrid), God causes him to see that there are to be women as well as men in Opus Dei. The first people of Opus Dei come one by one as the result of the founder's prodigious apostolate with people from every walk of life: men and women, priests and lay people, students and workers, the healthy and the sick. The first person to respond fully to God's calling to Opus Dei is Isidoro Zorzano, an engineer, who asks to be admitted to the Work on August 24, 1930.
1931	Father Escrivá has to leave the chaplaincy of the Foundation for the Sick in May. He becomes chaplain to the Enclosed Augustinians of St. Elizabeth on September 20. He visits patients in the General Hospital on Sundays with groups of students.
1933	The first apostolic work of Opus Dei, the DYA Academy, opens its doors in December in a flat in Luchana Street in Madrid. Months later, in September 1934, the academy and the residence move to 50 Ferraz Street. Hundreds of students are to receive Christian formation in these centers. So the task entrusted by God to Father Escrivá on October 2, 1928 takes off.
1934	December 11: Father Escrivá is appointed rector of the Royal Foundation of St. Elizabeth by the president of the Republic. His book *Spiritual Considerations* is published in Cuenca, followed by *Holy Rosary*.

1936	July 18: Outbreak of civil war all over Spain. For the first few months of the conflict Father Josemaría Escrivá stays on in Madrid, in great danger of his life. He takes refuge in different houses, not daring to stay anywhere very long. Later on he hides in a psychiatric hospital belonging to Dr. Angel Suils, in Arturo Soria Street.
1937	In March Father Josemaría Escrivá moves to the Honduran legation where he is protected by its diplomatic immunity. Towards the end of August, he obtains a document from the legation which allows him a certain amount of freedom. Together with other young men of Opus Dei he gets ready to go over to the other side, where religion is not persecuted and it will be possible to develop the apostolates of the Work. He leaves Madrid on October 7, going to Valencia and then Barcelona. From there they set out on November 19 to cross the Pyrenees, on a long and dangerous trek to Andorra. He is accompanied by José María Albareda, Tomas Alvira, Francisco Botella, Pedro Casciaro, Miguel Fisac, Juan Jimenez Vargas, and Manuel Sainz de los Terreros. From Andorra they go to France, and finally arrive back in San Sebastian in the National zone of Spain on December 12.
1938	From January onwards Father Escrivá lives in Burgos. From there, he visits the different battlefronts to carry on the apostolic work which the Civil War has interrupted. Father Escrivá has people he loves, friends and sons of his in Opus Dei, on both sides of the Civil War. Despite the uncertainty of the mail, he writes letters to many people, encouraging them to keep up their Christian spirit. Hundreds of letters from this time survive.
1939	Father Escrivá returns to Madrid on March 28. He obtains his Ph.D. in law at the Central University. The first edition of *The Way*, a spiritual best-seller, is published. It will eventually spread all over the world, selling over four million copies.
1939–46	Opus Dei spreads all over Spain: Valencia, Barcelona, Valladolid, Saragossa, Bilbao, Seville, Santiago.

1940–44	Several bishops from different dioceses ask Father Escrivá to give retreats to priests and seminarians: his preaching is heard by thousands during these years. He also gives retreats to several religious communities. In this period after the Spanish Civil War there is a general lack of understanding of the "universal call to holiness" which the founder of Opus Dei is preaching.
1941	March 19: Bishop Leopoldo Eijo y Garay of Madrid grants approval of Opus Dei as a "Pious Union." April 22: Doña Dolores Albas dies in Madrid while her son Father Josemaría is in Lerida preaching a retreat to diocesan priests. Several people of Opus Dei who live in the Diego de Leon residence look after the founder's mother as she is dying.
1943	February 14: While celebrating Mass in a women's center of Opus Dei in Jorge Manrique Street in Madrid Josemaría Escrivá founds the Priestly Society of the Holy Cross, inseparably united to Opus Dei. July 15: Isidoro Zorzano dies of Hodgkin's Disease. October 11: Opus Dei receives the *nihil obstat* from the Holy See as a diocesan foundation, which is formally established on December 8 in the diocese of Madrid. Two young doctors in law who are in Opus Dei, José Orlandis and Salvador Canals, move to Rome on Father Escrivá's instructions.
1944	June 25: The bishop of Madrid ordains the first three priests of Opus Dei: Alvaro del Portillo, José María Hernandez de Garnica, and José Luis Muzquiz. Father Escrivá publishes his doctoral thesis, La Abadesa de las Huelgas.
1945	In February, Father Escrivá visits Sister Lucia, one of the Fatima visionaries, in Tuy. She encourages him to set up Opus Dei in Portugal.
1946	The apostolic work of Opus Dei begins in Portugal, Italy, England, Ireland, and France. June 23: Father Josemaría Escrivá arrives in Rome.

1946 cont.	July 16 and December 8: Pius XII receives him in private audience.
1947	February 24: Opus Dei obtains the *Decretum Laudis* from the Holy See. From that moment Father Escrivá can accept married people into the Work. March 29: A general meeting of the Barbastro town council declares Father Josemaría Escrivá a "favorite son of Barbastro." April 22: He is appointed domestic prelate by Pope Pius XII. He acquires a villa in the district of Parioli in Rome, which becomes the headquarters of Opus Dei. That same year work to adapt and enlarge the building is started, lasting until 1960.
1948	June 29: Father Escrivá establishes the Roman College of the Holy Cross. Thousands of professional men from different countries belonging to Opus Dei will study there over the years. October 11: The cause of Isidoro Zorzano's beatification is initiated in the diocese of Madrid-Alcala.
1949	From Rome, the founder oversees the spread of Opus Dei all over the world. The first people of Opus Dei reach the US and Mexico.
1950	June 16: Pius XII grants his definitive approval to Opus Dei. From now on, diocesan priests can join the Work. Cooperators too are admitted—people who wish to cooperate materially or spiritually with the apostolates of Opus Dei, whether they are Catholic or not, even non-Christians. In this Father Escrivá anticipates the ecumenical spirit of the age, twelve years before Vatican II.
1951	A year of particular harassment against the Work: on May 14, Monsignor Escrivá consecrates the families of people of Opus Dei to the Holy Family. On August 15 he goes to Loreto to consecrate the Work to the Most Sweet Heart of Mary. A general congress of Opus Dei is held at Molinoviejo (Segovia), Spain. Escrivá is awarded the Cross of Alfonso X by the Spanish government.

1952	October 26: Josemaría makes a new consecration of the Work, this time to the Sacred Heart of Jesus. The work of Opus Dei begins in the German Federal Republic. The foundation which later becomes the University of Navarre is set up in Pamplona.
1953	Escrivá goes to Spain and celebrates the silver jubilee of the Work on October 2. December 12: establishment of the Roman College of Our Lady, where women of Opus Dei will take further degrees in philosophy and theology and receive intensive formation in the spirit of the Work. They will go on to develop the work of Opus Dei all over the world.
1954	April 27, feast of Our Lady of Montserrat: Monsignor Escrivá, who has suffered from a serious case of diabetes mellitus for the previous ten years, suddenly goes into a brief coma (anaphylactic shock) and appears to die. When he recovers consciousness, his illness is cured. This same year he receives the Cross of St. Raymond of Peñafort.
1955	April 22: Monsignor Josemaría Escrivá sets out from Rome to visit Milan, Como, Zurich, Basle, Lucerne, Berne, Freiberg, St. Gallen, Bonn, Cologne, Munich, and Vienna. Later this year he travels again to Switzerland, France, Belgium, Holland, Germany, and Austria. In Vienna on December 4, he invokes Our Lady with the aspiration *Sancta Maria, Stella Orientis, filios tuos adiuva*—"Holy Mary, Star of the East, help your children!" which he will use from then on to entrust the apostolate with East Europeans to her. In December he obtains a doctorate in sacred theology at the Lateran University in Rome.
1956	Monsignor Escrivá continues his rapid trips around Europe carrying out what he calls "the early history" of the Work in Switzerland, France, Belgium, Germany, and various cities in the north of Italy. In August a general congress of Opus Dei is held in the Swiss town of Einsiedeln. Among other conclusions, it was decided that the general council of the Work should reside in Rome. The Spanish government confers on Monsignor Escrivá the Cross of Isabel la Catolica.

1957	June 20: Carmen Escrivá dies. She contributed hugely to giving a warm atmosphere, attractiveness, and love to the centers of the Work, especially in the difficult early years. Her body is interred in Villa Tevere, the headquarters of Opus Dei in Rome.
	July 23: Monsignor Escrivá is appointed consultant to the Sacred Congregation of Seminaries and Universities and an honorary academic member of the Pontifical Academy of Roman Theology. The Holy See entrusts the prelature of Yauyos (Peru) to Opus Dei.
1958–62	Monsignor Escrivá spends the summers in England and also visits Ireland, personally promoting the spread of Opus Dei towards the English-speaking world.
1958	In August the work of Opus Dei begins in Kenya, the first African country; and in December in Japan, the first country of the Far East.
1960	March 9: Monsignor Josemaría Escrivá has his first audience with Pope John XXIII. October 21: he is given an honorary doctorate by the University of Saragossa.
	October 25: He chairs a meeting called to establish the University of Navarre and is appointed its chancellor. He receives other civil awards such as the Cross of Carlos III, membership of the College of Aragon and "favorite son" of Pamplona.
1961	Monsignor Escrivá appointed consultant of the pontifical commission for the authentic interpretation of the code of canon law. In November a general congress of Opus Dei is held in Rome.
1962	October 11: Second Vatican Council begins. Monsignor Escrivá asks all his children for prayers for the council.
1963	The work of Opus Dei begins in Australia.
1964	January 24: Monsignor Josemaría Escrivá has his first audience with Pope Paul VI. Opus Dei spreads to the Philippines.

1965

November 21: Paul VI inaugurates the buildings of the ELIS Center, a center for the professional training and qualification of workers which the Holy See entrusted to Opus Dei in the time of Pope John XXIII.

December 8: The Second Vatican Council is brought to a close. Monsignor Escrivá has maintained a close relationship with many of the council fathers during the time of the council. He has the joy of seeing the council endorse as doctrine of the Church what he has been teaching since October 2, 1928: the universal call to holiness, which is addressed to lay people in the midst of the world and through their ordinary work.

1966

In June an ordinary general congress of Opus Dei is held in Rome.

September 7: Monsignor Escrivá is proclaimed "favorite son" of Barcelona.

1967

In October Monsignor Escrivá gives the homily "Passionately Loving the World" on the campus of the University of Navarre before thousands of people. The homily is a compendium of the spirituality of Opus Dei which Vatican II has just sanctioned.

1968

Conversations with Monsignor Escrivá is published: a collection of interviews with journalists from different countries. The University of Piura (Peru) is founded; Monsignor Escrivá is its first chancellor.

1969

The founder of Opus Dei convenes a special congress of Opus Dei in Rome, with his express desire young people from different countries take part. Among the 87 men and 105 women (who hold their meetings separately) there is a wide range of nationalities and ages. The congress lasts from September 1–15 in its initial phase. Workshops and meetings follow in the countries where Opus Dei is established. Over 50,700 people of the Work participate,

1969 cont.	presenting 54,871 written communications. Meanwhile, Monsignor Escrivá follows the congress's progress with his prayers. He goes to the Marian shrines of Our Lady of the Pillar, Torreciudad, Fatima, and Guadalupe. He also went on pilgrimage to Lourdes, Sonsoles, Our Lady of the Pillar, Our Lady of Mercy, Einsiedeln, and Loreto. The second stage of the Congress is held from August 30 to September 14, 1970.
1970	April 7: Monsignor Escrivá goes on pilgrimage to Torreciudad. He prays to Our Lady in the same shrine his parents took him to when he was two and had just recovered from a serious illness. Here a great new Marian shrine is being built, on his initiative, with several houses attached for retreats and conferences. May 15 to June 22: He goes to Mexico on a penitential pilgrimage to the shrine of Our Lady of Guadalupe in line with others he has already made in Europe: Lourdes, Fatima, Einsiedeln, Loreto. He prays specifically for the Church and especially for the Pope.
1971	May 30: Monsignor Escrivá consecrates Opus Dei to the Holy Spirit.
1972	Monsignor Escrivá makes a tour of Spanish and Portuguese cities in October and November, meeting thousands of people in a public catechesis, which he develops along the lines of family gatherings with thousands of people.
1973	Some of Monsignor Escrivá's homilies published over the last few years are compiled in a single book under the title *Christ Is Passing By*. Other books follow after his death: *Friends of God, In Love with the Church, The Way of the Cross, Furrow,* and *The Forge*.
1974–75	Monsignor Josemaría Escrivá undertakes two long journeys of catechesis in Latin America: Brazil, Argentina, Chile, Peru, Equador, Venezuela, and Guatemala.

1975	March 28: Escrivá quietly celebrates the golden jubilee of his ordination to the priesthood. He goes to Spain for the last time from May 15–31, making a pilgrimage to the shrine of Torreciudad which has not yet been officially opened. He does so with no fanfare whatsoever: he inaugurates one of the confessionals by going to confession.
	May 25: In Barbastro Town Hall, he receives the city's gold medal.
	June 26: Just before midday, on returning from Castelgandolfo, where he had been having a get-together with the teachers and pupils of the Roman College of Our Lady, he dies of a sudden heart attack in the room where he usually worked in Villa Tevere. Next day he is buried in the crypt of the Oratory of Our Lady of Peace in Villa Tevere, the headquarters of Opus Dei in Rome. At the time of the Founder's death, there are about 60,000 people of Opus Dei living and working in 80 different countries.
	September 15: A general congress of official representatives of all the people in Opus Dei meeting in Rome unanimously elect Monsignor Alvaro del Portillo as Monsignor Josemaría Escrivá's successor. The founder of Opus Dei's reputation for holiness, and private devotion to him, are spread all over the world by means of a simple prayer card and a newsletter.
1982	November 28: Pope John Paul II makes Opus Dei a personal prelature, exactly as the founder had wanted for many years.
1990	April 9: Pope John Paul II orders the publication of the decree on the heroic virtues of Josemaría Escrivá who from then on is recognized by the Church as "the Venerable Servant of God."
1991	Sister Concepcion Boullon's cure having been examined and approved by the Medical Committee and the Committee of Theological Consultors of the Congregation for the Causes of Saints and by the Ordinary Congregation of Cardinals and Bishops, on June 6 Pope John Paul II proclaims the decree declaring the cure to be miraculous.

1992	May 17: The beatification ceremony of Josemaría Escrivá in St. Peter's Square in Rome. John Paul II presides and according to the estimate of *L'Osservatore Romano* 300,000 people from all over the world take part. In November, Dr. Manuel Nevado, aged 60, suffering from chronic radiodermatitis, and damage to his hands caused by repeated exposure to x-rays, is cured after praying for Blessed Josemaría's intercession.
1994	The canonical process on this miracle takes place between May and July, in the Archdiocese of Badajoz, Spain, where Nevado lives.
1997	On July 10, 1997, the Medical Committee of the Congregation for the Causes of Saints unanimously establishes the following diagnosis: "a cancerous state of chronic radiodermatitis in its third and irreversible stage," and therefore with a certain prognosis of "infaust" (without hope of a cure). The complete cure of the lesions are declared by the medical committee to be "very rapid, complete, lasting, and scientifically inexplicable."
1998	On January 9 the Committee of Theologians gives its unanimous approval for attributing the miracle to Blessed Josemaría.
2001	On September 21 the cardinals and bishops of the Congregation for the Causes of Saints confirm these conclusions. On December 20 the Holy See authenticates a second miracle attributed to Blessed Josemaría, thus clearing the way for the canonization.
2002	On February 26 the date for the canonization is announced. On October 6, 2002, before a congregation of over 300,000 from every corner of the globe overflowing St. Peter's Square and down to the River Tiber, Pope John Paul II canonized St. Josemaría Escriva, the saint of the ordinary.

INDEX

Te Deum, 37, 63, 64
Telva magazine, 44, 45
Teresa of Avila, St., 78, 162, 236, 354
Teresian Institute, 268
Termes, Rafael and Jaime, 81
thanksgiving, 141, 144, 159, 358
theology, 53, 222–23
Thomas, Rolf, 200
Thomas Aquinas, St., 117, 162
Thomas More, St., 132, 148, 219
Time magazine, 302
Tirelli, Luigi, 237
Tobias, 87
Toranzo, Lourdes, 168, 169
Tor d'Aveia conference center, San
    Felice d'Orce, Italy, 303
Tordella, Marisa, 352
totalitarianism, 89, 91, 217
Tourne, Teresa, 137
Trinity, 57, 130, 131, 134, 141, 143, 145,
    148, 159, 206, 358
trust
    freedom and, 226–27
    in God, 23, 34
    love and, 23
    sanctity and, 120
truth, 308
    freedom and, 45–47
    humility and, 17
    scientific, 46
tyranny, 46, 91, 223, 243

U

Ubi Caritas, 81
Udaondo, Juan, 96–97
Uffici, Villa Tevere, 38
Ullastres, Alberto, 216–17
ultra-conservatism, 223
United Nations Security Council, 308
United States, 63, 89
university halls of residence, 40, 41,
    42–43
University of Asia and the Pacific,
    Philippines, 42
University of Navarre, Spain, 42, 230,
    267, 302, 372

University of Piura, Peru, 42
University of Saragossa, 266, 367
Urbani, Cardian, 135
Urbistondo, Julian, 15–16
Urrutia, Maria, 68
Uruguay, 362

V

Valenciano, Fernando, 70, 77, 211, 360
Varvaro, Sofia, 205–8
Vatican, 13, 27, 327
    del Portillo, Alvaro and, 334–35
    diplomatic relations of, 15
    fraternal correction and, 270
    Greece, Opus Dei in and, 85
    Opus Dei, attack on structure of
        and, 312
    Opus Dei, campaign of insults and
        calumnies against and, 95
    Opus Dei, canonical recognition of
        and, 6, 8, 18, 74
Vatican II, 64, 67, 118, 135, 149, 212,
    227, 296, 298, 299–300, 312, 326,
    335, 340, 341, 342–43
Vatican Radio, 266, 362
Vavaro, Sofia, 319
Venezuela, 182, 356
Verdaguer, Juan Manuel, 360
Vergara, Maria Elvir, 252
Vernet, Gil, 329
Vettorelli, Anna, 164
Via Orsini center, 96
vigilance, 55
Villa delle Rose, Castelgandolfo, 37, 63,
    163, 168, 179, 180, 208, 228, 246,
    310–16, 358
Villa Gallabresi, Premeno, Italy, 316–19
Villanueva Street center, Madrid, Spain,
    9
Villa Sacchetti, Villa Tevere, 38, 68, 73,
    169, 172, 180, 190, 239, 244, 361
Villa Tevere, 20, 23, 49, 73, 91, 98, 133,
    137, 140, 149, 166, 228, 247, 274,
    296
    building of, 31–32, 32–36, 61–62, 74
    crucifix in, 32–33